# MODERN POLITICAL THEORY
# FROM HOBBES TO MARX
# KEY DEBATES

# MODERN POLITICAL THEORY FROM HOBBES TO MARX KEY DEBATES

*Edited and Introduced by*

JACK LIVELY

and

ANDREW REEVE

R

Routledge

London and New York

First published in 1989 by
Routledge
11 New Fetter Lane, London EC4P 4EE
29 West 35th Street, New York NY 10001

Set in 10/12 Times by
Input Typesetting, London
Printed in Great Britain by
The Guernsey Press, Guernsey,
The Channel Islands

*British Library Cataloguing in Publication Data*
Modern political thought: key debates.
1. Politics. Theories
I. Lively, Jack II. Reeve, Andrew
320′.01

*Library of Congress Cataloging in Publication Data*
Modern political theory from Hobbes to Marx: key debates/ [edited]
by Jack Lively and Andrew Reeve.
p. cm.
Anthology of articles on Hobbes, Locke, Rousseau, Burke, Bentham,
Mill, and Marx.
Includes bibliographies and index.
1. Political science – History. I. Lively, Jack. II. Reeve,
Andrew.
JA83.M63   1988
320.5–dc 1988–10109

ISBN 0–415–01351–8

# CONTENTS

# ACKNOWLEDGEMENTS

The editors and the publishers would like to thank the following copyright holders for permission to reprint material: Cambridge University Press for 'The ethical doctrine of Hobbes' by A. E. Taylor (*Philosophy*, 1938), 'Warrender and his critics' by Brian Barry (*Philosophy*, 1968), 'The *Discourse on Inequality* and *The Social Contract*' by J. I. MacAdam (*Philosophy*, 1972) and 'Burke and the ancient constitution' by J. G. A. Pocock (*Historical Journal*, 1960); Basil Blackwell for 'Locke and Professor Macpherson' by Isaiah Berlin (*Political Quarterly*, 1964); *Journal of the History of Ideas* for 'Appropriation in the state of nature: Locke on the origin of property' by Karl Olivecrona (1974); Butterworth & Co. for 'Will and political rationality in Rousseau' by F. M. Barnard (*Political Studies*, 1984) and 'Mill's principle of liberty' by G. L. Williams (*Political Studies*, 1976); The Canadian Political Science Association for 'Jeremy Bentham and the public interest' by J. A. W. Gunn (*Canadian Journal of Political Science*, 1968); the editor of the Aristotelian Society for 'On some criticisms of historical materialism' by Gerald A. Cohen (*Proceedings of the Aristotelian Society*, 1970) and 'On some criticisms of historical materialism'. A reply, by H. B. Acton (*Proceedings of the Aristotelian Society*, 1970).

# GENERAL INTRODUCTION

The aim of this book is to provide an accessible starting point for discussion of some of the major political thinkers from Hobbes to Marx. The articles included have been chosen because they raise a number of the main issues which arise in interpretation of each thinker. The introductions to the sections attempt, in a necessarily abbreviated fashion, to provide some historical context for the ideas under discussion, to sketch alternative interpretations to those presented in the articles, and to outline the other major questions at issue in the interpretative debate. They presuppose some preliminary reading of the principal texts, but not any extensive exploration of the secondary literature. They do not, of course, pose as a substitute for such exploration and brief suggestions for further reading are included.*

What, it is hoped, will be clear from the articles included and the introductions is that there is, as there always has been, considerable and persistent disagreement on how to understand these political thinkers. What Hobbes or Locke or Burke or Marx really meant or means is a controversial issue, no matter how confidently particular interpretations may be presented. Anyone concerned to understand the classical theorists is then faced not only with perhaps complex and difficult texts but also with a host of interpretative guides advising different paths to enlightenment. Such a prolixity of voices raises at least two pressing questions – how we are to go about understanding these theorists, and what the point is of trying to reach such an understanding. At the no doubt considerable risk of over-simplifying the variety of responses to these questions, let us isolate two major approaches and dub them the 'historical' and the 'philosophic'.

---

* The reading lists suggest accessible editions of the most important texts and a selection of the secondary literature. The books which may be most useful as general introductory accounts are starred.

1

The historical approach to the question of how we are to understand the classical theorists starts from an insistence on the crucial importance of the context in which the theorists wrote. To understand a particular thinker, we must recapture the language in which the political argument of his time was conducted; we must grasp the unargued assumptions on which that debate rested; we must appreciate the traditions of thought to which his ideas appealed or against which they were reacting; we must uncover the political or social or economic tensions of his time, his tactical reasons for publishing, the audience he was addressing, the groups he was attacking, what his own precise purposes and objectives were. We cannot, in sum, understand him simply by confronting his texts directly but must seek to understand them in terms of their genealogy and of the intellectual and political confrontations of his age.

Some of these pleas have a clear and immediate force. It is evident that we may seriously distort the arguments of past writers if we unthinkingly attach our own contemporary meanings to key words in past debates. If we take Hobbes to mean by 'science', or Locke to mean by 'reason', or Rousseau to mean by 'nature', or Marx to mean by 'labour', what we ourselves ordinarily understand by these terms, we shall inevitably misunderstand their ideas. Some effort at linguistic archaeology and also at the translation of past into modern idioms is a necessary prerequisite to understanding.* It is equally evident that we must, in any effort at understanding, recognize the intellectual and ideological landscape within which past debates were set; recognize, too, the ways in which that landscape had been shaped and formed over time. Unless, to take one instance, we have some grasp of the long tradition of natural law thinking, we may seriously misinterpret Hobbes or Locke; or, to take another, if we have no conception of the varied and convoluted attempts from the seventeenth century onwards to apply scientific method to the study of man and society, we shall make little of Bentham's ambition to construct a science of legislation or Marx's to construct a scientific socialism.

The claim that an appreciation of the more particular circumstances in which a text was written is essential to the comprehension of its meaning is perhaps less compelling. Of course such an appreciation may well help us to secure a better purchase on the nature and purport of the argument, as well perhaps as helping to explain

---

* The problems of such linguistic archaeology are of course compounded when it is a question not only of translating from the idioms of the past to those of the present but also those of one national tongue into another.

its ambiguities and silences. Whether Locke's second *Treatise* was a defence of the Glorious Revolution or a reaction to the Exclusion Crisis of 1683; the role of Burke's *Reflections on the Revolution in France* in the internal divisions amongst the Whigs in the early 1790s; the effects on the *Communist Manifesto* of Marx's relations with the League of the Just; the answering of such questions of historical context can clearly contribute to our understanding of the texts. There is, however, a danger that this kind of explaining can lead to explaining away. The 'meaning' of a text can be equated simply with its polemic thrust, its persuasive tactics, its role in the politics of 'who gets what, when, how'. Of course, even at the highest level of abstraction, theorizing about politics has seldom been purely meditative or disinterested. Theorists have had particular policies to defend, particular projects to further, particular institutions or groups or values or even interests to protect. But the mark of high political theory has been that these particular intentions have been pursued by relating them to general reflections on man and society and on the human condition; and, whatever the particular circumstances and purposes of this activity, these general reflections remain to be understood and evaluated.

This is the starting point for the 'philosophic' approach to the understanding of the classical theorists, which emphasizes the close study of the texts themselves. We do not need to join those on the wilder shores of contemporary literary theory in insisting that the intentions and concerns of a writer are irrelevant to an appreciation of his writings to accept that the text has some independent existence, can speak to us directly across historical space. Of course, we shall not be able to hear the thinker's voice distinctly unless we can recognize the intellectual and semantic dialect of his age. Given such knowledge, however, we can then address the question of the internal structure and coherence and persuasiveness of the arguments presented. This, the self-assumed task of the 'philosophic' approach, requires examination of the inter-relations not only of different aspects of a thinker's strictly political ideas but of those ideas and his epistemological, moral, metaphysical, and religious arguments and preconceptions. On this approach, understanding a thinker involves the attempt to discover the overall coherence of his ideas; or, and this is the obverse side of the coin, to uncover their unresolved inconsistencies and contradictions. This project leads straight to problematics that are at the centre of many of the interpretative debates outlined in the introductions to the sections of this book. Does Hobbes attach a single meaning to reason or natural law and what part do these concepts play in his overall

argument? How does Locke's theory of property relate to his constitutional ideas, and is there a contradiction between his attack on
the concept of innate ideas and his use of the natural law idiom?
Is Rousseau inconsistent in extolling at one point the virtues of
natural independence and at another those of closer social union?
How does Burke's plea for deference to tradition fit his vision of
the desirable structuring of society? Is Bentham's psychological
hedonism compatible with his ethical hedonism? Is there a tension
between John Stuart Mill's professed commitment to utilitarianism
and his defence of individual liberty? Does Marx present a coherent
economic or materialist theory of history and how does his use of
dialectics fit in with this theory? Such problems may be illuminated
or resolved or, in one sense at least, explained by an examination
of the historical context. But they can only be appreciated in the
first instance by an examination of the texts. To this extent, the
two approaches are not competitive but complementary.

The question of how we can go about understanding the major
political thinkers inevitably gives rise to the question of why we
should try to do so; and this is part – but only part – of the wider
question of why we should study the history of political ideas.
Again there are a variety of possible responses, but again two
basic approaches – the historical and the philosophical – may be
discerned.

The historical defence of the study of the major theorists might
be based on the argument either that they illuminate most sharply
the intellectual preconceptions and concerns of their time or that
they have had an important causal influence on social and political
and intellectual developments. Both arguments depend upon certain
assumptions about the relationship between 'ideas' and 'actions' or
'reality'. If ideas are simply epiphenomenal, reflections of, say,
underlying economic or class tensions and antagonisms, or if theorizing is simply the construction of apologies for the pursuit of
interests, the tribute that greed and the lust for power pay to moral
and spiritual and intellectual virtue, the study of theory can reap
little profit in terms of historical insight. If, on the other hand,
understanding actions involves the reconstruction of their meaning
and significance for the actors themselves, if ideas can inspire
political action or even just shape how people behave whatever
their motives, then an 'historical' defence of the history of ideas
may be mounted.

The argument that to understand the past we must try to enter
past minds, to see the world as those past others saw it, is powerful
and persuasive, but it may not provide strong support for concen-

tration on the major political theorists. Certainly, if those theorists can themselves only be understood in terms of their ideological context, it becomes difficult then to use them as evidence of that context. What most marks out the major theorists is precisely their originality, the degree to which they questioned accepted ideas or altered the terms of political discourse. And this is as true of those who sought to justify established authorities, as did Hobbes and Hegel, and those who claimed simply to be articulating the concrete conceptions and aspirations of particular social groups, as did in their different ways Burke and Marx, as of those who took up a self-consciously innovatory intellectual stance. It might be argued that such challenges, whether overt or covert, to accepted ideas themselves illuminate those previously unquestioned common-places. It seems, though, that a richer seam in which to mine for the generally accepted and unargued assumptions of a period or place or class might be found amongst the lesser writers and the more ephemeral literature.

Another possible historical defence of the study of the major theorists is forward rather than backward looking. On this view, it is the influence they have had, either in shaping subsequent widely held attitudes or in prompting political aspirations and movements, that make them worthy of the historian's attention. All of the thinkers discussed here have been – and still are – appealed to as alleged progenitors of particular social and political positions or attacked in defence of allegedly opposed positions. They have all had an assured and persistent place not only in academic discussion but in the world of political controversy. Of course, they have been called in aid of many different and even opposing causes. Locke has been used in defence of eighteenth-century constitutionalism, nineteenth-century egalitarianism and twentieth-century libertarianism; Marx was invoked by both Mensheviks and Bolsheviks to justify quite different strategies and tactics for a social democratic movement in late Tsarist Russia (to quote only one from a myriad of instances in the history of Marxism). However various and even contradictory the uses made of the classical theorists, it is still useful to return to them to assess how far their subsequent followers or opponents have accurately stated their positions or in what ways the exemplars have been subsequently distorted or only partially represented.

One powerful motive for pursuing this search for influences might be to understand better the ideas current in our own time or even perhaps the genealogy of our own personal values and visions of the world. Such pursuits of origins or roots have not on the whole been enthusiastically received by historians. Concentration on the explanation of present-day concerns and ideas may obviously under-mine any endeavour to see the past in its own lights and can lead to the writing of 'Whig history', the recounting of the (usually triumphal) progress of modern conditions and ideas. Many modern histories of Marxism and of liberalism show that Whig history is by no means dead. However, whatever the professional dangers, the illumination of the present is a legitimate ground for interest in the past. We depend heavily, even entirely, on our personal memories to establish our personal identities; and one of the most important uses of history, our social memory, is as an aid to communal identification. Of course, the study of *political* ideas is only part of this effort at identification, but, to the degree that modern thought has stressed the centrality of political structure and political action, it is an important part. So the search for the roots of 'totalitarian' modes of thought, or the genealogy of 'liberal' ideas, or the origins of the modern 'state', although perhaps fraught with dangers from the pure historian's point of view, is a valuable and in any case inevitable project.

These are all, in one way or another, historical modes of justifying the study of the classical theorists. But we may believe instead, or also, that they can speak directly to our own present concerns and preoccupations. The past may be a foreign country, and they may do things differently there, but these foreigners face recognizably perennial human problems and travel may well broaden the mind. The reading of thinkers as historically distant as Plato and Aristotle can, *mutatis mutandis*, give insight into modern problems, both intel-lectual and practical. This is even more the case with the post-medieval thinkers under consideration here. For they posed a range of questions which are clearly still present and pressing: the nature and actual functions of the modern state; what are, if any, the desirable functions of the state; how can it be restricted to those functions; its relationship with other forms of human associations – the church (or churches), the family, the economy, civil society, the nation, the world of learning; the freedom or rights which the individual can properly claim against the state or other associations or individuals; the nature and value of personal freedom or autonomy; the degree to which political action – the human will – is bounded, or even determined, by a providential ordering of things, whether providence is envisaged as the agency of God or nature or the Absolute Spirit or the laws of history. To understand such questions, certainly to understand the complexity of the issues they raise, we must first go back to those who have posed them most sharply and explored them most deeply. We must enter what has been called the conversation of mankind, a conversation in which the first task, and in the light of the interpretative debate no easy one, is to gather what the subject of discussion is and what the others are saying. Conversation may of course lead to argument. In such confrontation we may clarify our own ideas, or extend them, or change them, or even just be confirmed in them. To this extent, it can have an immediate and direct impact on our attitudes to the world around us, and those attitudes are likely to be impoverished by ignorance of the debate over time. To read Hobbes and Marx is not then just to sip idly at mature but dangerously aging wines. It is to engage directly in some of the central, if widest, problems of social and political life.

Over and above any such particular contributions that the study of the classical theorists might make to the informing and deepening of our present debate, there is value in trying to grasp the general vision of things they present. We might read Tolstoy to learn something about military campaigning or to gather some insights into the conditions of happy – or unhappy – families. But, beyond that, we might wish to comprehend Tolstoy's particular conception of the human condition. The same is true of the reading of, say, Hobbes or Marx. We may read the one to extend our understanding of the complex notion of sovereignty, or the other to deepen our understanding of the relationship between political and economic structures. But, on a wider level, we may hope to grasp one vision of how humanity can reasonably accommodate to its own God-given but destructive nature, or another vision of a providential pattern which seeks to impose order on the apparent randomness of history, give meaning to unconsidered and wretched lives, and offer grounds for hopes of a successful outcome to the human odyssey. At the most general level, the visions of thinkers such as Hobbes and Marx are as much mythopoeic as they are analytic or empirical, and the attempt to understand them may broaden our own conception of how the human drama can be felt and understood, may help us to reach that point at which the spiritual and moral and metaphysical and aesthetic and empirical worlds come together and can possibly cohere. From many points of view this conjunction and coherence may not be within the compass of a specifically political perception. For most persons at most times the central focus of such a comprehensive vision has been religious, the explorations of the intimations of divine ordination for our everyday practice of life. Indeed, it would be difficult to comprehend the thinkers who are presented here as primarily political in their vision without reference to other (and possibly wider) contexts. It would, for example, be difficult to grasp the real meaning of Hobbes or Locke or Rousseau without exploring the religious beliefs or bewilderments that underlie and haunt their political arguments. Nevertheless, for many thinkers in the modern world (and for many ordinary persons pursuing the problematic task of living – of both staying alive and making sense of doing so), the secular has displaced the divine as the major point of focus and the prophets speak a terrestrial rather than a celestial language. Many might reject this as too narrow a range, too sparse a language. Nevertheless the emergence of specifically political visions, in which communal will and intelligence are the crux of human destiny, is a central feature of modern western thought and these visions require, even if by some they are not thought to deserve, a sensitive exploration, not necessarily so that we might be converted to truths previously alien to us, but so that we may enlarge and deepen our own understanding of things.

The goods that may be gained from a study of the main political theorists are then as various as the methods by which they can be studied. Like the methods, the goods are not strict alternatives amongst which we are forced to make a choice, so that we can only enhance the historian's insight at the expense of the philosopher's wisdom and vice versa. The assumption made here is that there are many ways in which these theorists can legitimately be approached and many values which may be served by engagement in their study.

# THOMAS HOBBES

## Chapter One

# INTRODUCTION

Hobbes's *Leviathan* is widely acknowledged to be one of the finest works of English political philosophy. Like any masterpiece, it rewards study from many perspectives: for example, Hobbes addresses the explanation of perception, the concerns of epistemology, the operation of memory, and the role of political power in society. For political theorists, the importance of *Leviathan* arises largely from this last concern, an account of the nature of sovereignty and the indispensability of a coercive powerholder to a stable society. For this reason, the readings in this section are concerned primarily with the interpretation of Hobbes's theory of obligation. Such a theory sets out to explain both what it is to have an obligation, how obligations arise, and, in a political context, to show why, and to what extent, those who claim to rule should be obeyed, and how those with a *legitimate* claim should be recognized. It is quite clear that, for Hobbes, every society needs sovereign power; and it is clear, too, that Hobbes thought that the powers of the sovereign should be extensive, and that he had a preference for monarchical government. But it has been a disputed question whether Hobbes held (or perhaps merely implied) that we should obey those who, as a matter of fact, have power over us, or, alternatively, whether he had a standard by which legitimate power could be distinguished from mere power, and, if so, what that standard was.

The reasons for the dispute are best brought out by looking at the structure of Hobbes's argument, but a preliminary point should be made about an issue begged by speaking of 'Hobbes's theory of obligation' as if we knew in advance that he had just one theory. Hobbes wrote several works of political philosophy, and some exist in both English and Latin versions. Not only are there differences between particular books, but also there are differences between the English and Latin versions of works with the same title. Some interpreters have been more willing than others to draw the evidence for their conclusions from several works: for example, Professor Taylor draws his evidence largely from *De Cive*, but suggests it is Hobbes's theory generally, while Professor Barry insists in his essay that he is dealing mainly with the theory of obligation in *Leviathan*. A glance at the structure of the argument in that work will help to explain why there is disagreement about Hobbes's theory of obligation. In general, the following questions have arisen. First, is the obligation prudential or moral, dependent on rational self-interest or a moral code? Secondly, is Hobbes's *description* of man as self-seeking an important element in his conception of obligation? Thirdly, how important is Hobbes's materialism – does it determine his views on obligation, or entail his alleged atheism? Finally, how significant is Hobbes's commitment to science in an explanation of his political ideas?

*Leviathan* opens with a discussion of physiology, moves on to psychology, and then to politics. Hobbes's fundamental philosophical postulate was that what is, is matter in motion. This apparently wholehearted materialist commitment has played a large part in the characterization of Hobbes as an atheist, a characterization which has important consequences for the interpretation of his political philosophy in general. The first chapter of *Leviathan* tries to explain how our senses respond to the motion in objects (etc.) outside ourselves, to create the sensations which we experience. The idea of motion is further employed in Hobbes's discussion of desire and aversion: we are attracted towards some things and repelled by others, and we give the name of 'good' to those things which attract us and 'bad' to those things to which we are averse. We shall often differ as to what is good and bad, for our desires will not be uniform; but all men are anxious above all to avoid death.

Hobbes imagined a state of nature, a situation in which there is no powerholder able to 'overawe' everyone. He painted a very bleak picture of both the quality and brevity of life in such a world, in which there would be a constant war of all against all, because of competition for scarce resources combined with a basic equality of power (or insecurity). The law of nature, however, leads men to abandon the state of nature and live under a common power, a sovereign, in political society. Each man is conceived to contract with the others to give up (some part of) the right to govern himself, and the sovereign is the beneficiary of these renunciations. Men living in political society, the result of this contract, have an obligation to obey the sovereign as long as he is able to overawe them all. The issue of *political* obligation, then, is to explain the nature and derivation of this obligation.

'Natural law' has been treated in a number of different ways. Its oldest connotation was universality: no matter how the laws of societies differed, all societies actually recognized the same law in some respects. One extension of this idea might be to the law as between nations. A second understanding of the idea, however, would depend not on the empirical universality of certain laws, but on its prescriptive content: no matter what the *actual* laws of societies, the law of nature disclosed what they *should* be. On this understanding the law of nature provided a standard by which to judge not only the justice or legitimacy of particular laws but also of constitutional arrangements. The question then arises: what grounds the universal prescriptive force of the law of nature? One answer was 'reason' itself. Another answer, common in seventeenth-century Christian Europe, was that the law of nature disclosed God's command, injunction, or counsel. Interpretations of Hobbes's political theory have grappled with these putative distinctions. The status of 'laws of nature' in John Locke's thought is also disputed in a number of ways, as we shall see in the next section.

Two points may be made about the structure of Hobbes's discussion. At the more general level, commentators have been concerned to explore the logical connections between the physiology, the psychology, and the politics. This is for two main reasons. The first is that Hobbes had a strong commitment to science (which is not to say that he understood that term as we would), in which the process of deduction was prominent. It has also been suggested that he was attracted by a particular scientific method, associated with thinkers working in Padua. They explored a complex phenomenon by breaking it up into simpler parts which were then brought together to illuminate the nature of the whole. On this view, *Leviathan* may be seen as bringing together the 'parts' which make up the complex whole of man's political life: beginning with man's physiology and concluding with a civil community. This is relevant to the nature and derivation of the obligation, because *if* the politics is entailed by the psychology, and the psychology by the physiology, then Hobbes's conclusions about political obligation would follow from quasi-empirical premises about man's nature. Professor Macpherson has adopted a version of this thesis. The second reason for concern with the logical connections is that Hobbes's psychology has struck many interpreters as weak; and if the politics depends upon it, the political theory would be seriously undermined. Taylor expresses this concern, but rejects the dependence. The second point about the structure of the argument is more 'internal' to the politics. The social contract is, so to speak, a hinge or buckle connecting the state of nature with political society. The sovereign promulgates and enforces laws: the sovereign is brought into existence by a contract: the law of nature includes a provision that men keep their contracts. How far back should we go in search of the ground of obligation to the sovereign's laws? Or, to put the question another way, is the obligation in political society a new one, dependent on the existence of the sovereign or the contract (or both), or is it merely a particular form of an obligation which exists under the law of nature?

The possibilities here may be brought out by considering the two types of sovereignty Hobbes distinguishes. These are sovereignty by institution, and sovereignty by acquisition. Sovereignty by institution is the name given by Hobbes to the result of the contract each person makes with every other to create a sovereign who, though in one sense he is the beneficiary of the contract, is not himself a party to it. Sovereignty by acquisition, by contrast, arises when a person demanding obedience has the person from whom he is demanding it in his power. A conqueror, for example, is conceived to offer the defeated soldier a choice: either liberty under the conqueror's law, in return for a promise to obey, or death. (Hobbes makes distinctions between a promise, a covenant, and a contract which are not employed in this Introduction.) For many modern readers, this 'promise' is invalid: the threat (that if it is not given, death will follow) implies, they feel, that the promise is extorted, and is no more binding than the promise one might make to a kidnapper to secure one's release. Hobbes, however, saw the situation differently, for the following reasons. First, he held that fear and liberty are consistent, and that liberty and necessity are consistent. He originally defined liberty as 'the absence of external impediments to motion', suggesting a mechanistic notion of liberty. Clearly fear is not an external impediment, even if the cause of the fear is outside the person who is afraid. So liberty is not, on this definition, reduced by fear. Hence a man who is threatened is still free (to make his choice). But Hobbes also defines a free man as someone who is not hindered in doing what he has a will to do, and this leaves open the question of what exactly counts as a hindrance. Furthermore, he talks of liberty as 'the silence of law' in political society, which implies that the sovereign's coercive law does restrict liberty, and he talks of the 'true liberty' of the subject with respect to the right of self-preservation which can never be surrendered. So a problem of interpretation surrounds Hobbes's understanding of 'liberty', and its relation to 'obligation'. A second reason for Hobbes's unwillingness to allow that fear makes a promise invalid, apart from his argument that fear and liberty are, as a matter of definition, compatible, is that sovereignty by institution arises in fearful circumstances too. Men agree to create a sovereign because they are afraid of one another. So if fear were allowed to invalidate the promise given to a conqueror, it would also invalidate the contract which created a sovereign. Those who concentrate on this aspect of Hobbes's thought have felt that political obligation is much like the obligation to obey a gunman, and therefore morally uncompelling; they have felt that Hobbes's theory legitimizes any *de facto* sovereign, and therefore collapses the distinction between effective and legitimate power. Others have suggested, however, that further analysis is needed of the contract to create a sovereign or the promise to obey a superior power.

Two points about those promises or contracts are particularly important. The first is that Hobbes defines obligation as having given up a right, and promises and contracts seem obvious ways in which rights might be renounced or transferred. So it is possible to argue that political obligation arises from the surrender of a right, and is a moral obligation in precisely the same way as the obligation to keep a promise freely given. The second is that the law of nature has a provision that men keep the contracts they have made. So the obligation to the sovereign might be traced back as far as the law of nature. On this view, the obligation to the sovereign is connected to the obligation men have to obey the law of nature, whereas the argument mentioned as the first point does not require this. But does the law of nature have binding force?

Here we come to two further problems. The first is the description, *laws* of nature. Hobbes defined a law as a command issued by someone who had a right to do so. So the sovereign's commands are laws. In the pre- or post-political world of the state of nature, however, all men are equal in the sense that there is no natural political authority. So no one has a right to issue commands (or if one has, all have, which is to say no one has a duty to obey anyone else). So the laws of nature cannot be laws because of any human right to command. But they could be laws if they are conceived to be the commands of God, and God is conceived to have a right to be obeyed. The laws of nature are indeed laws, Hobbes maintained, if we make both those assumptions. (It is nevertheless contested as to whether Hobbes himself thought the assumptions were true, not least because his own belief in God is disputed.) An alternative description, which does not invoke those assumptions, is that the laws of nature are properly 'dictates of reason', that is, propositions that rational agents would accept (in a sense to be explored below) in the light of their own ends. Although Hobbes does say men are obliged to obey the laws of nature, he makes a distinction in relation to that obligation which further complicates the issue.

The distinction Hobbes makes is between an obligation *in foro interno* and an obligation *in foro externo*. These terms are not of his own invention, but in his usage correspond to something like disposition and action. That is, men are always obliged to obey the laws of nature *in foro interno*; they should always be ready to act as the laws require, if it is safe to do so. But they are obliged *in foro externo*, in the world of action, to behave as they require only when it *is* safe to do so. Men should always be ready to put the laws of nature into effect, but their willingness to do so should be tempered by consideration for their own safety. Although everyone might be able to understand the principles which it is necessary that everyone should follow if they are to live in peace, it might still be unsafe for any individual to follow those principles unilaterally.

A rational calculator therefore has to decide whether it is safe for him to act upon the laws of nature, even though he has an obligation to be prepared to act upon them when it is. The lack of safety is caused by the absence of trust: for one person to follow the laws of nature without having any reason to suppose that others will too would be to make himself more vulnerable. Contracts provide a good example of the problem of trust, which Barry explores. Individuals who do not trust each other will not want to be involved in any sort of agreement which specifies that they should do something now, in return for a benefit which another party is to confer in the future, because this will simply invite the other to fail to reciprocate. The absence of trust provides an incentive for simultaneity, as, for example, spies are 'swapped' by Intelligence Services. Hobbes suggests that contracts which are not simultaneously executed by the parties to them will not be made in the state of nature, but that they will be in civil society. The presence of a sovereign, with power to force the other contractor to do as he has agreed, removes the need for trust. More generally, the sovereign makes it safe to obey the laws of nature; the presence of the sovereign might be thought, therefore, to add the obligation *in foro externo* to that *in foro interno*. There is obviously a danger of circularity here, though: if the presence of the sovereign makes the laws of nature binding, and one provision of those laws is that men should keep their contracts, and the sovereign is created by a contract, then the effectiveness of the sovereign appears to be the precondition of the obligation of which

sovereignty is itself supposedly the result. This thought leads back
to the collapse of the distinction between 'being obliged' (in the
sense that an effective sovereign will oblige an individual to behave
in certain ways) and 'having an obligation', because the position at
which we have arrived identifies the circumstances in which men
have an obligation to obey with the circumstances in which they
can be obliged to do so.

Both Taylor and Barry explicitly reject the collapsing of the
distinction, and maintain that Hobbes kept the two ideas separate.
But they do so for different reasons. Taylor's interpretation (which,
it should be noted, deliberately focuses on works other than
*Leviathan*) is concerned to detach Hobbes's psychology from his
politics: his theory is deontological, not based upon self-interest,
and this is because men have a duty to obey the law of nature. The
law of nature requires men to keep their covenants (or contracts),
and the sovereign is created by a covenant. Therefore they have a
*moral* duty to obey him, not merely a prudential or self-interested
reason to do so. The sovereign himself has a duty to obey the laws
of nature, even though he is beyond the civil law. Taylor further
holds that this duty is in fact a duty to God: the laws of nature are
God's commands. On Hobbes's definition of 'law', this means that
God has a right to command, a right which, Taylor admits, arises
for Hobbes from God's irresistible power. But once again this may
appear to the reader to collapse the distinction Taylor is anxious
to maintain – between having a moral obligation, and being coerced
by a powerholder. The alternative possibility Taylor canvasses is
that the obligation is a moral obligation for those who have covenanted to obey God. Although he recognizes that this is not what
Hobbes actually wrote, he suggests that it is what he should have
held if he were to be consistent. This interpretation obviously
requires Taylor to spend some time refuting the charge that Hobbes
was an atheist.

Barry also emphasizes that Hobbes separated the idea of 'having
an obligation' from 'being obliged'. Barry is criticizing the interpretation offered in Howard Warrender's *The Political Philosophy of Hobbes*
which shares important features with that given by Taylor, in
particular the notion that the laws of nature are obligatory because
they are the commands of God. Barry rejects this view; some of the
reasons he gives for doing so depend, as we have seen, on distinguishing between Hobbes's various political works. The major argument, however, is that Hobbes gives, in *Leviathan*, a definition of
'obligation' which Warrender does not take sufficiently into account.
The burden of that definition is that a man has an obligation if he

has given up a right. Barry explores an instance of such a surrender, namely giving a contractual undertaking. To make a contract is to give up a right; therefore, the contractor has a (moral) obligation to keep it. But Barry wishes to detach that obligation to keep contracts, which follows from the logic of right-transfers, from the laws of nature. The laws of nature, Barry holds, are not obligatory in the sense of 'obligation' given in Hobbes's own definition. So while for Taylor the moral character of the obligation to obey the sovereign is generated by a moral obligation to obey the laws of nature (and some embarrassment is expressed about the apparent dependence of this allegedly moral obligation on God's irresistible power), for Barry the obligation to the sovereign is a moral obligation because it is a special case of an obligation arising from a contract, which is itself a moral obligation. The laws of nature, in Barry's view, 'oblige' only inasmuch as they identify what is necessary to a man's self-preservation, which suggests that a person who thinks clearly enough will be prepared to follow those laws. Although making and keeping some contracts might also tend to self-preservation, Barry distinguishes the primary sense of obligation as 'having given up a right' from a secondary sense as 'doing what tends to an agent's own preservation'.

The idea of obligation as self-interest once again brings up the interpretation Taylor sets out to criticize, according to which doing one's duty is identical to doing what is in one's interest. As we have seen, both Taylor and Barry reject this: Taylor because the laws of nature are *morally* binding, and Barry because, while the laws of nature oblige as a matter of self-preservation, the primary sense of obligation is a moral requirement to abide by a renunciation of a right. There is therefore a greater connection between the egoistic psychology and obligation in Barry's account than in Taylor's, although in neither case does the interpretation of the major sense of obligation depend upon it. This disconnection of the psychology and the politics is, however, resisted by C.B. Macpherson.

Macpherson's interpretation, presented in *The Political Theory of Possessive Individualism*, holds that Hobbes deduced (what he thought was a moral) obligation from the facts of man's condition – primarily his 'equal need for continued motion' in a market society. This gives Hobbes's materialism and his social assumptions a prominent place in the explanation of obligation, but both remain contentious issues. As we have noted, the connections, if any, between empirical statements (about physiology and psychology) and normative ones (about what men should do) are crucial in determining both the type of obligation (moral or prudential) and the relation between being obliged and having an obligation. Macpherson's interpretation differs radically from that of other modern scholars firstly in accepting a continuity between Hobbes's physiology and psychology (the need for motion) and his conception of man's rights and obligations; and secondly in regarding as unimportant the distinction between prudential and moral obligation, the distinction at the heart of the readings in this section.

## ACCESSIBLE EDITIONS

Thomas Hobbes, *Leviathan* (introduced by A.D. Lindsay) (London, Everyman, Dent, 1914)

C.B. Macpherson (ed.), *Leviathan* (Harmondsworth, Penguin, 1981)

## SUGGESTED READING

Keith Brown (ed.), *Hobbes Studies* (Oxford, Blackwell, 1965)

A.P. d'Entreves, *Natural Law* (revised edn) (London, Hutchinson, 1970)

M.M. Goldsmith, *Hobbes's Science of Politics* (New York, Columbia University Press, 1966)

Gregory S. Kavka, *Hobbesian Moral and Political Theory* (Princeton and Guildford, Princeton University Press, 1986)

C.B. Macpherson, *The Political Theory of Possessive Individualism* (Oxford, Clarendon Press, 1962)

Michael Oakeshott, 'Introduction' to *Leviathan*, ed. Oakeshott (Oxford, Blackwell, n.d.)

* Richard Peters, *Hobbes* (Harmondsworth, Penguin, 1956)

* D.D. Raphael, *Hobbes: Morals and Politics* (London, Allen & Unwin, 1977)

Quentin Skinner, 'The ideological context of Hobbes's political thought', *Historical Journal*, 9 (1966), pp. 286–317

Howard Warrender, *The Political Philosophy of Hobbes: His Theory of Obligation* (Oxford, Clarendon Press, 1957)

J.N. Watkins, *Hobbes's System of Ideas – An Essay in the Political Significance of Philosophical Ideas* (London, Hutchinson, 1973)

## Chapter Two

# THE ETHICAL DOCTRINE OF HOBBES*

## *A. E. TAYLOR*

The moral doctrine of Hobbes, in many ways the most interesting of our major British philosophers, is, I think, commonly seen in a false perspective which has seriously obscured its real affinities. This is, no doubt, largely due to the fact that most modern readers begin and end their study of Hobbes's ethics with the *Leviathan*, a rhetorical and, in many ways, a popular *Streitschrift* published in the very culmination of what looked at the time to be a permanent revolution, and do not pay such attention to the more calmly argued statements of the same doctrine contained in the *Elements of Law*, circulated before the outbreak of the Civil War, or the *De Cive*, produced (apart from the explanatory notes appended in the second edition of 1646) before the issue of the conflict could have been thought to be already decided by 'the sword'. As a corrective to misunderstandings based on exclusive attention to the *Leviathan*, I shall, in these pages, take my references to Hobbes almost entirely from the *De Cive*, and, for convenience' sake, I will use the text of the English version, *Philosophical Rudiments concerning Government and Society*, printed in 1651 and reproduced in volume II of Molesworth's edition of the *English Works*.‡ (I have remarked a few errors in this volume, notably the total perversion of Hobbes's sense by the omission of a whole line of text in XVI, 16, p. 245, of Molesworth.[1] But with these few exceptions it seems to me a sufficiently faithful rendering for my purposes.)

---

* Previously published in *Philosophy* (1938).

‡ It has become standard practice to supply references to the Molesworth edition of Hobbes's *Collected Works* (*The English Works of Thomas Hobbes*, ed. Sir William Molesworth, London, 1839–45, 11 vols; *Thomae Hobbes, Malmesburiensis, Opera Philosophica*, ed. Sir William Molesworth, London, 1839–45, 5 vols) – either the *English Works* (*EW*) or the *Latin Works* (*LW*) followed by volume and page number (e.g. *EW* III, 36). The standard edition of *Leviathan* is that edited by Michael Oakeshott (Oxford, Blackwell, n.d.) conventionally abbreviated to *Lev.* In these readings, references in these standard forms have been supplied if not given by the original author.

The impression which the average reader of the *Leviathan* carries away with him might, I think, be fairly summed up thus. The answer to the question *what ought a good man to do?* is the simple one that he ought to obey the political 'sovereign' without asking any questions or making any difficulties, and the reason why he ought to do this is equally simple. It can be shown, if not to demonstration, yet with overwhelming probability, that he stands personally to lose by doing anything else, and the object of every man's desire is 'always some good to himself'. It is my personal interest that the miseries of anarchy should be prevented; by disobeying the civil law in any particular, I am, so far, contributing to the recurrence of anarchy; *ergo*, it is always to my interest to conform to the law. And to say that this is to my interest is equivalent to saying that it is my duty; my duty, in fact, means my personal interest, calmly understood. That this should be popularly accepted as an adequate account of Hobbes's teaching about morality may be partly explained by historical causes. When Butler set himself to expose the fallacies of the 'selfish' psychology of human action, he found admirable examples of them in some of Hobbes's analyses of the 'passions', and he did the work of refutation so thoroughly that he has perhaps made the notion that there is nothing in Hobbes but this 'selfish psychology' (a charge which he himself is careful never to make) current from his day to our own. Partly also I think Hobbes himself must be held unintentionally responsible for the result. The *Leviathan* is far the most readable and amusing of his works, and it was written in a time of revolution and unsettlement as a persuasive to cessation from fruitless civil strife. For its immediate purpose, as an exhortation to peace, it was right and proper that the author should develop the contention that peace is the real interest of his fellow-countrymen as persuasively as he could; it is not surprising, therefore, that it attains such dimensions in his book as to give the impression that it is really all, or almost all, that he has to say.

And yet it is not all, nor nearly all. There are really two distinct questions before Hobbes, the question why I *ought* to behave as a good citizen, and the question what inducement can be given me to do so if my knowledge of the obligation to do so is not in itself sufficiently effective. According to his repeated declarations, it is a certain fact of psychology that I shall violate the law and break the peace if I believe that I stand to gain by doing so.[2] Hence the importance for him of arguing that I never really stand to gain by such conduct, since the recurrence of the state of 'war of every man against every man' is a disadvantage to me which cannot be offset by any compensating advantage. But the Hobbian answer to the other question, why I ought, or am obliged, to be a good citizen is quite different; it is, quite explicitly, that I have, expressly or tacitly, pledged my word to be one, and to violate my word, to refuse to 'perform my covenant as made', is *iniquity, malum in se*.[3] Hobbes's ethical doctrine proper, disengaged from an egoistic psychology with which it has no logically necessary connection, is a very strict deontology, curiously suggestive, though with interesting differences, of some of the characteristic theses of Kant.

This comes out particularly strikingly in the passage in *De Cive* (III, 5 [*EW* II, 32–3]), where Hobbes is explaining the difference between the justice of an act and the justice of a person. A just *act* is 'what is done in accord with right', but a man who does acts which are in accord with right is not *eo ipso* a just *man*.

When the words are applied to persons, *to be just* signifies to be delighted in just dealing, to study how to do righteousness, or to endeavour in all things to do that which is just; and *to be unjust* is to neglect righteous dealing, or to think it is to be measured not according to my contract, but some present benefit. . . . That man is to be accounted just, who doth just things because the law commands it, injust things only by reason of his infirmity; and he is properly said to be injust, who doth righteousness for fear of the punishment annexed unto the law, and unrighteousness by reason of the iniquity of his mind.[4]

This is precisely Kant's distinction between action done merely in accord with law and action done from law, with the characteristic difference that Hobbes is trying to reduce the law from which the virtuous man acts to the single law that a promise once duly fulfilled must be kept, and Hobbes is laying himself open to the very same line of argument which has, fairly or unfairly, been used against Kant, that a 'good will' which wills nothing but this conformity to laws because it is law, is formal and empty.

Indeed, Hobbes actually goes as far as to anticipate Kant's attempt to reduce all really wrong willing to the irrational attempt to will both sides of a contradiction at once. Thus we read (*De Cive*, III, 3 [*EW* II, 31], and the argument is equally used in other expositions of his theory)

There is some likeness between that which in the common course of life we call *injury*, and that which in the schools is usually called absurd. For even as he who by arguments is driven to deny the assertion which he first maintained, is said to be brought to an absurdity; in like manner, he who through weakness of mind does or omits that which before he had by contract promised not to do or omit, commits an injury, and falls into no less contradiction than he who in the schools is reduced to an absurdity. For by contracting for some future action, he wills it done; by not doing it, he wills it not done; which is to will a thing done and not done at the same time, which is a contradiction. An injury therefore is a kind of absurdity in conversation, as an absurdity is a kind of injury in disputation.

There is in every breach of covenant a contradiction properly so called; for he that covenanteth, willeth to do, or omit, in the time to come; and he that doth any action, willeth it in the present, which is part of the future time, contained in the covenant; and therefore he that violateth a covenant, willeth the doing and the not doing of the same thing, at the same time; which is a plain contradiction. And so injury is an absurdity of conversation, as absurdity is a kind of injury in disputation.
[*EW* IV, 96]

The thought here is at bottom the same as Kant's, but for the differences that (1) Hobbes, for his own reasons, reduces all 'injury' to the violation of an express or implied promise; (2) and he has not, like Kant, thought of the 'universalizing of a maxim' as a criterion of its freedom from contradiction. But the really important point is that Hobbes agrees with Kant on the 'imperative' character of the moral law, exactly as he also agrees with him in the assertion that it is the law of 'right reason'.

Hobbes's recognition of the imperativeness of the natural, which is also the moral law, is obscured for a hasty reader by the fact that he also repeatedly describes the contents of that law as 'theorems' discovered by our reason, like the theorems of mathematics, and even goes so far as to say that these theorems only become *laws* proper in civil society.

Thus (*De Cive*, III, 33 [*EW* II, 49–50])

those which we call the laws of nature (since they are nothing else but certain conclusions, understood by reason, of things to be done and omitted; but a law, to speak properly and accurately, is the speech of him who by right commands somewhat to others to be done or omitted) are, not in propriety of speech laws, as they proceed from nature. Yet, as they are

delivered by God in holy Scriptures . . . they are most properly
called by the name of laws;

again (*Leviathan*, XV [*Lev.*, 104–5: *EW* III, 147]),

> these Dictates of Reason, men use to call by the name of Lawes,
> but improperly: for they are but Conclusions, or Theoremes
> concerning what conduceth to the conservation and defence of
> themselves; whereas Law, properly, is the word of him, that
> by right hath command over others. But yet if we consider the
> same theoremes, as delivered in the word of God, that by right
> commandeth all things; then are they properly called Lawes.

So in the *Elements of Law* (XV, 2 [*EW* IV, 87]), the 'precepts of
Natural Law' are said simply to be 'those which declare unto us
the ways of peace, where the same may be obtained, and of defence
where it may not', without any reference to an imperative character,
though we read later in the same work (XVIII, 1 [*EW* IV, 111])
that they are 'also divine laws in respect of the author thereof, God
Almighty'. One might, at first, be disposed to understand these
deliverances to mean that in themselves the 'laws of nature' are
mere propositions indicative about the means which are commonly
found to be most conducive to a peaceful existence, and that their
imperative character as laws, in the proper sense of the word, is
entirely secondary; it only arises in a civil society when the sovereign
has bestowed it upon them, and reinforced it with penal 'sanctions'.
Thus outside a civil society with penalties for breach of contract,
the 'law' that 'men perform their covenants' would mean merely
the proposition that in the vast majority of cases, perhaps in all, a
man will find that it pays him better to keep his word than it would
do to break it; in civil society, so far as regards contracts of which
the law takes cognizance, this statement of fact is converted into an
imperative by the sovereign who imports the 'thou shalt' into it by
making covenant-breaking actionable in his courts. And this is, I
believe, how Hobbes has commonly been understood by most of
his readers.

But there are, as it seems to me, insuperable difficulties in the
way of such an interpretation.

(1) It is to be observed that from the first, and even when he is
speaking of the condition of things in his imaginary 'state of nature',
Hobbes always describes the items of the natural law as *dictamina*,
or dictates, never as *consilia*, or pieces of advice, and the very use
of this language implies their imperative character. So, too, Hobbes
regularly says of his natural law that it is a 'theorem' which *forbids*

certain actions, and uses imperative or quasi-imperative language in his formulation of them. Thus (*De Cive*, II, 1 [*EW* II, 16]) the law of nature is defined as 'the dictate of right reason, conversant about those things which are either to be done or omitted (dictamen rectae rationis circa ea, quae agenda vel omittenda sunt) for the constant preservation of life and members, as much as in us lies'. 'A Law of Nature (*Leviathan*, XIV [*Lev.*, 84: *EW* III, 116–17]) is a Precept, or generall Rule, found out by Reason, by which a man is forbidden to do, that, which is destructive of his life, or taketh away the means of preserving the same; and to omit that, by which he thinketh it may be best preserved.' And (ibid. [*Lev.*, 85: *EW* III, 117]) the 'Fundamentall Law of Nature' is that 'by which men are commanded to endeavour Peace'. The imperative character of the law is thus inseparable from it. Even in the 'state of nature' the 'fundamental law' is not 'men cling to life and are reluctant to leave it'; but 'I *am to* do what will, so far as I can see, preserve my life, and I am *not* to do what I judge will imperil it.' (Suicide would apparently be wholly excluded, even amid all the miseries of the 'natural state'.)

It is in strict accordance with this recognition of the imperativeness of the law that Hobbes always lays it down that *obligation* is not created by the sovereign when he issues his orders backed by threats of penalties. The moral obligation to obey the natural law is antecedent to the existence of the legislator and the civil society; even in the 'state of nature' the law obliges '*in foro interno*', though not, as Hobbes is careful to add, always '*in foro externo*'. This is not a mere idle playing with words. Hobbes could have conveyed his meaning more unambiguously perhaps, if he had laid more stress on the point that the fundamental law of nature and morals, as he conceives it, is a law of *reciprocal* obligation: what it commands is peace with him who is willing also to be at peace with me, 'that peace is to be sought after, *where it may be found*', 'that every man ought to endeavour Peace, *as farre as* he has hope of obtaining it'. The *caveat* that the 'Laws of nature oblige *in foro interno* . . . but *in foro externo*, that is, to the putting them in act, not alwayes' is, after all, only meant to remind us that the obligations of these laws are reciprocal, and that where there is no common power to act as protector, a man has to judge for himself whether his desire for peace with me is reciprocated on my part. It has also a fuller implication, which Hobbes's unfriends have not always been fair enough to keep in mind. Whereas the civil law can only be infringed by overt acts or words, the moral law is violated by an improper thought or purpose.

Whatsoever Lawes bind *in foro interno* may be broken, not onely by a fact contrary to the Law, but also by a fact according to it, in case men think it contrary. For though the Action in this case, be according to the Law; yet his Purpose was against the Law, which where the Obligation is *in foro interno* is a breach. (*Leviathan*, XV [*Lev.* 103: *EW* III, 145])

The laws which oblige conscience, may be broken by an act not only contrary to them, but also agreeable with them; if so be that he who does it, be of another opinion. For though the act itself be answerable to the laws, yet his conscience is against them. (*De Cive*, III, 28 [*EW* II, 46])

Hobbes is thus quite consistent with himself in maintaining that the natural law – unlike the civil – is

*immutable and eternal*; what they [the 'laws of nature'] forbid, can never be lawful, what they command can never be unlawful. For *pride, ingratitude, breach of contracts* (or *injury*), *inhumanity*, contumely will never be lawful, nor the contrary virtues to these ever unlawful, as we take them for dispositions of the mind, that is, as they are considered in the court of conscience, where only they oblige and are laws. (*De Cive*, III, 29 [*EW* II, 46])

(The meaning of the last clause is only that an outward act which would otherwise have been an exhibition of pride, or a breach of contract, and therefore contrary to the moral law, may acquire a different character, at a particular place and time, owing to the dispositions of the civil law. Thus to exact marks of respect which it would be pride in a private man to demand, may be a proper proceeding on the part of an ambassador or a judge who has the dignity of his sovereign and his sovereign's courts of justice to maintain, and is consistent with the most perfect personal modesty. To desist from fulfilling a contract which the law-courts have pronounced illegal and forbidden me to fulfil is not to show myself a promise-breaker and a man of bad faith, but to prove myself a good citizen; it is my duty as executor under a friend's will *not* to pay legacies which the law has declared invalid, and so on.)

To do full justice to Hobbes we have to remember that the private man in the civil state has other obligations besides that of 'keeping his covenant' by obeying all the commands and prohibitions of the civil law. There is a large range of action in respect to which the 'sovereign' has not laid down any specific commands, and here, Hobbes holds, I am obliged by the natural law to exhibit the 'equity' which he sums up in the traditional maxim not to do to another what I am unwilling to have done to myself. 'Justice' is not the whole of that to which a citizen is obliged but, and quite naturally, in view of the political disorders of the reign of Charles I and the Commonwealth, the practical importance of obedience to constituted authority is so great in Hobbes's eyes that it becomes his predominant theme; it is easy to forget that he equally teaches that we are under an 'eternal obligation' to practise an equity which demands mercy, benevolence, gratitude, and to practise it because the law demands it.

Since all obligation, including the obligation to honour my 'covenant' by strict obedience to the sovereign, is thus derived by Hobbes from a 'natural law' which is the 'dictate of reason', he really escapes from the charge brought against him by Cudworth of making moral distinctions the creation of 'meer will'. It is true that, according to him, there is one distinction which the sovereign does make by his 'meer will', that between *just* and *unjust, unjust* meaning by definition what the civil law forbids, and *just* what it permits. But the sovereign does *not* in this fashion make the antecedent and more important distinction between *equity* and *iniquity*; his will does not create the iniquity of refusing him the obedience we have promised. And the declaration that he does create the distinction between justice and injustice is, in exposition, so whittled down that it loses a great deal of its apparent sting. Thus we learn that the sovereign does nothing to create the obligation to keep a 'covenant'; all that he really does is to decree that the performance of certain 'covenants' is illegal, and to prescribe the precise forms of declaration of our intentions which his courts will regard as constituting a contract. So, we are told, he does not make adultery wrong; it was wrong antecedently by the 'natural law'; he merely decides 'what copulations' are to be regarded as adulterous.[5] I suppose this means that in any case, independently of the authority of any civil law, we could lay it down that sexual connections which are incompatible with the existence of a civilized community are wrong and should be forbidden; but I should be taking too much upon me if I presumed on my own authority to say just what sexual unions are so incompatible; if I am a loyal citizen, I shall regard that as settled for me by the civil law. The law may, of course, make a mistake, exactly as Hobbes himself says, one monarch may wage an iniquitous war against another. But, as he argues with reference to that illustration, the iniquity of the war is not the guilt of the subject who is commanded to bear arms in it; his business as a good subject is simply to obey the command of his own sovereign, to whom he has 'covenanted' to be loyal, and must therefore obey, if he is not to break the command of the natural law that 'covenants' are to be kept. He has thus discharged his own conscience; if the command were iniquitous, the inquity concerns only the sovereign who gave it, and he, according to Hobbes, will have to answer for it to God; if the subject had broken his 'covenant' to obey his lawful sovereign on the strength of his personal belief that the command given him was iniquitous, the iniquity of the disobedience would have been with him. This is, of course, just the familiar doctrine, 'Theirs not to reason why; Theirs but to do and die', a principle which perhaps few of us would care to apply as unrestrictedly as Hobbes does, but without some recognition of which all transaction of concerted human business would become impossible.[6]

It must be remembered, however, that this unqualified submission to the sovereign is regarded by Hobbes not as a mere counsel of safety, but as a strict moral obligation, and that the obligation is imported into it from the 'eternal' natural law that faith once given is to be kept, which is antecedent to the creation of political society. His view is not that in civilized societies the natural (or moral) law has been superseded by another, but that, in virtue of his theory of civil society as created by a 'covenant' of every member with every other to recognize the sovereign's commands as the rule of life, even when I disapprove of some particular command, I am strictly bound by a 'prior obligation', which I cannot violate without bad faith, to comply with it, exactly as a judge is bound by his office to give sentence in accord with the law, even when he personally thinks the existing law a bad one.

If we grant Hobbes's assumptions about the dependence of civil society on the 'covenant', and the character of the 'covenant' itself, the duty of obeying the civil law, even where I personally think it to be iniquitous, follows as part of a consistent deontology. It is not a logical necessity of the system that we should also accept his egoistic moral psychology. Even if we reject this psychology *in toto*, so long as we grant the premises that civil society rests upon a 'covenant' to obey whatever shall be enacted as the 'law of the land', and that breach of covenant is always a violation of duty, the conclusion he wishes to draw will follow, viz., that I am only free to be guided by my personal opinion as to what is equity when the civil law has seen fit to leave me free.

(2) The strictly deontological character of Hobbes's thought comes out equally in the doctrine, essential to his argument, that the civil sovereign himself, who obviously cannot be subject to the

jurisdiction of his own courts, but has been, in Hobbian language, 'authorized' in advance to command and forbid at his own discretion, is just as much under a rigid law of moral obligation as his subjects. He is obliged to equity, the strict observance of the natural (or moral) law, which means, in effect, that he is bound to command and forbid always with a view to the good of the community (and, therefore, as Hobbes is careful to explain, to the practice of just judgement, humanity, mercy, and benevolence). And Hobbes's professed doctrine is that though no human court can take cognizance of the sovereign's shortcomings in this matter, he has always to reckon with the account he will yet have to render to God, who is no excepter of persons. A hasty reader of the *Leviathan* (though he or she would be a hasty one) may come away with the impression that Hobbes's sovereign has extensive rights, but nothing to speak of in the way of corresponding duties. The impression should be corrected by a perusal of *De Cive*, XIII, *Concerning the Duties of those who bear Rule* [especially] sections 15–17 [*EW* II, 178–81], which deal with the way in which this duty is violated by 'princes' who unduly restrain the 'harmless liberty' of the subject by a multiplicity of superfluous laws, allow law to be stultified by the imposition of inadequate penalties or made odious by the infliction of unnecessary severities, or poison its administration by conniving at the corruption of judges by bribes and presents. All such misconduct on the part of 'princes' is constantly described by Hobbes as *iniquity* and *sin*.

Now since Hobbes also attempts to reduce all *iniquity* in the end to breach of an express or implied contract, and since he also, as we all know, makes it so capital a point that the parties to the original contract by which civil society was created are not the 'sovereign' and the 'subject' (who only come into existence in virtue of the contract itself), but the individual items of a 'dissolute multitude' which is not yet a society and has no legal personality, we might find a difficulty here. If the original contract, which must not be broken, imposed no conditions of any kind upon the future sovereign's arbitrary exercise of the power to command and forbid, how can he be said to be guilty of *iniquity* if he chooses to issue a host of grandmotherly commands, to enforce them savagely, or to neglect enforcing them, or if he winks at the bribery of his judges? He never covenanted with his subjects that he would not do these things; if he does them, then, he breaks no 'covenant', and cannot be iniquitous, if iniquity and breach of contract are the same thing. Hence it is not unnatural that Hobbes should have been suspected of meaning no more by all his talk about the 'duties' of sovereigns than that a sovereign who acts in the ways he condemns is likely to draw unpleasant consequences on himself. Yet it is, I think, impossible not to feel that Hobbes is writing in earnest all through the chapter of the *De Cive* which deals with the duties of 'them who bear rule', he does mean that in observing the rules he lays down, rulers are only discharging a *debitum*, and Hobbes would have been the first to insist that a man cannot properly be said to owe a debt to himself. It must be remembered that he is always very careful to insist that in ruling with a single eye to the public good, the sovereign is doing what he is *obliged* to do by the 'natural law', and that, in his terminology, there is an essential difference between following a *counsel* and obeying a *law*.

> *Counsel* is a *precept*, in which the reason of my obeying it is taken from *the thing itself which is advised*; but *command* is a *precept*, in which the cause of my obedience depends on the *will* of the commander. For it is not properly said that *thus I will and thus I command*, except the will stand for a reason. Now when obedience is yielded to the laws, not for the thing itself, but by reason of the adviser's will, the law is not a *counsel* but a *command*, and is defined thus: *law is the command of that person, whether man or court, whose precept contains in it the reason of obedience*. . . . *Law* belongs to him who hath power over those whom he adviseth; *counsel* to them who have no power. To follow what is prescribed by *law*, is *duty*; what by *counsel* is *free-will*.
> (*De Cive*, XIV, 1 [*EW* II, 183])

If Hobbes had meant, then, that the sovereign who does the various things which he condemns in a sovereign is acting in an *ill-advised* way, doing what he is likely hereafter to be sorry for, and nothing more, he ought, according to his own definitions, to have called the 'precepts' of *De Cive*, XIII, simply counsels, not duties. If the ruler can be said to have duties at all, he must be himself subject to a *law* that is to the *command* of some 'persons whose precept contains in it the reason of obedience'. (Here, again, we may remark an anticipation of Kant, though with a difference. Hobbes means to say that a 'counsel' is exactly what Kant calls an *analytic* imperative; it takes the form 'do this, if (or since) you desire that, to which this is required as a means'. But a dutiful act is one of obedience to a law for which obedience the motive is just that the law is law, is, in fact, in the Kantian not very well chosen phrase, a *synthetic* imperative.) If Hobbes is to be regarded as consistent with himself we must explain how, on his theory, the sovereign can be guilty of breach of faith, and how this breach of faith can be the violation of a command which is the command of a *person* (in the Hobbian sense), and 'contains in it the reason of obedience'.

Now as to the first point, there is something to be considered on which Hobbes himself has hardly laid all the stress he should have done. The sovereign, according to him, is created by a voluntary transference to him of what, in the 'state of nature', had been the personal right of each of his future subjects. What each of us transferred to the sovereign by this transaction was the right to prescribe at his discretion what we should do and omit. But the purpose of this transference was the promotion of the safety and commodious living of each of us. We did not renounce our claim to this when we renounced our claim to judge of our own discretion how it may be attained. And though the 'renunciation' was made not by a contract between the sovereign 'of the one part' and the 'people' of the other part, but by one between each individual man and every other, in which the sovereign is a beneficiary, but not a party, Hobbes is quite clear on the point that to make the transaction complete there must be an *acceptance* of the proposed transfer of rights by the beneficiary. 'In the conveyance of right, the will is requisite not only of him that conveys, but of him also that accepts it. If either be wanting, the right remains' (*De Cive*, II, 5 [*EW* II, 18]). Hence, though Hobbes does not say much on the point, there *is* a bargain to which the sovereign *is* a party in the constitution of civil society. He is not a party to the bargain, of which Hobbes speaks in particular, between you and me to divest ourselves of most of our 'natural right', he alone has divested himself of none of it. But, as the beneficiary under the bargain, to whom the 'rights' you and I lay down are transferred, he *accepts* the transfer, and in accepting it must be supposed to understand and accept the provision that the powers transferred to him are to be exercised for the preservation and commodity of all of us. This does not affect the conclusion Hobbes is most anxious to establish, that you and I cannot equitably cashier the sovereign or call him to account, since we are supposed to have agreed together to authorize beforehand whatever commands the sovereign may, in his arbitrary discretion, think good to give. We may not rebel because *we* think that what he commands is not conducive to the ends for which the transfer of right was made, since we expressly agreed that *he* was to be the judge of what is so conducive. But it is enough to show that there really is a bargain, to which the sovereign is a party by his acceptance of the sovereignty, that the transferred rights shall be exclusively used in the ways which the sovereign honestly believes to further the end aimed at in the transference, and this is enough to explain why, even on the assumption that all 'iniquity' can be reduced to breach of contract – an assumption which Hobbes can hardly be said to carry through with complete success – the sovereign can be said to be capable of 'iniquity', to be bound by the natural law, and to have a variety of exacting duties. By accepting the sovereignty he has virtually contracted, not indeed to submit his commands to the judgement of any council or body of ministers, but to use them only as he, in his conscience, deems to be for the common safety and welfare. Hence iniquity on his part, too, though not an offence of which any court can take cognizance, could be brought, at a pinch, without any departure from the main lines of Hobbes's thought, under the head of breach of the great law that 'men perform their covenants once made'.

(3) There still remains a further point for consideration. Sovereigns, we are told, have duties; a duty means 'following what is prescribed by law', and a law is 'the command of the person . . . whose precept contains in it the reason of obedience'.

If the fulfilling of the law of nature is a duty in the sovereign, it follows that the law of nature is a *command*, and a command the reason for obedience whereto is that it is the precept of a 'person' with the *right* to command. What 'person', then, is this, whose commands are binding on princes because they are *his* commands? Not the 'natural person' of any man, since Hobbes denies the existence of any universal monarch of the earth; not a 'court' composed of many 'natural persons', since there is no such 'court' with jurisdiction over the independent princes of the world. I can only make Hobbes's statements consistent with one another by supposing that he meant quite seriously what he so often says, that the 'natural law' is the command of God, and to be obeyed *because* it is God's command. Its clauses are 'theorems', because they are discoverable by the unaided use of clear and rational thinking. But if they are also commands, then on Hobbes's principles they are commands laid by one will upon another; no man, as Hobbes puts it, can oblige himself, because, being at once obliger and obliged, he could equally release himself at will from his obligation. 'It were merely in vain for a man to be obliged to himself, because he can release himself at his own pleasure, and he that can do this is already actually free' (*De Cive*, VI, 14 [*EW* II, 83]). 'No man can be obliged except it be to another' (ibid., XII, 4 [*EW* II, 154]). It would seem to follow that the rules of natural 'equity' cannot be commands, or laws, and therefore compliance with them a *duty*, so long as we know no more about them than that they are conclusions rightly collected by reason. To recognize them as *laws*, we must also know that they are the commands of God, and since Hobbes teaches that a law which binds *in foro interno* is not really complied with unless there was a formal intention to obey it as law, we do not really fulfil the demands of equity unless we obey the divine command as such, because it is a divine command.

On the question how we know that the 'theorems' which figure in Hobbes's text *are* commands of God, the answer seems to me to vary from one exposition to another. From a passage already quoted from the *Elements of Law* it would look as though the 'theorems' obtain this fuller character of being divine laws from their being laid down as commands in Scripture. If that is so, it should consistently be added that they are not laws, but remain simply true 'theorems' everywhere outside the 'kingdom of God by covenant', i.e. that they are only *laws* to the Jews and Christians who recognize the authority of the Scriptures to which Hobbes appeals. Yet in *De Cive*, XV, 4–5 [*EW* II, 206–7], we meet another different theory. There we are told that God has a two-fold kingdom, '*natural*, in which he reigns by the dictates of right reason; and which is universal over all who acknowledge the divine power by reason of that rational nature which is common to all', and '*prophetical*, in which he rules also by the *word of prophecy*; which is peculiar, because he hath not given positive laws to all men, but to his peculiar people and some certain men elected by him'. It is then added that in the *natural* kingdom God's right to rule is founded solely on His '*irresistible power*' (whereas in the *prophetical* kingdom, as is explained in detail in the sections of *De Cive* and *Leviathan* devoted to the subject of religion, God's sovereignty over the 'elected' rests on a *covenant*). It seems to follow that according to this version of the doctrine, the natural law is a *law* (and not merely a collection of true theorems) for all men except atheists (whom Hobbes always regards not as disobedient subjects of God, but as aliens, outside God's kingdom).[7] We should, in consistency, have to suppose that the knowledge that the natural law is the command of God may be attained independently of acquaintance with the Jewish and Christian Scriptures. I do not know whether there is any way of reconciling the various passages, nor how, if the view of the *De Cive* is adopted, Hobbes supposes persons unacquainted with the Scriptures to have discovered that the natural law *is* a command of God. But we are, I think, bound to believe that he means what he says when he calls it such a command; in no other way can we make his explicit statements about the connection between the notions of a *duty*, a *command*, and a *law* [cohere] with each other. A certain kind of theism is absolutely necessary to make the theory work.

The reasons which used to be given in the nineteenth century for supposing these theistic utterances to be insincere verbiage are really not creditable to the knowledge or intelligence of the writers who used them. In substance they only amount to this, that Hobbes always insists strongly on the incomprehensibility of the divine nature, and on the impossibility of our having a 'conception' of God, and that he points out in particular the danger of anthropomorphism attending the ascription of intellect and will to God. (The difficulty is that in us, according to Hobbes, will is *appetite*; the 'last appetite in deliberation', and intellection has its beginnings in 'sense'; but clearly we cannot ascribe appetite and 'sense' to the infinite and irresistible being.) Utterances of this kind are so far from being necessarily expressions of atheism that they are the common stock-in-trade of orthodox Christian scholastics. If Hobbes said that we have no conception of God, it was the universal scholastic doctrine that the *essentia* of God cannot be known to us in this life; though we can answer the question *an sit Deus*, we have to leave the question *quid Deus sit* to be solved in a better world. Neither will nor intellect, nor anything else, according to the greatest of the scholastics, can be *univocally* predicated of God and of any creature. When Hobbes in *De Corpore* threw doubt on the value of philosophic arguments for the beginning of the universe in time, he was only repeating what had long before been more fully urged by St Thomas. When he says – and the words have actually been used in support of the allegation of 'atheism' – that we may only attribute to God two kinds of predicates, negative predicates which deny of Him anything which is a mark of limitation, and superlatives which, by their form, indicate that there is no comparison between Him and the creatures of whom the same epithets are predicated in the positive degree, he is, consciously or not, reproducing the teaching and phraseology of the *de divinis nominibus* of 'Dionysius the Areopagite', a writer sympathetically expounded by St Thomas. Clearly arguments which, if valid, would prove the atheism of most of the schoolmen, including the *Doctor angelicus*, prove nothing about that of Hobbes. On the other hand, he *seems* always to accept at its face value the argument that the universe (= the aggregate of bodies) must have a cause, and since, on his own definition of causation, nothing can be *causa sui*, it follows at once (1) that the 'cause of the universe' is neither itself (the 'aggregate of bodies') nor any part of itself, and (2) that, if as Hobbes held, nothing can be conceived but body, this cause, though certainly known by the causal argument to exist, must be incomprehensible to us. The internal consistency of this doctrine seems to me to be the best proof that it was sincerely held. (There is, perhaps, a certain inconsistency between Hobbes's definition of cause and effect, for which it should follow that a cause is always temporally prior to its effect, and the doubt expressed in the *De Corpore* about the validity of the reasons given for a beginning of the world in time.[8] But the utmost that this proves, I think, is only that Hobbes had not thought out the implications of the problem to the end. He has been laughed at for leaving the question undecided until it shall be authoritatively determined by the sovereign. But he is here again in the company of St Thomas. Both leave the last word on the matter to the authorized interpreter of Scripture. The only difference between them is that St Thomas's authorized interpreter is the ecclesiastical power, and it has already given its decision; Hobbes's is the temporal, and its decision cannot be known until the 'sword' has finally settled who is to be the temporal sovereign in England.)

The 'incomprehensibility' of God, so far from being inconsistent with the thesis that the natural law is a divine command, actually serves to remove a possible objection. If God were comprehensible, it is conceivable that accurate knowledge of His nature might prove that nature to be such that we cannot think of it as the source of commands which oblige mankind. But if the nature of God is an inscrutable mystery, then this very inscrutability makes it impossible to use our inability to understand *how* God commands us as any argument against the fact that He does so command us, provided that the fact appears to be sufficiently authenticated. *If* a man finds evidence for the fact either in the witness of our sense of imperative obligation itself, or in the coincidence of the 'theorems' of 'right reason' with the injunctions of Scripture, a Hobbist cannot [reply to] him by alleging, to use the unlovely diction of modern slangishness, that 'ultimate reality is unethical', and therefore *cannot* be the source of moral commands and prohibitions. As we simply do not know what the 'ultimate reality' is (have no 'conception' of it), we are talking idly when we pretend to know that it is 'non-ethical'.

My own belief, for whatever it may be worth, is that Hobbes simply meant what he said about the natural law as a command of God, and that he was led to this conviction not so much by the Scriptural testimonies which he produces in such profusion, as by the unusual depth of his own sense of moral obligation. The impression repeated study of his works leaves on me is that Hobbes was a fundamentally honest man, and a man, as Professor Laird has said, with an almost overwhelming sense of duty. To such a man the thought that duty is a divine command is so natural that it is almost impossible not to form it. And I conceive that Hobbes's religion – for, in spite of De Quincey's jests, I think it clear he had one – consisted, as Kant's did, almost exclusively in the discharge of the duties of everyday morality with an accompanying sense of their transcendent obligatoriness. It is clear that he was not 'religious' in any deeper sense of the word; the worship of the heart was plainly not congenial to him, and his theories, in fact, make any direct personal relation between the worshipper and his god illusory. But such as it was, his religion does impress me as a genuine thing, and it is not very different from that of many worthy persons of today who would be sincerely shocked if they were to be accused of 'atheism'. It seems to me that when we make the necessary allowances for ways of thinking which were current in the middle of the seventeenth century but are now obsolete, Hobbes may have been more in earnest than is usually allowed in supplementing this religion of the duty of a citizen with the one 'article of faith' that Jesus is yet to reappear in Palestine and reign endlessly in temporal felicity over resuscitated believers. Such a 'faith' would have no chance of being accepted as 'the good Christianity' if it were to be proclaimed today. But I do not think it impossible that a man living in the welter of conflicting and bitterly hostile creeds of all kinds prevalent in England in the period 1640–50 may have fancied that something of this kind would emerge at last as the simple 'substance of the faith'.[9]

My serious concern, however, is not with what may have been Hobbes's personal opinions on these things, and I only make the remarks of the last paragraph by very free protest against the too facile assumption that there is nothing in the scriptural exegesis with which *Leviathan*, in particular, abounds beyond an ingenious treating of the ecclesiastics with their own weapons. The point I am really anxious to make is that Hobbes's *ethical* theory is commonly misrepresented and unintelligently criticized for want of sufficient recognition that it is, from first to last, a doctrine of *duty*, a strict deontology. It is true that Charles II had the good taste to enjoy the philosopher's conversation, and that the Whitehall of the Restoration is an unlikely quarter in which to find a deontologist. But Hobbes, after all, was not so very often at Whitehall, and he does not belong to the age of the Restoration wits. He is the contemporary of Clarendon, Falkland, and Selden, not of Rochester, Etherege, and Villiers.

N.B. I have in the text omitted to quote what is perhaps the most important single sentence of Hobbes about *obligation*. In view of its definiteness, I give it both in the Latin and the English forms. *De Cive*, XIV, 2, *annot.* – Clarius ergo hoc dico. Pacto obligari hominem, id est propter promissionem praestare debere. Lege vero obligatum teneri, id est metu poenae quae in Lege constituitur, ad praestationem cogi. *Philosophical Rudiments concerning Government and Society*, XIV, 2 [*EW* II, 185n.] – More clearly, therefore, I say thus: that a man is obliged by his contracts, that is, that he ought to perform for his promise' sake; but that the law ties him being obliged, that is to say, it compels him to make good his promise for fear of the punishment appointed by the law.

The clear distinction thus made between the *obligation* and the subsequent *compulsion* through the 'penal sanction' (a distinction merely overlooked in Bentham's statement that 'a Sanction is a source of obligatory powers or motives') explains at once how Hobbes could maintain that the 'laws of nature' oblige *in foro interno* even before the creation of civil society, that in civil society they continue to oblige wherever the civil law has issued no injunctions, and that they oblige the sovereign himself, who is unamenable to the civil law. The obligatory force of the civil law itself is, in fact, derived entirely from that of the natural. If we are always to obey the civil law, even when in our private opinion it is inequitable, that is because we are already obliged, in virtue of the natural law itself, to honour our 'previous engagement' to be directed by the commands of the sovereign. I am always sure that to break this engagement is inequitable, whereas my personal opinion that the act the sovereign commands me to do is inequitable is, in Hobbes's eyes, never more than a conjecture, and even if I have conjectured rightly, the answerability for the iniquity of the act so commanded lies not with me, but with the sovereign.

## NOTES

1 In the original Latin text of the sentence Hobbes says, as we should expect him to say in the course of an attempt to prove that the supreme power, both spiritual and temporal, was possessed, in the days of the Israelite and Jewish monarchies, by the kings, that the priests could only do rightfully what God commanded them, whereas the king had rightfully all the power over every man which that man had over himself (sacerdos id tantum iure poterat quod Deus iuberet, rex autem iure poterat quidquid poterat iure unusquisque in se). In Molesworth's edition this is represented by the sense-destroying statement that 'the priest could do rightly whatsoever every man could rightly do himself'.

2 Thus (*De Cive*, V, 1 [*EW* II, 63]): 'It is of itself manifest that the

actions of men proceed from the will, and the will from hope and fear, insomuch as when they shall see a greater good or less evil likely to happen to them by the breach than observation of the laws, they will wittingly violate them.' Hence Hobbes goes on to maintain that the moral guilt of offences into which subjects are led by the insufficiency of the penalties provided for them falls not on the subject but on the sovereign. 'If, therefore, the legislator doth set a less penalty on a crime, than will make our fear more considerable with us than our lust, that excess of lust above the fear of punishment, whereby sin is committed, is to be attributed to the legislator, that is to say, to the supreme' (*De Cive*, XIII, 16 [*EW* II, 180]).

3   When he is speaking strictly, Hobbes makes a distinction between *injustice* and *iniquity*, though the distinction is not always carefully kept up (less carefully, I think, in *De Cive* than in *Leviathan*). Injustice, in the strictest sense of the word, is possible only in the 'civil' state, since it is by definition disregard of the commands of the lawful sovereign. Iniquity, which can exist in 'the state of nature', or in the conduct of the sovereign, who, since he is not subject to his own commands, cannot be guilty of injustice proper, is violation of the 'natural law', which is also, according to Hobbes's repeated explanations, the *moral* law. But since my obligation to obey the sovereign is based on the assumption that by living under his protection I have expressly or tacitly 'covenanted' with all my neighbours to accept his commands as the rule of life, and the obligation to observe a 'covenant' is thus antecedent to the institution of civil society, the moral guilt of 'injustice' arises from the fact that all injustice is also *iniquity*, and therefore breach of the moral law, though not all iniquity is 'injustice'. Even in the 'state of nature' to which, according to the *Leviathan*, it is 'consequent' that no act can be just or unjust, *wanton* violation of a promise could be iniquitous. (It is true that since, according to Hobbes's psychology, a man inevitably acts to secure what he believes to be his own greatest good, really wanton promise-breaking could never occur. The promise-breaker would always be acting from the 'reasonable' motive that he hoped to secure more good by breaking his word than by keeping it.)

4   Cf. *De Cive*, IV, 21 [*EW* II, 60]. 'Although a man should order all his actions so much as belongs to external obedience just as the law commands, but not for the law's sake, but by reason of some punishment annexed to it, or out of vain glory; yet he is unjust.'

5   E.g. *De Cive*, XIV, 10 [*EW* II, 191]. 'For though the law of nature forbid theft, adultery, etc.; yet if the civil law command us to invade anything, that invasion is not theft, adultery, etc. For when the Lacedaemonians of old permitted their youths, by a certain law, to take away other men's goods, they commanded that these goods should not be accounted other men's, but their own who took them; and therefore such surreptions were no thefts. In like manner, copulations of heathen sexes, according to their laws, were lawful marriages.'

6   *De Cive*, XII, 2 [*EW* II, 152]. 'Whatsoever any man doeth against his conscience, is a sin; for he who doth so, contemns the law. But we must distinguish. That is my sin indeed, which committing I do

believe to be my sin; but what I believe to be another man's sin, I may sometimes do without any sin of mine. For if I be commanded to do that which is a sin in him who commands me, if I do it, and he that commands me be by right lord over me, I sin not. . . . They who observe not this distinction, will fall into a necessity of sinning, as oft as anything is commanded them which either is, or seems to be unlawful to them; for if they obey, they sin against their conscience; and if they obey not, against right. . . . For by our taking upon us to judge of *good* and *evil*, we are the occasion that as well our obedience, as our disobedience, becomes sin unto us.' Clearly Hobbes would have been on the side of those who have regarded Sophocles's Antigone as simply criminal in her defiance of Creon. The doctrine, in its unqualified form, may have its dangers, but in the middle of the seventeenth century many 'subjects' needed the warning that the commands of a lawful authority are not to be disobeyed whenever they do not approve themselves to the private judgement of a subordinate.

7    I confess here to finding a real difficulty in understanding how Hobbes could hold that mere *irresistible power* can be the foundation of a moral *obligation*. In strict consistency, should he not have held that the moral obligation to obey the natural, which is also the divine, law only covers the case of Israelites in the past, and Christians in the present, who are subjects of God in virtue of a 'covenant', by which they are pledged to 'faith and obedience' (or, when they have erred through frailty, repentance)? As the omnipotent Lord of all things, God is only king over 'infidels' in the same sense in which He is king over the beasts whose subjection to His 'irresistible power' is not supposed to give rise to any obligations.

8    The relevant facts are these:-

(1) Hobbes expressly says, here agreeing completely with St Thomas that no good reasons can be given why the world should have had a beginning (*De Corpore*, IV, 26, 1) (I quote from the text of 1668). Illos igitur qui mundi originem aliquam fuisse rationibus suis a rebus naturalibus demonstrasse se iactitant laudare non possum. . . . Nonne qui reternitatem mundi sic tollunt, eadem opera etiam mundi conditori aeternitatem tollunt. [Cf. *EW* I, 410–14]

(2) According to the definitions of cause and effect given in the same work (II, 9, 3), a *causa integra* (entire cause) is the 'aggregate of all the accidents both of the agents how many soever they be, and of the patient put together; which when they are all supposed to be present (omnibus suppositis) it cannot be understood but that the effect is produced *at the same instant* (quin effectus una sit productus) and if any one of them be wanting, it cannot be understood but that the effect is not produced', and we are consequently told 'quo instante causa sit *integra*, eodem quoque effectum esse productem' [Cf. *EW* I, 121–2]. Thus the 'entire cause', including the requisite conditions 'in the patient', and the effect are simultaneous. But Hobbes infers from this very proposition the 'causation and the production of effects consist in a certain continual progress' (ibid., II, 9, 6 [*EW* I, 123]), and this seems to imply that the 'agent', if not the 'patient', also has an existence which is temporally prior to the 'effect'. If this principle

can be extended to the causation of the universe, it would follow that the universe is *not* eternal. I suppose, however, that Hobbes, who held that philosophy is only concerned with those things of which there are 'generations', could quite consistently have said that the principle, being a philosophical one, must not be applied to God, nor yet to the 'world' *if* the world is 'eternal', and that the question therefore remains open for us as philosophers, though as good subjects we must acquiesce in the sentence of the sovereign, if he thinks fit to pronounce on the matter.

9   I certainly do not myself think that the feats of Biblical interpretation in the *Leviathan* are, in the main, a mere game. Hobbes's exegeses, where they are opposed to those generally current in his time, are often manifestly sound, and even where, to our better informed age they are not sound, they may well have seemed so to their seventeenth-century author. It is only in a small minority of cases that he seems to me to be merely 'answering a fool according to his folly'. It should always be remembered that Hobbes has an admirable practical purpose in his endeavour to reduce the articles of belief 'necessary to salvation' to a minimum. He wants, in an intolerant age, to put an end to persecution for speculative disagreements without challenging the generally accepted view that it is the sovereign's duty to 'cause such a doctrine and worship to be taught and practised' as he believes 'necessarily conducive to the *eternal* salvation' of his subjects (*De Cive*, XIII, 5 [*EW* II, 168]). And he held, as we see from his *Behemoth*, that the ultimate cause of the great rebellion had been the zeal of Presbyterian ministers to enforce all their own personal opinions on points of speculative divinity as 'necessary to salvation'. Persecution, he thinks, will cease if the sovereign insists on no article as fundamental beyond the recognition of Jesus as the future Messianic king, and the subject understands that conformity to the established worship does not imply speculative agreement in opinion, except on this single point.

# Chapter Three

# WARRENDER AND HIS CRITICS*[1]

## *BRIAN BARRY*

The decade of criticism [from 1957] directed at *The Political Philosophy of Hobbes*[2] has found the critics united in rejecting many of Warrender's conclusions, but it has not produced a generally accepted alternative interpretation. I shall argue in this paper that this has happened because the critics have not been searching enough in their criticism. Often they have taken over without discussion two crucial but highly questionable features of Warrender's book: first, his ignoring the definition of 'obligation' given in *Leviathan;* and, second, his presentation of logically independent conclusions about Hobbes's theory as if they were related. As a result of the first, Warrender's critics have sometimes followed him into error; and, as a result of the second, they have sometimes been led to dismiss correct conclusions in the belief that these were logically bound up with other conclusions that really were wrong. Too often they have thrown out the baby and kept the bathwater.

The first point, then, on which I maintain the critics have been less than properly critical, is the provenance of Warrender's definition of 'obligation'. We should notice at the start Warrender's claim that his interpretation of Hobbes is based on the *Leviathan*, and that everything he attributes to Hobbes can be found there. Quotations from elsewhere are used, he says, only where they make more clearly the same points as can be found in *Leviathan* (Warrender, vii-viii). Now, in *Leviathan* Hobbes gives the reader a single unequivocal definition of 'obligation', as follows:

> Right is laid aside, either by simply renouncing it; or by transferring it to another. . . . And when a man hath in either manner abandoned, or granted away his right; then he is said to be OBLIGED, or BOUND, not to hinder those, to whom

* Previously published in *Philosophy*, vol. XLII, no. 164 (April 1968).

such right is granted, or abandoned, from the benefit of it. . . .
(*Lev.*, 86³ [*EW* III, 118–19])

Warrender, however, makes little use of this definition.⁴ Instead,
he constructs a definition of 'obligation' from a passage in *De Cive*
and another in *Liberty and Necessity*. In the first, Hobbes speaks of a
kind of 'natural obligation' 'according to which the weaker,
despairing of his own power to resist, cannot but yield to the
stronger'. In this sense, Hobbes says, we are 'obliged to obey God
in his natural kingdom' (*De Cive*, XV, 7; *EW* II, 209). The second
passage runs thus: 'Power irresistible justifies all actions, really and
properly, in whomsoever it be found; less power does not, and
because such power is in God only, he must needs be just in all
actions . . .' (*EW* IV, 250).

According to Warrender, the basic concept of obligation in
Hobbes's political theory, which can be derived from these
quotations, is one which makes the relation rest on unequal power,
and especially the disparity of power between God and man. But
if we follow Warrender in taking our task to be the interpretation
of *Leviathan* (as against the *Elements of Law* or *De Cive*) we need
to be sure that the passages are relevant to *Leviathan*; even more
fundamentally, of course, we need to be sure they are about obligation. I think it can be shown that the first passage fails the first
test and the second fails the second test.

Let us begin with the first passage, from *De Cive*, according to
which we have a 'natural obligation' to obey God because 'the
weaker . . . cannot but yield to the stronger'. The striking fact here
is that, in the parallel passage of *Leviathan*, the reference to 'natural
obligation' is dropped. In chapter 31 of *Leviathan*, Hobbes again
speaks, as in *De Cive*, of God's 'natural kingdom', and again explains
that God is able to get men to do what He wants. But at no point
does he now say that God's operations in His 'natural kingdom'
lay obligations upon men.⁵ This, we can be sure, is not mere care-
lessness on Hobbes's part. Very few substantial points in the earlier
workings of Hobbes's political theory are omitted in *Leviathan*.⁶ Now,
it is not essential to my case to be able to show why Hobbes chose
to delete any reference to 'natural obligation' from *Leviathan*; it is
enough that he did. But I do not doubt that Hood⁷ is right in
suggesting that the explanation lies in Hobbes's controversy with
Bramhall about liberty and necessity. Since he now held that liberty
is not taken away by the fear of consequences, and wanted to
contrast liberty with obligation, he no longer had room for a concept
of 'natural obligation' based on fear of consequences.

Luckily, Hobbes has given us a comment on the doctrine of *De Cive*, XV, 7, in his *Answer* to Bramhall's *Catching of the Leviathan*, and this is of great interest. Bramhall quotes Hobbes as saying that men are obliged to obey God because of their weakness, and accuses him of impiety (*EW* IV, 290). In his reply, Hobbes coolly replaces the sentence quoted by Bramhall with a quite different one, writing:

> to the same sense I have said in my *Leviathan*, that the right of nature whereby God reigneth over man, is to be derived not from his creating them, as if he desired obedience, as of gratitude; but from his irresistible power. (*EW* IV, 295)

And then he argues that this is not discreditable to God. But notice that by his manoeuvre of citing *Leviathan*, Hobbes has neatly avoided having to defend the words quoted by Bramhall, which spoke of *obligation*. (Indeed it is hard to see any other point in making the substitution.) As if this were not enough evidence that Hobbes found the quotation from *De Cive* awkward, he added: 'But see the subtilty of his disputing. He saw he could not catch *Leviathan* in this place, he looks for him in my book *De Cive*, which is Latin, to see what he could fish out of that . . .' (*EW* IV, 295).[8] How ironical that Warrender, by making the same passage the cornerstone of his analysis, should have laid himself open to exactly the same charge!

Now let us turn to Warrender's second passage, from *Liberty and Necessity*, which says that 'power irresistible justifies all actions . . . and because such power is in God only, he must needs be just in all actions'. There is no problem about the relevance of this passage to *Leviathan*, since it occurs there, too, almost word for word. But there is a serious question about its relevance to obligation. It should be noticed that the word 'obligation' does not occur in the passage, so at best its relevance to the concept of obligation must be an inferential one. I shall now try to show that no inference can in fact be made from anything in this passage to an implied definition of 'obligation'.

There is an obviously apparent connecting link in the word 'just', which does occur in the passage. If all God's actions are just, doesn't this entail that we are obliged to obey Him? The answer is that Hobbes's definition of 'just' does not allow us to make any such inference. 'When a covenant is made, then to break it is *unjust*: and the definition of INJUSTICE is no other than *the not performance of covenant*. And whatsoever is not unjust, is *just*' (*Lev.*, 94 [*EW* III, 130–1]). Hobbes equivocates on the interpretation of the last sentence, so that saying someone is acting justly sometimes means that he is keeping a covenant and sometimes merely that there is no covenant which he is breaking – the latter of course including situations that are not covered by a covenant at all. In this latter sense of 'justice' there need be no connection with obligation at all. If we know that someone is behaving justly we can infer that he is not breaking an obligation, but we are not entitled to infer that he is keeping an obligation either.

In the *Leviathan*, Hobbes usually operates with this second, wider, sense of 'just', as when he says in the 'Review and Conclusion' that if a man lives in a country secretly (and has therefore not tacitly promised to obey the government)

> he is liable to anything that may be done to a spy, and enemy of the state. I say not, he does any injustice, for acts of open hostility bear not that name; but that he may be justly put to death. (*Lev.*, 462 [*EW* III, 705])

'Justly' here means simply 'not unjustly'; Hobbes is not suggesting that the sovereign is carrying out a covenant, merely rejecting the idea that he might be breaking one. The sovereign and the man living secretly are in a state of nature with one another. Now, God's actions with respect to men are 'just' in exactly the same sense, and for the same reason.[9] Leaving aside the Israelites, who had a covenant with God (and were therefore in God's *prophetic* kingdom) men's relation to God is that of a state of nature. Nobody has covenanted with God so therefore God cannot behave unjustly with respect to men. Nor, by the same token, can men behave unjustly with respect to God; breaking God's law may be foolish but Hobbes does not describe it as unjust. Thus, everything God does with respect to men is just; but this sort of 'justice' does not entail the existence of any obligation upon anybody.[10]

A slight variation on the suggestion that God's commands oblige because they are just is the suggestion that God's commands oblige because they are laws; but this is equally baseless. Warrender quotes Hobbes's statement that the 'dictates of reason' which he has been calling laws of nature are, strictly speaking, properly called *laws* only in so far as they are considered as 'delivered in the word of God, that by right commandeth all things' (Warrender, 98, quoting *Lev.*, 104–5 [*EW* III, 147]). And he then comments: 'Thus, if the laws of nature in the State of Nature are considered as the commands of God, they may properly be regarded as laws, *and it is this factor which is responsible for constituting their obligatory character*' (Warrender, 98).[11] Now, the clause which I have italicized, and which is essential to Warrender's argument at this point, has absolutely no foundation. To say that God commands 'by right' does not entail, in the terminology of *Leviathan*, that men have an obligation to obey His commands. God's 'right' to rule over men is merely the 'right of nature'. It 'is to be derived from his irresistible power' (*Lev.*, 234 [*EW* III, 345]). Men, Hobbes says, need to come out of the state of nature with respect to one another (by covenanting to obey a sovereign) because otherwise their approximate equality of strength results in their all getting hurt. But God has no need to come out of the state of nature with respect to men, for, being omnipotent, He cannot be hurt by them. God's 'right' over men is exactly on a par, Hobbes makes it clear, with the 'right' of one man to club another in the absence of an effective sovereign.[12]

Warrender, however, ignores Hobbes's account of the way in which God commands man 'by right'. Instead, he seizes on a statement made by Hobbes while defining *civil* law, that 'law in general, is [not counsel, but] command; nor a command of any man to any man; but only of him, whose command is addressed to one formerly obliged to obey him' (Warrender, 97, quoting *Lev.*, 172 [*EW* III, 251]). Hobbes is saying here that among men law is the result of covenant: a command of *A* is a law for *B* only if *B* is 'formerly obliged' (that is, if he has already covenanted) to obey *A*'s commands. Hobbes's use of the expression 'formerly obliged' shows clearly that he is using the concept of obligation in the way in which he defines it in *Leviathan* – to refer to the result of giving up a right. If we try to apply the concept of natural obligation from *De Cive*, the expression 'formerly obliged' makes no sense at all, for natural obligation depends on power relations at the moment of action, and not (as contractual obligation does) on anything that has occurred in the past.[13]

As an illustration of the tendency for Warrender's critics to take over some of the more questionable aspects of his treatment, let me cite John Plamenatz, one of the earliest and shrewdest critics. In his review of *The Political Philosophy of Hobbes*, Plamenatz, while dissenting from many of Warrender's interpretations, nevertheless agrees that the laws of nature oblige *qua* commands of God, uses the tag about 'power irresistible justifying all things' in the context of obligation, and follows Warrender in ignoring Hobbes's definition of 'obligation' as the logical consequence of a contract. 'Men are said to be *obliged*, when they stand in such a relation to someone that, if they see that relation clearly, they cannot choose but do what is commanded of them.'[14] This leads him to construct a theory in which one is obliged to obey the sovereign because of his ability to inflict punishments. But this was never Hobbes's view of the basis of political obligation, and, as we have seen, even the premise – natural obligation – was eliminated in the writing of *Leviathan*.

The other point on which Warrender's critics have failed to take up a sufficiently critical stance is a more general one. They have, I suggest, tended to take over uncritically his way of setting out the problems and connecting the issues. It will be recalled that Warrender begins his book by saying that there are three possible ideas about obligation in Hobbes: some people have said, he claims, that there is no such concept and that the theory is descriptive only, others that 'when civil society is established, a new type of obligation is created; and still others that obligation, as Hobbes understood it, is essentially the same in civil society and out of it'.[15] Warrender espouses the third view, and thus commits himself to showing that for Hobbes: (a) there can be obligations in the state of nature and (b) that no new kind of obligation is added with the formation of a state.

However, in the body of the book he spends most of his time trying to establish a number of quite different propositions, including the following:

(c) the laws of nature do not rest on individual self-interest either for their demonstration or for their effectiveness,

(d) the laws of nature oblige (in the primary Hobbesian sense of the word 'obligation') in the state of nature and *a fortiori* under a sovereign, and

(e) the obligation to keep the covenant by which a sovereign is set up (or equally any other covenant) depends on, and is merely a special case of, the obligation to obey the laws of nature.

Now if (c), (d), and (e) are true, then certainly (a) and (b) are true, for (d) entails (a) and (e) entails (b). But the falsity of (c), (d), (e) or any combination of them does not entail the rejection of either (a) or (b). It is logically possible for (c), (d), and (e) all to be false while yet (a) and (b) are true; and I shall argue later that it is this combination which Hobbes in fact espouses in the *Leviathan*. Subsequent writers, however, have tended to follow Warrender's way of grouping the possible relationships. Watkins, in *Hobbes's System of Ideas* rejects (c) explicitly and (d) and (e) implicitly.[16] But he goes on to put a negative sign in front of *all* Warrender's assertions by rejecting (a) and (b) too. He claims that the sovereign is 'himself responsible for the creation of obligations, where there were none before' (p. 68) and says that '*pace* Warrender, the sovereign's role *is* to create a public system of moral rules out of a moral vacuum' (p. 138). Thus, the sovereign not merely creates a new kind of obligation; he creates the only kind there is.

Hood, on the other hand, accepts all five propositions in his *The Divine Politics of Thomas Hobbes*. That is, he accepts the structure laid down by Warrender without question, and differs only on the content: where Warrender took the obligatory force of the laws of nature to depend on their being commands of God, Hood adds 'as delivered in Scripture'; and where Warrender leans towards saying that the sort of obligation the laws of nature have is Hobbesian 'natural obligation', Hood rejects this and says that it is a special sort of 'moral obligation' based on Scripture.[17]

I have pointed out that Warrender and his critics are alike in placing little store by Hobbes's explicit definition of 'obligation' in *Leviathan*, but I have not yet shown that they are wrong to do so. I have also asserted that Warrender's conclusions (a) and (b) are true while (c), (d), and (e) are false, but again substantiation needs to be provided. In the rest of this paper an attempt will be made to meet both points at once by showing that, starting from Hobbes's definition of 'obligation', we can develop a consistent theory – more consistent than either Warrender or his critics have given Hobbes credit for – in which Warrender's first two conclusions are true and the others false.[18] First I argue that there can, for Hobbes, be obligations in the state of nature, in the sense of 'obligation' defined by him. That is to say: in certain circumstances a man may create a binding obligation upon himself to perform a certain act as a result of his having given up a right, even where there is no 'common power set over' both parties. If this is accepted then the truth of (a) will have been demonstrated. I shall then try to prove (b) by arguing that the obligation to obey the sovereign is not a different kind of obligation from that given in Hobbes's definition – a citizen is obliged to obey the sovereign because he has given up his right not to obey him. Finally, reasons will be given for rejecting the three propositions culled from Warrender about the basis and status of the laws of nature.

To be under an obligation means to have given up a right; that is, to have given up some part of one's 'right to all things'. Simply giving up a right is 'renunciation'; giving it up in favour of a particular person is 'transfer'; and mutual transfer is contract. 'Covenant' or 'pact' is a particular kind of contract, namely a contract to perform some time in the future. *A* may covenant to perform later in return for *B*'s present performance (in this case *B* does not covenant, though he does enter into a contract); or *A* and *B* may both covenant to perform in the future (*Lev.*, 85–7 [*EW* III, 117–21]). Hobbes later distinguishes the second kind of situation

as one of 'covenants of mutual trust' (*Lev.*, 89 [*EW* III, 124]) or
'promises mutual' (*Lev.*, 95 [*EW* III, 133]).

Can there be obligations (in the sense defined) in the absence of
a 'common power set over both' parties, that is to say 'in the
condition of mere nature'? This does not reduce to the question
whether in the state of nature covenants are ever obligatory; still
less to the question whether covenants of mutual trust can be
obligatory. The question is whether *any* form of renouncing or transferring rights can create an obligation to perform in the state of
nature. Now, contracts, Hobbes tells us, are only conditionally
beneficial; it only pays me to do my part given that you do yours
as well. Therefore, it is not obligatory for one party to perform his
part if he has a 'reasonable suspicion' that the other party will fail
to do his.[19] The key is trust; in the absence of a 'common power'
over the contracting parties, the larger the element of trust involved,
the less chance there is that a contract will create an obligation to
perform. As Hobbes points out (see especially *EW* II, 20), where
both parties perform their part of the contract 'instantly' (by, for
example, exchanging physical goods), there is no need for either
party to trust the other. There is no room for one party to harbour
a 'reasonable suspicion' of the other party's good faith, so that a
contract providing for both parties to perform together must always
give rise to a firm obligation to carry it out.

If one end of the scale is represented by the case where both
parties perform simultaneously and the other end consists of the
case where both parties have yet to perform at separate or undeter-
mined times, the intermediate case is where one party has already
performed while the other has still to do so. Hobbes is quite explicit
about this – in these circumstances the second party is obliged to
do his part, too. Covenants are binding, he tells us, 'either where
one of the parties has performed already; or where there is a power
to make him perform' (*Lev.*, 95 [*EW* III, 133]). The absence of a
common power is, of course, the defining characteristic of the state
of nature; thus Hobbes is saying here that even in the state of nature
there is an obligation to perform your side of a covenant if the other
party has already performed his. For example,

> if I covenant to pay a ransom, or service for life, to an enemy;
> I am bound to it: for it is a contract, wherein one receiveth
> the benefit of life; the other is to receive money, or service for
> it; and consequently, where no other law, as in the condition
> of mere nature, forbiddeth the performance, the covenant [i.e.
> the promise to pay] is valid. (*Lev.*, 91 [*EW* III, 126–7])

Once the enemy has released me, I can obviously no longer plead mistrust of his good faith, and this would be the only acceptable excuse for not carrying out my part of the bargain. I am therefore obliged to do so.

Finally, there are covenants of mutual trust. The element of trust is at a maximum here; if you perform first you have no assurance that the other party will do his part. Hobbes is undecided as to whether this means that there is never an obligation to perform first or whether it is merely rare.[20] But, as we have seen, this does not entail that there can be no obligations in the state of nature. Even in the case of covenants of mutual trust, Hobbes never denies that there is an obligation to perform *second*. Thus, the enemy holding prisoners would never (or hardly ever) be obliged to carry out a promise to release them in return for a mere promise that they would pay a ransom when they get home. But if the prisoners *were* released (however quixotically) in return for a promise, they would be obliged to pay up.

The obligation to obey the sovereign's commands, or laws, is a special case of the obligation to keep one's word. Hobbes puts it neatly in *De Cive*: 'A contract obligeth of *itself*; the *law* holds the party obliged by virtue of the universal *contract* of yielding obedience' (*EW* II, 185. Italics in original. Cf. *Lev.*, 112–13, 462 [*EW* III, 157–9, 704–5]). Of course, the sovereign creates new obligations by his commands but he does not create a new *kind* of obligation.[21] An analogy would be this: if I sign a contract to teach 'under the direction of the professor' and the professor then says 'Teach *x*' the obligation to teach *x* is a contractual obligation. I now have an obligation that I did not have before but its basis is just the same as that of a contract to deliver a sack of potatoes. 'Obligation' is for Hobbes the result of giving up a right; and the obligation to obey the sovereign is the result of transferring to him all one's natural rights, except, of course, the inalienable right to defend oneself against 'death, wounds and imprisonment' (*Lev.*, 91 [*EW* III, 127]; cf. *Lev.*, 86–7 [*EW* III, 120]). In other words, and employing Hobbes's explanation of what it is to transfer one's rights, we can say that a man gives up all those rights that can be given up by means of a covenant (either with his fellow subjects or with the sovereign) in order that the sovereign should be less hindered in exercising his own natural 'right to all things'. The object in so doing is, of course, peace: even if the sovereign is oppressive he is better than the state of nature, and any attempt to guarantee against oppression invites a return to the state of nature.

Why does the covenant to transfer one's natural rights to a

sovereign create a real obligation? The general answer is that the sovereign operates in such a way as to remove the excuses for not performing which can so easily be maintained in the absence of a coercive power. It is not so much that the sovereign makes it pay to keep your covenant by punishing you if you don't, but that it always pays anyway to keep covenants provided you can do so without exposing yourself, and the sovereign ensures that you will not be exposing yourself by keeping your covenant. Exactly how this works out in detail is not shown by Hobbes, but it would seem that the precise formulation must differ between a commonwealth by institution and a commonwealth by acquisition.

A sovereign by institution is set up by a 'covenant of mutual trust' among the prospective subjects of the sovereign, in which they all promise, roughly speaking, blanket obedience in perpetuity to whatever commands (including standing commands, i.e. laws) the sovereign may see fit to give. 'Covenants of mutual trust' are defective in the state of nature because one party cannot be reasonably sure that the other party will perform in due course when his turn comes.

> But in a civil estate, where there is a power set up to constrain those who would otherwise violate their faith, that fear [of being double-crossed by the others] is no more reasonable; and for that cause, he which by covenant is to perform first, is obliged to do so. (*Lev.*, 90 [*EW* III, 125])

Hobbes does not argue that the covenant obliges you because 'there is a power set up to constrain' *you*; he says that the covenant obliges you because 'there is a power set up to constrain' the *other* parties to it, thus taking away the 'reasonable suspicion' of being double-crossed that would otherwise invalidate such a covenant. Of course, Hobbes does not discount the fear of punishment as a motive encouraging people to obey the law; but it is not the probability of having a sanction applied to oneself that makes one's obedience to the laws *obligatory*.[22]

A 'commonwealth by acquisition' comes about when a person or group of persons 'for fear of death, or bonds, do authorize all the actions of that man, or assembly of men, that hath their lives and liberty in his power' (*Lev.*, 129 [*EW* III, 185]). Exactly the same 'natural rights' have to be given up as before, but the covenant this time is with the powerful man or assembly (that is to say, with some already existing sovereign). 'So that *conquest*, to define it, is the acquiring of the right of sovereignty by victory. Which right, is acquired in the people's submission, by which they contract with the victor, promising obedience, for life and liberty' (*Lev.*, 462–3 [*EW* III, 705]). Now this is not in fact a 'covenant of mutual trust', for the victor lets you go (or refrains from killing you) now, whereas you promise to obey him in the future. (The victor cannot give you any guarantees about your 'life and liberty' *in the future*, because this would be a derogation of his sovereignty.) The case is, in fact, precisely analogous to that of the men released by their captors in return for the promise of a future ransom; and it will be recalled that even 'in the condition of mere nature' that promise was held to be obligatory, because the other party had already performed its part of the bargain. The logical role of the state's coercive power is thus a little different with sovereignty by acquisition. There is no need (as there is with sovereignty by institution) of a guarantee that the other party will perform, for he performs at once and once for all. But there may well still be a need for a guarantee that you can perform your part safely, and that is where the coercive power of the state comes in. Hobbes illustrates this a little after the ransom example: 'if a weaker prince, make a disadvantageous peace with a stronger, for fear; he is bound to keep it, unless ... there ariseth some new, and just cause of fear, to renew the war' (*Lev.*, 91 [*EW* III, 127]). The sovereign can use his coercive power to make sure as far as is humanly possible that the covenant to obey him will not be undermined by any 'new and just cause of fear'. Again, it is not that the sovereign obliges you to obey him by threatening sanctions if you don't, but rather that the sovereign removes the usual excuses which prevent promises from being obligatory.

To reduce Hobbes to saying, 'Obey the sovereign, or he'll punish you', is to miss the core of his doctrine, which is that you are obliged to obey wherever certain nullifying conditions are absent. Obedience pays because it helps to secure peace, which is the only sure means to personal survival. It pays, *other things being equal*, and it is the state's job to make them equal. If Hobbes's 'message' were that we ought to obey for fear of the police, why should he have thought that having his doctrine taught in the universities and preached in the pulpits would make England a less turbulent country? It was precisely because he had seen the fragility of régimes resting only on bayonets that he wrote *Leviathan*.[23] If we have to reduce Hobbes to a slogan, it must be something like this: 'Obey even when there isn't a policeman, because this contributes to peace: only provided that there are enough policemen around to give you more security than you would get in a free-for-all.' And it may be added that since a free-for-all is very, very insecure, the critical level of police protection need not be very high to make it preferable for you to cast your vote for peace by obeying the government's commands.

So far I have been in effect defending Warrender's theses (a) and (b), *viz.* that there can be obligations in the state of nature and that the sovereign does not create a new kind of obligation. Of course, my version of (a) is different from Warrender's in that I have been following Hobbes's definition of 'obligation' in *Leviathan* as the consequence of renouncing or transferring a right, whereas he takes obligation to be primarily connected with the laws of nature – that is to say, with all the laws of nature, and not just the third, which deals specifically with covenants. But I have still been holding, as Warrender does, that (a) and (b) are true. The other three theses, which I called (c), (d), and (e), I maintain to be false; I believe that the laws of nature *do* rest on the requirements for individual self-preservation, that they do *not* oblige (in the main sense of the 'oblige' used by Hobbes) and in particular that the obligation to keep covenants does *not* depend on there being an obligation to obey the laws of nature.

Since all these propositions involve the laws of nature it is worth asking where these come into Hobbes's theory. It seems to me that Hobbes gives three different, though not inconsistent, reasons why (to put it deliberately vaguely) it is a good idea to obey the commands of a sovereign. First, you are obliged to do so in that you have covenanted to, and not to keep covenants is injustice. Second, because the sovereign is your 'representative' who 'bears your person', you are the 'author' of his acts and you thus 'own' them. Since nothing done to a man, by his own consent, constitutes 'injury' (*Lev.*, 98 [*EW* III, 137]), you cannot complain that any act of the sovereign injures you. And third, the 'reason which dictateth to every man his own good' tells you (i) to enter into a covenant setting up a sovereign and (ii) to keep the covenant. Note that these are not to be regarded as 'three theories of obligation'; obligation arises from having covenanted, and is thus relevant only to the first of these three points. The second point takes up a logical consequence of the precise *form* taken by the covenant, and the third point emphasizes the personal gain from undertaking and adhering to an obligation to obey a sovereign.

The case against Warrender's view that Hobbesian laws of nature are not rules for individual self-preservation is a familiar one but none the worse for that. It consists, on the positive side, of citing Hobbes's numerous statements to that effect (including his definition of a law of nature); and, on the negative side, of showing that Warrender misapplies the quotations he uses to support his position. Thus, for example, Hobbes defines a law of nature as 'a general rule, found out by reason, by which a man is forbidden to do that, which is destructive of his life. . . .' (*Lev.*, 84 [*EW* III, 116–17]); and, although he does at one place say that the laws of nature that he has put forward are necessary for 'the conservation of men in multitudes', he goes on at once to say that these laws are only a selection, namely those that are politically relevant, and that there are others which conserve men singly.[24]

I come now to the case for saying that the laws of nature do not constitute obligations for men, in the primary sense of 'obligation' which is employed in *Leviathan*. By 'the primary sense' is meant simply that sense of 'obligation' which seems to make sense of the word in most of the contexts in which it occurs in *Leviathan*. It is easy to see that if we take 'obligation' as the result of giving up a right we are in accord with Hobbes's own definition of 'obligation', which is in precisely these terms. Of course, it may be that Hobbes failed to stick to his definition in most of his subsequent uses of the word 'obligation', but it seems on the face of it unlikely that a man so emphatic about the importance of using words in clearly defined ways would have treated his own definition of an absolutely central concept in so cavalier a way. Whether the unlikely is nevertheless true can only be decided by reading *Leviathan* with alternative definitions of 'obligation' in mind. My own conclusions are, first, that the *Leviathan* hangs together intelligibly when 'obligation' is read in the way proposed, and second, that (with the exceptions to be mentioned) all occurrences of 'obligation' fit this reading – that is, people are said to be obliged only when they *have* renounced or transferred a right.

In particular, I think it is true to say that, subject to the same exceptions, Hobbes does not refer to the laws of nature as creating obligations. There is, indeed, a slight complication here in that the third law of nature is 'that men perform their covenants made'. Thus the third law of nature underwrites the obligation to keep covenants, by making it a 'dictate of reason'. But it does not, of course, follow from this that the obligation to keep covenants is derived from an obligation to obey the laws of nature. Covenants create obligations by virtue of what they are – having given up a right is what being obliged *means*. Hobbes establishes this many pages before even introducing the third law of nature. How absurd, then, to maintain (and this is point (e), taken out of turn) that the obligation to keep covenants is merely a special case of an obligation to obey the laws of nature!

We must now, as promised above, look at the exceptions, the

deviant uses of 'obligation' which do not fit Hobbes's own definition. These are mostly clustered together in a familiar passage which begins with the comment that the laws of nature

> oblige in *foro interno*; that is to say, they bind to a desire they should take place: but in *foro externo*; that is, to the putting them in act, not always. For he that should be modest, and tractable, and perform all he promises, in such time, and place, where no man else should do so, should but make himself a prey to others, and secure his own certain ruin, contrary to the ground of all laws of nature, which tend to nature's preservation. And again, he that having sufficient security, that others shall observe the same laws towards him, observes them not himself, seeketh not peace, but war; and consequently the destruction of his nature by violence. (*Lev.*, 103 [*EW* III, 145])[25]

Hobbes is here saying that *all* the laws of nature oblige, so we must concede that a new, non-contractual, sense of obligation is being introduced. The only way of avoiding such a conclusion would be to maintain that, for Hobbes, the laws of nature oblige in virtue of men's voluntarily 'giving up the right' to do what is forbidden by them. This unlikely solution has actually been put forward, in an article by A. G. Wernham entitled 'Liberty and Obligation in Hobbes'. According to him, a man *makes* a law of nature obligatory for himself by 'willing to adopt it'. He thus 'gives up his right' to do actions of that kind, unless of course he believes such an action necessary to save his life.[26] But there is no reason for supposing that Hobbes either held this view or would have wished to. 'It is manifest that the *divine laws* sprang not from the consent of man, nor yet the *laws of nature*' (*EW* II, 184).[27]

The whole point of the laws of nature is that they are the means by which each person increases his own chances of staying alive; and on Hobbes's psychological premises trying to stay alive is not a matter of choice but (under normal conditions) a necessity of every human being's nature. Failure to act on the laws of nature is not due to a defect of will but a defect of reasoning akin to an inability to put two and two together. 'The whole breach of the laws of nature consists in the false reasoning, or rather folly of those men, who see not those duties they are necessarily to perform towards others in order to their own conservation' (*EW* II, 16).[28]

If we reject Wernham's suggestion, then, we have to conclude that Hobbes is using 'obligation' in the passage cited in a way other than that defined. He does not seem to be saying anything different about the status of the laws of nature from what he has already said; the innovation lies in using the term 'oblige' where he has previously been using 'dictate'. It may be significant that the terminology of 'dictation' would have been rather awkward for making the point Hobbes wants to make here. This is that although 'reason dictates' the laws of nature as 'convenient articles of peace' they will not tend to a given individual's self-preservation unless others follow them, too. Reason does not therefore dictate that one should always put the laws of nature 'in act' but only one should always be ready to do so when others will, too. If we analyse what is being said with 'obligation' here it appears that '*A* is obliged to do *x*' is equivalent to '*x* is a means to *A*'s self-preservation'. It should be noticed that in this sense of 'obligation' – which is 'natural obligation' slipping in again – it is not just the laws of nature that are obligatory, but any action which genuinely tends to the agent's self-preservation. Thus even actions carried out under the 'right of nature', where the agent had correctly assessed the situation, could also be obligatory in this sense.[29]

Since, on the 'self-preservation' definition of 'obligation', laws of nature (among other things) are obligatory, it follows that covenants – whose keeping is enjoined by the third law of nature – are obligatory too in this sense of the word. Thus, covenants are obligatory on either definition of 'obligation'. The question is: when Hobbes speaks of covenants 'obliging' does he simply mean that keeping covenants sometimes tends to self-preservation? Reasons have already been given for rejecting this view, but there is another which seems very difficult to meet. It is this. On the 'self-preservation' definition, keeping covenants represents only a small proportion of all the actions that are obligatory. Saving your skin by the 'right of nature' and keeping all the laws of nature are also obligatory. If Hobbes had intended to use this definition widely in *Leviathan* we would expect to find the word 'obligation' occurring wherever the right of nature or laws of nature were under discussion. Instead we find that exercising the right of nature is never described as obligatory, and that of the many references to the laws of nature only a tiny proportion call them obligatory. Aside from this small number of cases, what are said to give rise to obligations are invariably covenants, contracts, and the like. Why would Hobbes have confined the term 'obligation' to renunciations and transfers of right so exclusively if what he normally wanted to convey by using the word was that keeping your word was a means to self-preservation? Surely he would then have used 'obligation' freely when talking about the many other means to self-preservation.

If we were to suppose, then, that Hobbes intended the 'self-preservation' sense of 'obligation' to be read into his talk of the obligatory nature of covenants, etc., we should be faced with this insuperable mystery: why did he restrict the employment of such a wide-ranging concept to such a limited part of its field of application? The mystery disappears at once if we take it that the relevant sense of 'obligation' when Hobbes speaks of covenants, etc., is the sense defined by him in terms of having given up a right. From this perspective, the passages where the laws of nature are said to oblige are to be regarded as isolated instances of a secondary sense of 'obligation'. In reworking *De Cive*, Hobbes cut out the definition of 'natural obligation' (which would otherwise have occurred in chapter 31 of *Leviathan*), but he was not entirely successful in eradicating all uses of it from the revised version. The suppressed passage from *De Cive* and the occasional slips in *Leviathan* have been made the basis of an analysis, which, as I have tried to show, has been accepted in this vital respect even by its critics.

Finally, does it all matter? Perhaps the whole question is not of earth-shaking importance to human welfare; but, taking as given the narrower focus of appreciating Hobbes, I think it matters quite a lot. Hobbes, as everybody knows, was an early exponent of the 'command theory of law' which received its classic statement from Austin. However, if I am right, Hobbes's version is free from the most fundamental logical objections to Austin's theory. We do Hobbes not credit but discredit by reading Austin back into him. As Hart has pointed out, Austin assimilates the legal situation to a stick-up by a gun-man;[30] but Hobbes is clear that legal obligation is different from merely being in someone's power.[31]

> He [Bishop Bramhall] thinks, belike, that if a conqueror can kill me if he please, I am presently obliged without more ado to obey all his laws. May I not rather die, if I think fit? The conqueror makes no law over the conquered by virtue of his power; but by virtue of their assent, that promised obedience for the saving of their lives. (*EW* V, 180)

To put the same point linguistically: Austin assimilates 'being under an obligation [to keep a promise, obey a law, etc.]' with 'being obliged to [hand over the money to the gunman, throw the goods overboard in a storm, etc.]'.[32] The temptation to a tough-minded theorist to run the two together is manifest: 'to many later theorists [than Austin] this has appeared as a revelation, bringing down to earth an elusive notion and restating it in the same clear, hard, empirical terms as are used in science.'[33] But, although Hobbes dabbled with a type of 'natural obligation' in *De Cive*, he never took the short cut of reducing legal obligation to 'being obliged' in that sense. We may well think that 'having an obligation to do *x*' cannot always be reduced to 'having previously promised (contracted, etc.) to do *x*', as Hobbes suggested it should. But we must acknowledge that he had picked on the clearest, we might even say the paradigm, case of 'having an obligation' *as distinct from* 'being obliged'.

## NOTES

1 I am grateful to Professor H. L. A. Hart for his comments on an earlier draft of this paper.
2 Howard Warrender, *The Political Philosophy of Hobbes: His Theory of Obligation* (Oxford, Clarendon Press, 1957).
3 References in this form are to the pages of the edition of *Leviathan* edited by M. Oakeshott (see above p. 19).
4 He does quote Hobbes as saying that when a man has given up a right he is under an obligation, but loses the point of it by taking it to mean simply that being obliged is 'suffering impediment' (Warrender, 101). But giving up a right is not merely one among a number of possible ways of coming under an obligation, it is (by definition) the only way.
5 In *De Cive* Hobbes in fact distinguishes two kinds of 'natural obligation'. The first is exhibited by God's attaching unpleasant consequences to certain kinds of behaviour and thus controlling the rational members of His creation through their ability to foresee these consequences and take appropriate avoiding action. This is the kind of 'natural obligation' already discussed, and the kind which Warrender proposes to make central to his interpretation of the *Leviathan*. The second kind of 'natural obligation' is exhibited by God's making stones fall and planets revolve. In the *Leviathan* this kind of 'natural obligation' gets even shorter shrift than the other; so far from being an example of 'obligation', God's operations in this manner are only metaphorically allowed to be even an example of 'reigning'.
6 M. M. Goldsmith, in his *Hobbes's Science of Politics* (New York and London, Columbia University Press, 1966), has been very thorough in giving footnote references to the parallel passages; the quotation from *De Cive* (which he gives on p. 112) is one of the few which are not given with a cross-reference to *Leviathan*.
7 'The argument of *De Cive* is based upon a concept of arbitrary impediment to liberty which Hobbes had abandoned by 1646. . . . The most important point regarding the paragraph on natural obligation in *De Cive* [i.e. the passage quoted by Warrender] is that Hobbes had to jettison it when he wrote *Leviathan*. His first species of natural obligation, whereby the liberty of all created things is limited by the laws of their creation, had to disappear, because lack of intrinsic power does not restrict liberty. His second species of natural obligation, whereby the liberty of God's subjects is taken away by fear and hope aroused by His irresistible power, had to disappear, because there could no longer be arbitrary impediments to liberty;

fear and hope, too, do not restrict liberty.' F. C. Hood, *The Divine Politics of Thomas Hobbes* (Oxford, Clarendon Press, 1964), 45 and 50.

8 Notice that Hobbes here effectively admits that there *is* something in *De Cive* to be 'caught' that does not recur in *Leviathan*.

9 Hobbes actually took up the interpretation of his phrase about 'power irresistible' in his reply to Bramhall; and he clearly rejected the construction put on it by Warrender (and, as we shall see below, Plamenatz). 'He would make men believe, I hold all things to be just, that are done by them who have power enough to avoid the punishment. . . . I said no more, but that the power, which is absolutely irresistible, makes him that hath it above all law, so that nothing he doth can be unjust' (*EW* IV, 146).

10 In the other sense of 'justice', which presupposes the existence of a relevant covenant, there *is* a necessary connection between justice and obligation, but even if we supposed that this *was* the relevant sense here, the obligation that would follow from it would unfortunately come in the wrong place to help Warrender. For, in this sense of 'justice' what we can infer if we know that someone is behaving justly is that he himself is carrying out an obligation; we still cannot say that anybody else has obligations. At the *most* then, saying that God behaves justly in commanding men might entail that in so doing God is carrying out His own (contractual) obligations.

11 Note may also be taken of Hood's view that the laws of nature oblige *qua* commands of God *delivered in Scripture*. This is repeated at least five times (*Divine Politics*, 4, 49, 227, 228 and 253 – the last sentence in the book) each time without any reference. This compounds Warrender's illicit move from 'law' to 'obligation' with a groundless denial of God's being able to give laws without resorting to revelation. Hobbes makes it clear that the 'word of God' includes the 'dictates of reason and equity' (*Lev.*, 275 [*EW* III, 411]), so that there is a 'triple word of God, rational, sensible and prophetic' (*Lev.*, 233 [*EW* III, 344–5]). It is true that in *De Cive* Hobbes says that the laws of nature are properly *laws* 'as they are delivered by God in holy Scriptures'. But, quite apart from the fact that this is altered in *Leviathan* to the more general formulation of 'the word of God', Hobbes immediately adds, in *De Cive*, that the 'laws of nature are divine laws as well because reason, which is the law of nature, is given by God to every man for the rule of his actions; as because [they occur in Scripture]'. (Both passages from *EW* II, 50–1.) A more general point against Hood is that Hobbes sometimes maintains that the Bible is a law to us only on the authority of the sovereign: 'How came it then to be a law to us? Did God speak it *viva voce* to us? Have we then any warrant for it than the word of the prophets? Have we seen the miracles? Have we any other assurance of their certainty than the authority of the Church? And is the authority of the Church any other than the authority of the commonwealth . . . ?' (*Liberty and Necessity*, *EW* V, 179.) Even if we discount this as a polemical excess, the fact that Hobbes was willing to put it forward at all suggests that he did not regard it as undermining the thing closest his heart – the obligation to obey the sovereign. Yet this it would certainly do if (as Hood maintains) that

obligation depended ultimately on the Scripturally-based obligation to obey the laws of nature. For the obligation to keep (or even endeavour to keep) the laws of nature could not be valid until (*per impossibile*) a sovereign had already been brought into existence. And even if this difficulty could be circumvented, there could be no obligation to obey infidel sovereigns (since, by definition, they would not underwrite the Bible); yet Hobbes holds that there is in general such an obligation.

12    As originally defined, the 'right of nature' was a right to act in self-defence only; you could hurt another man legitimately only if you sincerely believed him a threat to your existence. It was a 'right to all things' only in the sense that there was no general category of action (e.g. killing) that it ruled out. But this limitation is soon dropped. For example, God's 'natural right' is 'to afflict men at his pleasure' (*Lev.*, 234 [*EW* III, 346]); but obviously He has no need of self-defence. It is easy to see why Hobbes drops the restriction. He wants to say that the covenant setting up a sovereign simply leaves him to exercise his 'right of nature' without impediment, but to restrict the powers of the sovereign to acting in his own self-defence would obviously defeat Hobbes's whole purpose. The 'right of nature' *must* therefore be unlimited to save the sovereign's absolute authority; God is an incidental beneficiary.

13    Even if we accepted for the sake of argument that the definition of law quoted by Warrender applied to God's law as well as civil law, we should get the conclusion that men have a contractual obligation to obey God's laws, which is something that Hobbes explicitly denies, and in any case is not what Warrender wants to maintain. Warrender quotes the passage to prove that men have a *natural* obligation (in the *De Cive* sense) to obey God's laws, but the passage would not support this even if it were about God. And since, if it were about God, it would have to mean that every man has covenanted with God to obey Him, we can add that it certainly is not about God.

14    J. Plamenatz, 'Mr Warrender's Hobbes' (*Political Studies*, vol. V, no. 3 (1957), 297; reprinted in K. C. Brown (ed.), *Hobbes Studies* (Oxford, Blackwell, 1965), 75). The same view is expressed in *Man and Society* (London, Longman, 1963), vol. I, 130. In a subsequently written account, he suggests that this sort of obligation to obey someone can be treated as a special case of a more general concept such that 'when Hobbes says a man is obliged . . . to do something he implies that, if he saw his advantage clearly, he would necessarily do it' (Introduction to *Leviathan*, Fontana paperback, London, 1962, 32). The obligation to keep covenants is still treated as logically on a par with (say) the obligation to kill another man; it is obligatory when it pays and all that is meant by saying it is obligatory in some situation is that it does pay. (Incidentally, the idea that the laws of nature are obligatory *qua* commands of God, and the move from God's 'irresistible power' to man's obligation to obey Him, recur on pages 28 and 30.)

15    Summary by Plamenatz, *Political Studies*, vol. V, no. 3 (1957), 296; Brown (ed.), op. cit., 73–4.

16    (c) is dealt with on pages 89–94 of *Hobbes's System of Ideas* (London, Hutchinson, 1973). With (d) and (e) we must be more inferential since Watkins employs the concept of 'obligation' very little in his exposition. (There is no entry in the index.) However, on 87–9 he denies that the laws of nature are morally obligatory without suggesting they are obligatory in some other way; and in dealing with the reasons for obeying the sovereign he mentions only two: firstly that he 'bears the person' of the subjects (160–1) and secondly that he can 'cause men, by threat of punishment' to obey the law (162).

17    Hood also calls this 'natural obligation', but it is clearly not the 'natural obligation' of the *De Cive* passage. He does not, in my view, produce any textual evidence for believing that Hobbes at any time recognized any form of obligation except those resulting from physical manipulation, fear of consequences, and contract. Obligations to God are not an additional *form* of obligation; they must take one or more of these three forms. Incidentally, Warrender seems to have set the fashion for speaking of 'moral obligation' as if this were a Hobbesian category – both Watkins and Hood do it. As far as I am aware, the term 'moral obligation' appears nowhere in Hobbes. He does sometimes say that the laws of nature are (among other things, such as natural and positive divine law) moral laws, 'because they concern the manners and conversation of men, one towards another' (*Elements of Law*, 5–1 [*EW* IV, 111]). But just as divine law does not entail divine obligation neither does moral law entail moral obligation. (The sovereign's laws do, of course, involve an obligation, which we may if we like call political or legal obligation, though as far as I know Hobbes does not. But if we do, we must be clear that it is not a new *form* of obligation, but one of the three forms mentioned – in fact, the contractual form – applied to certain special covenants.)

18    It is perhaps worth noting that C.B. Macpherson's essay in Marxist psychoanalysis, *The Political Philosophy of Possessive Individualism* (Oxford, Clarendon Press, 1962), which aimed to supply the 'hidden premises' allegedly needed to make Hobbes's theory work, took its warrant from the consensus among commentators on Hobbes that his political theory is incoherent. But if the theory is in fact coherent already, the case for an elaborate reconstruction to *make* it coherent immediately collapses.

19    Incidentally, to say that a promise obliges only when keeping it conduces to your security does not entail saying that everything which conduces to your security is obligatory. If an action conduces to your security, then it would indeed be contrary to 'that reason, which dictateth to every man his own good' (*Lev.*, 95 [*EW* III, 132]), not to do that action; but doing it is *obligatory* only if you have promised to do it.

20    First, Hobbes says that 'on any reasonable suspicion it is void', and adds discouragingly that 'he which performeth first, does but betray himself to his enemy'. But a little later, he stipulates that 'the cause of fear, which maketh such a covenant invalid, must always be

something arising after the covenant made' (*Lev.*, 89–90 [*EW* III, 124–5]). Cf. Goldsmith, op. cit., 135–7.

21  To say, as Warrender does, that the sovereign operates 'in a system of rights and duties that he does not himself control or create except in the most trivial sense' (Warrender, 28), is surely to overstate the point. The sovereign's commands obviously do create 'a system of rights and duties' which is new, though the obligation to observe them is not of a new kind. Watkins quite properly objects to Warrender here (Watkins, 154–7) but he again rejects too much. It is quite true that 'what the legislator commands, must be held for *good*, and what he forbids for *evil*' (Watkins, 155), but it does not follow from this that nothing is generally agreed on as good or evil until the sovereign commands it. 'All men agree on this, that peace is good, and therefore . . . the laws of nature are good' (*Lev.*, 104 [*EW* III, 146]).

22  In *De Cive*, Hobbes makes the point of saying that 'a man is obliged by his contracts' but the law 'ties him being obliged' (*EW* II, 185). Contrast Austin's view that legal obligation *consisted in* the chance or likelihood of suffering an 'evil' at the hands of the sovereign.

23  'The ground of these rights [of the sovereign] have the rather need to be taught diligently, and truly taught; because they cannot be maintained by any civil law, or terror of legal punishment' (*Lev.*, 220 [*EW* III, 323]). And in *Behemoth*, Hobbes wrote, 'If men know not their duty, what is there that can force them to obey the laws? An army, you will say. But what shall force the army?' (*EW* VI, 237). Thus Hobbes, like Hume in the well-known opening of the essay 'Of the First Principles of Government', is clear that it is 'on opinion only that government is founded' (*Hume's Essays*, Oxford, Oxford University Press, 1963, 29).

24  What makes rules for collective conservation a means to individual conservation is the fact of virtual equality. Since no man can hope to dominate others securely by a sheer superiority of natural strength everyone must accept terms which are equally favourable to all (i.e. which will conserve men in multitudes) if there is to be peace. (See *Lev.*, 100–1 [*EW* III, 140–1].)

25  The laws of nature are also said to 'oblige' at *Lev.*, 219–20 [*EW* III, 322–4].

26  Brown (ed.), *Hobbes Studies*, 135.

27  A covenant is the giving up of a right, so that the third law of nature, 'that men perform their covenants made', means that when you have given up a right it should stay given up. Now, according to Wernham one adopts a law of nature by 'giving up the right' to do what it forbids, but then where does this put the adoption of the third law of nature? On Wernham's view, adopting the third law of nature would have to consist in giving up the right to go back on one's word when one had given up a right. But this is absurd. If the man's giving up rights is already effective in controlling his actions, his giving up the right to break the third law of nature is redundant; but if it is not already effective then giving up the right to break the third law of nature is ineffective, too, and we have an infinite regress.

28   M. M. Goldsmith also tries to reconcile the ideas 'that all obligations are self-imposed' and that the laws of nature are obligatory. He writes: 'If these natural regularities [the laws of nature] apply whether they are known or not, how can a man be obliged to obey them only by his own act? In the sense of physical necessity [i.e. the actual regularities themselves], surely no one has a choice. Nevertheless, there is another sense in which these laws oblige only by a man's own act; it is by his own discovery of their existence and their necessity that he realizes that he is bound to respect them in the sense of taking account of them in his deliberations' (*Hobbes's Science of Politics*, 132–3). If this kind of tortured reasoning is necessary to reconcile the two ideas, this is equivalent to their being irreconcilable; to say that the 'act' which puts a man under an obligation is discovering a regularity is, at best, a rather weak joke. The laborious attempt is especially perverse because the phrase quoted – that there is 'no obligation on any man, which ariseth not from some act of his own' – is perfectly clear in its context (*Lev.*, 141 [*EW* III, 203]; reference on 134 of Goldsmith). Hobbes is arguing that the obligation of the citizen depends on the terms of the covenant setting up the sovereign; thus the 'act of his own' by which alone a man undertakes obligations is the act of making a covenant.

29   Perhaps a comment is unavoidable at this point on Hobbes's statement (*Lev.*, 84 [*EW* III, 117]) that 'obligation and liberty . . . in one and the same matter are inconsistent'. If Hobbes had wanted to make obligations and liberty strict contradictories he could have done it by two alternative pairs of definitions. One pair would be that obligation in a matter is having given up a right to do it, and liberty is not having given up a right to it; the other pair would be that liberty is not suffering corporal impediment (chains, imprisonment, etc.) and obligation *is* suffering them. Unfortunately, in *Leviathan* he picked his definition of 'obligation' from the first pair and his definition of 'liberty' from the second pair. But in practice he brings his use of 'liberty' in line with his definition of 'obligation': in his chapter on 'The Liberty of Subjects' he sticks at the beginning to saying that 'in the proper sense for corporal liberty' it is 'freedom from chains and prison' (*Lev.*, 138 [*EW* III, 199]), but he then uses the word to cover (a) those matters where there is no command of the sovereign (i.e. no law) so no contractual obligation, and (b) those matters (e.g. self-destruction) where no covenant can give rise to obligations. Hobbes would have been much better off if he had couched his formal definition of freedom in terms of the absence of contractual obligation. His actual definition produces absurd results when substituted for occurrences of the word 'liberty'. For example, substitute it in his definition of 'laying down a right' as 'divesting yourself of the liberty of hindering someone else's right'; the latter would then read, 'divesting yourself of the absence of external impediments [e.g. chains or prison] to hindering someone else's right'. Thus undertaking an obligation would entail literally, not metaphorically, chaining yourself up! This point is worth making because it is as well to be clear that the correlative of 'corporal liberty' is not 'natural obligation', for 'natural obligation' is not

physical restraint but fear of consequences. So Hobbes's misjudgement in clinging to 'corporal liberty' is no encouragement to those who wish to read 'natural obligation' into a central position in *Leviathan*.

30  H. L. A. Hart, *The Concept of Law* (Oxford, Oxford University Press, 1961), 80.
31  Plamenatz would attribute to Hobbes the view that the state obliges *qua* gunman; Warrender that God, *qua* super-gunman, obliges you to obey the state.
32  See Hart, op. cit., 79–88.
33  Hart op. cit., 81.

# JOHN LOCKE

## Chapter Four

# INTRODUCTION

John Locke is often characterized as a liberal political thinker, especially because of his treatment of the possession of political power as a trust, and in many respects the problems of interpretation which surround his political theory may reasonably be regarded as problems concerned with the nature of, or degree of, that liberalism. Other difficulties arise, however, from the relationship between his most famous work in political theory, *Two Treatises of Government*, and his many other writings. Interpreters have invoked writings other than the *Two Treatises* in an attempt to resolve the many ambiguities present in that work. This has raised questions about the adequacy and limitations of this procedure; furthermore, it has led to debate about the coherence of Locke's writings *taken together* which overarches the discussion of the coherence of the *Two Treatises* read in isolation. One influential interpretation, provided by John Dunn, finds a coherence flowing from Locke's 'Calvinist' disposition.

It will be helpful to recall that Locke was not merely, nor perhaps primarily, a political philosopher. The range of his interests may be illustrated by reference to some of the other works for which he is now remembered. The first and most important, perhaps, is his *Essay Concerning Human Understanding*, the thesis of which is that the only reliable knowledge we can have comes to us through our senses. Two other possible sources of knowledge – innate ideas and authoritative pronouncement – are rejected. This thesis was adopted by many writers in the eighteenth century, and had important consequences for their conception of the scientific method appropriate to the study of man's social world. (This theme is elaborated in the Introduction to section V.) Indeed, Locke himself aimed at providing a study of morality on the model of mathematics, even if he was not successful. We shall see below that doubts have been raised about the consistency of the argument against innate ideas in the *Essay* and the argument that the law of nature is knowable by rational agents in the *Two Treatises*.

A second area of intellectual concern for Locke is now recognized as 'economics', although that category was not available to him. He has been described as one of the founders of 'scientific economics', largely because of his studies of market price determination. This problem is today approached through supply and demand, but again we should remember that these were not Locke's categories or concepts. Additionally, Locke was concerned with the value of money – both in relation to the prices of (other) commodities and in relation to the rate of interest. He was consulted by the government during debates about recoinage with, it has been suggested, unfortunate results for the economy, partly because of the defects in his advice. Locke's economic writings are potentially important to the interpretation of his political theory because, as we shall see, some of the central disputes about the *Two Treatises* are disputes about the sort of 'economy' Locke assumed or envisaged when he wrote.

A third set of writings to which appeal is likely to be made in search of an understanding of Locke's political thought is concerned with toleration. Toleration is treated as a value in modern liberal thought because (it is argued) it is necessary to accommodate a plurality of life-styles, a plurality required if each person is to have the opportunity to find happiness or pursue his or her own plan of life; for these and other reasons, coercion is considered *prima facie* undesirable. The problem of toleration with which Locke was concerned was in one sense more specific: to what extent should society (or the state – another term which Locke himself did not use) tolerate individuals who cleaved to a religion other than the established religion, or indeed to no religion at all? The relevant political concern in the late seventeenth century was, of course, the treatment of Roman Catholics. Since the *Two Treatises* was written and published at a time when the acceptability of a Catholic monarch was under discussion, the *Letters on Toleration* have an obvious relevance.

The three sets of writings to which we have referred do not, of course, exhaust the *corpus* of Locke's work or the range of his interests. We might also mention Locke's writings on the subject of education and his interest in medicine. The preceding discussion does, however, serve to introduce the problems with which interpreters have been concerned: most generally, how is Locke's political thought best characterized? Is the *Two Treatises* internally consistent, and can information derived from other works help to resolve apparent inconsistencies, or help us to determine how to treat ambiguous passages? The question of general characterization may be crudely stated as follows. Is Locke a liberal, a narrowly bourgeois liberal, or a radical democrat? Problems of internal consistency surround Locke's account of the origins of property, his account of political obligation, and, crucially for the question of general characterization, the relationship between these two. The extent to which the *Two Treatises* is consistent with, or may be illuminated by, other works in Locke's *corpus* is controversial with respect to his epistemology, his so-called social assumptions, and the elucidation of his personal theology. These issues may be most readily approached by looking at questions surrounding the idea of natural law employed in the *Two Treatises*.

The most fundamental question is: how do men come to know the law of nature? Subsidiary issues are: is the law of nature equally accessible to everyone? Does it have a clear content? Is it to govern man only in the absence of political society, or are the laws of political society to be consistent with the law of nature?

Locke imagines men in a state of nature, but this non-political condition was nevertheless a social condition. The state of nature had a law to govern it, the law of nature. Locke has no doubt that this law *is* accessible, but we might ask how exactly men are to come to know it since, as we saw, Locke rejects innate ideas as a reliable source of knowledge. It seems clear that reason is necessary, but it is not clear that reason is sufficient. Experience and revelation are possible additional requirements. Experience is a candidate because Locke explicitly excludes children from the capacity to govern their conduct in accordance with the law, which suggests the importance of the passage of time in providing material for reflection. On the other hand, perhaps Locke imagines that the reasoning capacity itself develops as the child matures, so that only adults have sufficient reason to understand the law. Revelation is a candidate because Locke is quite clear that the law of nature represents God's requirements for the preservation of his Creation; for example, Locke's theory of property is informed by a particular teleology. While Locke himself undoubtedly felt that reason and revelation would concur about the content of the law of nature, we may still ask whether reason could *independently* lead to knowledge of that law, and whether Locke's assumptions about its accessibility are consistent with the argument of the *Essay*.

The general issue of how men come to know the law of nature slides easily into the particular problem of whether the law is equally knowable for everyone. In so far as reason is required, then all adults may be equally expected to have that knowledge. But if reasonableness in this sense is unequally distributed, perhaps some persons will fail to grasp the law of nature. This is important for two reasons. The first concerns Professor Macpherson's allegation that Locke thought that men exhibited differential rationality, and that this fact is important in the interpretation of Locke's theory of property, to which we come below. The second reason is concerned with the plausibility of Locke's account of the state of nature and men's motives for leaving it to create a political society. Although Locke's state of nature is obviously not as bleak as that suggested by Hobbes, it is not entirely harmonious; it is less bleak because men are conceived to be capable, amongst other things, of respecting property and using money. Locke suggests that there are 'inconveniences' in the state of nature, and 'inconvenience' was certainly a stronger word in the seventeenth century than it is now. So whatever defects the state of nature has, they are not so serious as to make a settled social life impossible.

It will be helpful to distinguish two possible explanations of the main defects, that there is no known and settled law nor impartial judge. The first is that some persons do not follow the law of nature because they do not know it. The second is that some persons give way to the temptation to break it, even though everyone knows what conduct the law prescribes. The first reason would give a motive for the creation of coercive political power – to protect the law-abiding from the rest. The second reason would also provide a motive – but it would be universal in application. Both would encourage the creation and use of coercive political power: the first to protect the law-abiding from the rest, the second to protect us all from each other. The plausibility of Locke's story of the deliberate creation of political authority depends on the defects of the state of nature, and those defects depend upon the fact that not everyone follows the law of nature all the time. If this is because of differential rationality, then political power may be represented as inspired by the self-interest of the more rational. If, moreover, differential rationality is also associated with inequalities in property-holding, then political power is associated with the self-interest of the wealthy. If, on the other hand, the problem is not differential rationality but deficiencies in capacity to conform behaviour to the law of nature, then there is less reason to associate the motive for the creation of political society with the interests of a particular social group.

The questions of the *content* and the *universality* of the law of nature are connected. The law of nature may be given a very general expression: it prescribes the preservation of men as far as possible. But this requirement may be elaborated in more detail: for example, Locke argues that in the absence of political society there is a natural right of inheritance, such that children have a right to take over their parents' goods when they die. This right may be used to illustrate the problem of universal application. It might be that such a right should always be recognized, both in and out of political society. Alternatively, it may be that the detailed provisions of the law of nature are moulded by the existence of political society. In the present example, this would mean that, if political society meets the obligation to preserve children, the right to inherit may lapse in favour of a parent's right to choose to whom to leave property. One particular problem about stating the law of nature and its more particular provisions concerns the relationship between the preservation of the individual and the preservation of all. If the law of nature prescribes the preservation of men, is the individual obliged to preserve only himself, or to preserve as many men as possible? It is clear that he has a duty (to God) to preserve himself, but the content of his duties to others is less clear. Again, this issue connects with Locke's theory of property, and with the rights and duties of those who possess it.

The tradition of natural law within which Locke was writing provides an important key to understanding his approach to both property and to political obligation. The advertised target of the *Two Treatises* is Sir Robert Filmer. Filmer had argued, in *Patriarcha*, against views associated with Grotius and Pufendorf. Those authors held that both private property and political authority were created by consent. Men had agreed to both institutions. They also held that all men were born free and equal. Filmer had cast doubt on the coherence of this position. He argued first, that it was absurd to imagine men coming together to agree to divide up the world, and secondly that it was impossible to reconcile the propositions. If men are born free and equal, then parental consent to private property cannot legitimate it for the next generation; alternatively, if children are to be bound by the consent of their parents, then all are not born free and equal and political authority need not rest on consent either. Locke's labour theory of the origins of private property, coupled with his argument for a natural right to inherit, and his notions of 'express' and 'tacit' consent, may be seen as ways of avoiding the problem posed by Filmer and thus preserving the view that political obligation depends exclusively on the consent of the governed. Hence considerable critical attention has been paid to

Locke's theory of property, his theory of political obligation, and the relationship between them.

If 'Filmer's problem' provides the important intellectual context of Locke's *Two Treatises*, modern scholarship has equally demonstrated the significance of the political context in which the book was written. Although debate about the precise dating of composition continues, it is generally agreed that the book was written before the so-called 'Glorious Revolution' of 1688 and it is widely accepted that its proper historical context is a phase in the attempts to exclude the Duke of York from the succession. The book is therefore not to be seen as a retrospective attempt to legitimize the ascent of William of Orange. One of the central doctrines in the *Second Treatise* is that the people have the right to rebel. But we have to understand Locke's theory of political obligation to know who are 'the people', and therefore, taking due note of the historical context, how radical his theory was. And concern with his theory of obligation leads us inexorably to his theory of property because, as we saw, political society is created, in Locke's view, to preserve property.

Locke's account of the origins of legitimate property is justly famous. He supposes that God gave the world to everyone in common, but that individuals might legitimately take from the common what they need to preserve themselves. The expenditure of labour creates an entitlement, because individuals have a property in themselves, and therefore in their labour, and if they mix this property with the common stock then they fix a property in that part of it. They are required, however, to avoid waste, and to leave 'enough and as good' for others. These requirements relate to the point about the law of nature prescribing the preservation of men noted earlier. Although this mixing of labour is initially conceived as gathering nature's fruits, Locke subsequently suggests that a man may legitimately enclose land itself, subject to the requirements mentioned. He also suggests that men agree to the use of money. For some commentators, the introduction of money occurs in the state of nature, while others argue that Locke intended to associate the use of money, division of land, and the creation of political society. Macpherson, who holds the former view, goes on to suggest that Locke's theory legitimizes a capitalist market economy: beginning with an equal right to property, Locke ends, he claims, by legitimizing unequal private property and by accepting the practice of wage-labour which denies to the worker a property in that with which his labour is mixed. He then argues that since political society is created to protect property, and since property is unequally distributed, and since full membership of political society depends on propertied status, Locke should be seen as an apologist for a particularly 'bourgeois' liberal polity.

This reading is, however, controversial. Among the difficulties to which critics have pointed is the inadequacy of the evidence for Macpherson's claim that Locke assumed a widespread labour market. Others, for example James Tully, have suggested that Locke envisaged an artisanal economy, in which those who mixed their labour also owned its product. This is one example of the reasons commentators have had for seeking Locke's 'social assumptions' in his *corpus*, and for interest in his overtly 'economic' writings. A second difficulty is with the argument that political society is designed to protect property. As Macpherson is aware, Locke used the term to cover both 'life, liberty and estate' and, more narrowly, 'estate'; and 'estate' in any case might include goods and land. Macpherson holds that the relevant sense in the present context is the latter; others have not been convinced. A third problem, one which brings us directly to the theory of political obligation, is the claim that membership of political society (and thus perhaps possession of the right to rebel discussed above) depends on propertied status.

Locke undoubtedly supposed that political authority is legitimate only if grounded in consent, but he was notoriously unclear about the procedures by which this consent was given, and thus about the membership of political society, and about the connection, if any, between such membership and the possession of property. He distinguished between express consent, which was perpetual and conferred membership, and tacit consent, which lasted only as long as the person concerned did not withdraw himself from the jurisdiction of the society. Locke assumed the self-evidence of what express consent means, but gave as examples of tacit consent walking down the road, taking a lodging, or possessing land. To this it has been retorted that if these actions are taken as signs of consent, it is effectively impossible not to give it, thus undermining the legitimacy conferred by consent. Locke has been defended, however, by the suggestion that tacit consent is designed only to legitimate the punishment of foreigners. Further difficulty arises from Locke's remark that consent is given when children reach adulthood, and from his observation that since political societies do not allow themselves to be dismembered, a person can inherit his parents' property only on the same terms as they held it, that is, subject to the law of a particular community. It is this connection between the inheritance of property and consent which is noticed by Macpherson. In his view, express consent is for the propertied member, while tacit consent is for the propertyless worker. On the other hand, there is the suggestion concerning foreign visitors noted above, and the claim that nothing in the *Two Treatises* precludes membership for all indigenous persons. On this last reading, Locke has been represented as a radical democrat.

The issue of the proper characterization of Locke's political theory is, therefore, bound to come to grips with his theory of property, his theory of obligation, and the connections between the two. Whilst many of the debates surrounding his work have this focus, rival interpretations naturally seek support beyond the covers of the *Two Treatises* simply because it is ambiguous in crucial areas. For Macpherson illumination is to be found in Locke's social assumptions, stated or not; for others, it is to be found in the broad historical context or the more specific intellectual background to the argument.

## ACCESSIBLE EDITIONS

Peter Laslett (ed.), *John Locke's Two Treatises of Government* (revised edn) (Cambridge, Cambridge University Press, 1963; Mentor paperback, New York, 1965)

John Yolton (ed.), *The Locke Reader* (Cambridge, Cambridge University Press, 1977)

## SUGGESTED READING

Richard Ashcraft, *Locke's Two Treatises of Government* (London, Allen & Unwin, 1987)

Richard H. Cox, *Locke on War and Peace* (Oxford, Oxford University Press, 1960)

Maurice Cranston, *John Locke: A Biography* (London, Longmans, 1957)

John Dunn, *The Political Thought of John Locke – An Historical Account of the Argument of the Two Treatises of Government* (Cambridge, Cambridge University Press, 1969)

C. B. Macpherson, *The Political Theory of Possessive Individualism: Hobbes to Locke* (Oxford, Clarendon Press, 1962)

* Geraint Parry, *John Locke* (London, Allen & Unwin, 1978)

Martin Seliger, *The Liberal Politics of John Locke* (London, Allen & Unwin, 1968)

James Tully, *Discourse on Property – John Locke and his Adversaries* (Cambridge, Cambridge University Press, 1980)

## Chapter Five

# LOCKE AND PROFESSOR MACPHERSON*

## *ISAIAH BERLIN*

If Mr Macpherson's treatment of Hobbes is at times over-ingenious and compels admiration for the author's skill rather than his views, in examining Locke's assumptions he is on firmer ground. 'Locke's astonishing achievement was to base the property right on natural right and natural law, and then to remove all the natural law limits from the property right' (p. 199). How was this done? Mr Macpherson points out the heavy emphasis that Locke laid on the invention of money. He argues convincingly that Locke distinguished three stages: a state of nature without money, one with money and contracts, and the full political state. Natural law allowed men a right only to so much land as would leave 'enough and as good' for others. But a money economy (together with an additional argument which Mr Macpherson gleans from the fourth edition of the *Two Treatises*) prevents the rotting of accumulated resources, since gold lasts for ever; and also increases productivity of land to such a degree that even the landless 'day labourer' gets more absolutely – however much less relatively – than he would get in the natural 'enough and as good' natural law economy. Money prevents spoiling, and it increases productivity; this, for Locke, overcomes the traditional objections, based on natural law, to unlimited private accumulation. Professor Macpherson discovers in Locke's state of nature a market in labour power; labour is for Locke an alienable commodity, but he is still medieval enough to think that human life itself cannot be alienated. In this he is alleged to be less consistent than Hobbes (p. 220), who said, 'the value or worth of a man is as of all other things, his price', or Marx, who

---

* The following reading is an extract from a longer essay in which the author discusses C. B. Macpherson's *The Political Theory of Possessive Individualism* (Oxford, Clarendon Press, 1962), focusing particularly on the interpretation of the political theories of Hobbes and Locke. Previously published in *Political Quarterly*, vol. 35 (1964).

said that if labour is alienated, then so are life and liberty. But life was just as inalienable for Hobbes: a man cannot, according to him, rationally be expected to yield it up.

On the other hand, Mr Macpherson seems to me to be right when he says that Locke travelled from the position that my title to a property is derived from the fact that I mix my labour with the raw material, to the notion that not only my own labour, but 'the turfs my servant has cut' still make the land mine; and from there to unlimited ownership of anything that can be turned into unspoilable money. And Locke certainly also holds that labour is a commodity, that is, that I can sell my work – and my ability to work – for a wage determined by the market. Whether this is to be regarded as a sufficient symptom of developed capitalism seems not so clear. The Greeks and the Romans (apart from one or two philosophical schools – which did not include the Stoics) placed no barriers upon capital acquisition, and yet it surely dilutes the term too much to speak of these societies as characteristically capitalist. Having established by clear and cogent argument Locke's claims to be regarded as the spokesman of unlimited capitalist appropriation, Professor Macpherson falls once again into exaggeration. He represents Locke as loading his political scales against the poor – which is true – and trying to save natural law by viewing them as being *pro tanto* not wholly rational: and adds that this view of the poor would be taken for granted by Locke's readers.[1] He admits that Locke nowhere explicitly says that there are two kinds of rights – one for men of property, one for those without – or that only property gives rights, yet he believes that this is one of Locke's 'assumptions', which to him is as good as an assertion. He infers from the proposition that property will become unequal as accumulation increases, that a fundamental right not to be subject to the jurisdiction of another will be so unequal as between owners and non-owners that it will be different in kind and not in degree; because Locke recognizes that the propertyless will depend for their very livelihood on those who have property, there will for him be unequal rights.

This may well be true in fact: inequality of power may lead to real inequality of rights or the perversion of even-handed justice. But what solid evidence is there that Locke thought this? In a state of nature, Locke declares, each man is his own judge; in theory all rights are equal, and so long as there is no actual slavery this remains true. The fact that most modern readers would consider economic dependence of wage-earning workers upon their masters to be a kind of slavery (that is to say, more than a mere metaphor for oppression of a non-slave-owning type) has no tendency to show that Locke thought that this was the case in the state of nature. The consequences of losing that 'full proprietorship of his own person' which Locke thinks the basis of equal natural rights, are not something about which he speculates; perhaps he should have recognized its likelihood under capitalism, but he does not. To say that he disguised the *de facto* situation by *de jure* considerations is not to interpret Locke but to attempt (perhaps quite justly) to expose him – a very different procedure. Mr Macpherson's central thesis is that Locke, having quietly got rid of the natural law restraints upon unlimited accumulation with which he began (because money does not spoil, and because 'ten acres well culti-vated yields more than a thousand in a wild waste', so that enclos-ures may actually improve the life of a landless labourer and make him richer than an Indian king), then proceeds to establish 'implicitly' differential natural rights. Only rational men have full natural rights (p. 234); but, according to Mr Macpherson, those who labour but do not appropriate and are landless (without being actually 'depraved') are not, for Locke, wholly rational; and the rest of Locke's argument is then held to proceed on the assumption that the beings endowed with full natural rights – those whose consent is needed for the purpose of setting up governments among men, those whose natural rights may not be infringed, whose majori-ties legislate and determine what shall be done – are not all the members of a society, but only those who are fully rational, ration-ality being defined in terms of capacity for, or success in, the accumulation of property.

This will surely not do. Locke nowhere says this; nor does Mr Macpherson maintain that he does; only that this is 'an implicit assumption' of his position and will alone explain some of the contradictions or apparent contradictions of his system. It may be conceded that the general thrust of Locke's argument is towards a democracy of property-owners; that he takes as little interest in landless men and the poor section of the community as, say, Winstanley did in servants and beggars. Nevertheless, Locke would have had every reason to protest at this startling piece of psycho-logical analysis of his hidden motives. Even if it is valid, Locke was not conscious of such assumptions, and a political theory stands or falls by what it says and omits to say, rather than by what may have conditioned its author to perpetrate particular errors and obscurities. The concept of a natural right for Locke is not bound up exclusively with property in the modern sense of the word. All students of Locke know by now that 'property' for him means sometimes (a) what belongs to a man as such – 'life, liberty, and estate' – at other times (b) what we should mean by it – i.e., possessions, what can be bought and sold; but it is impossible to show that when Locke meant (b) by 'property', he meant nothing but (b). Professor Macpherson says (pp. 247–8): 'The property for the protection of which men oblige themselves to civil society is sometimes (*Second Treatise*, sect. 123) stated to be life, liberty, and estate, and sometimes (*e.g.*, *Second Treatise*, sects. 138–140, 193) it is clearly only goods or land.' Whence it follows for him that the poor 'are rightfully both in and not in civil society'. But this is not to elucidate but to torture Locke's text. Locke does not, so far as I know, define property as 'only' goods and land, and the late George Paul, who used to insist on this point in his lectures, seems to me clearly right. Since Professor Macpherson bases his theory that Locke intended explicitly to exclude the propertyless from full participation in the state on these passages, the point is a crucial one for his entire thesis.

One of the ends of society is for Locke the preservation of property, in the sense of goods, and one of the justifications for rebellion is insecurity of property in this sense. But at the same time, Locke states quite clearly in the *Second Treatise* that all men can know natural law save lunatics and idiots (sect. 60); they may choose to ignore it or disobey it, but they know it; and it includes the right to life and liberty as well as property – men cannot forfeit these to society save through the commission of crimes. Nothing is said about the fact that only accumulators are fully able to see these truths. Foreigners are not full members of the society; Mr Macpherson draws a parallel between poor men and foreigners as men in, but not full members of, the state; but this is too strained; the allegiance of foreigners is elsewhere and the analogy between them and labourers does not work. Locke's labourers, unlike Marx's, have a country. When Locke speaks of the enjoyment of property, he speaks not merely of landholdings, but 'a week's lodging or the use of a highway', which labourers certainly have as much as anyone else.

Professor Macpherson, believing as he does that Locke identifies rational men with property-owners, then takes Locke to assume that civil society or the state consists in the management of affairs for the benefit of these property-owners; in contrast with true democracy, which consists in the management of society for the benefit of all its members – a utopia, so long as unavoidable conflict between the exploiters and the exploited renders the notion of a common interest self-contradictory. Locke's passionate attacks upon absolute government, which are unqualified, then have to be represented by Mr Macpherson as the protection not of the whole society, but of property-owners only, against usurpation of power by an individual, say James II. But if in a market society the bourgeoisie is already in the saddle and riding on the backs of the proletariat, it seems odd to defend the ruling group against dangers that *ex hypothesi* the social structure has rendered impossible. It may not be incorrect to say that Locke is in fact identified with men of property, that he looks on them as endowed with such political virtues as judgement and solidity – as Aristotle and Hume also did; and that he wishes to found the state on them. It may be said also that he has insufficient sympathy for the poor – there are some brutal passages which may be quoted against him – and perhaps Marxists rightly maintain that his entire position is utopian: that a less biased thinker would have realized that the interests of the rich and poor do not coincide, that there is no common interest in class-divided societies; and that like other liberals he rationalized this away, and saw a coincidence of interests where there was none, because this suited his class. But this is not the same as saying that Locke said, or even assumed, that labourers are not to be included among the wholly rational, and have a set of rights different from and inferior to men in general. Yet this is what Mr Macpherson's position seems to me to amount to. To support his extraordinary position Mr Macpherson (p. 224, para. 3) cites Locke's *The Reasonableness of Christianity*, where he says:

> The greatest part of mankind have not leisure for learning and logick, and superfine distinctions of the schools. Where the hand is used to the plough and the spade, the head is seldom elevated to sublime notions or exercised in mysterious reasoning. 'Tis well if men of that rank (to say nothing of the other sex) can comprehend plain propositions . . . , etc.

Mr Macpherson equates 'mysterious reasoning' and 'superfine distinctions' with reason – reason as such – the possession of which entitles us to call men rational, and the absence of which disqualifies them from having a say in creating and controlling civil society.[2] Special pleading can scarcely go further.

If anything, Locke's tone is that of a man half-sighing for a simpler, earlier, conflict-free, perhaps imaginary, almost idyllic society, not for the devil-take-the-hindmost mentality of a world of unbridled *laissez-faire*. Mr Macpherson speaks, as he has every right to do, of the confusion in Locke between two states of nature: the 'pleasant' and the 'unpleasant', as he calls them. In one, Locke speaks of peace, goodwill and mutual assistance, and so on; the other he calls 'very unsafe, very insecure', in which the enjoyment of individual rights is 'very uncertain and constantly exposed to the invasion of others', 'full of fears and continual dangers'. This is due to not the degenerate and wicked few, but to a liability on the part of the many not to follow the laws of reason. He explains this by saying that Locke held two contradictory concepts simultaneously: (a) of 'equal undifferentiated beings', men as conceived by Christian and natural law, e.g., by the judicious Hooker: free men, equal to one another, with equal ability to shift for themselves. Hence Locke's anti-paternalism, his opposition to any view, such as Filmer's,[3] which would justify the management of men as children by a sovereign upon whom they must look as a father. This is the concept of a market society modified by vestigial remnants of natural law. (b) That of two classes differentiated by level of rationality, determined by capacity for accumulation. Not only is there no evidence for this, but anti-paternalism as such does not depend upon adherence to a market society. Kant[4] is passionately anti-paternalist – exploitation of one man by another is to him the worst of vices – but even more unfriendly to the notion of men and their faculties as commodities for sale. These positions are commonly held to be harmonious if not mutually entailed – does either imply a support for market society? Why is one not allowed to say that Locke, in talking about the state of nature, was simply repeating the Christian Fathers and Seneca, for whom peace and equality reigned in a state of nature until sin and the Fall broke it all, and made men covetous and aggressive? This was the traditional view, to which Locke, not very consistently, it is true, added the discomforts and insecurities of such a life, which made it worth men's while to compact with one another in order to create civil society. Mr Macpherson says that the Christian view of man is of 'a mixture of appetite and reason'; why should not what Mr Macpherson calls the two views in Locke's account be an attempt to meet both these characteristics, together with the usual mythology about the innocence of the state of nature? To demonstrate that only property-owners are full and rational members of society, Mr Macpherson quotes Locke on the fact that every man must submit his possessions to the community: but this surely does not mean 'only those who have property to submit can be full members'. If I have no property, I submit potential property, or just my begging bowl. I am not allowed to keep my property outside the bounds of state authority; but this does not imply that rights directly depend upon submitting some kind of possessions as if in payment for them – a doctrine of 'No possessions, no rights'. Mr Macpherson interprets the notorious notion of tacit consent simply as a method of subjecting the passive non-possessors to the active possessors: if this is generalized, which society, save that of Rousseau's ideal rustics, would escape this fate?

But Mr Macpherson is severely consistent. When he comes to the problem of the incompatibility of majority rule with indefeasible natural rights of the individual that may not be set aside by any man or institution, Mr Macpherson argues that if the majority are by definition all property-owners, there can be no danger to individual property, and no man will then be taxed save by his own consent; for both he and his representatives, bound by class solidarity, will be equally anxious to preserve the rights of property. But Locke does say 'every man by [tacitly] consenting with others to make one body politic . . . puts himself under an obligation . . . to submit to the determination of the majority', etc. That is to say, he equates the 'tacit' consent of the many with the actual consent of the few (their representatives). This may be an improper use of the word 'consent', and even a dangerous one, but it seems more in harmony with Locke's normal usage than Mr Macpherson's belief that the conception of government as the committee of the ruling class is not merely a realistic account of the facts but the central notion of Locke's (implicit? or unconscious?) outlook. To defend, as I am attempting to do, traditional interpretations against new and interesting and brilliantly constructed ones, is a tedious business: but this last is perhaps the least plausible thesis in a good and important book. Thus Mr Macpherson supposes that it is only the rational property-owners who realize that submission to the decision of the majority is a rational step: since without it there will be no adequate protection of property. But why should this be confined to property, and not include life and liberty, too? Everything except religious freedom, on which Locke is very uncompromising? It is this utilitarian proposition that lies at the base of the routine democratic theory of majority rule. It may be full of flaws, majorities may be tyrannous, the notion of human rights may be left insufficiently articulated or protected; but it is difficult to see how, e.g., a communist society would dispense with it – if it is not to be governed by a majority, then by whom? Only by a Jacobin unanimity – is it this that Locke failed to perceive? For Professor Macpherson, Locke is the prophet of what Mussolini was later to call pluto-democracies (or was it demo-plutocracies?), and indeed, he plainly attaches great importance to ownership of property, far greater than to wealth as such. But there is no less present in him the notion that an individual's rights – not merely property rights, but rights to life and elementary liberties – are in danger from all governments as such. When these governments represent genuine majorities in a classless society, this danger is regarded as non-existent – logically ruled out – by Marxists; but on other assumptions, Christian, for example, or Freudian, the danger is not so easily spirited away. And Professor Macpherson himself, although he does not allow that such passions as greed or ambition may not be due solely to the market society, and find other, no less destructive channels even when it has been abolished, does ask in his last pages whether 'liberal institutions and values' can be preserved in a society where men are truly equal at last.

It seems unhistorical not to allow that Locke may have been troubled by similar problems. For Mr Macpherson, the individuals whose rights Locke wishes to defend are the pike, not the carp, the owners, not the owned. 'A market society generates class differentiation in effective rights and rationality, yet requires for its justification a postulate of equal natural rights and rationality. Locke recognized the differentiation in his own society, and read it back into natural society' (p. 269). This is Locke's alleged contradiction. But why did the market society require equal rights for its justification? Why not unequal rights based on differences in capacity to acquire? Why should society conceived as a Joint Stock Company need the assumption of equal rights? Equal rights to trade, perhaps, to accumulation; but not necessarily equality under the law in other respects. Thrasymachus would have recognized the need for equal opportunity for the strong and the weak, so that the strong might organize and dominate the weak. This may be unjust or morally repulsive, but it is an assumption that in other contexts, and for a variety of reasons, other thinkers, Burke, for example, or de Maistre, made very firmly. Certainly there is an incompatibility between the unbridled freedom of the individual and the notion of equal rights, and no solution of this dilemma has thus far proved either morally or practically satisfactory. This is an insight with which Locke may be credited, but it is a conclusion far tamer than anything which Mr Macpherson wishes to advance. He accuses Locke of reading back the characteristics of civilized society into natural society; but perhaps it is Professor Macpherson who is reading back nineteenth-century conflicts into the seventeenth century.

In this over-long review, largely devoted to specific criticisms, I have, despite acknowledging Mr Macpherson's philosophical and literary gifts, perhaps not made it sufficiently clear that the book is singularly rich in ideas, with most of which I have been unable to deal; and I should like to say again that it is a work of exceptional originality, imagination, and intellectual power, from which, despite all my disagreements – and I cannot accept its central theses – I have profited greatly, and which I greatly admire: it is a superb piece of work. The sensation of suddenly feeling that one is sailing in intellectually first-class waters is wonderfully exhilarating. I should like to salute a work which by its critical standards and the quality of its writing has lifted the history of political ideas treated from a Marxist point of view to a level seldom attained in the west, at any rate in our time.

## NOTES

1   Thus Hobbes is a ravening wolf who looks like one. Locke is a capitalist wolf in medieval, natural law, sheep's clothing. This puts Mr Macpherson into paradoxical proximity to Dr Leo Strauss and his followers: if Hobbes and Locke turn out to be bedfellows, so are those who (from very opposite corners) so regard them.

2   On p. 197, para. 1 (*The Reasonableness of Christianity*), Locke speaks of 'common reason and equity', which Mr Macpherson quotes as 'reason and common equity'; this is a very trivial lapse: but to apply to him, a little unfairly, the method he applies to Locke, it may indicate the trend of his own thought: he wants 'reason': 'common reason' may seem less general.

3   And perhaps William Petyt's: although the passage quoted by Mr Macpherson (p. 228) seems capable of another interpretation.

4   Especially in his essay *Was ist Aufklärung* [What is Enlightenment?].

## Chapter Six

# APPROPRIATION IN THE STATE OF NATURE: LOCKE ON THE ORIGIN OF PROPERTY*[1]

## KARL OLIVECRONA

In the discussion of John Locke's concept of property, which lies at the root of his political theory, controversy prevails. Laslett records as the conventional judgement of Locke's view of property that it 'described a natural, inalienable right'; this Laslett himself finds 'exactly wrong'.[2] It has been suggested that Locke used the term 'property' in two senses, both in the narrow one of 'material belongings' and in a more extended sense including such ideal benefits as liberty and honour: but this distinction has been contested.[3] With regard to the acquisition of property there is some lack of clarity concerning the significance of the labour theory of value ascribed to Locke.

As a contribution to the explanation of Locke's theory of property I propose in this paper to discuss his views on the acquisition of property. His opinion in this respect has to be seen against the background of the doctrines of the great teachers of natural law in the seventeenth century. We know that Locke possessed the works of Grotius and Pufendorf on the law of nature and made use of them.[4] He especially admired Pufendorf, whose great treatise *De Jure Naturae et Gentium* (1672) he described as 'the best book of its kind', better than the work of Grotius on *War and Peace* (1625).[5] Hobbes was of less importance for Locke.[6]

Pufendorf usually followed Grotius. His general view on the law of nature and the origin of rights is on the whole the same as that of Grotius. But regarding the introduction of the right of property there are some differences of opinion which are not without significance for our subject.

---

* Previously published in *Journal of the History of Ideas*, vol. 35 (1974).

# THE VIEWS OF GROTIUS AND PUFENDORF

The starting point for Grotius and Pufendorf was the assumption of the original liberty of man. Liberty implied equality. Everybody was sovereign within his own sphere. But he must not encroach upon the sphere of others. To do so constituted an *iniuria*. The fundamental precept of the law of nature (the will and commands of God) was to accord to everybody what belonged to him: *suum cuique tribuere*. This was not a command to exert oneself on behalf of others. The precept had a purely negative significance: to refrain from causing injury to one's fellow men. That was to act justly. Grotius says that justice consists entirely in abstaining from taking that which belongs to others (*alieni abstinentia*).[7]

Thus each individual was supposed to possess, in the state of nature, a sphere of his own. By Grotius this sphere was called the *suum*, that which belongs to oneself. Every infringement on the *suum* was an *iniuria*. The consequence of an *iniuria* was that the principle of *alieni abstinentia* was no longer applicable in favour of the aggressor. Without committing an injury the offended person could now use violence against him to avert the attack, to recover what he had lost, or to extract compensation. The reaction need not be proportionate to the damage caused or threatened by the attack. If it was necessary to prevent an injury, even of the most trifling kind, the assailant might be killed.[8]

Everybody was, so to speak, surrounded by an invisible fence which marked off his sphere against others. If an intrusion was made or attempted, the invader forfeited the sacredness of his own person. He lost the protection of the fence and was nakedly exposed to the violence of the offended party. But in the state of nature existence was precarious. Society was formed for the purpose of protecting the *suum*.[9] The participants to the compact forswore the licence of using force themselves. Vindicating the *suum* was entrusted to the community acting on behalf of injured parties under the direction of the courts, exception being made only for situations where the community could not intervene.

As will be seen, the two great principles governing relationships in the state of nature were the sacredness of the *suum*, on the one hand, and the licence to react with violence against injuries, on the other. The same principles obtained in society. But force had now to be used, on principle, by the community alone. The pivot of the system was the *suum*. Everything depended on how it was circumscribed. This was what gave substance to the principle *suum cuique*. We shall now see how Grotius and Pufendorf defined the *suum*.

Since there was a certain difference of opinion between them, we had better first discuss Grotius alone.

## The suum *according to Grotius*

In the language of Grotius the term *suum (meum, nostrum)* denotes that which 'belongs' to a person. An equivalent expression was 'to be proper' to somebody (*alicui proprium esse*). In the state of nature that which belonged to an individual was, in the first place, his life, limb, and liberty, but also his reputation and honour. Consequently, every attack on the life, limb, liberty, reputation, or honour of somebody was an injury to him. Furthermore the *suum* included one's own actions. They were co-ordinated by Grotius with body, limbs, reputation, and honour. Therefore they were counted as belonging to a person in the same sense as his life and limb, etc.[10]

The positive content of liberty (*libertas*) was the power one had over one's own actions (*potestas in se*). But the power over a certain action could be transferred to another person. In this way the *suum* of one person could be diminished and that of another correspondingly enlarged. The transference implied the establishment of a *right* for one person over another. The means of effectuating the transference was an act of will. Since the power over one's own actions resided in the will and everybody was sovereign within his own sphere, the will alone could detach part of its power from itself and bestow it on somebody else. But acceptance was necessary. The will of the recipient must be active in order to include the transferred power within its own domain.

This was the import of a contract. The *force créatrice* in a contract was the will of the parties. But for practical reasons the inner action of will could not be sufficient in human relations. The will had to be made manifest in some appropriate way. A *signum* or *declaratio voluntatis* was necessary. A contract therefore was made up by two declarations of will, promise and acceptance. The promisor alienated part of his liberty (*particula libertatis*) and transferred it to the opposite party who took possession of it. The promisee thereby acquired a power over a certain action by the promisor. If the promisor, for instance, engaged to pay a sum of money, he lost the power of freely deciding whether or not to perform this act. The promisee could now request him, or command him, to do so. It then became necessary for the promisor to comply.[11]

The necessity was not of a factual kind. The promisor could actually refuse payment. But it was morally necessary for him to pay. He had deprived himself of the inner freedom to choose between different modes of acting. He was morally speaking in a state of subjection to the promisee. The latter held a moral power over him, a *qualitas* or *facultas moralis*. This was the significance of a right, *ius*, in the proper sense. All rights in the sense of moral faculties derived, directly or indirectly, from promises, that is, from acts of will through which parts of the original liberty were transferred to others. An exception was made only with regard to the right of parents over their children, which the parents possessed because they had generated the children.

In the state of nature there were no rights in the sense of moral faculties except in so far as agreements had been concluded and parents had rights over their children. Everybody simply had his sphere of *suum* and was at liberty to vindicate it by force against actual or threatening aggression. But through agreements the sphere of the *suum* could be extended so that it came to include more than life, limb, etc. Every *facultas moralis* that one had acquired through an agreement also belonged to the *suum*.[12] The general rule of the consequences of an *iniuria* was applicable. Disobedience to the request of the possessor of a moral faculty was an injury done to him, and he was entitled to react with force, in society with the help of the courts. The connotation of the term *suum* was 'that which belongs to the personality': life, limb, liberty, reputation, honour, and the moral faculties over other people acquired by agreements. The connotation of the word *iniuria* was 'attack on the personality' of somebody.[13]

The right of property was a moral faculty used against other people in requesting them to refrain from interfering with the object owned and to restore it if they had taken it. This right, like every other right, rested on an agreement. God had given to mankind all things and animals on earth to use (Gen. 1:29, 30; 9:2). Originally all men possessed everything in common. The right of property was introduced when this state of community of goods was found inconvenient. The agreement could either be an express compact to divide existing resources or a silent convention that everybody should have as his own what he had occupied.[14] Evidently what one acquired in one way or other was included in the *suum*. But even before the introduction of the right of property the sphere of the *suum* could be enlarged. From God's original grant it followed that everybody could take for himself what he desired and could consume. This general practice, Grotius says, filled the role of the right of property. If somebody had appropriated an object it was an injury to deprive him of it.[15]

This sort of appropriation is only briefly mentioned by Grotius.

He does not enlarge on the subject. It would seem as if he only had in mind taking things needed for immediate consumption or else for personal use. He does not explain how the appropriation was accomplished. The verb that he employs is *arripere*, not the technical *occupare*. He obviously means 'laying hold of' something, taking it to oneself. This could not give rise to the right of property: a *facultas moralis* could only originate from an agreement. But the object possessed was included in the *suum*.

Grotius here makes use of a natural and common idea. We can observe it in children. When a child has picked some strawberries, they are said to be 'his' or 'hers'. If they are taken from the child by a naughty boy this is acutely felt, not only because of the loss of the strawberries. The act is experienced by the child as an attack on itself, that is, on its personality. In this way we feel, all of us, with regard to objects that 'belong' to us. They are supposed to be joined to ourselves. We have the feeling of our personality being in some inexplicable way extended to encompass the objects we own. Therefore, if anything is taken from us or damaged, we have the experience of an attack on ourselves. The feeling differs, of course, in strength depending on circumstances. It is especially pronounced with regard to cherished things in daily use or connected with memories. In the case of land it can rise to a high degree of intensity. If a farmer is deprived of the soil which he and his forefathers have cultivated for generations, he will feel it as a severe amputation.[16]

## Pufendorf on the acquisition of property

Pufendorf gives very clear expression to the idea of uniting an object with one's personality. Discussing the transference of the right of property he stresses that the concourse of the will of both parties is necessary. The transferor's volition is not sufficient. The recipient must consent. The object is physically separated from me, he says, and it would be out of order if it should be, so to speak, adjoined to me unless I embrace it with my will and consent.[17] The connection between my ego and the object is spiritual. To establish it an act of will is required. But Pufendorf does not make the same use as Grotius of the idea of appropriation. Like Grotius he holds that the right of property was introduced by a compact. But he differs from Grotius with regard to the preceding stage. He denies the possibility, assumed by Grotius, of uniting an object with the *suum* by means of simple appropriation. An antecedent agreement is always necessary. Pufendorf adheres rigidly to this principle.

The argument was as follows. If simple appropriation were really

sufficient to make the object mine, this could only be so in consequence of the terms of the original grant. It would presuppose that
God had given men in common a right in a *positive* sense to all
things on earth. Pufendorf's meaning is that God must have given
men a common *facultas moralis* with regard to everything on earth.
But this was not the case. The things on earth were given to
mankind in the sense only that all men were allowed to use them.
Nobody had more right to them than another. Community of goods
existed only in this *negative* sense (Pufendorf, 4, 4, 2).

It was indeed impossible that men could have a *facultas moralis*
in common over things on earth. For a *facultas moralis* is a power
over another man's actions. The force of the right of property (*vis
dominii*) is such that we are masters over things that belong to us
and can prohibit others from using them. God did not give the
things to mankind in this sense. An indication of this is that God
allowed the animals to use and consume things (Gen. 1:30). But
there is no right of property for animals. If one animal puts something away for the future, the others are not prohibited from taking
it (Pufendorf, 4, 4, 5). Pufendorf also adduces the case of Adam.
He was allowed to make use of everything. But he had not the right
of property to anything because there was nobody over whom he
could have a *facultas moralis*. Therefore, if one of his sons collected
more apples than he was permitted to, he did not steal; he was only
disobedient to his father (Pufendorf, 4, 4, 12).

In this way Pufendorf shows that no *facultas moralis* could be
directly derived from the original grant to mankind. It was left to
men's own judgement how special rights were to be established
(Pufendorf, 4, 4, 4). An agreement among them was necessarily
required. Since men were equal it was impossible to understand
how the mere physical act of occupation could have the effect of
excluding others from an object. An agreement must first be
concluded if occupation were to create an individual right to an
object (Pufendorf, 4, 4, 5). This is why it was necessary to assume
that the right of property had been introduced by the human will.

When speaking of the introduction of property Pufendorf has in
mind the general establishment of property rights. But like Grotius
he discusses the situation in the earlier stage when community of
goods prevailed. Men could not make use of the fruits of the earth
without collecting them. But it would be useless to collect the fruits
if others were permitted to take them away. Therefore, the first
convention among mortals is understood to have been to the effect
that if someone had taken possession of things with the intention
of making use of them, nobody should take them from him. If there

had been no such convention, men would have had to abstain from using anything at all (Pufendorf, 4, 4, 5; 4, 4, 13).

At this pristine stage the community of goods was 'tempered'. There was a mixture of community of goods and right of property. The substance of things was common to all. But the fruits belonged to him who had collected them. The oak belonged to nobody. But if I picked up an acorn, it became mine (Pufendorf, 4, 4, 13). This followed from the primaeval convention. Only gradually were separate rights of property established by compacts, in response to the requirements of changing conditions (Pufendorf, 4, 4, 6 and 12).

To sum up. Pufendorf's argument is that the good things on earth could be of no use to men unless they acquired a right of property in them; that this right could not be directly derived from God's original grant; that it could not be created solely through occupation; and that an agreement among men was necessary to give rise to the right of property. He draws the conclusion that the principle of *suum cuique* did not become applicable with regard to things until it had been determined through a convention what belonged to whom (Pufendorf, 4, 4, 14).

Thus Pufendorf did not accept the idea of Grotius that the *suum* could be extended to encompass external objects without a preceding convention (Pufendorf, 4, 4, 9).

### Locke on the acquisition of property

Locke makes the same general assumptions as Grotius and Pufendorf. Men are naturally 'in . . . a *State of perfect Freedom* to order their Actions, and dispose of their Possessions, and Persons as they think fit' (II, 4); Man is 'absolute Lord of his own Person and Possessions' (II, 123). There is 'a *State* also *of Equality*, wherein all the Power and Jurisdiction is reciprocal, no one having more than another' (II, 4).

But the state of nature, though a state of liberty, is not a state of licence. It has 'a Law of Nature to govern it, which obliges every one: And Reason, which is that Law, teaches all Mankind, who will but consult it, that being all equal and independent, no one ought to harm another in his Life, Health, Liberty, or Possessions' (II, 6). This is the principle *suum cuique tribuere*. At the same time as being the dictates of Reason, the law of nature is the will and commands of God (II, 135).

The law of nature is violated when somebody makes an attack on the life, liberty, or possessions of another. The consequence is that he exposes himself to the reaction of the offended party. He forfeits the protection of the law of nature. Locke's mode of expressing this is that the offender puts himself into a state of war. He 'declares himself to live by another rule than that of *reason*' (II, 8). He has 'declared War against all Mankind, and therefore may be destroyed as a *Lyon* or a *Tyger*' (II, 11). He 'has exposed his life to the others Power to be taken away by him [the offended party], or any one that joyns with him in his Defence' (II, 16).

Everyone has 'a right to punish the transgressors of [the Law of Nature] to such a Degree, as may hinder its Violation' (II, 7). In one passage Locke claims that the reaction has to be proportionate to the transgression (II, 8). But later this limitation seems to be discarded. I may kill a thief, Locke says, 'when he sets on me to rob me, but of my Horse or Coat' (II, 19).

The state of nature is, however, unsafe. Men will not accept the law of nature as 'binding to them in the application of it to their particular Cases'. Moreover there are no independent judges: everybody is a judge unto himself. But he may lack the power to give due execution to the law of nature (II, 124).

These are the reasons why men are willing to quit the state of nature. They unite 'for the mutual *Preservation* of their Lives, Liberties and Estates', which Locke calls 'by the general Name, *Property*' (II, 123). The preservation of their property is 'the great and *chief end*' of 'Mens uniting into Commonwealths, and putting themselves under Government' (II, 124).

This corresponds to the statement by Grotius that society has been formed with the object of preserving the *suum* for everybody. What Grotius calls the *suum* Locke calls a man's property. Originally he used the term 'propriety', though he later exchanged it in most places for 'property'.[18] 'Propriety' seems to have been the usual word in the seventeenth century. It was employed by Hobbes, Filmer, and others. The connotation was primarily 'that which is proper to a person' (= *proprium alicui, suum*) or 'that which belongs to somebody'.[19]

What 'belonged' to a person was not in the first place physical things. It was his life, limb, and liberty. In the *Second Treatise* Locke says: 'By *Property* I must be understood here, as in other places, to mean that Property which Men have *in their Persons* [emphasis supplied] as well as Goods' (II, 173). This was in accordance with seventeenth-century usage. 'Of things held in propriety', Hobbes says, 'those that are dearest to a man are his own life, and limbs; and in the next degree (in most men), those that concern conjugall affection; and after them riches and means of living.'[20] Laslett records that Locke's contemporaries could talk of the Protestant religion established by law as their 'property'.[21] Richard Baxter, writing before 1680, said that every man was born 'with a propriety in his *own members*, and nature giveth him a propriety in *his Children*, and his *food* and other just *acquisitions* of his industry'; he also said that 'men's *lives* and *Liberties* are the chief parts of their propriety'.[22]

Locke too regarded life, limb, and liberty as the core of one's property (II, 123). But just as Grotius did, he thought that the sphere of property, or *suum*, could be extended to encompass physical objects. The problem of the acquisition of property was the problem of how such enlargement could be achieved. The solution was presented in the famous ch. V of the *Second Treatise*.

As mentioned above, it has been suggested that Locke used the term 'property' in two meanings, both as signifying 'material possessions' or 'units of the conveniences or necessities of life', and – in an extended meaning – as 'Lives, Liberties and Estates' (Laslett, 84, 101, and Viner above, note 3).

Locke's use of the word is not consistent. There are two connotations which are not distinguished by Locke himself. One is 'that which belongs to a person' or 'that which is a person's own'. In this sense the word 'property' refers to the *objects* included within the spheres of the *suum*. The other connotation appears, for instance, when Locke talks of how property in 'the *Earth itself*' is acquired (II, 32). Here 'property' signifies a *right* to land, not the object of that right.

The 'extended' meaning suggested by Viner refers to the denotation of the word 'property' when used in the former sense. But it is turning things upside down to say that the meaning is 'extended' when life and liberty are comprised within a person's property. Life, limb, and liberty are from the beginning his property. But the sphere of his property can be extended to encompass material things.

## THE BIBLICAL FOUNDATION

The ultimate ground why men could acquire things as their own was the original grant of God to mankind. This was the common assumption of Grotius, Pufendorf, and Locke. Only by the will of God could men have come to possess any things on earth as belonging to themselves.

Therefore, the terms of the original grant were of fundamental importance. Since they were set out in Gen. 1:28, 29 and 2:9, the interpretation of these passages was decisive for the basis of the doctrine of property.

On this point there is no discernible difference of opinion between

Grotius and Pufendorf, on the one hand, and Locke, on the other. All of them held that God had given all animals and things on earth to men 'in common' without any special right for anybody. Locke had therefore no occasion to argue against Grotius or Pufendorf concerning God's grant. But Filmer had a different opinion concerning its terms. Locke in his *First Treatise* put forward his arguments against Filmer.

Filmer interpreted Gen. 1:28 as implying that Adam by donation from God 'was made the general lord of all things' with 'private dominion to himself' and the right of 'donation, assignation or cession'. At the time of the Flood Noah was left the sole heir of the whole world. It is not probable, Filmer says, that God abrogated his donation to Adam and instituted a community of all things between Noah and his sons, as Selden would have it. Filmer finds it most reasonable that 'Noah himself, as lord of all, was the author of the distribution of the world, and of private dominion.'[23]

Locke refutes this theory by applying a principle of the common law to the original grant (I, 85). The argument is that if God had made a personal donation to Adam of the whole world, Adam's rights could not have been inherited by his children; for a 'positive grant' must be interpreted strictly in accordance with the express words used and cannot confer any right beyond that. Therefore, at Adam's death the donation would have reverted to God. This, Locke obviously thinks, would be an unacceptable conclusion.

Filmer has nothing more of a positive kind to say on the origin of property. Locke had therefore no reason to argue any more against him on that question in the *First Treatise*. As we shall presently see, there is a brief reference to Filmer in the *Second Treatise*. For the rest Filmer's doctrine is without importance for Locke's theory of property.

Laslett contends that Locke's chapter on property was written with Filmer's works in mind, and as a direct refutation of them. This is unlikely. In Laslett's opinion Locke had in mind a passage in *Patriarcha* where Filmer argues against the theory that the right of property was introduced by a compact. The passage runs as follows (273):

Certainly it was a rare felicity, that all men in the world at one instant of time should agree together in one mind to change the natural community of all things into private dominion: for without such a unanimous consent it was not possible for community to be altered: for if but one man in the world had dissented, the alteration had been unjust, because that man by the law of nature had a right to the common use of all things in the world; so that to have given a propriety of any one thing to any other, had been to have robbed him of his right to the common use of all things.

This is one of the many arguments which Filmer proffers against Grotius' assumption of the original community of goods. Filmer wants to show that if community of goods had really existed from the beginning, it could not have been replaced by private property through a compact. For this would have required consent by every man on earth, which, Filmer implies, could never have been obtained. Therefore, the theory of original community of goods is false. This theory Filmer held to be 'an error which the heathens taught' (*Patriarcha*, 262).

If Locke had intended to refute Filmer's doctrine in ch. V of the *Second Treatise*, he would have argued in support of his own theory that God had given the earth to men in common. But there is nothing in ch. V on that point besides a few words in the beginning (II, 25).

As regards Filmer's argument against Grotius that the right of property could not have been instituted by a compact, Locke could have had no objection. He reasoned in a similar way. It would have been impossible, he thought, to obtain the consent of all men on earth (II, 28).

## LOCKE'S PROBLEM

Locke starts his exposition of the origin of property by stating his fundamental thesis that God had given the earth to mankind in common (II, 25). This is evident both from reason and revelation. Reason tells us that men, being once born, have a right to their preservation and consequently to such things as nature affords for their subsistence. Revelation is very clear to the effect that God, as King David says (and he might be supposed to understand the donation, I, 28) 'has given the Earth to the Children of Men' (Psalm 115).

Locke further brushes aside Filmer's theory, criticized in the *First Treatise*, that God gave the world to Adam and his 'Heirs in Succession' to the exclusion of 'all the rest of his Posterity'. On that supposition only a universal monarch could possess property, which Locke plainly finds absurd. But there was another, far more serious difficulty in the demonstration of origin of private property in things. If the earth had been given to men in common, how had it come to be that the community of goods thus established had been replaced by private property rights? Unless valid titles to private rights could be shown, the actual distribution of possessions would seem to rest on robbery; and justice would require the return to the community of goods. Locke had no intention of acceding to such claims.

Grotius and Pufendorf had solved the difficulty by deriving the institution of private property from a compact through which the community of goods had been set aside. But there was another reason too for them to require an agreement as the foundation of the right of property. *Dominium*, as every other right, was a *facultas moralis*. It was a moral power in the owner over the minds of all other men to request them to abstain from the object and restore it if they had gained possession of it without the consent of the owner. No *facultas moralis* of one man over another could, however, be established without his consent.

Locke rejects the compact theory of Grotius and Pufendorf. His argument is as follows. Like Pufendorf Locke holds that men in the state of nature must be able to 'appropriate' things necessary for their sustenance. 'Appropriation', which is a word frequently employed by Locke in his chapter on property, literally means 'making a thing proper to oneself', that is, making it one's own. 'Fruits' and 'Beasts', Locke says, 'being given for the use of Men, there must of necessity be a means *to appropriate* them some way or other before they can be of any use, or at all beneficial to any particular Man' (II, 26).

The idea is that a man cannot use a thing for his own benefit *without injury to others* unless that thing, being by nature common to all, has first been made his own. God cannot have put man on earth under such conditions that he would be unable to support himself without breaking the law of nature, God's own will. Therefore, God must have instituted a means of appropriating the necessities of life. But appropriation cannot have presupposed general agreement. It would have been patently impossible to obtain the consent of all men on earth. Consequently, 'if such a consent as that was necessary, Man had starved, notwithstanding the Plenty God had given him' (II, 28). This is a retort to Pufendorf, who, without exception, had required general consent for appropriation in the state of nature. This compact theory cannot be upheld, Locke thinks.

The real problem for Locke was, therefore, how to explain the origin of property without interposing a fictitious compact. The solution was facilitated for him because there was a significant difference between his concept of a right and that of Grotius and Pufendorf. Locke did not adopt the concept of *facultas moralis*. It was not a basis of his reasoning as it was for Grotius and Pufendorf. As far as I know he never criticized this concept. But he ignored it. In the *Two Treatises* it is never mentioned or presupposed. This difference is highly important. It made it easier for Locke to explain the origin of private property without assuming a compact. Still the problem remained. How could the original community of goods have been superseded by private rights to land and goods without an agreement to divide the common or to allow occupation? This must have been brought about without inflicting injury on anybody. Locke had to steer between the Scylla of the compact theory of property and the Charybdis of robbery.


## APPROPRIATION

To solve the problem Locke made use of the same idea of appropriation as Grotius employed, but on a far larger scale. Grotius allowed appropriation without the consent of others only in the earliest stage of the world and presumably for very limited purposes; it lost its importance with the introduction of *dominium* by way of convention. Locke, on the contrary, made appropriation the beginning and foundation of the right of property. In immediate continuation of his statement that there must be some means of appropriating the necessities of life Locke explains by an example what appropriation implies. 'The Fruit, or Venison, which nourishes the wild *Indian*, who knows no Inclosure, and is still a Tenant in common, must be his, and so his, *i.e., a part of him* [emphasis supplied], that another can no longer have any right to it, before it can do him any good for the support of his Life' (II, 26).

Here we have a most unequivocal expression of the idea that the personality is extended to encompass physical objects. The deer that the Indian has killed is *his* in the sense that it is part of himself. Locke is not encumbered by the notion that *dominium* is a moral faculty against all other men. He only maintains that the object is included within the sphere of the personality, or within the *suum*, as Grotius would have said, by being appropriated. But when the object has been included within that sphere, it will be an injury to the possessor to deprive him of it. For his own person is exclusively his own. 'Though the Earth, and all inferior Creatures be common to all Men, yet every Man has a *Property* in his own *Person*. This no Body has any Right to but himself' (II, 27). Therefore, an attack on that which belongs to the personality constitutes an injury; and the injured party is licensed to react with violence.

Locke goes on to explain the concept of appropriation. His idea is that I infuse something of my personality into an object in spending some 'labour' on it. For a man's labour is his own (II, 27):

> The *Labour* of his Body, and the *Work* of his Hands, we may say, are properly his. Whatsoever then he removes out of the State that Nature hath provided, and left it in, he hath mixed his *Labour* with, and joined to it something that is his own, and thereby makes it his *Property*. It being by him removed from the common state Nature placed it in, it hath by this *labour* something annexed to it, that excludes the common right of other Men. For this *Labour* being the unquestionable Property of the Labourer, no Man but he can have a right to what that is once joyned to, at least where there is enough, and as good left in common for others.

The 'labourer' has mixed his labour with the object; he has joined something to the object that is his own; by his labour something has been annexed to the object. In this way the object has been removed out of the state of nature. It contains something more than it does by nature alone because the personality of the labourer has been infused into it. Therefore, it has become the property of the labourer. Since the labour is the unquestionable property of the labourer, no other man can have any right to that to which his labour has been joined. The exertion through which a thing is made my own need not necessarily be labour in the usual sense of the word. If 'the wild Indian' kills a deer with his arrow it becomes his. The case would be the same if he picks an acorn from the ground: this act makes the acorn his own. 'Labour' is = action (II, 44). The term corresponds to *actio* in the language of Grotius and Pufendorf.

The example with the acorn is especially illuminating. Locke borrowed it from Pufendorf (4, 4, 13).[24] But he makes use of the example against Pufendorf in order to show how things unquestionably can be made our own by apprehension without preceding compact between all men. It is his chief example in this respect. Locke says (II, 28):

> He that is nourished by the Acorns he pickt up under an Oak, or the Apples gathered from the Trees in the Wood, has certainly appropriated them to himself. No Body can deny but

the nourishment is his. I ask then, When did they begin to be his? When he digested? Or when he eat? Or when he boiled? Or when he brought them home? Or when he pickt them up? And 'tis plain, if the first gathering made them not his, nothing else could. That *labour* put a distinction between them and common. That added something to them more than Nature, the common Mother of all, had done; and so they became his private right.

What Locke here calls 'labour' is mere apprehension of an object. The acorn becomes the property of the collector when he picks it from the ground. This is the moment when something of his personality is infused into the acorn. Locke sums up his theory in the following expressive words (II, 44):

From all which it is evident, that though the things of Nature are given in common, yet Man (by being Master of himself, and *Proprietor of his own Person*, and the Actions or *Labour* of it) had still in himself *the great Foundation of Property*.

Man's power over his own person and actions (his *potestas in se* in the language of Grotius and Pufendorf) is the great fountain of his right of property in things given by God in common to all: for by laying hold of a thing under certain circumstances in the state of nature he mixes something of himself with the object, removes it out of the state of nature, and makes it his own. 'He that so employed his Pains about any of the spontaneous Products of Nature, *as any way to alter them* [emphasis supplied] . . . *by* placing any of his *Labour* on them, did thereby *acquire a Propriety in them*' (II, 37).


## APPREHENSION AND ENCLOSURE

Locke never states with exactitude how the act of appropriation is to be performed. He only gives a few examples. They indicate, however, when it seems natural to him to say that an object has been 'appropriated' by somebody. Appropriation in Locke's sense is definitely not to be identified with 'occupation' in current natural law doctrine. Occupation could only take place with regard to things that belonged to nobody (*res nullius*), except when people had made an agreement that common things might be occupied by individuals. But Locke had to show how things could be made one's own without preceding agreement.

In the case of movables Locke obviously thought that appropriation could be achieved by apprehending an object for one's use. He works with the vague notion of taking possession of something. A reflex of the legal doctrine of possession is evident when he talks of 'the Grass my Horse has bit; the Turfs my Servant has cut' as being mine (II, 28). The taking of possession through an intermediary like a servant is a well-known proposition of law. Physical apprehension was not always necessary. 'Even amongst us the Hare that any one is Hunting, is thought his who pursues her during the Chase' (II, 30). Locke adopts the opinion of the country gentlemen of his time. Other examples are drawing water from a common fountain (II, 29) and catching fish 'in the Ocean, that great and still remaining Common of Mankind' (II, 30). Locke appeals to the reader: can anyone deny that the water in the pitcher becomes his who has drawn it and the fish his who has caught it? The argument is throughout of this kind. It consists in referring to certain common and natural, but not strictly legal, ways of looking at things and speaking about acquisition. The prototype of such reasoning is Cicero's saying that the theatre is common to all, but a seat belongs to him who has occupied it.[25]

Having thus explained the appropriation of movables (II, 26–31) Locke turns his attention to 'the *chief matter of Property*', which is 'the Earth itself; as that which takes in and carries with it all the rest' (II, 32). It is plain, he thinks, that property (= the right of ownership) in land is acquired in the same manner as property in movable things. This means that a piece of land becomes a man's own when he cultivates it. He then lays out 'something upon it that was his own, his labour', he 'thereby annexed to it something that was his *Property*, which another had no Title to, nor could without injury take from him' (II, 32). The basic idea is the same as with regard to movables. One infuses something of oneself into the land by cultivating it. Thereby it is removed out of the state of nature and joined to the personality of the cultivator. To deprive him of it is an injury.

In this connection the word 'labour' seems to have its usual connotation. Much is made of man's labour on the earth for its improvement. God commanded man to labour, and the penury of his condition required him to do so. Therefore both 'God and his Reason commanded him to subdue the Earth, i.e. improve it for the benefit of Life' (II, 32). This makes it quite obvious that the land, in the state of nature, becomes the property of him who lays out his labour on it by cultivating it. 'God, by commanding to subdue, gave Authority so far to *appropriate*' (II, 35).

But Locke has another idea too of how land was appropriated.

There must be a limit to the appropriation made by one man through his work. On this question Locke says (II, 32): '*As much Land* as a Man Tills, Plants, Improves, Cultivates, and can use the Product of, so much is his *Property*. He by his Labour does, as it were, inclose it from the Common.' Here the work on the land is represented as accomplishing *enclosure*. In the same paragraph 'appropriating' is expressly equated to 'inclosing' ('he cannot appropriate, he cannot inclose'). The identification of 'inclosing' and 'appropriating' recurs in II, 35 ('inclose or appropriate'). The 'wild Indian' knows 'no Inclosure', that is, no private property rights to land (II, 26). On the measures governing the possession of land it is said: 'Whatsoever he tilled and reaped, laid up and made use of, before it spoiled, that was his peculiar Right; whatsoever he enclosed, and could feed, and make use of, the Cattle and Product was also his' (II, 38). In the inland parts of America, where there could be no hope of commerce with other parts of the world, the land would not be worth 'the inclosing' (II, 48).

As Laslett points out, Locke is using the language of agrarian enclosure in England.[26] The lords of manors, profiting from a dubious rule of the common law, appropriated parts of the manorial 'waste' or 'common' by enclosing it for their own benefit.[27] This method of acquiring private rights of property in common lands Locke transplanted to an early age. Doing so is a typical example of his way of using familiar ideas and customs to substantiate his contention that private rights of property could be acquired in the state of nature without preceding agreement. The underlying meaning must have been that a man annexed a piece of land to his personality by enclosing it.

## AVOIDING INJURY

The theory of appropriation needed a complement. Appropriation presupposed that no injury was inflicted on others. How could that be explained? If all things on earth were common, taking something for one's own use would seem to imply an injury to all fellow-men. The answer is very simple. No injury is committed when there is enough left for others. Considering 'the plenty of natural Provisions there was a long time in the World, and the few spenders', there could be then 'little room for Quarrels or Contentions' about property (II, 31). No man could consume more than a small part; 'so that it was impossible for any Man . . . to intrench upon the right of another'. That measure 'did confine every Man's *Possession*, to a very moderate Proportion, and such as he might appropriate to himself, without Injury to any Body in the first Ages of the World' (II, 36). The sphere of 'mine' could be extended so as to include both land and movables as long as other people could do the same without colliding.

## ENLARGING PROPERTY

So far Locke has explained how men could appropriate the fruits of the earth, animals, and the soil itself in the state of nature. He referred to the first few centuries of the world, when there was still a plentiful supply of everything man needed (including some parts of the world, such as America, where the situation was still the same). But the explanation was patently not capable of justifying the actual distribution of property in a densely populated country like England. Undoubtedly it was Locke's intention to show that this distribution of property was not contrary to the law of nature.

Locke, of course, did not contend that the titles of English land-owners could be traced back to original enclosure in the state of nature. He reasoned in the abstract on how property in material things *could* be justly enlarged beyond the narrow limits set by the requirement that enough should be left for others. The argument proceeded in three steps.

First, he put another limit on appropriation besides the requirement that enough should be left for others. This was that one must not appropriate more than was needed for one's own use. 'Nothing was made by God for Man to spoil or destroy' (II, 31). To let something spoil was to offend against the common law of nature, and the culprit was liable to be punished (II, 37). (Somewhat illogically Locke adds that 'he invaded his Neighbour's share, for he had *no Right, farther than his Use* called for any of them [Fruits and Venison]'. The neighbour's share was not necessarily invaded because a man collected more fruits than he could consume; there might be enough left for others to collect as much as they could make use of.)

Secondly, the limitation by usefulness became in fact the means for Locke to extend the possibility of acquiring goods. For later on Locke gave a wide meaning to 'making use of'. It was not restricted to personal consumption (including needs of the family, we must suppose). A man could 'use' things by bartering them away for other things before they spoiled (II, 46):

> He that *gathered* a Hundred Bushels of Acorns or Apples, had
> thereby a *Property* in them: they were his Goods as soon as

gathered. He was only to look that he used them before they spoiled; else he took more than his share, and robb'd others [the same illogicality]. And indeed it was a foolish thing, as well as dishonest, to hoard up more than he could make use of. If he gave away a part to any body else, so that it perished not useles[s]ly in his Possession, these he also made use of. And if he also bartered away Plumbs that would have rotted in a Week, for Nuts that would last good for his eating a whole Year, he did no injury; he wasted not the common Stock; destroyed no part of the portion of Goods that belonged to others, so long as nothing perished useles[s]ly in his hands.

A man could only have gathered and hoarded very limited amounts of acorns, or fruits, or grain, etc. But he could exchange such goods for durable things that could be preserved indefinitely without inconvenience. Locke continues by saying:

Again, if he would give his Nuts for a piece of Metal, pleased with its colour; or exchange his Sheep for Shells, or Wool for a sparkling Pebble or Diamond, and keep those by him all his Life, he invaded not the Right of others, he might heap up as much of these durable things as he pleased; the *exceeding of the bounds of his* just *Property* not lying in the largeness of his Possession, but the perishing of any thing useles[s]ly in it.

The third step in the argument is that men have made the inequality of possessions practicable by introducing the institution of money. Locke held the metallistic theory of money; he identified a monetary unit, as the pound sterling, with a quantity of precious metal, gold, or silver.[28] Money is a lasting thing that can be kept without spoiling, he says. The tacit agreement of men has put a value on it (II, 36, 50). By mutual consent men take it in exchange for 'the truly useful, but perishable Supports of Life' (II, 47). Thus the invention of money gave men the opportunity to continue and enlarge their possessions. No limits were set to this. Gold and silver may be hoarded 'without injury to any one, these metalls not spoiling or decaying in the hands of the possessor' (II, 50). Therefore a man might acquire more land than he can use himself. For he can sell the surplus of its produce for money that he might keep without inflicting injury on anybody else.

## COMPACT THEORY REVIVED

Locke says that men have agreed 'to disproportionate and unequal Possession of the Earth' by the introduction of money because money 'has its *value* only from the consent of Men' (II, 50). This 'inequality of private possessions' men have made practicable irrespective of the formation of society ('out of the bounds of Societie') and 'without compact'. It has been achieved 'only by putting a value on gold and silver and tacitly agreeing in the use of Money' (II, 50).

Locke persists in rejecting the compact theory concerning the origin of property, because he negates the existence of a *direct* agreement as to the division of the earth. But indirectly an agreement is nevertheless taken to be the basis of the actual distribution of property, namely, the agreement to use money. The inequality of possessions is expressly grounded on that agreement. Moreover, in society the property of private men has been regulated by laws (II, 45, 50). But the laws derive their binding force from the social compact. Indirectly, therefore, the distribution of property is based on agreement. In this sense the compact theory is ultimately revived. The distribution of property through the introduction of money and through positive law has superseded that distribution which derived from apprehension and enclosure in the state of nature.

Now this investigation has reached its end. But there is a prominent feature in Locke's theory of property that has not been examined here: the emphatical assertions that the value of things is mostly due to the labour spent on them. It is labour indeed 'that *puts the difference of value* on every thing', Locke says (II, 40). This contention is evidently connected with the theory of property. But the nature of the connection is problematical. The usual interpretation is that Locke's theory of property is based on the labour theory of value. For my own part I cannot share this view. I have come to the conclusion that the relationship between the value propositions and the theory of property must be defined in a different way. But the question is rather complicated. To discuss it would require a separate article.

### NOTES

1   Locke's *Two Treatises of Government* are cited from Peter Laslett's edition (Cambridge, Cambridge University Press, 1960; 1968). The introduction is cited 'Laslett'. Sir Robert Filmer is cited from

*Patriarcha and Other Political Works*, ed. Peter Laslett (Oxford, Blackwell, 1949).

2   Laslett, p. 102, note. Literature on Locke's doctrine of property is listed by Laslett, p. 103, note. More recent contributions: R. H. Cox, *Locke on War and Peace* (Oxford, Clarendon Press, 1960); R. Polin, *La politique morale de John Locke* (Paris, Presses Universitaires de France, 1960); H. Moulds, 'Private Property in John Locke's State of Nature', *The American Journal of Economics and Sociology*, 23 (1964); J. P. Day, 'Locke on Property', *Philosophical Quarterly*, 16 (1966); cf. below, note 3. [And see Suggested Reading, p. 71.]

3   J. Viner, review of C. B. Macpherson, *The Political Theory of Possessive Individualism* (Oxford, Clarendon Press, 1962), in *Canadian Journal of Economics and Political Science*, 29 (1963), 544ff. and 562ff.; Macpherson, op. cit., 559ff.; cf. Laslett, pp. 101f., 226, 341, 368.

4   Laslett, pp. 74, 137, 142f.

5   Laslett, p. 74; cf. M. Cranston, *John Locke: A Biography* (London, Longmans, Green, 1957), p. 428. In 1697 Locke advised the young Lord Mordaunt to read 'Tully, Pufendorf, Aristotle and above all The New Testament'.

6   Laslett, p. 72ff.

7   Grotius, *De jure belli ac pacis* (cited from the Amsterdam edition 1712, with comments by J. F. Gronovius), prol. 44: iustitia tota in alieni abstinentia posita est. Cf. A. Hägerström, *Recht, Pflicht and bindende Kraft des Vertrages nach römischer und naturrechtlicher Anschauung* (Uppsala, 1965), p. 50f. The views of Grotius and Pufendorf are discussed at some length in my *Law as Fact* (London, Stevens, 1971), pp. 8ff., 142ff., 275ff.

8   Grotius, 1, 2, 1, 5; Pufendorf, *De iure naturae et gentium*, cited from the Frankfort edn (1744) by G. Mascovius, 2, 5, 3.

9   Grotius, 1, 2, 1, 5.

10  Grotius, 1, 2, 1, 5: in the state of nature *vita, membra, libertas* were *propria cuique*, 2, 17, 2, 1.

11  Grotius, 2, 11; Hägerström, p. 63ff.; *Law as Fact*, p. 276ff.

12  Grotius, 2, 17, 2, 1.

13  The usual translation of the maxim *suum cuique tribuere* is 'to render to every man his due'. This suggests that the maxim enjoined the fulfilment of a duty towards others. Such was not its meaning according to Grotius. He interpreted it as saying that one should abstain from that which belongs to others – *alieni abstinentia*. Pufendorf's interpretation was similar; see below, note 26.

14  Grotius, 2, 2, 1, 5.

15  Grotius, 2, 2, 2, 1.

16  William James has written a few striking pages on the extension of personality in his *The Principles of Psychology* (London, Macmillan, 1891), I, p. 292f.

17  Pufendorf, 4, 9, 2.

18  Laslett, p. 101 and notes to pp. 213 and 310.

19  Hobbes gives a translation of the adage *suum cuique tribuere*. Referring to the 'ordinary definition of justice in the Schools' that justice is 'the constant will of giving to every man his own', he says: 'And therefore where there is no *own*, that is no propriety, there is no

injustice. . . .' (*Leviathan*, ed. M. Oakeshott, Oxford, n.d., ch. 15). Here is direct evidence that 'propriety' was used as the English word for *suum*.

20  *Leviathan*, ch. 30.
21  Laslett, p. 101.
22  Laslett, p. 101 and note to p. 305. Cf. *OED*, v. propriety.
23  *Patriarcha*, p. 63ff.
24  Laslett, note to p. 306.
25  *De finibus bonorum et malorum* 3, 20, 67.
26  Notes to pp. 306, 308.
27  E.g. Jenks, *History of English Law* (London, Methuen, 1928), 267ff.
28  Cf. my *The Problems of the Monetary Unit* (New York and Uppsala, Macmillan, 1957), p. 81ff.

# JEAN-JACQUES ROUSSEAU

## Chapter Seven

# INTRODUCTION

One modern commentary on Rousseau has as its title the question, *Rousseau – Totalitarian or Liberal?* The question suggests a number of problems in the interpretation of this original and paradoxical thinker. The first is the apparent diversity of possible interpretations of his thought, given the polar opposition we assume to exist between totalitarianism and liberalism. The second is the degree to which interpretation of him may be illuminated, or alternatively distorted, by hindsight; for, of course, the terms 'totalitarian' and 'liberal' entered political vocabulary long after Rousseau's death, and have been used to describe political practices and structures far outside eighteenth-century experience. A third and related problem is the degree to which exegesis of Rousseau seems to involve us in contemporary ideological battles and concerns.

Yet, even giving due weight to constant warnings about the dangers of importing modern concepts and concerns into the elucidation of past ideas, the question asked does reflect some persistent puzzles about the general character of Rousseau's thought. For, from his own day, he has been portrayed, and criticized, both as an exponent of extreme individualism, impatient of all the constraints imposed by civilized society, and as an advocate of a novel form of political life which would require the subservience of the individual to the community, his total absorption in communal life and communal objectives.

The two apparently contradictory charges have often been evidenced from different works of Rousseau. In the early discourses, *On the Origin and Foundations of Inequality* and *On the Arts and the Sciences*, he seems to be concerned with emphasizing the contrast between nature and civilization and the corrupting effects of the actual historical development of modern societies. This last was a theme echoed by other *philosophes*, such as Diderot, in their contrast of the effete, neurotic (civilized) European man and the morally integrated, self-sufficient (natural) non-European man. By apparent contrast, in the *Social Contract*, Rousseau seems to be sketching a political ideal in which the individual could achieve moral integrity and psychic harmony through participation in a tightly-knit community, in which conformity to a moral consensus and obedience to generally agreed rules would ease the tensions and stresses of anarchic individuality.

A primary problem then in interpreting Rousseau is whether or not there is any overall continuity in his ideas. The authors presented here argue, MacAdam explicitly and Barnard implicitly, that there is such a continuity: they agree too that the connecting concept is the idea of freedom or independence or autonomy. That independence was a central value for Rousseau can hardly be gainsaid; it recurs in his writings and also, through his at times near paranoic fear of domination by others, in his life. Differences of interpretation arise, however, over the meaning and implications of his concept of freedom or independence.

As MacAdam presents it, this concept has resonances over and beyond the ordinary 'negative' understanding of freedom. Freedom consists not just in the absence of constraints imposed by others; it has two aspects – not only not being controlled by others but also not being subject to one's own passions. To be free is to achieve self-government, in the sense of governing oneself as well as not being subject to the governance of others.

The connecting link between the discourses and the *Social Contract*, argues MacAdam, is that the vicissitudes of 'independence' are central to the hypothetical history of mankind presented in the former, and the restoration of 'independence' is the aim of the latter. In this sense, Rousseau's sketch of the past and the future poses a dialectical progression from the independence of natural man, through the growth of dependence in historical societies, to the re-achievement of independence in his democratic utopia. His treatment of the first two moments in this triadic progression has been the basis of portrayals of him as the advocate of a return to the simplicities of 'nature' and natural savagery. To the extent that Rousseau believed that in some way the individual could escape from corrupting dependencies by limiting his own demands on and need of others, this portrayal has some reality. In *Emile*, for instance, he suggested that, if he were fully insulated from corrupting social influences and subject to careful moral education, the child could be father to the virtuous and autonomous man, even in present degenerate societies. But if, as Barnard argues, he opted finally for the collective solution of the *Social Contract*, his treatment of the past is the basis of a plea for social reconstruction rather than for social deconstruction.

Rousseau's depiction of the state of nature contrasts sharply with that of others in the contractarian tradition. He differs from Locke in that his state of nature is not just the absence of political society but the absence of any kind of social relationships, even apparently settled familial relationships. He differs explicitly from Hobbes in denying that human attributes in the natural state can be discovered by observation (even through introspection) of men in developed societies. For Rousseau, man in his natural state was isolated, had no persistent relations with others or concern for the opinions of others. In this situation, MacAdam concludes, natural man was independent in the senses that, even if occasionally subject to the physical power of another, he was not in any permanent state of subservience, and that he did not want more than he could attain or feel any inconsistency between his desire and his obligations.

Despite his critique of Hobbes, Rousseau does attribute some general characteristics to natural man, does in other words have some conception of an abiding human nature. The primary characteristics he isolates are self-concern (*amour de soi*), compassion (*pitié*), the capacity of self-improvement, and free will. Men, in or out of the state of nature, are concerned for their own welfare and preservation, can feel for the sufferings of other creatures (non-human as well as human animals), desire the realization of their abilities, and have both the capacity for choice and consciousness of this capacity. The meaning and significance of these characteristics is a matter of contention. However, given Rousseau's attribution of such largely sympathetic natural qualities to humanity, his depiction of the independence enjoyed by natural man and his account of the degeneracy of social man, it is understandable that many have seen him as pleading for a return to a primeval Golden Age. MacAdam claims, in contrast, that any such return was for Rousseau certainly impossible and perhaps also undesirable. The development of society had produced 'consciousness of self' in men; this self-consciousness was a prime cause of the loss of independence, but it would also have to be accommodated in any re-creation of human autonomy.

In his hypothetical history, Rousseau poses several possible causes for the growth of society – population expansion, the development of the family, technological innovation, the invention of language, the division of labour, the foundation of property and inequalities of property, and at the final stage the institution of government. The chronology he suggests is by no means clear, but one claim seems unequivocal, that historical societies cannot be seen as the product of voluntary agreement. In the main, however, his concern seems to be not so much with the mechanism of social development as with its psychic consequences. In the discourses, a sense of loss and decline dominates his historical account. The rise of societies had involved the loss of the autonomy enjoyed by natural man. Straightforwardly, the creation of systems of property and government had led to the curtailment of natural independence. The stratification of society in terms of wealth and political power meant that the many – the poor and the weak – were subordinated to and controlled by the few; their freedom was decreased by constraints imposed by others. But natural independence had been subject to another and more complex process of erosion. For the development of unequal social relations had given rise to the individual's awareness of the differences between himself and others, his awareness of the opinions of others about himself, and his own evaluation of himself and his actions in terms of the opinions of others. It had, in other words, given rise to *amour-propre* which, in contrast with *amour de soi*, was a self-esteem dependent on the esteem or at least deference of others. Pride and the desire for possessions, domination, and status bred a host of artificial needs and aspirations imposed on the individual by the prevailing values and fashions of his society. In this context, all, even the rich and the powerful, had suffered a loss of independence in the sense that they had ceased to have mastery over their own desires and ambitions.

If the dominant mood of Rousseau's hypothetical history is nostalgic, another and more positive conception of the psychic consequences of social development has been discerned in his account. On this view, Rousseau sees social experience as the cause of the metamorphosis of amoral natural man into a moral agent. For the growth of self-consciousness meant that men had become possible judges of themselves. Even if the standards on which they judged themselves were in practice largely imposed by social mores, there nevertheless remained the possibility that the individual could now apprehend and impose upon himself objective standards of right and wrong; and the bases for such objective standards were such natural propensities as compassion and the desire for self-improvement. Social experience could then lead to the transformation of natural instincts into self-chosen and considered rules of behaviour.

These apparently contradictory accounts of the psychic effects of social experience are, it can be argued, the foundation of Rousseau's assertion of contradictions within the human psyche. His conception of freedom, including as it does the notion of self-mastery, rests on the idea of the divided self, a duality in men, for it presupposes a higher self and a lower self with the former controlling and restraining the latter if true autonomy is to be achieved. Barnard defines this antinomy in terms of the contradiction between the rational and the impulsive self; others have done so in terms of conscience and passion. Rousseau's hypothetical history suggests that the conflict might also be seen as one between the self moved by standards imposed on it by others, even if these are internalized, and the moral self seeking to govern its actions by a code of behaviour which it prescribes for itself. In his presentation of the divided self, Rousseau was following in a long Christian tradition in which man, made in the image of God, had fallen from grace; man, capable of seeing God's laws for humanity, was prompted by his sinful nature to break them. What was novel, even momentous, in this presentation was Rousseau's ascription of this moral schizophrenia to social causes. For this suggested that the malaise was not necessarily a permanent aspect of the human condition, but could be transcended by further social development or overcome by social reconstruction. In this, Rousseau was foreshadowing later discussions of 'estrangement' or 'alienation', central to Hegelian and Marxist thought (see section VI).

It is against this background, MacAdam argues, that Rousseau's purposes in the *Social Contract* can be understood. For it was the aim of the ideal polity there outlined to restore men to a full independence which existing societies made impossible to attain. What could be restored was independence, not 'natural' independence. Indeed, men lose natural liberty on entry into this ideal polity, gaining in its place civil and moral liberty, civil liberty consisting in equality before laws in whose formulation all citizens have been involved and moral liberty consisting in obedience only to laws which men have prescribed to themselves. How to achieve a society in which these liberties are guaranteed whilst the persons and goods of citizens are protected is the problem Rousseau sets himself at the beginning of the *Social Contract*.

Such an association could be created only by a social contract, the unanimous agreement of all those who were to be its members. Immediately, questions of consistency between the discourses and the *Social Contract* arise. For in the latter, Rousseau seems to suggest that there have been at least a few historical examples of legitimate political associations (Sparta, the Roman Republic, Geneva); and this apparently contradicts the sketch of social development given in the second discourse, which denied the origination of political structures in voluntary agreement. Whatever the inconsistency, it is clear that Rousseau turns in the *Social Contract* to the contractarian claim that legitimate authority must be based on consent.

Indeed Rousseau extends this claim by arguing that universal consent must be incorporated into the association itself. The contract of association is an agreement to submit equally and totally to the general will of the community, in whose formulation each person must participate. This is the solution to the problem Rousseau had posed for himself, since each will gain civil liberty by being constrained only by impartial laws and each will gain moral liberty by being subject only to laws to which he has himself agreed. By equal subjection to rules authorized by all, the complete autonomy of the individual in society can be assured. It is then through the concept of the general will that Rousseau seeks the reconciliation of social discipline with total individual liberty; and many of the disagreements in interpretation of Rousseau centre on the understanding of this concept and on how he thought it could be realized politically.

Much that is problematic in Rousseau's argument arises from his claim that the general will always acts for the public good and from the apparent implication that it should be unanimous. The first is necessary to his conclusion that the general will is the only foundation for legitimate authority and the second is apparently necessary to his conclusion that in a society governed by the general will each person is independent because subject only to self-prescribed laws.

If the general will is always right, does this then imply either that a vote amongst citizens is always morally and politically correct or that there is no test for the rightness of a law other than that it has proceeded from a popular vote? It would seem that Rousseau accepts neither of these conclusions. In his distinction between the general will and the will of all, the former being aimed at the common good and the latter being based on a consideration of particular interests, he indicates that not all votes by citizens will elicit the general will. Only when the voting decisions of individuals follow from a consideration of what is required for the good of all rather than what is to their own particular advantage does the general will emerge.

In this distinction, Rousseau reverts to the notion of the divided self. The individual is subject to two wills – a higher, general will and a lower, particular will. It is only when, in his role as citizen, the former dominates over the latter that he can express the general will; and it is also only then that he can achieve self-mastery. For some commentators, this talk of general and particular wills has decidedly illiberal connotations. These, it is thought, emerge particularly from Rousseau's remark that citizens may be 'forced to be free'. If by this is meant that the actual wants of individuals may be ignored or frustrated on the grounds that their being coerced into following what their better selves would desire enhances their freedom, such doubts about Rousseau's liberalism may be justified. If on the other hand he is arguing only that, once individuals have assented to certain social rules, forcing them subsequently to follow those rules, even if this conflicts with their particular wishes, enhances their freedom, then the sinister implications are less obvious; or, at any rate, there is no contradiction given Rousseau's insistence that the following of self-prescribed rules is an important element of liberty.

If this latter reading is correct, then it would seem that in his general-will society all laws would have to be agreed by all citizens. In fact, when he considers voting in popular assemblies, Rousseau recognizes the impracticality of any unanimity requirement and, whilst clearly hankering after unanimity in legislative decisions, accepts that majority decisions must be binding. Yet, in answer to the question of how a dissident minority could be free if subject to laws which they had opposed, he has to argue that apparent disagreement masks real agreement. Voters who have been facing the question of what the general will requires and find themselves in a minority have simply been mistaken in their judgement; and, recognizing that they have been mistaken, they will accept the majority decision as what they really wanted. Whatever the plausibility of this argument, it is essential to one of Rousseau's main endeavours, to construct a society in which persons would be, in his sense, *totally* free.

It is generally accepted that Rousseau's ideal polity would require a high degree of moral and political consensus and of public-spirit-edness, that is willingness to subordinate private concerns and interests to considerations of the public good. The first requirement at least separates him from any liberalism that values individuality, debate, plurality of opinions and styles of life. How far it moves him towards the advocacy of what has been called 'totalitarian democracy' is a question whose answer depends upon a judgement of his many suggestions on how moral consensus and public spirit could be created or sustained.

Rousseau argues at points that they would be nurtured by democratic institutions themselves, that direct democracy would itself create the attitudes it needs for its vitality and preservation. But he often takes a more pessimistic stance and stresses the difficulties of creating an ideal polity in a world of fallen men and the fragility of even the best of institutional structures. In this mood, he sought devices and agents which would ensure that the people possessed the moral probity his democratic system required, or, as Barnard puts it, that self-choosing citizens would also be right-acting citizens.

One illustration of this mood is Rousseau's distrust of partial associations and political argument. Rejecting many of the arguments that were to become the stock-in-trade of defences of pluralist democracy, he attacks parties, factions, and intermediary associations as likely to prevent the emergence of a genuine, consensual will. He links this attack also with a plea for political silence; political debate and rational, discursive argument are equally likely to frustrate any disposition to agreement and push individuals towards a concern for their particular wills and interests. For the citizen, inner sentiments are a more reliable guide in the determination of his general will than discursive reasoning.

Barnard sees such instances as evidence of Rousseau's ambivalence towards the role of rationality in political willing. Autonomy requires that the individual be both self-consciously aware of making choices and endeavouring to impose on himself objectively valid standards. Whilst this seems to imply that independence needs the actor's rational consideration of his own decisions, Rousseau remained unconvinced that, unaided, the individual, at any rate in degenerate societies, had a sufficient capacity both to comprehend and to will the good. In such circumstances, Rousseau accepted, however uneasily, that men might have to be manipulated into an appreciation and concern for the public good and he introduced, as either the agents or the means of such manipulation, the Legislator, civil religion, and morally didactic education. Barnard points out the tension between such paternalism (as he terms it) and autonomy, but holds also that Rousseau retained a distaste for paternalism. This continuing distaste is evidenced in his appeal to patriotism, the instinctive and unreasoned love of country, as a preferable alternative to ideological manipulation. Barnard concludes that, although Rousseau never abandoned the idea that the capacity for rational choice is a condition of active citizenship, his emphasis on unity and political commitment, and his appeal to unreasoned sentiment as a means to these ends, leads him to picture the participant in his ideal society as a conditioned conformist rather than an autonomous decider of his own destiny.

This conclusion has been repeated, often in stronger language, by many modern interpreters of Rousseau. On this view, despite his proclamation of the value of freedom and autonomy, his real concerns were with moral consensus and political engagement and this led him to a support of ideological manipulation and irrational politics which demonstrate either his liberal apostasy or the inherent flaws in his conception of liberty. An alternative general view is that, however exaggerated his hopes for the complete autonomy of the individual in society, however obsessive his consequent concern with social unity, his identification of freedom with self-direction and of autonomy with democratic participation were central to his political hopes and are not in themselves illiberal.

## ACCESSIBLE EDITIONS

J.J. Rousseau, *The Social Contract and Discourses* (London, Dent, Everyman's Library)

J.J. Rousseau, *The First and Second Discourses* (New York, St Martin's Press, 1964)

## SUGGESTED READING

J.H. Broome, *Rousseau: a Study of his Thought* (London, Arnold, 1963)

J.W. Chapman, *Rousseau – Totalitarian or Liberal?* (New York, Columbia University Press, 1956)

J. Charvet, *The Social Problem in the Philosophy of Rousseau* (London, Cambridge University Press, 1974)

* R. Grimsley, *The Philosophy of Rousseau* (London, Oxford University Press, 1973)

R. Masters, *Political Philosophy of Rousseau* (Princeton University Press, 1968)

J. Shklar, *Men and Citizens* (London, Cambridge University Press, 1969)

J.L. Talmon, *The Origins of Totalitarian Democracy* (London, Secker & Warburg, 1952)

## Chapter Eight

# THE *DISCOURSE ON INEQUALITY* AND *THE SOCIAL CONTRACT**[1]

## *J. I. MACADAM*

My purpose is twofold: first, to interpret Rousseau's *Social Contract* in terms of a serious interpretation of the *Discourse on the Origin and Foundations of Inequality* and second, to use as the principal interpretative concept for both, the concept of independence. One gets the impression in reading commentators that the *Discourse on Inequality* is not taken seriously in its own right but rather is treated as what it is, an essay which was suitable for submission as a prize essay, with the required clever rhetorical style, flashes of paradox and yet withal solemnly addressing itself to a virtually impossible question. However, if it is taken, in part, as Rousseau's social and psychological analysis of modern society, as an account of 'men as they are' (*Social Contract*, ed. Cranston, p. 49), then it is not only worthy of serious study in itself, it also helps one to see that still puzzling book, the *Social Contract*, from a new perspective. Moreover, Rousseau's concept of independence is both interesting and helpful. What Rousseau means by 'independence' may differ from what he means by 'freedom', but for most of this essay I shall draw from the latter a working definition of the former and thus shall mean by independence: (1) not being subject to or under the control of another person or persons, and (2) not being subject to or under the control of one's passions. The advantage of attending to the concept of independence is that it enables one to recognize that Rousseau is asserting three seemingly incompatible propositions: first, man is independent; second, no man is independent and in the given circumstances can be; and, third, man must become dependent in order to become independent.

Prior to beginning this interpretation, I need to introduce four categories which are necessary to it. They are to be called: the state of nature, the nature of man, the state of man, the nature of the

---

* Previously published in *Philosophy*, vol. 47 (1972).

state. To explain, one of the most fertile sources of confusion in Rousseau's thought is that he uses the concept of the state of nature for three main purposes: first, to give an account of the original, primitive condition of the human race, second, to identify the basic principles of human nature which exist in man in that original condition, third, to describe and evaluate what he calls 'the new state of nature' by which he means, roughly, the present condition or state of man in modern society. These purposes correspond respectively to the first three categories named above. One source of confusion may be uncovered by asking: why does Rousseau describe man's present state as a state of nature? There are at least two reasons. One is that although he thinks it is necessary to refer to three conditions: man as he must have been, as presently he is, and as he ought to be, his theoretical framework includes only two terms – the state of nature and legitimate civil society – to account for this relationship of three conditions.[2] Another is that he wishes to contend that even when men have experience of civil society they remain in the state of nature, if their relationships are less than those characteristic of legitimate civil society. In consequence, the fourth category, 'the nature of the state', deals with Rousseau's conception of the legitimate state, as outlined in the *Social Contract*, and a major problem of this interpretation will be to understand how the *Social Contract* deals with the question of independence as it emerges from the three previous categories. Finally, and in spite of the complexity of this interpretative framework of categories, it should be obvious that my intention is to study the concept of independence in relation to each category separately and thereby to indicate the method of removing the apparent incompatibility amongst the three propositions concerning independence.


## THE STATE OF NATURE

There are three points worth discussing under this heading: (1) what Rousseau says about the use which other philosophers make of the concept of the state of nature, (2) what Rousseau himself says about the state of nature, and (3) his comments on natural law.

In criticizing what other philosophers have meant by the state of nature, Rousseau writes near the beginning of the *Discourse on Inequality* as follows.

The philosophers who have examined the foundations of society have all felt the necessity of going back to the state of nature,

but none of them has reached it. . . . All of them . . . speaking
continually of need, avarice, oppression, desires, and pride,
have carried over to the state of nature ideas which they
acquired in society: they spoke about savage man and they
described civil man. (*The First and Second Discourses*, ed. Masters,
p. 102 [Cole, p. 161])

Later Rousseau returns to this subject again and discusses it with
reference to Hobbes (Masters, pp. 128–9 [Cole, pp. 181–2]), and it
seems clear that Hobbes's views are his main target. And yet it
would be a mistake to take Rousseau's comments purely at face-
value. He seems to be saying that the basic sense of the state of
nature is that it refers to that period of human existence which
preceded not only all political relationships but all social ones as
well. Thus, he seems to be implying that other philosophers in
talking about the state of nature have 'cooked' history, or rather
pre-history, to suit their own nefarious ends. There are two problems with this interpretation.

First, the obvious way to correct the mistake would be to seek to
establish the historical or anthropological facts of the matter.
However, Rousseau not only acknowledges the practical impossibility of this task: he says, on the page following that from which
the original quotation is taken: 'Let us therefore begin by setting
all the facts aside, for they do not affect the question' (Masters,
p. 103 [Cole, p. 161]). From this confusion at least this much is
evident: Rousseau is not accusing the other philosophers of being
dishonest historians, for he himself insists that history, in the normal
sense of establishing facts about the past, is not relevant. What then
is Rousseau's criticism? This question brings one to the second
problem.

To the extent that Rousseau's criticism is intended to apply to
Hobbes's concept of the state of nature, it misfires in suggesting
Hobbes meant to describe primitive society. It can be, and often
has been, argued that Hobbes's state of nature is understood most
accurately if one supposes merely that people and society remain
as they are and, in imagination, one removes the governing power.
This absence of government would put men, *vis-à-vis* one another,
in the state of nature, and, according to Hobbes, all the horrors he
depicts would follow. If this characterization is at all accurate, it is
clear that Rousseau is unfair and misrepresents Hobbes's intention.
Or, if one wishes to be charitable, one might say that Hobbes and
Rousseau are working with different concepts of the state of nature:

the first, things as they are minus government, the second, man's original condition.

What I do not think is true of the passage from Rousseau is that it shows that Rousseau fails to understand the ultimate intention of Hobbes's state of nature. That which accounts for the passion in the passage is that Rousseau realizes that Hobbes has two purposes in mind: namely, to describe the basic drives of human nature and therefrom to provide a basis for political obligation. As in the case of Rousseau himself, Hobbes claims (*Leviathan*, The Introduction) that one knows human nature by introspection. Thus one knows how all would behave in the absence of a power to overawe them all, thus is provided the ground for political obedience. As a consequence, it can be seen that the issue between Rousseau and Hobbes is not only theoretical. Rousseau wishes to undermine Hobbes's concept of the state of nature by holding that that which one might call the causal passions of disunity and strife are brought about by the nature and quality of evolved social relationships. As shall be argued later, Rousseau's implicit criticism is that vanity, avarice, envy, ambition, jealousy, shame, contempt, and misery are not innate but are characteristic of certain kinds of social relationships. If Rousseau is correct then Hobbes's conclusion, that avoidance of the state of nature entails the necessary submission of all to a King of the Proud who can enforce obedience, need not follow. Instead, what is called for is a new set of relationships which can nurture humane values and liberate man from enslavement to selfish passions.

At this point we may turn to Rousseau's own characterization of the state of nature. Once you assume, as Rousseau does, that the state of nature is to be understood as both pre-political and pre-social then most of what he says goes on from there. Natural man would be a savage and only slightly different from other animals. This original man would live a nomadic life, living in caves and off the land; he would be timid but resourceful. Even the family, as a group to be with and come to care about, would take time to develop. He would have no settled form of life and thus would develop none of the vices, nor the virtues either, which follow from intimate social relationships. He would have no property and no conception of anything belonging to him rather than to anyone else. Everything would exist in common and since there would be plenty of everything for everyone there would be no cause of quarrels, jealousy, or ambition. In very brief terms, the above summarizes Rousseau's view of the original, primitive state of nature. Man is to man as beast is to beast, and life may be sometimes 'nasty, brutish and short', but if so, the causes are natural hardships and not man's inhumanity to man.

What then of natural law? Now one of the puzzling features of Rousseau's thought is his final stand on natural law and thus his place in that important tradition. All I propose to say here is that it is clear that what philosophers had meant by natural law – approximately, moral principles which dictate the proper and improper conduct of all rational beings – has no practical place in Rousseau's conception of an original state of nature. What Rousseau says is that a being in this primitive condition would lack the reasoning ability to apprehend such rational principles. Of course, this claim doesn't settle the matter whether Rousseau's political philosophy is or is not based on natural law, and Masters' comment that: 'it should be evident that Rousseau radically rejects all accepted, traditional justifications for the existence of political society and natural law'³ is unjustified in the absence of detailed argument. Nevertheless, on the subject of natural law, Rousseau can be described best as cagey. As Masters points out,⁴ the question put by the Academy of Dijon, and to which the *Discourse on Inequality* was an answer, asked whether inequality is 'authorized by Natural Law'. Rousseau's title omits any reference to natural law and, except by its absence, it is of no practical importance to his general argument. Natural law, understood as rational, universal moral principles, is simply inapplicable in Rousseau's primitive state of nature.

However, in discussing the state of nature he does draw attention to two principles which perform in natural man something of the same role which other philosophers attribute to natural law. This reference to the principles, however, brings us back to the earlier claim in this essay that Rousseau uses the state of nature concept, not only to describe man's original condition but also to describe the nature of man. As a consequence, they will be treated within the next category, the nature of man.

## THE NATURE OF MAN

The two principles appear to be both defining and motivational principles of man as such. Rousseau claims to derive them by meditation 'on the first and simplest operations of the human soul' (*The First and Second Discourses*, p. 95) and he describes them thus:

> I believe I perceive [in the human soul] two principles anterior to reason, of which one interests us ardently in our well-being and our self-preservation, and the other inspires in us a natural

repugnance to see any sensitive being perish or suffer, principally our fellow-men. It is from the conjunction and combination that our mind is able to make of these two principles . . . that all the rules of natural right appear to me to flow: rules which reason is later forced to re-establish upon other foundations when, by its successive developments, it has succeeded in stifling nature. (Masters, pp. 95–6 [Cole, p. 157])

The suggestion in the final sentence of this passage is both important[5] and obscure. The idea that human reason, on the one hand, has 'stifled' the action of the natural principles and, on the other, that reason re-establishes them on other foundations – reason destructive, reason constructive – is one that will be taken up briefly later.

The two principles, then, of human nature are held to be what may be called self-concern and compassion (or fellow-feeling or sympathy). To these Rousseau adds another defining and motivational characteristic: 'perfectibility', a universal desire to realize or fulfil one's human capacities. With original man, this faculty of self-perfection, of each man striving to realize his human qualities, remains dormant. Finally, reason, passion, and free will also characterize man and contribute to the desire for self-perfection. But throughout most of history, Rousseau believes, reason and will have been ruled by desire. That is to say, reason acts only in response to problems created by desire. Thus, man progressed from a state of primitive savagery but only by responding to his physical and social environment rather than, through reason, attempting to take control of it. As Rousseau puts it:

We seek to know only because we desire to have pleasure . . .
in all nations of the world progress of the mind has been precisely proportioned to the needs that peoples had received from nature or to those to which circumstances had subjected them, and consequently to the passions which inclined them to provide for those needs. (Masters, p. 116 [Cole, pp. 171–2])

## INDEPENDENCE AND THE ORIGINAL STATE OF MAN

With these references to the categories of the state of nature and the nature of man in hand, we may now turn to the concept of independence as the principal interpretative concept. To review, 'independence' has two meanings: one, not subject to the will of another, two, not subject to the passions. Further, a problem of interpretation follows from Rousseau's claims that: man is independent; no man is independent, and in the given circumstances can be; and man must become dependent in order to become independent. It would constitute some, and perhaps sufficient, verification of the importance of independence to the understanding of Rousseau, if independence could be shown to have a significant meaning in the categories which are held to be necessary. This task will now be undertaken, beginning with the sense of independence as it is found in the original state of nature.

It is clear that man would be independent in the original condition and that he would be according to both meanings. In the circumstances described by Rousseau, such that savage man meets another of his kind only by accident, no man would be subject to the will of another. Even if one had killed a deer and was forced by a stronger to give it to him, the first would regard the situation as no different from being forced to relinquish the deer to a bear or lion.[6] In other words, relationships in these circumstances would be seen as one of *natural* inequalities and they would not affect independence. Nor would man be dependent in the sense of being subject to unruly passions. Natural man would be a harmonious being in that his wants and needs would exactly coincide: 'desiring only the things he knows and knowing only those things the possession of which is in his power or easily acquired, nothing should be so tranquil as his soul and nothing so limited as his mind.'[7] He would see no difference or distinction between what he wanted to do or what interested him to do, and what he ought to do. He would not be, as Rousseau put it later in the *Social Contract*, a slave to his passions.

When Rousseau contrasts natural man with his characterization of modern or sociable man as a neurotic and miserable creature, it is perhaps not surprising that so many have interpreted the *Discourse on Inequality* as Rousseau's impassioned invitation to his contemporaries to return to the primeval forests and become Noble Savages. There are reasons why this interpretation won't do, including Rousseau's denial of it (Masters, p. 93 [Cole, p. 155]): but the most important one is not made explicit by Rousseau. It is that savage man lacks what I shall call for want of a better name 'consciousness of self'. Since ordinary usage does not seem to mark the distinction, an example may help to make it. In learning a new activity, such as how to paddle a canoe, one may experience three distinguishable states of consciousness: (1) being conscious while doing something, in this case, attempting to paddle, (2) doing it self-consciously, that is, very deliberately following directions and receiving advice from one's instructor, and (3) being conscious of one's self, that is, conscious of one's individuality, of what others think of you: 'If I fail, they'll take me for a muscular moron.' The important consideration, then, is that natural man lacks this third form of mental state. That is to say, he would be independent, as explained above, but he would not be aware of himself *as one who is independent* since he would not be aware of himself as a self. Thus, although man is independent, in the state of nature, independence is not a value to him. Thus too, the irony of the *Discourse on Inequality*. Independence is the supreme value for man. When he had it, he was not conscious of it; when he was conscious of it, he could not have it. Man's innocent ignorance, Rousseau argues, cannot be regained. The most modern man could conceive of, and in my view this is what Rousseau seeks in the *Social Contract*, is a new set of circumstances for a new independence. However, before we come to that, it is necessary to consider the meaning of independence in modern society, which brings us to the third category.

## THE STATE OF MAN

It is here that Rousseau tells us that man is not independent and in the given circumstances never can be. To understand this statement we need to look at the rational history of mankind which Rousseau offers in the *Discourse on Inequality*. Of course, he argues, there have always been natural inequalities of bodily strength, skill, beauty, intelligence, etc. amongst men. Amongst savages meeting only occasionally and then accidentally, nothing would be made of them. But gradually, out of organic needs, men would begin to live together, first, as a family and then as groups of families. Sooner or later, these differences would come to make a difference. That is to say, on the basis of these, comparisons would come to be made and with comparisons, evaluations. Out of this fateful sequence inevitably would come 'consciousness of self' and with it dependence.

> Each one began to look at the others and to want to be looked at himself, and public esteem had a value. The one who sang or danced the best, the handsomest, the strongest, the most adroit, or the most eloquent became the most highly considered; and that was the first step toward inequality and, at the same time, toward vice. From these first preferences were born on the one hand vanity and contempt, on the other shame and envy . . . from this any voluntary wrong became an outrage, because along with the harm that resulted from

injury, the offended man saw in it contempt for his person which was often more unbearable than the harm itself. (Masters, p. 149 [Cole, pp. 197–8])

Since this event is the most important in Rousseau's narrative and since Rousseau himself does not make explicit the socio-psychological mechanism he is asserting, it might be made clearer by a brief reference to evaluation. Often we speak of evaluation as a two-termed process, consisting simply of a subject who judges an object. On this basis we normally hold either that a certain object has intrinsic qualities, qualities which make the object valuable in itself, or that the object has a value for the subject because of certain desires of the subject. Thus, we say either that the object is valuable in itself or valuable to the subject.

Now it is important to notice that Rousseau is suggesting something different in giving his analysis of the state of modern man and, in consequence, of the personal development of any individual in modern society. He is saying that when the object of evaluation becomes one's self then necessarily 'I', who consider myself a subject, become for you merely an object. In other words when my Self, understood now as my individuality, subjectivity, personality, etc., becomes for me an overriding concern then I become necessarily dependent upon others. I exist, what I am exists, only in the consciousness of others. I, and the same of course is true of everyone else, exist only as others think me and others exist as I think them. It is on the basis of this insight concerning the 'consciousness of self' that Rousseau rests his fundamental distinction between the original state of nature and the state of man; that which he calls 'sociable man' and the '*new* state of nature'. In a very important passage Rousseau compares savage and sociable man and says that savage man:

> would have to learn that there is a kind of men who set some store by the consideration of the rest of the universe and who know how to be happy and content with themselves on the testimony of others rather than on their own. Such is, in fact, the true cause of all these differences (between the two): the savage lives within himself; the sociable man, always outside of himself, knows how to live only in the opinion of others; and it is, so to speak, *from their judgment alone* that he draws the sentiment of his own existence.[8]

Moreover, Rousseau's recognition that one's self, as the way in which one sees oneself, is formed by others leads him to see that this feature of self-evaluation affects evaluation of everything. For if my image of myself depends upon others and I seek the approval of others then it becomes clear that I shall choose as I think others think I should choose. In other words, sociable man does not choose in terms of the qualities of the object nor in terms of its value to the subject, rather each evaluates as he thinks every other would have him do. And when one reflects on Rousseau's analysis of modern man one realizes that it yields a paradox: each lives outside himself, no one lives inside himself. We are, as T. S. Eliot put it, 'hollow men'.

In addition, Rousseau's critique has as yet unexplored implications for the concept of personal property. In Locke's account, for example, personal property is justified on grounds of self-preservation and need, and if Macpherson be correct, he even seeks to justify the right to unlimited acquisition of personal property. Yet Locke does not explain why man comes to desire possessions beyond his needs. Rousseau's analysis of dependence does provide the basis of explanation. According to Rousseau, what I am becomes identified with what I have so that I am what I have. Thus to the natural inequalities of man there comes to be added the most significant artificial inequality – inequality of possessions. It is significant because my possession of material goods can overcome my lack of natural gifts. Marx seems to reach a similar conclusion when he writes:

> Money's properties are my properties. . . . Thus, what I am and am capable of is by no means determined by my individuality. I am ugly, but I can buy myself the most beautiful of women. Therefore I am not ugly. . . . Money is the supreme good, therefore its possessor is good. (Dirk Jan Strvik, *The Economic and Philosophic Manuscripts of 1844*, trans. Martin Mulligan, 1970, p. 167)

Rousseau goes deeper than Marx in holding that personal property is itself an *effect* of 'the furor to distinguish oneself'. Vanity is the typical vice of modern man. It is a distorted form of self-concern and the desire of self-perfection. But it does account for acquisitiveness. The reason why vain people desire seemingly useless objects is because possession of them makes them different from others. Moreover, such possessions enable those who have to dominate those who have not, because being is having. But, as before, Rousseau recognizes that this inequality is a species of dependence in the sense that your superiority over me, through your possessions, depends solely upon my recognition that those possessions do make you superior. If I do not grant this, then you are not superior (Masters, p. 140 [Cole, pp. 189–90]).

So far this discussion of dependence in 'the new state of nature' has been restricted to dependence in the personal or moral sense. However, the dependence has a political dimension as well. Towards the end of the *Discourse on Inequality*, Rousseau speculates that actual political societies may have originated in a conspiracy by the rich few against the many poor such that the forces of all would protect the possessions of the few. However, except for one interesting passage, he does not explain why the poor would consent to an arrangement which is so little to their advantage. But this passage offers a reason if it is viewed in the light of the concept of dependence:

> citizens let themselves be oppressed only insofar as they are carried away by blind ambition; and looking more below than above them, domination becomes dearer to them than independence, and they consent to wear chains in order to give them to others in turn. (Masters, p. 173 [Cole, p. 215])

Independence means not being subject to the will of another; domination, that another is subject to my will. One accepts a political structure of domination and inequality, one of dependency, provided one can dominate another in return. In this sense, dependence may even be mistaken for independence. Thus the effective climax of the *Discourse on Inequality* is as follows:

> Here is the ultimate stage of inequality. . . . Here all individuals become equals again because they are nothing; and subjects no longer having any law except the will of the master, nor the master any other rule except his passions . . . everything is brought back to the sole law of the stronger, and consequently to a new state of nature different from the one with which we began, in that the one was the state of nature in its purity, and this last is the fruit of an excess of corruption. (Masters, p. 177 [Cole, p. 219])

In summary, let me note the two senses in which modern man is dependent. Each man is dependent upon every other in the sense that his existence as a self, as a person is so dependent. Moreover, in the course of seeking a self, each becomes subject to passions, unruly and unreasonable passions of greed, vanity, and ambition. Finally, independence, in the sense of not being subject to another's will, is mistaken for domination, which means the control of one person over another. We may now turn to the final category.

# THE NATURE OF THE STATE

Except for occasional suggestions in the dedication to the republic of Geneva, Rousseau does not offer any corrective to the dismal portrait of man that he leaves one with at the conclusion of the *Discourse on Inequality*. However, it is open to one to interpret the *Social Contract* from the perspective developed in this essay. Indeed there are many passages in it which make sense only if one does[9] and still others where it seems impossible to take Rousseau's statements at face-value. To give only two brief examples of the latter sort. In the first paragraph of the *Social Contract* Rousseau says: 'My purpose is to consider if, in political society, there can be any legitimate and sure principle of government *taking men as they are* and laws as they might be.' Given what he says in the *Discourse on Inequality*, he cannot be understood to mean that what he advocates in the *Social Contract* will leave them as they are, and he makes this plain in the *Social Contract*, Book two, chapter 7. Again, there is the famous passage at the start of Book one, chapter 1: 'Man was born free, and he is everywhere in chains. Those who think themselves the masters of others are indeed greater slaves than they. How did this transformation come about? I do not know. How can it be made legitimate? That question I believe I can answer.' The first two sentences now make complicated sense, involving as they do reference to both political and moral or personal dependence. But the question and answer which follow directly must mean that he lacks the historical facts.

However, it is not necessary or practically possible at this time to offer a detailed interpretation of the *Social Contract* and it should be enough if one considers briefly how Rousseau's legitimate state deals with the problems of dependence and independence.

If one assumes that an individual is politically independent if he is not subject to the will of another person or persons, the concepts of the *Social Contract* which are relevant are those of 'a sovereign among equals' and 'the sovereignty of the general will'.[10] To take both concepts at once, Rousseau holds that the sovereignty of the general will is a practice such that each citizen by right is a citizen–sovereign, a legislator, and thus authorizes the law which he, along with other sovereign equals, obeys. The law which he legislates and which he imposes upon himself is such that it should ensure equality in two senses: the law should come from all equally and apply to all equally. If the law is equal in these ways then the condition of political independence may be satisfied, for all are equally subject to the law and none are subject to the will of another person. In order for this to be true, legislation must be impersonal, in the sense of impartial, both at the source, in the agent's judgement, and in application.

Looked at in terms of man as he is, in 'the new state of nature', impersonal legislation seems impossible. However, there is a plausible reply in the *Social Contract*. If one thinks for a moment of the sovereignty of the general will as a model of how a group of persons might try self-rule then the model would appear to logically imply the following 'rule of rules': if something is to be a rule then it must be acceptable to other sovereign equals. This rule appears to be implied by the two senses of equality which Rousseau has specified.

What makes this rule a plausible reply to the selfish 'sociable man' is that the method employed seems to allow him to obey laws which are just, in the sense of being in the interest of everyone, and to act in his enlightened self-interest, since they are in the interest of everyone, himself included. If the sovereignty of the general will meant approximately this method, whereby enlightened egoists could co-operate to their mutual benefit, no doubt it would be an advance over 'the new state of nature'. For the practice of making rules for others as well as oneself would free one to transcend one's own selfish interests and to be as disinterested with respect to them as with respect to those of others. And, too, it can be argued that such disinterested consideration of the interests of all is a rational act, so that reason might come to control the passions. Further, one may now see the method of the general will as 'reason constructive', as beginning to fulfil the promise implied in: 'rules which reason is later forced to re-establish upon other foundations when, by its successive developments, it has succeeded in stifling nature.' Again, one may even see it in terms of Rousseau really taking 'men as they are' and the method, finally, as that which 'forces men to be free', that is, forces man to surmount his own selfish desires to consider desires of others.

When I say that within the limits of the point under discussion, the general will can be thought of as a method which 'forces men to be free' I am not overlooking the fact that Rousseau confines the use of forcing freedom to some minority which refuses to obey legitimate law (*Social Contract*, p. 64). The problem is that between the reality of the self-seeking selfishness of 'the new state of nature' and the ideal of the citizen–sovereign state there exists a gap. Ultimately, what Rousseau seems to seek is not merely that in prescribing a law each citizen endeavours to treat all interests equally, but also that each citizen should come to respect every other as equal to himself. In conceiving of the general will as a method of group decision-making which forces men to be free, I intend to suggest only that the adoption of it as a method *necessitates* treating the interests of the other, if not the other himself, as equal to one's own. As a method, it could be thought of as a transformational device between the selfishness of sociable dependence and enlightened self-interest. But then it remains only half of a solution, for in treating interests impartially, it does not follow necessarily that one accepts others as one's equals.

Within this category, then, one may be able to understand the third proposition, that man must become dependent in order to be independent. He must subject himself to the law, the rule of the general will. In so doing he does not subject himself to the will of another person or persons, but rather to the impartial will of all citizens. With this kind of dependence, politically he is free of all personal domination, and morally, free from domination by his passions.

One might feel justified in arresting the interpretation at this point for the concept of independence has been used to show the continuity between the *Discourse on Inequality* and the *Social Contract* and, in addition, the sovereignty of the general will may be seen as the correction of the political and moral dependence of sociable man. There may even be grounds for believing that Rousseau himself intended to go no farther than removing the abuses to mankind which he portrays.

The objection to stopping may be stated as follows. If one describes independence as not being subject to the will of another and to one's own passions and intends this description to stand for the full ideal towards which Rousseau's major political writings are aimed then the independence of the citizen–sovereign which is to be realized in the legitimate state of the *Social Contract* does not mark an advance over the independence of the savage in the primitive state of nature. For the savage is not subject to another nor to his passions.[11]

Moreover, it is surely true that Rousseau, more fully perhaps than any other political philosopher, valued political activity for its moral effects on the political agent. Rousseau could argue that representative democracy renders the average citizen a passive receiver. Perhaps he receives moral goods, for example in a welfare state, but politics as an activity from which his decision-making is excluded, except at elections, does not improve morally. Politics, in representative democracy, is something which is done for him and happens to him.

Taken together these points lead one to look for in the *Social*

*Contract* a positive, creative independence which, in turn, would provide a rich moral justification of Rousseau's concept of democracy. To the extent that this idea of independence is present in the *Social Contract*, it is one of the most original and exciting parts of his work. It seems implicit in the notion that human freedom includes duties to others (*Social Contract*, p. 55) and in that moral freedom which involves making rules for the benefit of others besides oneself and yet prescribing them to oneself. Thus, the political activity of being a citizen–sovereign would seem to entail being responsible both to and for others. The duty of making rules for the good of others would contribute to one's own development as a moral being, as one whose nature is such that when realized reason will rule selfish passions. The general will, considered as a method which 'forces man to be free', is only compatible with such a moral justification if it is taken as an intermediate stage between the sociable man and the moral man. If the practice of the general will eventually makes man moral, then the moral man will recognize that his duty is other than his self-interest and in the circumstances will act to the benefit of others even at the cost of his own interest.

Although this moral justification of democracy, of each legislating on behalf of those to whom moral duty is owed, seems to be what is required for true independence, the idea is not developed in the *Social Contract*. To do so, Rousseau would have had to work out there an ideal of human nature; a sense of self and self-interest which one morally ought to seek to realize in oneself and others. This idea is promised in the manuscript chapter which Rousseau omitted from the final version (*Rousseau, The Political Writings*, ed. C. E. Vaughan, vol. 1, p. 454) when Rousseau distinguished between one's apparent interest and one's interest 'well-understood'. It is suggested in the lines from the discourse:

> Vanity and love of oneself, two passions very different in their nature and effects, must not be confused. Love of oneself is a natural sentiment which inclines every animal to watch over its own preservation, and which, directed in man by reason and modified by pity, produces humanity and virtue. Vanity is only a relative sentiment, artificial and born in society, which inclines each individual to have a greater esteem for himself than anyone else. . . . (Masters, p. 222 [Cole, p. 182])

If true independence could be clarified, one suspects that it, perfectibility (understood as desire for self-improvement), human self-realization, and freedom, would be connected closely in meaning.

## NOTES

1 I have used the following editions: Jean-Jacques Rousseau, *The First and Second Discourses* (including the *Discourse on the Origin and Foundations of Inequality, Second Discourse*), translated by Roger D. and Judith R. Masters, New York, St Martin's Press, 1964, and Jean-Jacques Rousseau, *The Social Contract*, translated by Maurice Cranston, Harmondsworth, Penguin, 1968. [Additional references are given to the *Discourse on Inequality* in the edition of *The Social Contract and Discourses*, ed. and trans. by G.D.H. Cole (London, Everyman Library, 1947).]

2 Sometimes he uses 'civil society' ambiguously, either for 'what is' or 'what ought to be'. The point is that either 'the state of nature' or 'civil society' must be ambiguous if one is to refer to all three conditions.

3 Masters, *The First and Second Discourses*, Introduction, p. 21.

4 Masters, *The First and Second Discourses*, p. 234, Editor's Notes no. 19.

5 It is important to Rousseau's position on natural law. On the basis of the interpretation offered in this paper I would argue as follows. Rousseau's two principles – although comparable to natural law – are not principles of reason but of sentiment, not dissimilar from that which Hume means by natural virtue. In the *Discourse on Inequality*, reason is responsive to circumstances and sentiment is stifled when reason is employed by man's selfishness. Through the educative influence of the general will, reason ultimately finds its true role in the general will as a source of rational rules by which a community of sovereign equals can order their conduct. Thus, the general will could displace natural law in Rousseau's political philosophy.

6 Masters, *The First and Second Discourses*, p. 139 [Cole, p. 189] and p. 195, [omitted by Cole] Rousseau's Notes (i).

7 ibid., p. 213, Rousseau's Notes (k). [omitted by Cole]

8 ibid., p. 179, my emphasis. [Cole, p. 220] Compare also pp. 221–2, Rousseau's Notes (o). [Cole, p. 182]

9 Primarily in Book one and in Book two, chapters 6 and 7.

10 For a more careful treatment of the general will, see: J. MacAdam, 'What Rousseau Meant By The General Will', *Dialogue*, 1967.

11 I owe this observation to my colleague David Cameron.

## Chapter Nine

# WILL AND POLITICAL RATIONALITY IN ROUSSEAU*

## F. M. BARNARD

Rousseau insists on the indispensability of 'will' in action and on its own distinctive causality in political action. It will be suggested that Rousseau's ambivalence over political rationality renders his success in advancing an unambiguous theory of autonomous and accountable agency in politics highly arguable despite his unquestionably ingenious attempt to create an analogue between willing in nature and willing in society. It will be argued further that this ambivalence bedevils also his attempted synthesis between self-choosing and right-acting in politics and between the requirements of political legitimacy and sheer political viability.

This article will first explore Rousseau's analogue between self-mastery in nature and self-mastery in society before turning to his problematic fusion of two distinct and potentially conflicting visions of political motivation and political purpose.

When Rousseau speaks of natural freedom he does not mean by freedom what many, following Hobbes, mean by it: the absence of external impediments. Natural man is by no means free from the external impediments of nature; all that he is free from, in a negative sense, is the dominance of others, while, positively, he is free in that his desires do not exceed his powers or abilities.[1] The word 'independence', Rousseau thinks, is therefore more appropriate. Natural man is not 'free' in the social sense, but he is 'independent' in only willing what he has the power to do unaided. Unfortunately, Rousseau complains, these terms are not kept apart, and their conflation conceals the possibility of their mutual exclusiveness.[2] Being free from the dominance of others does not necessarily imply self-mastery or self-sufficiency; yet this is precisely what independence in nature does imply or in fact means.[3] A child, for example,

* Previously published in *Political Studies*, vol. XXXII (1984).

like man in the state of nature, is not curbed by social institutions, and in this sense is free, but unlike natural man, the child lacks the power to realize his desires: they exceed his strength, making him dependent on the power of another.[1] Now, the condition of man in civil society is comparable to, though considerably worse than that of the child, and it is so for two quite distinct reasons. One is that life in civil society is characterized by the presence of others who, at every turn, thwart our will; the other that society, by creating artificial needs, destroys the balance between will and power: it makes a person feel enfeebled since his strength is insufficient for his needs. The balance between will and power is lost and, with it, independence is lost as well, and human beings become weak, wretched, and everywhere in chains.[5]

Could independence be recovered in society? Could the structural equilibrium be restored? In addressing these questions Rousseau suggests two solutions. One is designed to promote recovery through individual action, the other through collective action. The second solution is of course well known. It consists in restructuring society by creating a new understanding (or ethos) of what it is to live with others as *citizens*. The first solution is to minimize the corruption caused by existing society; it consists in setting limits to one's desires. Will and power are brought into equilibrium and dependence upon others is curtailed. Unfortunately this solution incurs the risk of being self-defeating. In striving to live and act as though society did not exist, one is liable to deceive oneself and ignore the crucial difference between dependence in society and dependence in nature. For dependence in society is upon persons and not upon things, and it is dependence upon persons which is the source of all moral problems, while dependence upon things involves no morality at all.[6] Inevitably, therefore, people become subject to increasing tensions: outwardly they profess to live for others while in fact they think of themselves alone.[7]

On balance, Rousseau suggests, it may therefore be wiser to opt for the collective solution. To be sure, this would not mean that people at all times would be able to do what they want; rather it would help to prevent their being compelled to do what they do not want through the will of another.[8] Of course, they had better realize from the start that as individuals living in society they are merely numerators of a fraction whose happiness and wellbeing depends on its denominator, the community as a whole.[9] But the crucial point about this individual surrender is that it is a surrender to the *community* and that the dependence it establishes is an *equal* dependence, when no one depends on the other to any greater extent than the other depends on him.[10] Only through the community protecting us from the capriciousness of those we come to be mutually dependent upon does it make sense to enter an association with others.

The envisioned association, then, has to do two things at once: it has to replace nature in its content *and* approximate it in its structure. The question to be posed is this: if men can be independent within the bounds of natural necessity, how can they analogously attain freedom within the bounds of social necessity? In answer to this question Rousseau substitutes the generality of political law for the generality of natural law. Political law is to emulate the impersonal objectivity that is found in natural law and thus gain for it a status that places it above men and the government of men. Even if law falls short of acquiring this status fully, it is still preferable to subservience to the best master. For 'every master has his favourites, and the law has none'.[11] No one living in society is objective enough about himself to determine what he can demand of his fellows and what his fellows have a right to demand of him. Only law is capable of such objectivity for it brooks no exceptions whatsoever.[12]

To prevent, however, that 'the rich keep the law in their pockets and the poor prefer bread to liberty', a measure of equality is essential.[13] Property may be sacred – Rousseau is quite emphatic on this – but property is not above the law. Once property succeeds in usurping political authority or in commanding political influence, it is bound to corrode the fabric of political legitimacy in that it undermines the very purpose the institution of law is designed to ensure: the equity and objectivity of justice. No citizen, therefore, should be rich enough to be able to buy another, and none so poor to be forced to sell himself.[14] If esteem and authority can be bought and sold like commodities in the market, they lose all meaning. A situation, therefore, in which gross inequality is not curbed is a situation in peril.

> Strange and fatal must be that constitution, in which the accumulation of riches always facilitates the means of further accumulation and in which it is impossible for him that has nothing to acquire anything; in which an honest man has no means to extricate himself from poverty; in which knaves are most honoured, and in which a man must necessarily renounce all virtue to become a respectable person.[15]

It follows that the equilibrium of will and power that governs man's natural state can be re-created only if justice and equality are kept in harness. Only then is 'recovery' at all conceivable.

Of course Rousseau seeks more than recovery; and the 'more' is precisely what attracted Kant to Rousseau: the idea of moral autonomy through the fusion of will and law. But what *is* will? Rousseau is not prepared to define willing in abstraction from acting, but neither is he prepared to *identify* willing with acting. 'Every free act', he stipulates, 'is produced by the concurrence of two causes, one mental, namely that which determines the act, and the other physical, namely the force that executes it.'[16] Thus having the capacity to act does not make one act. Unlike Locke, Rousseau does not equate freedom with capacity. An able-bodied person has the capacity to run, but the capacity to run does not make him run. 'If I am to walk to an object, the first condition is that I must will to go to it.'[17] To be sure, merely willing an action does not bring it about, if we lack the capacity or power to translate willing into doing; a paralytic who wills to run gets no further than an able-bodied who wills not to run.[18] Rousseau does not profess to know what in turn determines willing, but then, he says, are we not equally in the dark about the causes that determine our judgement? 'I know will only through the feeling of my own will, and understanding is no better known to me. When I am asked what cause determines my will, I ask in turn what cause determines my judgment, for it is clear that those causes are one.'[19] Willing, on this view, is not a blind impulse but a reasoned decision to act one way rather than another. I will as I judge, and I judge as I will. It is in and through acting that will combined with judgement manifests itself, and it is only thus, and not by its 'essence' that will is known to me.[20] Things done unwittingly, under the influence of drugs, or under external compulsion, may or may not be subject to censure, but they do not qualify as true actions because they are not freely chosen and because they do not enlist our judgement.

Will, then, is not the same as pure impulse. But neither, evidently, is it the same as pure rationality. Conscious choice is reasoned choice, yet the act of choosing is something wholly distinctive. For Rousseau it is the distinctiveness of conscious choosing – rather than rationality *per se* – which confers upon conduct the defining characteristic of action as it also embodies the defining difference between humans and animals.

Nature commands all animals, and animals obey. Man feels the same impulses, but he knows he is free to acquiesce or resist;

and it is above all in his *awareness of this freedom* that the spirituality of his soul is manifested. For physics can, in a way, explain the mechanism of the senses and the formation of ideas; but in our power of willing, or rather of choosing, in our *awareness of that power*, we find only *spiritual acts* about which *nothing can be explained by the laws of mechanics*.[21]

'Will' implies therefore consciousness of what we do freely and what we want to do for a reason that we understand as our own. To understand ourselves as free or rational agents it suffices that we possess this consciousness; it does not require that we know how we come to possess it. Will as consciousness of choice is something *sui generis*, reducible neither to *a priori* rationality nor to antecedent psycho-physical motives or impulses. While motives may or may not be conscious, will, for Rousseau, is always conscious and, if translated into action, forms the source of our accountability as agents. If, on this view, we are at all accountable for what we do, what we are accountable for is our will as judgement, as reasoned choice, and not as antecedent motive or impulse, not for what prompted it but for what it expresses. Not understanding its antecedent causes does not stop us therefore from considering ourselves as persons capable of choosing between courses of actions and of accounting for the way we choose. Nor do we have to know – in the sense of predicting – ultimate outcomes of what we do in order to be accountably conscious of our actions. We may after all, as Rousseau observes, know little of the world's purpose or purposes, but this does not stop us from judging the order of the world or from attempting to shape its course.[22] Rousseau makes here two important points. One is that we possess a knowledge as actors which is different from the knowledge we have as observers; the other that the knowledge we have as actors is not purely subjective in that we can view ourselves – by having an awareness of what we consciously do – from the standpoint of an hypothetical observer as well as from that of a doer. Thus we are neither *mere* observers nor *mere* subjects but rather a bit of both at one and the same time. It is the possibility of this twofold knowledge which characterizes reflective awareness and which, for Rousseau, defines human self-consciousness.

But this is not the end of the matter, for 'autonomy' implies more than reflective consciousness of subjective willing, in that it enshrines a recognizably objective standard or criterion of self-choosing. To will autonomously is to will according to an objective and generalizable principle or law that the self imposes upon itself.[23]

Yet, just as self-conscious subjective willing by itself fails to qualify as autonomous willing, so does mere compliance with an objectively 'good' law. Willing, to be autonomous, must satisfy the conditions of both voluntariness and objectivity: *how* one wills is as important as *that* one wills. The idea of autonomy, as advanced by Rousseau, accordingly combines two distinct dimensions of willing, one defined by its source, the other by its quality or content, and it is through the combination of these two dimensions that autonomous willing acquires its substantive sense. Through it Rousseau believed that he had provided a solution to the central problem of the social compact: to find a form of association in which 'each one, uniting with all, nevertheless obeys only himself and remains as free as before'.[24] Man is as free as before in the sense of once again being, as he was in the state of nature, his own master. Willing, in its twofold sense of self-conscious choice and objective ordering or control, is the means whereby the experience of being a free agent is given a new lease of life. The structure of man's self-mastery is thus kept intact: he preserves his self-rule. It is this single structural property which links two otherwise distinct states of human existence and two conceptions of self-rule which otherwise differ profoundly in intrinsic quality and extrinsic source.

Though preserved, the structural property of self-rule is preserved in a radically transmuted form in that a person now, in contrast to a person in the state of nature, has to think of himself in terms of the other; he has to impose on his acts a principle or law that includes the other. Will and law thus coalesce. By submitting to an ordering principle that one accepts as objectively valid, one combines self-choosing with right-acting. And it is this integral combination that is to restore freedom as self-mastery in society.

This conception of freedom is of course notoriously problematic. Underlying it is a particular philosophical anthropology, a histori-cally persistent vision of man as a duality made up of a rational self and an impulsive self. Rousseau at times posits the impulsive self as something external to the rational self. Drawing apparently on his own experience, he remarks (through the Savoyard Vicar): 'When I yield to temptation I act according to the compulsion of external objects. When I reproach myself with that weakness I listen only to my will. . . . The feeling of freedom is effaced only when I degrade myself.'[25] By this statement Rousseau brings toge-ther will, freedom, and morality. Autonomy is not simply imposing upon myself a law, but a law of specific content, a moral content, which is discerned and enjoined not by any will, but a specific will which speaks to the self from within. To listen to this will is to listen to 'reasons', 'conscience', 'judgement', or 'common sense' – Rousseau uses these terms interchangeably. By heeding this inner will and acting upon it, a person becomes conscious of what it is to be 'truly' free; to act according to one's inner will is to reveal to oneself the meaning of freedom as well as one's own identity as a moral self. A self-determined act is free precisely because it involves the consciousness of a moral choice.

The question, as others have pointed out, is whether this is a theory of freedom at all; for what it does is to urge or prescribe what freedom ought to mean rather than define what it is or actually means to people when they use the word. Rousseau was not unaware of this distinction. For he knew that, as Herder once put it, man is capable of legislating himself into a beast.[26] He knew that 'the people is always free to change its laws, even the best ones, for if it chooses to harm itself, who has the right to prevent it?'[27] Here Rousseau clearly reveals his awareness of another kind of 'freedom', the freedom to make 'wrong' choices, wrong, because they bring in their train the loss of 'true' freedom, the loss of autonomy. There is no easy way out, and Rousseau does not pretend that there is. But he cannot leave matters there. If he cannot find a logical solution, at least he can suggest a political solution. People may be 'forced to be free' in order to forestall the risk of personal dependence.[28] Manipulation or social engineering are, however, infinitely preferable to brute force, even if these involve such doubtful means of generating freedom as penetrating a person's 'will' at his earliest and most formative age through 'religion' and other kinds of appropriate 'education'.[29] Rousseau may have a serious problem legitimating this kind of intervention within his scheme of things, but he has no difficulty in justifying it. He points in this connection to an interesting asymmetry between private willing and public willing. Individuals can see a good but not will it; a people collectively can will a good but not see it. And in neither case, apparently, can reason be relied upon to act spontaneously. Both the individual and the collectivity need guidance; both must be *made* to bring will into conformity with reason. Individuals must be taught to will the good they see and the people as a whole must be taught to perceive what it wills.[30]

Evidently, Rousseau has little faith in self-direction being 'naturally' moral or rational. Just as J. S. Mill had to concede that self-regarding actions may affect others, so Rousseau, for similar reasons, argued that self-choosing needs to be curbed for the sake of others. Some 'authority' external to the self-choosing selves, some paternalist intervention of one sort or another, notably in the person of an outsider such as the Legislator, may therefore be indispensable. Here again it is not physical compulsion that Rousseau has in mind; the Legislator should win over people *without* violence.[31] And just as Mill, in conceding the possible need for regulating self-regarding actions, did not view such intervention as a threat to the paramountcy of the principle of autonomy, so Rousseau did not doubt that he was promoting rather than weakening the emergence of autonomous man. What is intriguing, therefore, is not so much the sinister-sounding phrase 'forced to be free' as the implied assumption of a conceivable compatibility between autonomy and paternalism. People may be interfered with to ensure that they will what they ought to will in order to remain truly free; they may need to be helped along in order to preserve their authentic selves. It is not to usurp self-mastery that paternalism has to infuse objective willing into subjective willing, but in order to make it socially viable. Since the coincidence of self-choosing and right-acting cannot be relied upon, external guidance has to come into play.

Rousseau's suggested compatibility theory is of course strikingly at odds with Kant's conception of autonomy.[32] This is not altogether surprising if certain, more fundamental, differences are borne in mind. Thus, although Rousseau intimately linked the morality of freedom with the rationality of law, he did not *derive* morality from rationality and, while he viewed law in terms of universality, it is not the universality of Kant's categorical imperative. Rousseau's 'general will' is not meant to serve as a universal principle of human conduct irrespective of national conditions of time and place; its bearers are not members of a global kingdom of ends but members of a specific association who, as citizens and patriots, aim primarily at the good of their nation. Rousseau's notion of political universality, in short, unlike Kant's notion of moral universality, is neither unconditional nor absolute. The idea of autonomous action has, accordingly, a decidedly circumscribed source or *locale*. 'Self-legislation' in Rousseau's use is not, as in Kant's use, a merely metaphorical borrowing from politics, it is a political concept through and through, rooted in the political context from which it takes its origin. All the same, the rightness that is politically generated is to enshrine a recognizably moral content. Collective authorization through mutual agreement is to confer upon political law a rightfulness that blends with or enjoins what is right and obligatory for the individual as a moral law.

It is not easy to see how this twofold legitimation is to come about. Since 'will' here is not detachable from its political context, as it is for Kant, nor confined to the role of an instrumentality in legitimating consent, as it is for natural law theorists of popular sovereignty, Rousseau faces the difficulty of identifying the source of legitimate interference with the people's will. For if the people's will is itself the supreme sovereign, there is clearly nothing above or beyond it, and no appeal can strictly be made to any higher authority. Laws are designed to rule above men once they are created, but they are still the creation of men, the product of their collective will. What is supreme, then, is ultimately an act of political will and not laws, for laws are only the conditions of civil association; they are what they are through the will of those who come together to form a society, and they can be unmade as they are made, by the same collective will.[33] Nor can a government authorize paternalist intervention, since it, too, is merely the instrument of a nation's collective will. It follows that once the Legislator has done his work of 'public enlightenment', the 'union of understanding and will' must be relied upon to do the rest. This, at any rate, appears to be the only legitimate sanction of bringing about the desired fusion between self-choosing and right-acting.[34] Conceivably, social institutions which the Legislator helped to create, such as civil religion and a politicized form of education, could be looked upon as powerful safeguards. Conceivably, too, 'paternalism' could, under those conditions, be viewed as something integral rather than external to the general will; a sort of self-imposed or internalized collective discipline. If so, the opposition between autonomy and paternalism clearly loses its force. By the same token, whatever distinctive meaning each notion has runs the risk of being blurred beyond recognition.

Did Rousseau, then, deliberately wish to blur the distinction between paternalism and autonomy? Did he feel that the marriage between self-choosing and right-acting could not be effected without artful political contrivances, noble lies, or psychological devices of penetrating a person's inmost being? Undoubtedly, passages in *Emile*, the *Social Contract*, the *Political Economy*, the *Letter to d'Alembert* and the *Considerations on the Government of Poland* point in this direction. At the same time there is enough telling evidence that Rousseau felt exceedingly uneasy over the use of 'inane tricks' and that he took a rather poor view of the intervention of 'superior talents' in political life. Not surprisingly, it might be said, since the incongruity of calling upon the assistance of very unequal if not god-like men, while proclaiming the essential equality of all men, could scarcely have escaped him. Still, does this explanation really or wholly account for Rousseau's distaste for paternalism? Might it not equally be true, if indeed not closer to the truth, that, sensitive as he was to the difficulty of reconciling self-choosing and right-acting, he was torn between what is required to make politics legitimate and what is required to make it at all viable? Rousseau had no illusions about the obstacles confronting the desired fusion of self-choosing and right-acting. 'Wouldn't it often happen', he writes in the *Geneva Manuscript*, 'that a well-intentioned man would make a mistake about the rule of [the general will's] application, and follow only his inclination while thinking that he is obeying the law?'[35] Nor did he underrate people's reluctance to be constantly involved in politics, to have to make each and every decision themselves.

> Soon the inconvenience of everyone deciding on everything forces the sovereign people to charge a few of its members with the execution of its wishes. . . . Imperceptibly, a body grows up which acts the whole time. A body which acts the whole time cannot give an account of every action; it only gives an account of the main ones; soon it ends up by giving an account of none.[36]

Once people abandon self-choosing and leave things to the government, Rousseau therefore warns, political legitimacy is in peril.

Despite these worries and misgivings, if not perhaps because of them, Rousseau hoped that by strengthening the sentiment of patriotism he might provide an effective antidote to political inertia on the one side and political paternalism on the other. But here, too, he knew perfectly well what an uphill struggle he was taking on. For he was convinced that patriotism had virtually perished from the earth, that for most of his contemporaries, at any rate, patriotic virtues had come 'to pass for fables', to be 'made mock of', or be ignored altogether as purely 'fanciful'. This in no way stopped Rousseau, however, from declaring that of all political virtues patriotism was the 'most efficacious' in preserving political legitimacy *and* political viability.[37]

How crucially Rousseau's principled opposition to paternalism is tied to his faith in patriotism as *the* political force of autonomous self-legislation is most impressively brought out in his discourse in *Political Economy*. It is here that the most explicit statement of his anti-paternalism is conjoined with his most spirited vindication of patriotism. There are, however, several other instances pointing in the same direction that are perhaps less frequently noticed. Take, for example, Rousseau's hesitation (in the *Social Contract*) over the timing of the Legislator's appearance: should he intervene only once people already possess unwritten standards of mutuality or would he first have to provide a code of written laws for these unwritten standards to emerge? That they, rather than written laws, are of paramount importance is made unmistakably clear in what Rousseau has to say about the real, though secret, task of the Legislator. Although formally required to give advice on the drawing up of a constitution, he is actually intended to promote the growth of such unwritten standards and sentiments which most crucially help to fashion patriotism.[38] For without patriotism, in Rousseau's view, the emergence of authentic citizenship remains a forlorn hope. Now, if this is so, would not the role of the Legislator be rendered rather marginal, if not wholly dispensable, if patriotism and the unwritten standards which sustain it were already in place? Surely, whatever work still awaited him under these conditions could hardly consist in *creating* the foundations of a polity; at best it would amount to devising means of reinforcing them, of 'routinizing' them, possibly in order to make the state more effectively durable over time.

More strikingly still, one could point to occasions on which Rousseau discloses outright hostility to paternalist intervention. Superior men are now held to be not merely dispensable but decidedly undesirable. In the *Social Contract*, for example, simple peasants are portrayed as eminently capable of 'deciding the affairs of state under an oak tree', evidently fully in possession of that practical reason or judgement required to size up a situation by merely looking at it – a capacity which Max Weber called *Augenmass*, but which he, unlike Rousseau, confined to the professional statesman.[39] Clearly, if peasants naturally possess this precious gift, why should they need a Legislator to remind them of what they already know? Similarly, in the *Project For Corsica*, Rousseau unequivocally rejects the intervention of exceptional individuals. Men working in the fields can learn all there is to know about self-government without enlisting the aid of superior talents. Such talents, Rousseau remarks, are more often a liability rather than a boon to a healthy community. Only sick societies require superior men; there they are necessary to 'lead a people' precisely because the people had 'ceased to love its country'. Exceptional talents are called for to 'serve as a substitute for patriotic zeal'.[40]

On this view, paternalist intervention is plainly a necessary evil, a sort of last-ditch effort to save a political order, a salvage operation designed to put off a state's premature demise. But what is foremost at stake in such efforts is no longer legitimacy but sheer survival. Rousseau points here revealingly to the possible conflict between the requirements of legitimacy and the requirements of viability in politics.[41] In such a conflict, it seems, Rousseau is prepared to compromise legitimacy. If paternalist intervention of one sort or another is the only way of preventing justice and utility from being wholly or permanently rent apart, then viability has to be bought at the cost of autonomy.

It would appear, therefore, that if Rousseau indeed considered autonomy and paternalism in some sense or at some stage to be mutually compatible, he did so with an acute awareness of the tension inherent in such a 'compatibility'. Yet to resolve this tension, Rousseau would have had to resolve the problem of political rationality; he would, that is, have had to decide whether political judgement is a form of practical reasoning which men inherently possess unaided or whether it is something they acquire in the process of becoming citizens, but acquire only with the aid of authoritative guidance.

There can be little doubt that the merging of subjective voluntariness and objective validity entails for Rousseau some form of rationality in the causality of willing. On his own showing, a will is rational if its 'causation' is not reducible to the senses or dominated by them. 'We succumb or resist, but however we decide, it is always perfectly clear to us whether or not we did what we wanted.'[42] The causality of will, therefore, is rational if it is recognizably distinct from whatever psycho-physical 'motives' may have acted upon it. To be rational, in other words, will must contain a *causa rationis*, that is, a purpose or end which determines or defines its conscious direction, whose efficacy is other and distinct from that of whatever *causa naturalis* may also be at work. Acts of rational will, thus understood, differ from other forms of human striving in that their mode of causality is that of purposive reasoning.[43] Although their source is psychologically distinct from their orientation and, as Rousseau concedes, not always clear to us, the moment we act source and orientation collapse into one, so that what then effectively operates is a form of teleological causation.[44] And when the causality of purposive reasoning is that of *discursive* reasoning, a warrant for the assumption of rational accountability appears to be given. We can give reasons for our actions because in choosing them we have rehearsed the purposive grounds for our choice. Discursive rationality makes sense of accountability in that it has its origin in the weighing of alternatives. In accounting for our actions we recall the reasons which, in debating with ourselves (or with others) what to do, we found purposively compelling in doing or saying what we did on grounds that seemed valid to us at the time.

Now it is quite apparent that 'reason' frequently assumes a meaning for Rousseau that is radically different from discursive rationality. In particular his thinking on patriotism suggests a rationality that is inherently different from the rationality he generally associates with citizenship. Yet although he seems to be aware of the contrasting generative source of willing in each case, Rousseau apparently does not think in terms of a dual form of willing or in terms of a dual form of political rationality, let alone of the possibility of internal conflict. Evidently, he is more impressed by what they have in common than by what differentiates them. Both the will of the patriot and the will of the citizen are conceivable for him only within the context of that social entity which we call the state; neither has any meaning within the larger society of 'humanity'. Especially within the city-state citizenship and patriotism are said to be so closely enmeshed that the rational authorization of right, defining citizenship, is suffused with the passionate zeal animating the patriot, and the patriot's love for his native land embraces reverence for its laws and institutions.[45]

All the same, what favours the coincidence of patriotism and citizenship is something very different from what *constitutes* them. The mere fact that Rousseau sees in patriotism the most powerful sentiment grounding and reinforcing citizenship itself suggests their difference. Rousseau compares love for one's country to love for a woman.[46] What these kinds of love have in common is that they require no reason beyond themselves; indeed any reason beyond themselves robs them of their intrinsic value and distinctive nature. If we love our country as we love a woman, we do so, presumably, for its own sake, with no other end in mind. Loving it any other way would be suspect: our sincerity would be in doubt. Yet while we surely are aware of the object of our affections, we are scarcely able to account for them in rationally discursive terms, nor are we normally expected to, since love is taken to be its own reason or explanation. It is precisely this intrinsic self-justificatory quality which makes patriotism so powerful a reinforcement of citizenship and which, by the same token, makes sincerity of motives or sentiments so important. While sincerity is undoubtedly desirable in the will of the citizen, in the will of the patriot it is definitionally crucial.

If sincerity and depth of sentiments, then, characterize the ethos of patriotism, citizenship is the work of sober reasoning. It is rational discourse which mediates agreement, the sole source and justification of human association within a state. People do not unite politically because they like or resemble each other; nor do they agree, when they do, for the sake of agreeing.[47] They agree if they are aware of reasons for which it makes sense to them to unite. And there is nothing spontaneous or 'natural' about attaining this awareness. Individuals do not naturally aspire to public objects, their wills do not naturally develop in the direction of a general will. Rousseau knew this well. 'For every two men whose interests may coincide', he writes in the Preface to *Narcissus*, 'there are a hundred thousand, perhaps, whose interests are totally opposite.'[48] Sharing customs, tastes, a language, or mere prejudices, certainly helps people to be *a* people, but it falls short of creating a collective purpose, a general will. To experience a culture as a common *political* culture, people must be conscious of shared interests and shared objectives. Only then does a culture become a political habitat if people are made to feel that public objectives are also their own individual concerns; for only then do they truly view themselves as interdependent parts rather than as independent wholes.[49] It is when people do not regard public objectives as their own that a Legislator has to persuade them that what they gain through agreement is of far greater value than what they surrender; that by working with others they truly work for themselves. And in order to persuade them, he has to induce them to consult their reason and not merely to listen to their inclination. Emotional affinities cannot by themselves instruct people whether or not they have interests in common. Yet only the discovery of common interests can form the foundation of *political* association.[50]

What defines citizenship, then, is not sentiments of affinity but reasoned agreement. Clearly, citizenship is mediated in a way patriotism is not. Although the notion of *patrie* comprises for Rousseau, as it did for the ancient Hebrews and Greeks, veneration for a country's laws, the prime emphasis is on spontaneous attitudes and feelings, on reasons of the heart rather than on reasons of interest. Patriotism is not a matter of discursive consensus. Preferably, people should 'suck in love of the *patrie* with their mother's milk', and laws should touch their hearts long before they are able to understand them.[51] Nor is patriotism an act of reasoned choice. Patriots do what they do, as lovers do what they do, because they are what they are. Being here defines doing. They may search their hearts to validate their sentiments but they have no need to reason why, for this to them is obvious enough. Yet what is obvious to the patriot is by no means obvious to the citizen; he has to know *what* he identifies with and *why*. In order to act right, a patriot, not unlike a father, has only to consult his heart; a citizen, not unlike a magistrate, is liable to become a traitor 'the moment he listens to his'.[52] A citizen's commitments may derive their strength from patriotic sentiments but they do not wholly rest on these. Commitments to be strictly political must be defensible on impersonal grounds, on grounds of purely 'public reasons'.[53] Although patriotic sentiments arguably qualify as impersonal reasons in that they draw on motives other than personal interest, they are not publicly discussable; they can neither be discursively challenged nor discursively defended. Rousseau sees no need to justify acts of patriotic dedication, but he goes out of his way to explain why a citizen must be prepared to die for his country. And the reasons he gives are reasons of prudence. Prudence tells a citizen that it is in his interest to protect his life. Since it is the prime function of the state to protect the life of its citizens, it is the prime duty of the citizen to protect the life of the state. What is involved is a reciprocal exchange, a trade-off: the citizen returns to the state what he receives from it.[54] To defend the state is as much rational on personal grounds as it is rational on public grounds. The patriot's willingness to sacrifice his life is evidently implicit in his love of *patrie*, a source not amenable to discursive reasoning. Love for one's country is no more disputable than love for a woman. We love or we do not love, but arguments or reasons do not make us love. Rational agreement, however, *requires* argument, for its compelling force depends on its justifying reasons; and justifying reasons as discursive reasons *are* disputable.

It follows that, while they are both characterized by generality of willing, patriotism and citizenship draw on radically different justifying sources, the former on non-discursive intimations of intrinsic sentiment, the latter on discursive deliberations of instrumental interest. Rousseau, though aware of these differences, tends to blur them by so closely associating citizenship with patriotism. Admittedly, care must be taken not to overdraw the differences. Patriotism, although in essence an affair of the heart, is not for Rousseau a purely impulsive passion. It may be unmediated by discursive reason, but it is not unmediated by *any* reason. Patriotism is not like the non-rational impulses of natural man which never transcend his physical needs for food, sex, and rest. A patriot's passions do transcend these 'simple impulses of nature' and embody therefore some form of reason.[55] There are, evidently, for Rousseau such things as reasons of the heart which, though inherently different from reasons of interest, are not incapable of being suffused with or supportive of these. Civic virtue, on this understanding, cannot but gain from the marriage of reason as political sentiment and reason as political interest. Rousseau undeniably points here to the possibly most common grounds upon which people act (or say they act) in the public space. But while this may indicate a profound sense of political realism, at any rate as far as political *participation* in one form or another is concerned, it fails to resolve the ambiguity over political *accountability*. To resolve this ambiguity, we would need to know what mattered most in the suggested duality of political rationality; only then could we learn in what manner or measure it allowed for the possibility of demanding and questioning reasons for what is claimed to be in the public interest.

As things stand, Rousseau's ambiguity over political rationality presents us with some worrisome puzzles. How are we, for example, to resolve a possible conflict between the 'general will' of the citizens and the 'general will' of the patriot? More fundamentally still, how are we to account for such a conflict on Rousseau's own terms, according to which there could only be one way of legitimately thinking of the public good so that any challenge to the general will could come only from particular wills? To grant therefore the duality of political will and political rationality would imply a denial of a single source of legitimate generality unless one set of reasons, discursive *or* intrinsic is accorded primacy as qualifying or justifying source. And if intrinsic reasons were to be accorded primacy or indeed supremacy, how could general claims based on these ever be challenged or supported? Whose intrinsic reasons would count? Merely to pose these questions is to disclose the dangers lurking in their answers.

Similarly, what are we to make of Rousseau's statement that simple peasants generally act more wisely than professional politicians because they intuitively know the common good? Do intuitive reasons of the heart reveal what discursive reasons of interest or intellect refuse to divulge? Or, again, if people are supposed to love their laws before they are old enough to understand them, what need is there for laws to pass the test of discursive rationality? Finally, when Rousseau insists that the general will be questioned so that it would reply, does he have argument in mind or mere voting? Does he, that is, expect public discourse or mere numbers to decide whether claims of generality are truly warranted?

In principle, it seems, Rousseau wishes to uphold the primacy of discursive rationality in politics. In practice, however, he clearly harbours doubt about its efficacy in generating authentic commitment and associative unity. And since commitment and unity figure so prominently in his political scheme of things, it is scarcely surprising that he sets greater store by intrinsic reasons of sentiment than by discursive reasons of interest. In the final weighing intrinsic reasons tip the scales; they and they only are held truly capable of sustaining a person's abiding loyalties and of serving as ultimate standards for deciding whether or not man-made institutions really befitted man. But in elevating intrinsic reasons of sentiment above discursive reasons of interest, Rousseau succeeds in effectively beclouding what in principle he professes to illuminate. His preference for voting over discussion points in the same direction. Conceivably, this preference does not imply a total denial of a citizen's right to 'express or oppose opinions, make propositions, or analyze and discuss proposals',[56] but it does look as though Rousseau regards discussion and argument as something people would have little use for in a politically wholesome society. Under proper conditions, so Rousseau would apparently have us believe, people would have no cause for disagreement; an intuitive understanding of what the public good demands would render discourse otiose.

That the restoration of balance between will and power should be capable of engendering so high a degree of consensus cannot but kindle one's suspicions. For it suggests that in order to become an integral part of a social whole, a person may virtually have to deny his distinctive individuality; that in order to become a good citizen, he may have to cease being a person in any meaningful sense. Although autonomous self-direction which denies individual differentiation need not perhaps be thought of as an utter contradiction in terms, it surely assumes a somewhat hollow ring. Even if violence is bracketed out from Rousseau's envisioned 'restoration' and the notion of being 'forced to be free' drained of its sinister-sounding implications, Rousseau's blurring of autonomy and paternalism coupled with his persistent ambivalence over political rationality undeniably raise the spectre of new social man emerging as a moulded man, given to right-acting rather than self-choosing.[57]

Implicit, therefore, in Rousseau's position on will and political rationality is something of a paradox. For, while it contains the potential of an impressive vindication of the non-vacuity thesis of willing in action and, with it, of accountable human agency, it contains, at the same time, the potential of a serious threat to free choice and public discourse as modes of political action and to the giving and probing of reasons as modes of political accountability.

## NOTES

1 Allan Bloom (trans.), *Rousseau: Emile* (New York, Basic Books, 1979), pp. 84–5.

2 Pléiade (ed.), *Rousseau: Letters from the Mountain, Oeuvres Complètes* (Paris, Gallimard, 1959–69, vol. III, p. 837). (Subsequently referred to as *Letters*.)

3 *Emile*, p. 81.

4 *Emile*, pp. 84–6.

5 *Emile*, pp. 84–6.

6 *Emile*, p. 84.

7 *Emile*, pp. 40–1; Preface to *Narcissus, The Miscellaneous Works of Mr. J. J. Rousseau* (New York, Burt Franklin, 1767) (1972 reprint), vol. II, p. 138. A contemporary (but not necessarily superior) translation will be found in *Political Theory*, VI (1978), 543–54.

8 *Letters*, pp. 837–8; Rousseau reiterates this distinction in one of his last writings, *Reveries of the Solitary Walker*: 'I have never believed that man's freedom consists in doing what he wants, but rather in never doing what he does not want to do.' Translated by Peter France (Harmondsworth, Penguin Books, 1979), p. 104.

9 *Emile*, pp. 39–40; *Social Contract*, Bk I, ch. 7; Bk II, chs 7, 12.

10 *Emile*, p. 85. Rousseau attempts to re-create the three basic conditions nature imposes on man: (1) dependence on only impersonal or objective laws; (2) absence of personal subjection implicit in men's isolation and independence of each other; and (3) a fundamental equality of conditions for all, since all are equally subject to the forces of nature.

11 *Emile*, p. 85; *Letters*, p. 841.

12 'Geneva Manuscript', in Roger D. Masters (ed.), *On the Social Contract* (New York, St Martin's Press, 1978), p. 161.

13 *Letters*, p. 889.

14 *Social Contract*, Bk II, ch. 11.

15 Preface to *Narcissus*, p. 139; *Constitutional Project for Corsica, Oeuvres*, vol. III, pp. 920–4, 930–1.

16 *Social Contract*, Bk III, ch. 1.

17 *Social Contract*, Bk III, ch. 1.

18 *Social Contract*, Bk III, ch. 1.

19 *Emile*, pp. 273, 280.

20 *Emile*, p. 274.

21 *Discourse on the Origin and Basis of Inequality Among Men* (translated by Lowell Blair) (New York, New American Library, 1974), p. 153. (Subsequently referred to as *Inequality*.) Emphasis added. (G. D. H. Cole (ed.), *The Social Contract and Discourses* (London, Dent, 1946), p. 170.)

22 *Emile*, p. 275.

23 *Social Contract*, Bk I, ch. 8.

24 *Social Contract*, Bk I, ch. 6.

25 *Emile*, p. 280.

26 F. M. Barnard (ed. and trans.), *Herder on Social and Political Culture* (London, Cambridge University Press, 1969), p. 266.

27 *Social Contract*, Bk II, ch. 12.

28 *Social Contract*, Bk I, ch. 7.

29 'In the long run', Rousseau says, 'all peoples become what government makes them.' To turn men as they are into what they should be, authority must penetrate 'man's inmost being, and

concern itself no less with his will than with his actions'. 'Men have to be *made*, they only need to know what is their duty to do.' G. D. H. Cole (ed.), *Political Economy* (London, Dent, 1946), p. 243.

30  *Social Contract*, Bk II, ch. 6.

31  *Social Contract*, Bk II, ch. 7.

32  Although the parallels between Kant's and Rousseau's understanding of autonomy may not be as close as some commentators are inclined to believe, in his political–anthropological thinking Kant comes at times remarkably close to Rousseau, thus causing the dichotomy between autonomy and paternalism to be somewhat muted. I have discussed Kant's conception of autonomy more fully in 'Self-Direction: Thomasius, Kant, and Herder', *Political Theory*, XI (1983), 343–68.

33  *Social Contract*, Bk II, ch. 6.

34  *Social Contract*, Bk II, ch. 6.

35  'Geneva Manuscript', p. 161.

36  *Letters*, p. 813; *Emile*, p. 463.

37  *Political Economy*, p. 246. For a fascinating historical account of patriotism, see J. Huizinga, 'Wachstum und Formen des Nationalen Bewusstseins', *Im Bann der Geschichte* (Basel, Burg, 1943), pp. 131–210. According to Huizinga, the Latin *patria* met with opposition before it assumed its French meaning as *patrie*, in which it recalled its original Greek meaning of *patris* more strongly or more typically than the Roman *patria*. It is possible, however, that the word gained currency in France not so much as a result of Italian as of English influence, in particular through Bolingbroke's writings on patriotism. Rousseau's distinction between using 'inane tricks' and 'political wisdom' in creating the unwritten laws conducive to the growth of patriotic sentiments is made in the *Social Contract*, Bk II, ch. 7.

38  *Social Contract*, Bk II, ch. 12.

39  *Social Contract* Bk IV, ch. 1.

40  *Corsica*, pp. 940–1; *Political Economy*, p. 245.

41  The first book of the *Social Contract* already points to this conflict, as Hilail Gildin, in his careful commentary on the *Social Contract* observes. *Rousseau's Social Contract: The Design of the Argument* (Chicago, University of Chicago Press, 1983), p. 50.

42  *Emile*, p. 280. But the reasons for which at any given time we say or do something may in retrospect reveal themselves not to have been our 'real and basic motives'. Or reasons that appeared clear at the time may subsequently appear much less so. So Rousseau reflects in the 'Sixth Walk' of the *Reveries*, p. 94.

43  *Emile*, pp. 280–1.

44  I discuss this aspect of teleological causation in 'Accounting for Actions: Causality and Teleology', *History and Theory*, XX (1981), 291–312.

45  *Political Economy*, p. 246; *Inequality*, pp. 128–36 (Cole, pp. 144–53); 'Geneva Manuscript', p. 159. A state as large as Poland, Rousseau tells the Poles, cannot possibly bring about the coincidence of citizenship and patriotism. *Considerations on the Government of Poland*, *Oeuvres*, vol. III, pp. 969–70. (Subsequently referred to as *Poland*.) A fuller discussion of Rousseau's thinking on a state's size, timing,

and form of nationhood compatible with the coincidence of patriotism and citizenship may be found in my 'National Culture and Political Legitimacy: Herder and Rousseau', *Journal of the History of Ideas*, XLIV (1983), 231–53.

46  *Political Economy*, p. 246.
47  'Geneva Manuscript', p. 159.
48  Preface to *Narcissus*, p. 138.
49  *Social Contract*, Bk II, ch. 10; *Inequality*, pp. 177–8 (Cole, p. 197); *Emile*, pp. 39, 85; Preface to *Narcissus*, p. 138.
50  *Social Contract*, Bk I, ch. 8; Bk II, chs 1, 4, 7.
51  *Social Contract*, Bk II, ch. 12; *Poland*, pp. 961, 965; *Reveries*, p. 154.
52  *Political Economy*, p. 235.
53  *Political Economy*, pp. 235 and 240.
54  *Social Contract*, Bk II, chs 4, 5.
55  *Inequality*, p. 154 (Cole, p. 171).
56  *Social Contract*, Bk IV, chs 1, 2; *Letters*, p. 830.
57  This is brought out well in John Charvet, 'Individual Identity and Social Consciousness in Rousseau's Philosophy', *Hobbes and Rousseau*, edited by Maurice Cranston and Richard S. Peters (New York, Doubleday, 1972), pp. 472–3. (I owe this reference to Professor J. M. Porter of the University of Saskatchewan, with whom I gave an early and extended draft of this essay at the annual conference of the Canadian Political Science Association in Vancouver, June 1983.) The degree to which paternalism threatens the belief in man's autonomy is the subject of Gerald Dworkin's 'Paternalism', in Peter Laslett and James Fishkin (eds), *Philosophy, Politics and Society*, Fifth Series (New Haven, Yale University Press, 1979), pp. 78–96, and of Douglas N. Husak's 'Paternalism and Autonomy', *Philosophy and Public Affairs*, X (1981), 27–46. On this and some of the other points raised in this essay I am indebted to comments by members of my graduate seminar on autonomy and accountability in politics, in particular to those made by Janet Menard and Bruce Fyfe. I also wish to acknowledge assistance granted by the Social Sciences and Humanities Research Council of Canada which in the form of a Research Time Stipend afforded me time to work on this essay in conjunction with my research project 'Accounting for Actions'.

# EDMUND BURKE

## Chapter Ten

# INTRODUCTION

Professor Pocock starts his discussion of Burke with what might be called the Macaulay Gambit ('Every schoolboy knows who imprisoned Montezuma . . .'). Whatever else might be held to be controversial in Burke's thought, Pocock claims, his commitment to a doctrine of traditionalism has been universally acknowledged. In fact, not even this degree of consensus exists among commentators. Indeed, for some, no general theory of politics emerges from the occasional writings and speeches of a politician whose main role was as a publicist and propagandist within factional politics. Others have repeated the charge made against Burke in his own lifetime that the old Burke was an apostate from the views of the young Burke, that there was no position in common between the earlier scourge of the Crown and defender of the American Revolution and the later scourge of the people and critic of the French Revolution.

Burke himself rejected these two charges, the first implicitly, the second explicitly. He would not have refused the name of 'party' man, indeed offered a spirited defence of party and the party politician; nor did he, even while attacking general or 'abstract' political theories, move from the ground that particular issues should be evaluated in terms of general principles about both the proper modes and the proper objectives of political action. Against the charge of inconsistency, he argued that it was the circumstances not his principles that had changed, that his early attack on the growing influence of the Crown was based on the same commitments as his later attack on the revolutionary notion of the sovereignty of the people. Even when, during the French Revolutionary period, he broke with his former political associates, he still appealed as a Whig (albeit a 'new' Whig) to Whigs (albeit 'old' Whigs).

Most commentators have followed Burke, and Pocock, in seeing a consistent body of principles within Burke's occasional writings, although most have drawn most heavily on his anti-Revolutionary writings to elucidate these principles. Most too have, as Pocock claims, seen 'traditionalism' (or, as most have more generally termed it, 'conservatism') as central to these principles. Most too agree with Pocock's definition of 'traditionalism' – the assertion that political practice should be based, not on the application of rationally derived first principles of government, but on the protection of established institutions and the application of established habits of thought and action.

Any such traditionalist stance is likely to have two aspects, a defence of relying on tradition as a guide to political practice and a definition of the political objectives enshrined in the particular tradition which the traditionalist is defending. Pocock conflates these two questions by arguing that the tradition to which Burke appealed was one concerned primarily with the modes rather than the objectives of political action, with how statesmen should act rather than what ends they should try to achieve. The common law tradition, allied with the doctrine of the ancient constitution, was itself a tradition of traditionalism.

This placing of Burke is open to question as an explanation and explication of his thought as a whole, or even, more narrowly, of his 'traditionalism'. In the first place, there is the question of whether or not this was the, or the only, tradition to which Burke owed allegiance. He himself pointed to Locke as a forefather. His attack an 'Old Jewry' principles was an attack, not so much upon Lockean ideas, as upon what he saw as a dangerous distortion of a Whig tradition to which he himself subscribed. The *Reflections* themselves can be seen as in part at least an attempt to dissipate the initially euphoric Whig reaction to the French Revolution, that it was simply the tardy installation in France of the principles of the Glorious Revolution. However close the parallel between Burke and the common lawyers, his acknowledged debt to the political theorists cannot be ignored.

The *Reflections* no doubt cannot be fully understood outside the context of the English political debate of the time. However, the book was, after all, *Reflections on the Revolution in France*, and Burke's defence of traditionalism was meant to serve as a critique of French revolutionaries as well as of Old Jewry radicals. This constitutes a second difficulty for Pocock's interpretation, for it could hardly have been part of that critique that the French had failed to follow traditional English practices (as Burke saw them), unless there were good reasons for following those practices quite apart from their being traditionally English. Of course, Burke attacked the revolutionaries on the grounds of their overturning French political traditions, but, however mistaken he might have been about those traditions, he obviously did not define them in common law terms. In other words, his use of traditionalism in the French context implied a free-standing defence of traditionalism independent of its being the English tradition; it implied too an independent criticism of the rationalist approach to politics he took to be characteristic of revolutionary thought. All this took him beyond history into political theory, and the exploration of that theory must be part of the explication of his traditionalism.

Pocock notices and addresses a third problem, which is that Burke was not alone in adhering to the doctrine of the ancient constitution and that many radical reformers used the same invocation of the past in service to their demands for change. Up to the first Reform Act, the common coin of radical rhetoric was an appeal, not to the rights of men or even to general utility, but to the rights of Englishmen, democratic rights which had been usurped at the Norman Conquest or in medieval restrictions of the franchise. Pocock portrays Burke as answering this claim by asserting that no general, or at any rate 'original', principles of the constitution could be discovered and none could therefore be used as evidence of the degeneracy of the present state of affairs. But Burke went beyond this argument and presented what he saw as the true principles of this English constitution (and indeed of English society). In doing so, he offered a set of substantive principles which defined the social and political ends statesmen should be concerned to preserve and even, after attacks upon them, consciously to reinstate. This perhaps illustrates a general dilemma of traditionalism. Nothing much follows from urging the following of traditional practices and principles without the definition of those traditions. Any such definition is contestable. Given a contest, the argument is likely to move from historical controversy to a debate on the merits of the different principles allegedly enshrined in the tradition. Just as traditionalism as a mode of political practice requires a non-traditionalist justification, so any persuasive defence of particular traditional norms is likely to include more than just the claim that they are in fact traditional.

Even if Burke was following within the common law tradition, his thought as a whole, as of course Pocock recognizes, was then more than a simple restatement of that tradition. On the one side he elaborated, and provided a justification for, the whole concept of traditionalism (or conservatism) as a mode of political practice; and, on the other side, he articulated and defended a range of social values he claimed to be traditional. On the one side, he urged respect for tried institutions; consideration for vested interests; political responses only to particular and concrete grievances; distrust of rationalist thought and utopian projects; the acceptance by politicians of the severe limitations on political action imposed by human nature; tenderness towards the attitudes – even the prejudices – prevailing in society. On the other side, he defended a hierarchical ordering of society; the dominance of a 'natural' aristocracy; the crucial role of the family; the firm protection of civil rights, and most especially property rights; the safeguarding, even encouragement, of a pluralist social structure; and at the same time the maintenance of the organic unity of society. The very complexity of these arguments, together with Burke's deliberate and, in terms of his own ideas, justifiable refusal to engage in any systematic 'abstract' exposition of them, allows for a wide variety of divergent interpretations of the general character of his thought. Much depends on which particular aspects of these arguments are stressed, and he has been depicted variously as a hard-headed pragmatist, a cautious and sceptical empiricist, a political moralist, a romantic nationalist, a theocratic theorist, a political sociologist.

Pocock builds his own characterization of Burke on an examination of the tradition which, it is claimed, he was following. An alternative strategy for assessing these varying characterizations is to explore the nature of Burke's attack upon radical and revolutionary thought, for his traditionalism can perhaps best be understood in terms of his attack upon rationalist politics and his substantive social values in terms of the ends on which he supposed the revolutionaries to be bent and which he so vehemently rejected. Burke's conservatism, like continental reactionary thought, was articulated fully only as a response to the Revolution, and understanding the nature of that response is perhaps the best route to understanding his conservatism.

His criticism of the rationalism and idealism of the revolutionaries is central to that response. The Revolution marked the disastrous irruption into political life of the rationalist theorists, the *philosophes*. In part, his attack was on the refusal of this style of thinking to face the complexity of politics, its attempts to reduce moral judgement in politics to the simple application of utopian blueprints, its search for some simple formula to explain political behaviour, a formula which ignored both the diversity of historical circumstances and the ambiguities of human nature and motivation. The consequence of such rationalism and idealism was ineptitude, the failure of those who wanted to do things too quickly, or too well. These criticisms seem to be the indignant reaction of an experienced politician to political tyros; and they provide the justification for those who picture Burke as the worldly-wise pragmatist or empiricist.

Such pictures miss, however, the moral fervour which informs Burke's assault on rationalism. The revolutionaries were, he claimed, bedevilled not only by a 'want of comprehension' but by 'some malignity of disposition'. The 'abstract reasoning' on which the revolutionary faith was founded involved the search, not only for explanations stripped of historical contingency, but for moral truths equally immune to qualification by circumstances and equally applicable at all times and in all places. The basic sin of this style of thought was, he insisted, pride, a wilful refusal to accept limitations on human action and a wilful ambition to transform and regenerate human nature itself. It was this aspiration, rather than any practical necessity or concrete grievances, that had prompted the Revolution. This moral absolutism, based on rationalist arrogance, resulted in the breach of all ordinary moral rules, all previously accepted moral constraints on rulers. The assertion of general benevolence or humanitarianism was not the advocacy of a new and refined morality but a surrender to feeling, a displacement of reason and justice by sensibility. A proper moral perspective required and resulted in praise and blame; it recognized men as moral agents and so acknowledged their capacity for, and even propensity to, evil. The profession of humanitarianism was not necessarily supportive of personal morality or even personal kindliness. It could weaken those private virtues which, springing from a recognition of flaws in the self, rested on self-restraint. In consequence a professed love of humanity was compatible with indifference to the actual feelings and needs of other individuals, a 'love of kind and hatred of kindred' which Burke believed was exemplified by Rousseau himself. What was true of private was true also of public morality. The revolutionary leaders excused their imposition of suffering and oppression by the highest ideals. Their will to power and their retention of it, no matter how base the means they used, was justified by the nobility of their humanitarian motives. Their policies were aimed, not at the remedying of clearly recognizable abuses, but at some future hypothetical benefit of humanity. So there emerged the discrepancy between the highmindedness of their intentions and the savagery of their means. This paradox was reflected in their attitude towards the present and the future. Existing, imperfect men were readily sacrificed in the service of some future ideal society and regenerated humanity. 'Their humanity is at their horizon, and, like the horizon, it always flies before them.'

To this flawed morality, Burke contrasted a true morality

respectful of inherited institutions. The revolutionary contrast between a corrupt present and a perfect future was paralleled by an opposition posed between conscience and instinct. The instincts – acquisitive, sexual, gregarious – and their social products – private property, the family, minor social groupings – were seen as acting inevitably against conscience and therefore against men's realization of themselves as moral agents or good citizens. For Burke, the contrast was false. The instincts, at least when expressed within and moderated by conventional social institutions, were not the enemies but the agents of moral education; and any attack upon those institutions, far from releasing men from the tyranny of instincts, would unleash them in the unrestrained forms of a lust for unlimited possession, the collapse of personal morality and a desire for submersion in the community as a whole.

Thus, for Burke, the vast political paradox of the Revolution – the coupling of unbounded hopes for the perfection of mankind with the malignant use of cruelty and violence – was the product of a fundamental moral flaw, the wilful refusal to recognize the moral constraints imposed by circumstances and human nature. This moral critique of rationalism and idealism is the basis for the picture of Burke as a political moralist. Yet there are elements in this critique which justify the somewhat different depiction of him as a theocratic thinker. For, to the charges against rationalism of practical and moral obtuseness, he added the charge of impiety. The pride exhibited by the revolutionaries was literally Satanic, since the aspiration to reconstitute human nature was a revolt against the author of that nature. The refusal too to accept the limitations of circumstances was a revolt against a providentially ordered human history.

Burke's defence of traditionalism as a mode of political practice is embedded in this critique of rationalism on practical, moral, and religious grounds; and the critique must be considered, together no doubt with his claim that the mode of practice had in fact been part of the English tradition, in any full explication of his conservatism. This is true also of his statement of the substantive social values which politicians should be concerned to protect. Of course, he presented these values as ones rooted in English traditions; but, in his attack upon what he saw as the revolutionary flouting of them, he was pushed into a defence of them beyond the claim that they were in fact traditionally sanctioned.

Implicit in Burke's statement is a distinction between society and the state. The distinction had already been suggested by Locke and Adam Smith, and was to be developed by Hegel and Marx. Those thinkers all saw civil society primarily in economic terms, although of course they differed in their views of the proper or actual relationship between civil society and the state. Burke, in contrast, saw society primarily in moral terms and argued that the social structure constituted an actual and proper constraint upon political action. Society was a complex of moral relationships and it was there that men received their moral education and most men found scope for expressing themselves as moral agents. This moral order was particularly manifested in the family, in intermediary associations, and in the social hierarchy.

The family was the basic moral unit of society, and in consequence its protection was a prime duty of the state. It was the family that demonstrated most clearly the folly of the rationalist's divorce of conscience and instinct. For it was within the family that men's affections were most closely linked to their duties, and it was there that their interests and obligations were most closely identified. The partiality of this acceptance of obligations was not a reason for condemnation, for the exercise of such limited altruism was a necessary preliminary to any acceptance of more extensive moral responsibilities; 'no cold relation is a zealous citizen'.

The same was true of intermediary associations in society. As against what he saw as the revolutionary desire to destroy partial associations and to counterpoise loyalty to the state and subordinate loyalties, Burke defended a pluralist society. As with the family, the most important function of partial association was moral education, the drawing of men into social commitments and a sense of duty to others. This is the view that had informed his earlier defence of parties and his claim that parties were not a danger to public unity. In contrast to Rousseau, he argued that attachment to party did not diminish but enhanced love of country.

Nevertheless, the main source of social unity was the habitual social discipline imposed within the 'natural' hierarchy of society. In every society, there was a natural aristocracy of 'the wiser, more expert, more opulent' and it was only by the recognition of and submission to this natural leadership that social cohesion could be attained. Only under such natural discipline could a mass of individuals be incorporated as a people.

It should be the first duty of statesmen to protect this moral order of society, but it had been the prime objective of the revolutionaries to subvert the settled order in France. They had engaged not just in political revolution, but the 'destruction and decomposition of the whole society'. They had done so in pursuit of false ideals of individual liberty and popular sovereignty. A good deal of Burke's defence of traditional values is couched in terms of a demonstration of the falsity of these revolutionary ideals. The liberty sought by the revolutionaries was freedom from external constraints; against this, Burke posed a notion of liberty which approached that of Rousseau, liberty as freedom from the bondage of passion, a freedom which could be attained only by adherence to the demands of an objective moral order. He attacked also the related notion of natural rights. Men could not enjoy rights outside society, and those rights-claims they could make inside society were to participate in the benefits which the moral social order provided. Most particularly they could not claim a right of democratic participation based on some natural right of self-government. Government might indeed rest on consent or contract, but that consent was expressed in national traditions. Just as popular unity was achievable only through the operation of habitual social discipline, so the popular will could be discerned only in traditional modes of thought and habits of behaviour.

In this way, Burke substantiated his own values in a theoretical critique of revolutionary objectives. His defence of traditionalism as a political practice depended on more than an appeal to traditional English practices; so too his defence of what he claimed to be traditional values involved more than just an appeal to prescription.

Burke did not have to face a dilemma implicit in this conservative position, the possibility of a clash between the recommended methods of political action and the recommended political ends. On the continent, and particularly in France, the dilemma arose in a stark form as the Revolution proceeded and as the changes brought by the revolutionary and Napoleonic regimes took root in French society. After 1815, the French right had virtually to choose between conservative practice and conservative ends. Some, like Guizot, chose the first. The French should cease refighting the battles of the Revolution. The Revolution had happened, its effects could be neither denied nor obliterated, and there could be no return to the *ancien régime*. In post-Revolutionary France, the conservative must conserve a society profoundly affected by the Revolution, and a cautious, pragmatic political style excluded any attempt to restructure present society on a model of the past just as much as it excluded any attempt to restructure it on a vision of the future. Others such as de Maistre, strictly the reactionaries, remained loyal to the political ends and sought a return to those substantive values – hierarchy, order, authority – thought to have been embodied in past societies. But this past was becoming more and more distant from the present and increasingly a return to the past demanded a repudiation of the present. So the reactionary stance required radical change and a repudiation of the limitation of political objectives. In an England less profoundly affected by the Revolution, the dilemma did not emerge in this sharp form, and the Burkean synthesis could long survive the upheaval that had occasioned it.

## ACCESSIBLE EDITION

E. Burke, *Reflections on the Revolution in France* (London, Dent, Everyman's Library)

## SUGGESTED READING

F. Canovan, *The Political Reason of Edmund Burke* (London, Dent, 1974)

M. Freeman, *Edmund Burke and the Critique of Political Radicalism* (Oxford, Basil Blackwell, 1980)

*C.B. Macpherson, *Burke* (Oxford, Oxford University Press, 1980)

C. Parkin, *The Moral Basis of Burke's Political Thought* (Cambridge, Cambridge University Press, 1956)

P. Stanlis, *Edmund Burke and Natural Law* (University of Michigan, 1958)

## Chapter Eleven

# BURKE AND THE ANCIENT CONSTITUTION – A PROBLEM IN THE HISTORY OF IDEAS*

## J. G. A. POCOCK

The intention of this paper is to enquire into Burke's doctrine of traditionalism – as it may be termed – from a point of view not quite identical with that usually adopted. The aspect of Burke's thought thus isolated may or may not be the most important or the most characteristic, but it is the most familiar and that with which the student first becomes acquainted. Burke held – to summarize what may be found in a hundred text-books on the history of conservatism – that a nation's institutions were the fruit of its experience, that they had taken shape slowly as the result, and were in themselves the record, of a thousand adjustments to the needs of circumstance, each one of which, if it had been found by trial and error to answer recurrent needs, had been preserved in the usages and established rules of the nation concerned. He also held that political knowledge was the fruit of experience and that reason in this field had nothing to operate on except experience; from which it followed that, since the knowledge of an individual or a generation of individuals was limited by the amount of experience on which it was based, there was always a case for the view that the reason of the living, though it might clearly enough discern the disadvantages, might not fully perceive the advantages of existing and ancient institutions, for these might contain the fruits of more experience than was available to living individuals as the sum of their personal or reported experience of the world. It also followed that since the wisdom embodied in institutions was based on experience and nothing but experience, it could not be completely rationalized, that is, reduced to first principles which might be clearly enunciated, shown to be the cause of the institutions' first being set up, or employed to criticize their subsequent workings. There was, in short, always more in laws and institutions than met the eye of

* Previously published in *The Historical Journal*, vol. III, no. 2 (1960).

critical reason, always a case for them undiminished by anything that could be said against them.

All this is, of course, no more than elementary Burke, the first lesson learnt by every student of his thought. This paper is concerned with the way in which its presence in his thought should be historically explained. The account of political society here given is in a fairly obvious sense anti-rationalist: it endows the community with an inner life of growth and adaptation, and it denies to individual reason the power to see this process as a whole or to establish by its own efforts the principles on which the process is based. Burke's thought can, therefore, properly be set in opposition to any rationalist system of politics, which presents political society as based originally on the assent of individual minds to universal principles rationally discerned. Such systems, of course, abounded in the eighteenth century, and Burke opposed these where he met with them. But this does not of itself justify us in supposing that the historical origins of Burke's thought are necessarily to be found in a reaction against political rationalism, as if the latter had conditioned all political thinking before his time and some special explanation needed to be found of his breaking with it. Yet many studies of his thought have been and perhaps still are based upon some such presumption. Meinecke and Sabine, for example, both supposed that the thought of Burke must be regarded as an effect and consequence of Hume's critique of rationalism,[1] and when Meinecke was constrained to admit that there was not enough evidence of Burke's having read Hume at the critical time, he fell back on the untestable hypothesis that Hume's teachings were 'in the air'[2] and had infected Burke as a species of *influenza*. He was assuming that only some basic change of philosophical viewpoint could account for Burke's not conforming to a political rationalism which had hitherto dominated thought; and the assumption rests on a complex of misunderstandings which are still all too common among historians of ideas. We tend in the first place to assume that the ideas of a major thinker must be explained by co-ordinating them in a unified philosophy and discovering the common metaphysical or epistemological foundation on which they all rest; and we tend in the second place to simplify our field by the method of dialectical projection, by assuming that the thought of a particular period may be characterized as founded on certain common philosophical foundations and that the thought of the succeeding periods must be shown to have come into being as a result of some shift in these foundations. These methods are justified in some circumstances, but it is a misunderstanding to suppose that they must be adopted in all; and where we do not suppose this some other means must be found of offering historical explanations of a man's ideas. We now know, for example, that Locke's political thought is not a simple extension of his philosophy, but an explanation of contemporary political experience offered to his contemporaries in one, and not the only one, of the modes of discourse they were accustomed to adopt.[3] The history of ideas may legitimately, though not exclusively, be viewed as the history of the modes of explaining the world and its behaviour which have from time to time existed. Burke says clearly of his doctrine of traditionalism that it is a way of thinking which existed in the England of his time and had existed for so long that it was itself traditional. In this paper an attempt will be made to see if he was right in this assertion, and if so what the consequences may be for the historical understanding of his thought.

We may conveniently begin with a passage from the *Reflections on the Revolution in France* which, like most of the quotations from Burke in this paper, is familiar to all students and is cited here in an attempt to establish the proper context in which it may be understood.

The third head of right, asserted by the pulpit of the Old Jewry, namely, the 'right to form a government by ourselves', has, at least, as little countenance from any thing done at the Revolution, either in precedent or in principle, as the two first of their claims. The Revolution was made to preserve our *antient* indisputable laws and liberties, and that *antient* constitution of government which is our only security for law and liberty. If you are desirous of knowing the spirit of our constitution, and the policy which predominated in that great period which has secured it to this hour, pray look for both in our histories, in our records, in our acts of parliament, and journals of parliament, and not in the sermons of the Old Jewry, and the after-dinner toasts of the Revolution Society. In the former you will find other ideas and another language. Such a claim is as ill-suited to our temper and wishes as it is unsupported by any appearance of authority. The very idea of the fabrication of a new government is enough to fill us with disgust and horror. We wished at the period of the Revolution, and do now wish, to derive all we possess as *an inheritance from our forefathers*. Upon that body and stock of inheritance we have taken care not to inoculate any cyon [scion] alien to the nature of the original plant. All the reformations we have hitherto made, have proceeded upon the principle of reference to antiquity; and I hope, nay I am persuaded, that all those which possibly may be made hereafter, will be carefully formed upon analogical precedent, authority and example.

Our oldest reformation is that of Magna Charta. You will see that Sir Edward Coke, that great oracle of our law, and indeed all the great men who follow him, to Blackstone, are industrious to prove the pedigree of our liberties. They endeavour to prove, that the antient charter, the Magna Charta of King John, was connected with another positive charter from Henry I, and that both the one and the other were nothing more than a re-affirmance of the still more antient standing law of the kingdom. In the matter of fact, for the greater part, these authors appear to be in the right; perhaps not always; but if the lawyers mistake in some particulars, it proves my position still the more strongly; because it demonstrates the powerful prepossession towards antiquity, with which the minds of all our lawyers and legislators, and of all the people whom they wish to influence, have been always filled; and the stationary policy of this kingdom in considering their most sacred rights and franchises as an inheritance.[4]

Now, before assuming that this passage must be explained by attributing to Burke possession of any general theory of man and society, we can take one by one the statements of which it consists, and see both what is being said in them and to what order of statement they belong. Burke is simultaneously advocating and making an appeal to history – to 'records, and acts of parliament, and journals of parliament' – and making a series of statements about history; for he is saying that the practice of establishing the rules of political behaviour by an appeal to history conducted in this manner has been followed so regularly in the course of English history that it now constitutes a tradition of behaviour, a 'stationary policy' which he hopes and believes will be maintained in future. The Revolution of 1688, he says, was conducted on the principle that there existed a body of ancient laws and liberties, and an ancient constitution guaranteeing them, and that all that was necessary in the conditions of that critical year was to reaffirm their existence; it was not conducted on the principle that under certain circumstances power 'reverts to the society' and the people have a right to 'erect a new form . . . as they think good'.[5] Rights are not justified by abstract reason, but as an inheritance under positive laws; but for this assertion to have validity, it is necessary that the positive laws be as old as, or older than, the rights which they substantiate and – almost – the society which contains them. From

Coke to Blackstone, Burke observes, the great English lawyers have steadily maintained that this is in fact the case with English law; that the laws and liberties of England are rooted in Magna Carta, and the Charter of 1215 in a body of law very much more ancient than itself. Burke inspects this historical statement; he thinks it very largely accurate, but adds that the fact that it has so constantly been made is of greater significance than the accuracy of its contents, because it demonstrates that Englishmen have always been concerned to establish their rights by appeal to their own past and not to abstract principles. This habit of mind he considers the most important fact in the history of English political behaviour.

Burke is talking history; he is discussing both a traditional interpretation of English history and the part which that interpretation has itself played in shaping English history; and the historical facts to which he alludes are such as we may ourselves discern and describe in terms not unlike his own. There really did exist a habit of conducting political discussion in England 'upon the principle of reference to antiquity', upon the assumption that there existed an ancient constitution which was the justification of all rights and was itself justified primarily by its antiquity. The public and authorized theory of what had occurred in 1688–9 – that on which the houses of the convention parliament had been able to agree and which was contained in the public documents of the time – really did base its interpretation on the doctrine of the ancient constitution, far more than on the doctrines of contract, natural right, and reason propounded by Sidney or Locke. The interpretation of history which that doctrine necessitated – involving the assertion that Magna Carta confirmed a charter of Henry I, which confirmed a charter of William I, which confirmed the laws of Edward the Confessor, which were themselves no more than a codification of law already ancient – had, as Burke remarks, been constantly put forward by lawyers from Coke to Blackstone. It was consequently still a living issue in Burke's own time; he feels called upon to comment on its truth or falsity, and though he has enough historical detachment to feel interested primarily in its significance as a long-held belief, its truth as history seems to him to be well established. What he is saying, then, is not a piece of antiquarian's lore, but an account of contemporary practice. This is how we conduct our politics, he is saying; how we have always conducted them. He is not calling upon his contemporaries to return to a seventeenth-century habit of mind, but assuming that it is still alive and meaningful among them. It will be of some significance to our understanding of Burke's thought if we decide that he was right in this assumption.

The plot thickens and becomes more suggestive when we observe that the habit of mind denoted by the term 'ancient constitution' had already – during the seventeenth century – produced and given expression to ideas very like those of Burke's traditionalism, and (though this is of less importance) that Burke had some opportunity of knowing this. It is the evidence for such an assertion that we must next review, though it involves some repetition of what has been said elsewhere.[6]

The doctrine of the ancient constitution received its classical formulation, though probably not its original conception, about the year 1600. It was the work of common lawyers, and seems to have been shaped throughout by assumptions concerning the common law of England and deeply implanted in the mind of everyone trained in that study. These assumptions were first, that all the law in England might properly be termed common law; second, that common law was common custom, originating in the usages of the people and declared, interpreted, and applied in the courts; third, that all custom was by definition immemorial, that which had been usage and law since time out of mind, so that any declaration of law, whether judgment or (with not quite the same certainty) statute, was a declaration that its content had been usage since time immemorial. These assumptions were now made the framework of an interpretation of history, one based on record, axiom, and judgement rather than the statements of chroniclers and, therefore, containing at every turn the presumption that law was immemorial. It therefore became possible to believe that the whole framework of English law and (when that term came into use) the 'constitution' – meaning the distribution by law of powers of declaring and applying the law – had existed from the obscure beginnings of English history; from a time earlier than the earliest historical evidences. Legal history, read upon the assumptions which were native and instinctive to a common lawyer, became a series of declarations that the law was immemorial. In this way grew up an elaborate body of myths, maintained with great tenacity by Englishmen of the seventeenth century and after, which taken together form the cult of the 'ancient constitution'. It has elsewhere been argued that the idea of immemorial law was one of the cardinal political ideas of Stuart England; and since it has been found to have appeared, based consistently on the same assumptions, in every major controversy and in the mind of every important political thinker from Coke to Locke, the hypothesis has received some verification. This, then, is the doctrine and the habit of mind which Burke describes as 'the stationary policy of this kingdom'.[7]

It may be further characterized as the habit of interpreting English politics and society not with the aid of any political theory designed for the explanation of society in general, but in the light of those assumptions about English society which were already contained in its most distinctive and characteristic body of rules. That body of rules was the common law and when English political thought committed the supreme insularity of assuming that English politics and history already contained all that was necessary to their understanding, and did not require to be studied in the light of any foreign law or universal principle, it was to the unique character of the common law that English thinkers were referring. Of this Burke seems to have realized something; in a passage[8] closely following on the one already quoted, he speaks again of the age-old English practice of claiming their liberties

> as an *entailed inheritance* derived to us from our forefathers, and to be transmitted by us to our posterity; as an estate specially belonging to the people of this kingdom without any reference whatever to any other more general or prior right.

He goes on to say that this practice is 'the happy result of following nature, which is wisdom without reflection and above it'.

> Whatever advantages are obtained by a state proceeding on these maxims, are locked fast as in a sort of family settlement, grasped as in a kind of mortmain for ever. By a constitutional policy, working after the pattern of nature, we receive, we hold, we transmit our government and our privileges, in the same manner in which we enjoy and transmit our property and our lives.[9]

Now the way of thinking and behaving which Burke is here recommending was founded upon an identification of the rules and spirit of English society with the rules and spirit of the common law; and the common law had taken shape as a law of real property. It cannot be quite coincidental that in these passages Burke is talking of the advantages which accrue when a people lay claim to their liberties on exactly the same principles as those on which they inherit their estates. From the words which have just been quoted he goes on without interruption to embark upon the famous passage which runs:

> The institutions of policy, the goods of fortune, the gifts of

Providence, are handed down, to us and from us, in the same course and order. Our political system is placed in a just correspondence and symmetry with the order of the world, and with the mode of existence decreed to a permanent body composed of transitory parts; wherein, by the disposition of a stupendous wisdom, moulding together the great mysterious incorporation of the human race, the whole, at one time, is never old, or middle-aged, or young, but in a condition of unchangeable constancy, moves on through the varied tenour of perpetual decay, fall, renovation, and progression.

This has many times been cited as evidence of Burke's vision of society as an organic community, not composed atomistically of self-regarding individuals; and so indeed it is. But if we seek for the historical genesis of these thoughts, may it not lie in the chain of association formed by the words 'entail', 'family settlement', 'mortmain', 'incorporation', which occur in that order in the passages that have been quoted? 'In this choice of inheritance', Burke says, 'we have given to our frame of polity the image of a relation in blood.'[10] That is, we have made the state a family; but have we not done so by constituting it a family in the sense in which a family is a relation in law? By entailing our inheritance of liberties we have established a family settlement, based upon a mortmain; and it is when this is done, not in virtue of the tie of blood solely, that the family becomes an immortal corporation. We have made the state not only a family, but a trust; not so much a biological unity, or the image of one, as an undying *persona ficta*, which secures our liberties by vesting the possession of them in an immortal continuity. And all this has been done by the simple device – the most superb of all legal fictions – of identifying the principles of political liberty with the principles of our law of landed property. Burke sees this as an act of conformity with the order of nature, and it is not the intention of this paper to deny the importance which his conception of nature had in the formation of his political philosophy. But the above passages may at the same time be cited as evidence that he had achieved a genuine historical insight into the character of English political thinking. He says, quite explicitly, that it is the greatest accomplishment of our thought to have based our claim to liberty on an idea drawn from the law of real property; and historical enquiry seems to confirm that it was the influence of that law on political thought which had given rise to the very English way of thinking and behaving which Burke accurately describes, and with which he identifies himself.

It has now to be shown that a doctrine of traditionalism, very much akin to Burke's own, grew out of the concept of the ancient constitution. To do this we need to remind ourselves that this concept was founded on the identification of English law with custom, and that the term custom had more than one connotation for common lawyers. Primarily, it implied that all that was custom was immemorial; but this need not – though it often did – imply a static and unchanging content. A second implication, of no less importance than the first, was that custom was constantly being subjected to the test of experience, so that if immemorial it was, equally, always up to date, and that it was ultimately rooted in nothing other than experience. We may put the point in the words of Sir John Davies, James I's Attorney-General for Ireland, who had written 'the *Common Law of England* is nothing else but the *Common Custome* of the Realm'.[11] The essence of this law was in immemorial usage; it consisted of a series of 'reasonable acts once done', which, having been found 'good and beneficial to the people', had been repeated 'without interruption time out of mind' and so had become a law recognized, declared, and recorded as such in the courts of common law. The act itself was nothing but a response to experience, and the test by which it had been found good and beneficial nothing but further experience. From about 1600, if not from much earlier, this concept lay at the heart of English thinking about law and exerted a potent influence on thinking about politics and society. It will be observed that though Davies refers to the act in usage as 'reasonable', he nowhere suggests that its rationality was the proof that it was good and beneficial, still less that reason gave it the force of law. No doubt he regarded usage and experience as in some sense or other rational behaviour, but he does not equate law with reason; and both in his writings and in Coke's, signs may be found that common lawyers were already disposed to draw a distinction between the wisdom of the law, founded in experience, and the reflective reason of individuals, which they regarded as a different instrument designed to produce different and perhaps lesser results.

Two famous quotations from Coke may make the point for us. The first is from his notorious and variously reported interview with James I.

Then the king said, that he thought the law was founded upon reason, and that he and others had reason as well as the judges: to which it was answered by me, that true it was, that God had endowed his Majesty with excellent science, and great endowments of nature; but his Majesty was not learned in the laws of his realm of England, and causes which concern the life, or inheritance, or goods, or fortunes of his subjects are not to be decided by natural reason, but by the artificial reason and judgment of law, which law is an act which requires long study and experience before that a man can attain to the knowledge of it.[12]

The other is from *Calvin's Case*:

our days upon the earth are but as shadows in respect of the old ancient days and times past, wherein the laws have been by the wisdom of the most excellent men, in many successions of ages, by long and continuall experience, (the trial of light and truth) fined and refined, which no one man, (being of so short a time) albeit he had in his head the wisdom of all the men in the world, in any one age could ever have effected or attained unto.[13]

In both these passages Coke's contention appears to be the same. Philosophic reason could not by its own efforts reconstruct the law, because the law's origin is not in any philosophical assumption but in a multitude of particular decisions. The only way to know the law, therefore, is to know the law, by becoming acquainted with the innumerable decisions and digests of decisions which it contains. Selden believed that a deeper understanding of the law could be attained by historical knowledge of the circumstances in which the various decisions had been taken, but Coke gives no sign of believing even that; for him, there was little to be known about the history of the law except that it was immemorial. No one man, by taking thought, could reproduce the infinitely complex train of experiences and decisions which had led the law to be what it was; and Coke seems also to be denying that there exist any means whereby the intellect can, by laying down axioms, assumptions, or universal propositions, reproduce the law as a process of reasoning. The law, in short, cannot be reduced to general principles, or scientific laws, and their consequences; and in this very lawyer-like proposition we seem to have one origin of the long tradition of sceptical and conservative empiricism in English social thought. If so, the long outmoded concept of immemorial law has done much to make our thought what it is today; for it was the principle that the law was immemorial that made common lawyers realize that its origin was not in men's assent to universally acceptable propositions, but in 'one emergency following upon another as wave follows wave; only one great fact with respect to which, since it is unique, there can be no generalizations'.[14]

It seems, then, that an empirical and traditionalist way of thought, sceptical of systematic reason, formed part of the intellectual equipment of common lawyers and was grounded on the same assumptions as belief in the ancient constitution. With the next step in the story, we arrive at the first direct clash in the history of English thought between this outlook and the political rationalism which we learn from Burke to regard as its antithesis. A few years after the Restoration Thomas Hobbes completed his *Dialogue of the Common Laws*, and in this work set out to deny the law of England was either immemorial custom or Coke's 'artificial reason'.[15] To Hobbes, consistent in this dialogue with the ideas of his major political works, society was composed of and by individuals employing their 'natural reason', which dictated to the individual that certain things must be done for his own preservation and, later, that certain things must be done by all for the preservation of all. To enforce the doing of these things a sovereign was set up, and doing them became a law for all when established as such by his command. But he did not possess more 'natural reason', let alone reason of another sort, than that possessed by other men, and it was by the natural reason that he shared with his subjects that the laws he enjoined were seen to be necessary. All that was artificial about the sovereign was his power to command. Any doctrine of an artificial reason, known only to professionals as their craft mystery and ultimately inscrutable to reflective reason, appeared to Hobbes dangerous alike to the human mind and to the stability of the state, as tending to monopolize power in the hands of Bentham's Judge and Co. He therefore found it necessary to maintain that law was the product of natural reason and should be such as any intelligent individual might frame for himself; and in so far as the reason he spoke of was scientific, arguing logically from universal truths, Hobbes maintained the possibility of a social science. This was the ground on which he was met by Chief Justice Sir Matthew Hale – though Hale's reply remained unfinished and unpublished[16] – and both here and in his *History of the Common Law*, Hale set out in opposition to individualistic rationalism an empirical and traditionalist view of the law which can be shown to be founded on the common-law concept of custom.

Hale was a philosopher as well as a judge – though his philosophy was as case-made as his law – and he began his reply to Hobbes with epistemological considerations. Reason, he said, was the faculty of discerning the necessary connections between things, and a man became expert at law, medicine, or some other form of learning as he applied this faculty to different classes of things; so that, though the same faculty of reason might be at work in all cases, a man expert in one field might be hopelessly inept in another – it was the things of which a man had experience that determined the character of his knowledge, and the notion of a naturally reasonable individual who became, simply by applying his reason, good at making and applying laws must therefore be dismissed.[17] Law was a matter of applied morals, and this field was a specially complicated one; for the fact that a man was expert at moral philosophy, that is at discerning the connections between moral ideas, was no guarantee of his success in applying these ideas to practical decisions. This was a class of problem in which Hale thought a power of discerning necessary connections likely to be of very little use, for he was above all impressed with the complexity and instability of the human context in which such decisions had to be taken, and was disposed to regard each decision not as the recurrence of a regular phenomenon but as something unique. Two quotations may help to make his thought clear.

> it is a thing of greatest difficulty, So to Contrive and Order any Lawe that while it remedyes or provides against one Inconvenience, it introduceth not a worse or an equall . . . the texture of Humane affairs is not unlike the Texture of a diseased bodey labouring under Maladies, it may be of so various natures that such Phisique as may be proper for the Cure of one of the maladies may be destructive in relation to the other, and the Cure of one disease may be the death of the patient.[18]

This instability of context affected not only the practical but the moral problem:

> every Morall Action is or may be diversified from another by Circumstances which are of soe great an Influence into the true nature and determination of Morall Actions that they very frequently specifically difference Actions that are materially the Same, and give such Allayes and abatements or advances and improvements to them that Scarce two Morall Actions in the world are every way commensurate. And these Circumstances are Soe various and their Influx into Morall Actions so different and Soe difficult to be discerned, or adequately estimated, that the makeinge of Laws touching them is very difficult.[19]

Here, plainly, we have the social philosophy of a judge, a man accustomed to viewing each moral problem on its merits as it comes before him, and to viewing it as entangled in the endlessly complex web of practical social reality. This alone might explain Hale's disposition to view each problem as a unique complexity and to doubt whether there exist universally valid patterns of thought with which natural reason may legislate for society – to doubt, in short, the efficacy of a social science. But we cannot leave out of account the further fact that Hale was accustomed to dealing with such problems with the aid of a law which already insisted that there were no universally valid rules, only accumulated experience, and that the only outcome of experience was a precedent which never achieved finality as a universal rule. It is law of this kind which Hale goes on to recommend as an artificial reason more effective and reliable than Hobbes's natural reason. Directly after the words last quoted, we find him advocating reliance on ancient law in preference to the dictates of individual reason, and his argument for doing so comes in a double form. In the first place, he argues that experience does what reason cannot do – it finds out the 'conveniences and inconveniences' that attend the operation of a particular law, which the complexity and instability of the social context render it impossible 'for the wisest Councill of Men att first to foresee'. Secondly, and in consequence of this, he argues that ancient laws very often defy our criticisms, for the reason that while we have the law itself we no longer know the circumstances in which, or the reasons for which, it was originally made. Therefore we cannot criticize those reasons; but the mere fact that the law survives furnishes a presumption, not only that the law was originally good, but that it has adequately answered the needs of all the situations in which it has subsequently been invoked. There is a further presumption that it will adequately solve our problem, even though to our intellects, evaluating the problem and the law, it may not appear so.

From all this it seems to follow that the law is inscrutable; it is reasonable, Hale says, but our reason cannot tell why. Historical reconstruction cannot tell us, since the law itself may be the only evidence we have concerning its history; philosophical consideration cannot tell us, because the law is nothing but a record of particular decisions and is not founded on any universal rational propositions. It can only be known as a collection of particulars.

Now if any the most refined Braine under heaven would goe about to Enquire by Speculation, or by reading of Plato or

Aristotle, or by Considering the Laws of the Jewes, or other Nations, to find out how Landes descend in England, or how Estates are there transferred, or transmitted among us, he wou'd lose his Labour, and spend his Notions in vaine, till he acquainted himselfe with the Lawes of England, and the reason is because they are Institutions introduced by the will and Consent of others . . . the Positions and Conclusions in the Mathematicks have more Evidence in them, and are more Naturally Seated in the minde than Institutions of Laws, which in a greate measure depend upon the Consent and appointment of the first Institutors.[20]

The law does not consist of first principles and their logical consequences, the necessary connections between which can be known by reason. It consists of a series of particular decisions, each of which was framed in circumstances no longer known and has been tested by experience in circumstances which may similarly have been forgotten. All that need – very often all that can – be known of it is that it has survived an indefinite number of such tests, and this is enough to create a presumption that it is more efficacious than our intellects can comprehend. Such is Hale's reply to the rationalism of Thomas Hobbes, a reply which visibly gives expression to the social philosophy of the common law and is essentially a development of common-law assumptions concerning the law and its workings. Only an immemorial customary law could satisfy Hale's requirements or give birth to his ideas, for if law were founded on the decisions of known men in recorded circumstances it could be evaluated and criticized both on rational and on historical grounds and would lose the ultimate inscrutability with which Hale, a sceptical traditionalist, is seeking to invest it. There is little about custom in the reply to Hobbes, but in his *History of the Common Law*[21] Hale worked out, at length and with subtlety, a view of law as immemorial custom in perpetual adaptation.

On his interpretation of immemorial law, it was not necessary that it should have retained its present content since time beyond memory, for law consisted solely in a series of responses to particular exigencies and what rendered it immemorial was not the stability of its content but the continuity (since time beyond memory) of the process of adapting old precedents to new situations. As this process continued the old precedent became, by degrees and generally insensibly, both refined and enlarged, until it took on a meaning beyond anything those who first established it could have intended. Therefore, one would not seek to know the meaning of a law by going back to the circumstances of its first institution, and indeed in most cases neither these nor the subsequent stages of its development could be accurately known. Hale united a subtle sense of historical growth with a high degree of scepticism as to the possibility of historical knowledge, and in this as in all else he was a true common lawyer in his thought. He regarded the records of the law as very nearly all the evidence existing concerning the history of the law, and these records, as he knew, did not often rehearse the circumstances in which they had been made and were in essence little more than a series of declarations of what the immemorial law was, through which nevertheless ran a thread of almost imperceptible change. Hale, therefore, despaired of knowing when any particular point in the law had originated, or of recovering its original meaning from its successive reformulations, or of establishing what the state of the law as a whole had been at any moment in time past; nor did he think that this mattered.[22] To him the law was in flux, constantly being restated by people, parliament, and judges in response to their immediate practical needs, and what was of importance was that they had chosen to do this rather by restating old decisions than by creating new out of their rational estimate of each situation as it arose. Because they operated in this manner the law was perpetually in change and you could neither analyse what it was nor reconstruct its history; but they were constantly drawing on and applying the accumulated experience of their ancestors, even though they could not explain what it was nor demonstrate its rationality. Hale repeatedly uses the image of law as a river, and what matters to him is not the analysis of the water it contains but the unchecked continuity of its flow. Society constantly produces law; doing this by refining on old precedents, it accumulates a wisdom which is rooted in experience and never rationally demonstrable or capable of analysis into its elements. It is the fact that it is the record of society's experience that makes law immemorial.

Such is Sir Matthew Hale's philosophy of the common law; its kinship with the traditionalism we ascribe to Burke should be evident. The question now to be settled is that of the connections between Burke and the common-law thought of the seventeenth century, and here we may begin by reminding ourselves that Burke alluded to the belief in an immemorial constitution as a thing well known to himself and his readers, of peculiar importance to the understanding of seventeenth-century constitutional history, and as a way of thinking still alive in his own time. Burke was then aware of common-law thought both as a phenomenon of the seventeenth century, and as a phenomenon of the eighteenth; and it may be worth commencing under the former head and investigating his knowledge of Hale as the common-law theorist whose ideas most resembled his own. There is no reason to suppose that he knew the manuscript reply to Hobbes, though there were copies in the Harleian MSS and in the collection of Francis Hargreave;[23] but the *History of the Common Law* was one of the standard books of the eighteenth century, and in an early work from Burke's hand we have his opinion of it. That opinion is unfavourable, but illuminating. There is a fragment, which may date from about Burke's thirtieth year, known under the title of *Essay towards a History of the Laws of England*; after remarking that few attempts have been made to provide such a history, he continues:

Lord Chief Justice Hale's History of the Common Law is, I think, the only one, good or bad, which we have. But with all the deference justly due to so great a name, we may venture to assert that this performance, though not without merit, is wholly unworthy of the high reputation of its author: the sources of our English law are not well, nor indeed fairly, laid open; the ancient judicial proceedings are touched in a very slight and transient manner; and the great changes and remarkable revolutions in the law, together with their causes, down to his time, are scarcely mentioned.

Of this defect I think there were two principal causes; the first, a persuasion hardly to be eradicated from the minds of our lawyers, that the English law has continued very much in the same state from an antiquity to which they will allow hardly any sort of bounds. The second is, that it was formed and grew up among ourselves; that it is in every respect peculiar to this island; and that if the Roman or any foreign laws attempted to intrude into its composition, it has always had the vigour to shake them off, and return to the purity of its primitive constitution.

These opinions are flattering to national vanity and professional narrowness . . . we have been, and in a great measure still are, extremely tenacious of them. If these principles are admitted, the history of the law must in a great measure be deemed superfluous. For to what purpose is a history of a law, of which it is impossible to trace the beginning, and which, during its continuance, has admitted no essential change? Or why should we search foreign laws, or histories, for explanation or ornament of that which is wholly our own; and by which we are effectually distinguished from all other countries? Thus the law has been confined, and drawn up into a narrow and inglorious study . . . which deduced the spirit of the law, not from original justice or legal conformity, but from causes foreign to it, and altogether whimsical . . . the truth is, the present system of our laws, like our language and our learning, is a very mixed and heterogeneous mass; in some respects our own; in more borrowed from the policy of foreign nations and compounded, altered and variously modified, according to the various necessities, which the manners, the religion and the commerce of the people have at different times imposed.[24]

Here the young Burke, perhaps not long out of the Middle Temple, shows the same vigorous awareness of the tradition of common-law thought and belief in the ancient constitution as he was to display in the *Reflections*, thirty years later, when he wrote: 'In the matter of fact, for the greater part, these authors appear to be in the right; perhaps not always.' But here his attitude is hostile, and his criticism is founded on the quite accurate perception that if the law is absolutely unique and absolutely immemorial, there is nothing about its history that can usefully be said. In one sense, he was being unfair to Hale, who had many times denied that an immemorial law meant a law whose content never changed and had asserted, in words foreshadowing Burke's own, that the law had been transformed utterly in the course of its history. But the difference between Hale and Burke lies deeper: Burke here is asserting, what Hale had virtually denied, that the course of change in the law can be historically explained by relating it to the operation of factors outside the law and independently known. To Hale a legal decision was a response to some momentary situation, of which as a rule no record was preserved other than the decision to which it had given rise, so that there was little prospect of historical reconstruction. Burke is visibly of the opinion that there is more evidence about the history of the law than the law by itself supplies, and the crucial point of his difference with the common-law school lies here. In making this point, we should note that he speaks with two distinguishable voices. His insistence that the law is derived in large part from foreign nations may have been drawn from Spelman – whom he discusses[25] – or the other seventeenth-century scholars who had investigated the Germanic, feudal, or Norman origins of much English law. But a certain emphasis should be given to Burke's use of the words 'the spirit of our laws' and his reference to 'the various necessities, which the manners, the religion and the commerce of the people have at different times imposed'. Here is thoroughly eighteenth-century language: the idea that peoples or their institutions possess a 'spirit', or historical character, which may be understood by relating it to just such things as 'the manners, the religion and the commerce of the people', might come direct from Montesquieu or any of the Scottish historical sociologists with whom Burke was later to be acquainted.[26] The words prefigure the *Speech on Conciliation with America* and the orator who was to depict the 'spirit' of the American colonists in as impressive a passage as eighteenth-century historiography contains. At this point in his thought, then, Burke is thoroughly of his age in believing that laws can be understood by reference to the operation of general social factors, and he rejects the empiricist mystique of the immemorial partly on these grounds. He implies clearly that the history of the law can be made intelligible.

But he knew, when writing this early essay, that if the law were truly immemorial and as Hale had described it, the reverse was true and its condition in the past could not be reconstructed. He therefore understood on what his position was based, and what its contrary was, and this helps us to understand the fact that in 1782 we find him reversing it and returning to a doctrine very like Hale's. In May of that year he composed but did not deliver the speech *On a Motion Made in the House of Commons . . . for a Committee to Enquire into the State of the Representation of the Commons in Parliament*.[27] He divided the arguments he meant to oppose into two kinds. First there was the claim that representation was the natural right of the individual, and it was in answering this that Burke used the following words:

> Our constitution is a prescriptive constitution; it is a constitution whose sole authority is that it has existed time out of mind. . . . Your king, your lords, your judges, your juries, grand and little, all are prescriptive; and what proves it is the disputes not yet concluded, and never near becoming so, when any of them first originated. Prescription is the most solid of all titles, not only to property, but, which is to secure that property, to government. . . . It is accompanied with another ground of authority in the constitution of the human mind – presumption. It is a presumption in favour of any settled scheme of government against any untried project, that a nation has long existed and flourished under it. It is a better presumption even of the choice of a nation, far better than any sudden and temporary arrangement by actual election. Because a nation

is not an idea only of local extent, and individual momentary aggregation; but it is an idea of continuity, which extends in time as well as in numbers and in space. And this is a choice, not of one day, or one set of people, not a tumultuary and giddy choice; it is a deliberate election of ages and generations; it is a constitution made by what is ten thousand times better than choice, it is made by the peculiar circumstances, occasions, tempers, dispositions, and moral, civil and social habitudes of the people, which disclose themselves only in a long space of time. It is a vestment, which accommodates itself to the body. Nor is prescription of government formed upon blind, unmeaning prejudices – for man is a most unwise and a most wise being. The individual is foolish; the multitude, for the moment, is foolish, when they act without deliberation; but the species is wise, and, when time is given to it, as a species it always acts right.[28]

Now these sentences (though never spoken by their author) are treasured in the anthologies of English conservatism and repeated in nearly every textbook on the history of political thought; but the meaning which they had for Burke and his intended auditors can be appreciated only when we regard them as a restatement of the classic and familiar doctrine of the ancient constitution, in which its two fundamental assumptions are brought out and elaborated. Burke's prescriptive constitution has two characteristics: it is immemorial – and this is what makes it prescriptive and gives it authority as a constitution – and it is customary, rooted in something 'better than choice . . . the peculiar circumstances . . . and . . . habitudes of the people'. This is Burke's argument against a reform of the representation founded upon the principle of natural right. Every word he uses may be paralleled from the traditional doctrines of the common lawyers, the doctrines he had once rejected in his criticism of Hale but was to espouse once again in the *Reflections*: and common-law thought, as Burke could have found it in Hale and was (wherever he learned it) expounding it here, contained an explicitly formulated theory of conservative traditionalism.

Was Burke an antiquarian, expounding seventeenth-century ways of thinking to a generation of uncomprehending Lockeans? This conclusion easily follows from some of the unstated assumptions upon which the history of ideas is commonly conducted,[29] but it can be disproved by the simple exercise of observing how Burke's draft of May 1782 develops. There is, he says, a second argument in favour of reform, which he now proceeds to answer in the same way as the argument based on natural right; and it consists in the assertion that the constitution has fallen away from its original principles – here supposed to include the principle of representation on the basis of numbers – and must now be restored to them. This argument Burke answers with an assertion of startling simplicity and yet venerable antiquity – one implicit in the debate between Hale and Hobbes; that an immemorial constitution is not based upon any original principles and that consequently none can be alleged as a means of evaluating its workings.

> To ask whether a thing which has always been the same stands to its usual principle, seems to me to be perfectly absurd; for how do you know the principles but from the construction? and if that remains the same, the principles remain the same. It is true, that to say your constitution is what it has been is no sufficient defence for those who say it is a bad constitution. It is an answer to those who say it is a degenerate constitution. . . .
>
> On what grounds do we go to restore our constitution to what it has been at one definite period, or to reform and reconstruct it upon principles more conformable to a sound theory of government? A prescriptive government, such as ours, never was the work of any legislator, never was made upon any foregone theory. It seems to me a preposterous way of reasoning, and a perfect confusion of ideas, to take the theories which learned and speculative men have made from that government, and then, supposing it made on those theories, which were made from it, to accuse the government as not corresponding with them.[30]

The sentiments of the second paragraph can be rediscovered in Professor Oakeshott's *Political Education*,[31] but the passage as a whole might have been written by Hale. The requirements which the constitution has existed to satisfy can only be inferred from its structure, and if the structure is immemorial nothing can be inferred about its functioning at any particular time. Consequently, we can never know the principles on which it has functioned, either at its origin or at any subsequent period; and only by partial and speculative abstraction can we discover any principles which we may call common to its entire history. Its true basis, moreover, will not lie in these principles but in the mere fact of prescription. Burke, in fact, has reverted to the position he formerly rebuked Hale for adopting – that little or nothing can be known of the history of an immemorial constitution save that there is a great weight of presumption in its favour; and like Hale, he roots his argument in the idea that the law is immemorial and customary.

He developed this argument as a reply to the contention that the constitution had degenerated from its original principles. This doctrine was indeed employed by Pitt and other speakers for the motion of May 1782, and is a staple argument in the literature of the county movement. It may be traced back through James Burgh to Bolingbroke, and on through Major Cartwright and the literature of the next half-century of frustrated reformers.[32] Its importance for our purposes is that it was clearly no more than a partial rationalization of the traditional common-law doctrine. There exists an ancient constitution, it said, whose claim upon us lies largely in its antiquity; but this constitution was founded upon principles which can be known, and we are therefore able to know when it has degenerated from them and to restore it to them. This Burke denied. He was, therefore, faced not only with a rationalist doctrine based on a Lockean theory of natural right, but also with a modified form of the seventeenth-century 'ancient constitution'. It emerges that a political language was still in regular use in 1782, based on assumptions which had been established in English thought as far back as the age of Coke by the theory and practice of the common law and had not – as it is too easy to suppose they had – been submerged in a tide of rationalism.

In the conflicting ideologies of the first period of parliamentary reform it is possible to discern reaffirmations of a number of typical seventeenth-century ideas. For example, Leveller anti-Normanism – the doctrine that existing laws and institutions are unjust, being founded in Norman conquest and usurpation – reappears in Paine and Cartwright; and it has been argued elsewhere[33] that there is no need to suppose direct contact or transmission between the ideas of 1648 and 1780. In both periods it was usual to declare that the essential soundness of the laws was proved by their having survived the Conquest, and it is not to be wondered at if the same affirmation called forth the same negation; Overton, Paine, and their adversaries all spoke the same language. Burke, too, was in the part of his thought under inspection repeating the assumptions of the seventeenth century. Faced with an argument for reform that presupposed the existence of an ancient constitution, he responded by pointing out the foundation on which that belief was really based: the identification of law with immemorial custom, from which it was possible to deduce an entire philosophy of sceptical conservatism and empirical traditionalism. Hale had deduced that philosophy and Burke, who also deduced it, was acquainted with part of

Hale's work and had criticized it for the very positions he was afterwards to take up. But the present essay is not designed to show that Hale 'influenced' Burke or that Burke 'derived' his ideas from Hale; such phraseology is universally agreed to be inadequate. If any importance attaches to Burke's readings in the ancient-constitution thought of the previous century, it may be that they helped to create his intense historical awareness of the common-law tradition as 'the stationary policy of this kingdom' – as a factor in shaping English political thought and behaviour. The point which it seems most important to establish is that Hale and Burke reached similar conclusions because they were arguing from similar assumptions, from a common acceptance of a belief in immemorial customary law which, as Burke found it necessary to explain and Hale did not, was one of the cardinal beliefs of the society and tradition in which both men lived. Burke's traditionalism is rooted in a way of thought already traditional; it may be possible to discern, from the way in which he restated it, that it was a tradition beginning to fade.

It is important that this analysis should not seem to claim too much. It is confined to one aspect of Burke's thought – his doctrine of the superior wisdom of traditional institutions – and it treats even that in isolation. There are many things in his social and political philosophy besides his traditionalism, and it is not suggested that his membership of the common-law tradition explains all or any of them. To understand their meaning and their presence among his ideas, it may well be necessary to invoke the natural law, the philosophy of Hume, the sociology of Montesquieu, or the rise of a romantic sensibility, and even more complex operations will obviously be needed if any one aspect of his thought is to be reduced to philosophical unity with any other. It is certainly not suggested that Burke's unified view of reality – if he had one – was derived from the common law; on the other hand it is suggested that in order to explain his traditionalism, regarded simply as an isolated factor, there is no need to suppose more than his continued employment and highly developed understanding of certain concepts which came from the common law (as he recognized) and were generally in use as part of the political language he spoke with his contemporaries. In this respect, Burke's thought was formed by the contemplation of English society and history with the aid of concepts traditionally used for that purpose, and by the contemplation of those concepts themselves.

# NOTES

1  F. Meinecke, *Die Entstehung des Historismus* (2nd edn, Munich, R. Oldenbourg, 1946), part I, ch. VI; G.H. Sabine, *A History of Political Theory* (New York, R. Holt, 1945), ch. XXIX, pp. 605–7, 612, 614, 618.

2  Meinecke, op. cit., p. 278.

3  P. Laslett (ed.), *John Locke: Two Treatises of Government* (Cambridge, Cambridge University Press, 1960), introduction, *passim*.

4  Burke, *Reflections on the Revolution in France*, in *Works* (Bohn's Libraries edn, London, George Bell and Sons, 1901), II, pp. 304–5.

5  The words in quotation marks are, of course, from the closing sentence of Locke's *Second Treatise*. Burke did not allude to that work in this part of the *Reflections*.

6  What follows is to some extent a development and reformulation of some points made in Pocock, *The Ancient Constitution and the Feudal Law* (London, Cambridge University Press, 1957) – hereafter referred to as *ACFL* – especially chs II, VII, and IX.

7  For the foregoing see *ACFL*, ch. II and generally.

8  Burke, op. cit, p. 306.

9  ibid., p. 307.

10  ibid.

11  Davies, *Irish Reports* (1614 – London edn of 1674), preface.

12  Coke, *Twelfth Reports*, Prohibitions del Roy (12 Co. Rep. 65).

13  Coke, *Seventh Reports*, Calvin's Case (7 Co. Rep. 3b).

14  H.A.L. Fisher's preface to his *History of Europe* (London, Eyre & Spottiswoode, 1946), p. v.

15  Hobbes, *English Works* (ed. W. Molesworth, London, 1839–45), VI, pp. 5–7, 14–15, 62–3.

16  It is printed as an appendix (pp. 499–513) to vol. V of W. S. Holdsworth's *History of English Law* (London, Methuen, 1924). A hint at the date of its composition may be found in John Aubrey's letter of 3 Feb. 1673, in which he seeks to further the publication of a work on law by Hobbes, saying that Hale 'has read it and much mislikes it' (*Brief Lives*, ed. Clark, 1898, I, p. 394). It is still very improbable that Aubrey is referring to the *Elements of Law*, as some scholars have concluded.

17  Holdsworth, op. cit., V, pp. 501–2.

18  ibid., p. 503.

19  ibid., p. 504.

20  ibid., p. 505.

21  This too was published posthumously in 1714. Since Hobbes's *Dialogue* was unpublished until 1682, the whole story of the contact between these two minds, of some importance to the understanding of the recurrent themes in English political thought, was overlooked until Holdsworth and Pollock brought it to light.

22  The key passage for the above interpretation of Hale's thoughts is in ch. IV of his *History of the Common Law* (2nd edn, 1716, pp. 57–65). See also *ACFL*, pp. 174–8.

23  Holdsworth, op. cit., V, p. 499.

24  Burke, *Works* (Bohn's Libraries edn, London, George Bell and Sons,

1877), VI, pp. 413–16. This fragmentary study is usually exempted from the controversy concerning the authenticity of the *Essay towards the Abridgment of the English History*, with which it has been printed.

25 Burke, loc. cit., p. 414.

26 C. P. Courtney, *Montesquieu and Burke* (Oxford, 1963)

27 The speech does not occur in *Hansard*. In the editions of Burke's collected works it appears in an incomplete form.

28 Burke, loc. cit., pp. 146–7.

29 It is easy, for reasons glanced at earlier in this paper, to think of Locke as if he transformed the whole character of English political thinking and inaugurated a period in which it was conducted exclusively in rationalist terms. The present writer was once led (*ACFL*, p. 243) to speak of the customary concept of English law as 'running underground' between Hale and Burke, and an American reviewer developed the idea of a 'rationalist hiatus' in English thought. To such over-simplifications the history of ideas seems prone.

30 Burke, loc. cit., p. 148.

31 P. Laslett (ed.), *Philosophy, Politics and Society* (Oxford, Blackwell, 1956), pp. 7–10.

32 H. Butterfield, *George III, Lord North and the People* (London, Bell, 1949), pp. 341–52; Christopher Hill, *Puritanism and Revolution* (London, Secker & Warburg, 1958), ch. III, 'The Norman Yoke', pp. 94–122.

33 *ACFL*, p. 127.

# JEREMY BENTHAM AND J. S. MILL

## Chapter Twelve

# INTRODUCTION

Although its genealogy can be traced back at least as far as Hobbes, utilitarianism, as an explicit doctrine, emerged from the eighteenth-century movement of ideas known as the Enlightenment. Two central projects of the Enlightenment were, firstly, to articulate and forward a scientific understanding of the nature of things, more particularly of man and society; and, secondly, to fill the vacuum left by what the philosophers saw as the crumbling of the older foundations of ethical certainties.

The attempt to construct a science of society was dominated by the example of the physical sciences, and particularly by an appeal to those who, it was thought, had established firmly the character and universal scope of scientific enquiry – Bacon, the propounder of scientific method, and Newton, its brilliant exponent. These exemplars were, however, by no means unambiguous and the attempt to follow them led to the development of a number of different models of a social science which, if never subject to rigid *apartheid*, none the less followed lines of separate development in the nineteenth century. One possibility was the apparently strict application of the Baconian method, to derive inductively from an examination of empirical historical material some general, historically unconditioned, repetitive laws of human society and social behaviour. The most effective exponent of this model was Montesquieu; and it was this view of a political science that was to be used by Macaulay to belabour the utilitarians. Another possibility was to uncover the laws of human development or progress as a whole, or at the least to trace and explain the actual patterning of human history over time. This, as we have seen, was an essential element of Rousseau's investigation; it was exploited by Adam Smith and other thinkers of the Scottish Enlightenment; it was used more systematically by the theorists of progress, Turgot and Condorcet; and it was to be for the great nineteenth-century philosophers of history – Comte, Hegel, and Marx – the foundation of scientific social analysis. A third possibility was to discover some single, central organizing principle of social movement which would explain human behaviour as gravity had explained the movement of physical bodies. This suggested that the key to a successful social science lay, not in the tangled web of history, but in an account of the motivating forces driving individuals. This the utilitarians found in the hedonist psychological axiom, that men's behaviour is to be explained by their pursuit of pleasure and avoidance of pain.

The ethical dilemmas of the Enlightenment arose from the weakening, at least amongst intellectuals, of the old certainties of Christianity and the natural law tradition. These certainties suffered particularly from the gradual acceptance of sensationalist epistemology, with its insistence that all knowledge, including moral knowledge, derived, not from revelation or sacerdotal authority or innate ideas, but from human experience through the senses. One attempt to fill this ethical vacuum lay in the assertion of a new source of human values – that which was productive of human happiness. Pleasure and pain are the sole standards of right and wrong.

There is no better illustration of the confluence of these two intellectual streams than the opening words of Bentham's *Introduction to the Principles of Morals and Legislation*. 'Nature has placed men under the governance of two sovereign masters, *pain* and *pleasure*. It is for them alone to point out what we ought to do, as well as to determine what we shall do.' So the pursuit of happiness, the maximizing of pleasure and the minimizing of pain, explains why people act as they do and also provides the basis for ethical norms.

Even at this basic level, Bentham's utilitarianism poses a number of problems to which interpreters, followers, and critics of Bentham have repeatedly returned. One obvious problem is how satisfactory psychological hedonism is as an explanation of human behaviour. How far is it other than empty and tautological? Man necessarily pursues happiness. But in what does happiness consist? It consists, Bentham tells us, in achieving one's objects of desire and avoiding one's objects of aversion. Here, it has been claimed, what starts as apparently an empirical generalization – men pursue happiness – ends as an empty tautology – men want what they want and do not want what they do not want. On this view, psychological hedonism is empty unless some definite content can be given to 'objects of desire and aversion', unless we can specify what sort of ends people do actually set themselves. Utilitarian theory does offer such specification to the degree that it poses the rational egoist as the prototypical person, although it is a matter for debate how far

Bentham, still less John Stuart Mill, is fully committed to such a postulate. Other problems then arise with the question of how far this postulate of the rational, self-interested, happiness-maximizing individual can capture the complexities of human motivations and social interactions.

The relationship between Bentham's ethical and his psychological hedonism raises another set of problems. Taking the two theories together, the ethical theory might seem redundant. If it is indeed the case that pleasure and pain tell us what we ought to do as well as determining what we shall do, then surely what we must do because of psychological imperatives is what we are morally required to do. Whatever we do is right, and the common confrontation between desire and duty, interest and obligation, is a false opposition. Clearly, Bentham does not hold any such belief in the redundancy of ethics and wishes to maintain the distinction between an individual's interests and his moral duties. He does so by making a further distinction between individual and general utility, the first consisting in the augmentation of the individual's own happiness, the second in the augmentation of the happiness of the community at large. Crudely, it would seem, the psychological theory rests on the claim that the pursuit of individual utility is the mainspring of behaviour, whilst the ethical theory poses general utility maximization as the ground of individual moral obligations. In behavioural terms, what is at issue are the individual actor's pains and pleasures; in ethical terms, what is at issue are communally summed pains and pleasures. Now, although this distinction may save utilitarianism from the conflation of desire and duty, it raises further difficulties frequently referred to in the discussion of utilitarian ethics. Does not utilitarianism lay down as ethical ends for individuals objectives which they are psychologically incapable of pursuing? If men must act to maximize their own interests, how can they be urged to act so as to achieve a general interest, except in the presumably exceptional circumstances that what the general interest demands is what the individual's own interest requires?

These then are the major questions that arise from the juxtaposition of psychological and ethical hedonism in Bentham's thought – how far are the psychological axioms he poses sufficiently precise to allow any specific prediction of human behaviour; how coherent is the ethical theory and, more particularly, is there a contradiction between the ethical theory and the psychological axioms?

Bentham set the general utility principle at the centre of his ethical theory; he set it also at the centre of his political theory, in that it should, he urged, be the standard aimed at by legislators.

The more precise formulation of this principle that Bentham used in most of his writings was 'the greatest happiness of the greatest number', and the exploration of the implications and ambiguities of this formula and Bentham's attempt to apply it practically have formed a major part of discussion of classical utilitarianism.

One first implication that can be noticed is that Bentham saw this principle as the proper foundation of moral and legislative codes, that is that it was to be the basis of social rules. This raises the distinction, dear to modern discussants of utilitarianism, between act and rule utilitarianism and the possibility of conflict between the two. The possibility exists because, whilst some general rule (say one safeguarding private property) may be justified by the argument that its observance furthers the general interest over time, a breach of that rule (say the theft of food from a rich man by a starving man) might in particular instances further the aggregate interest. When early utilitarians noticed the distinction, as did the jurist John Austin, they emphatically articulated Bentham's assumption that rule utilitarianism had precedence.

Another aspect of Bentham's utility principle is, as Gunn points out below, that it is an aggregative principle. The utility of a moral or social rule can only be calculated by reckoning the utility effects of the rule on all members of the community and summing those effects. The community is a fictitious body and there can be no communal interest which is not in some way derived from a calculation of the interests of its individual members.

One difficulty that presents itself is how far it is possible to construct a 'felicific calculus', as Bentham termed it, a summation of individual interests. For this to be possible, some cardinal, and not just ordinal, weighting of the satisfaction of individual wants must be achievable. In other words, for an individual with three wants (A, B, C) it must be possible to say more than that his first preference is A, his second B, and his third C; it must be possible to say that the satisfaction of A will, for example, give him 60 units of utility, of B 40 units, and of C 20 units. A further difficulty arises from the claim that it is meaningful to add together these cardinally weighted individual utility values. What is assumed is that the utility of any one individual is strictly commensurate with the utilities of all other individuals. The questioning of this assumption was to be central to the debate amongst economists about the possibility of an inter-personal comparison of utilities.

Gunn suggests a way round some of these difficulties in arguing that, for Bentham, what the public interest primarily consists in is the furtherance of interests common to all members of the community. A paradigm case of such a common interest is security of property for it is an interest shared by all that they should be secure in whatever it is they do possess. If this is an accurate reading of Bentham, the difficulties of aggregation are bypassed, since the utility principle ceases essentially to be an aggregative principle. It is open to question how far Bentham did depart from his aggregative formula. In regard to property, for example, Bentham was not arguing just that any community needs some legal protection for private possessions, but also (despite allowing for some long-term measures of redistribution) that the existing – highly unequal – distribution of property should be safeguarded. His justification for this was entirely in aggregative terms, that is that any large-scale redistribution of wealth would have catastrophic effects on the wealth-creating capacities of the community.

This points to another contentious issue arising from Bentham's formulation of the utility principle, how far 'the greatest happiness of the greatest number' has distributive implications, more specifically how far it suggests that the interests of the majority should be favoured or how far it provides support for measures of equalization.

The inclusion in the formula of the phrase, 'of the greatest number', has been taken to have majoritarian implications. As against this, Bentham did disregard an alternative formulation of the utility principle current in his time, 'the greatest happiness of the majority'; and by the end of his life, he was willing to abandon the phrase leaving the bleak definition of general utility as 'the greatest happiness'. It is certainly not necessarily the case that the distribution which most benefits the majority is that which achieves the highest interest aggregate; and it is a question at issue whether or not Bentham believed this to be so.

Equally contentious is the question of whether or not Bentham's utility principle has egalitarian implications. Certainly, his dictum, 'everybody to count for one, nobody for more than one', seems to have such implications. The egalitarian inferences may, however, be fairly modest. What Bentham is claiming is that, in any felicific calculation, the effects of a legal rule on every member of the community must be taken into account and its beneficial or harmful effects on any particular person or section must not be accorded any special consideration, must not be multiple counted. But this does not imply that the benefits or disbenefits conferred by the rule need be equally distributed for the general utility to be enhanced.

If the general utility ought to be the objective of government, what does this require in more specific terms? Bentham points to four subordinate ends of legislation, all of them primarily economic

– to provide subsistence, to produce abundance, to favour equality, and to maintain security. In practice, Bentham argues, there is little that government can or should do directly to further most of these ends. The law has little need to induce people to provide subsistence for themselves; all it can do is to provide for subsistence indirectly by assuring them the secure enjoyment of the fruits of their labour. On abundance, Bentham rejects almost without discussion the notion that government can directly induce economic growth; again the most that can be done is to maintain economic incentives by securing property. Both of these claims are, of course, problematic. It is a matter of dispute how far Bentham's posing of equality as an end of legislation is sufficient grounds for claiming him as an egalitarian. What is interesting is that he justifies equalization, in an argument whose full implications were to be explored only later in the nineteenth century, on aggregative utility grounds. He does this through the assertion of diminishing marginal utility. The greater the amount of wealth possessed by a person, the lower would be the utility value to that person of any given increment of wealth; and, it followed, given a fixed volume of wealth in a community in which wealth was unequally distributed and equal abilities to derive happiness from wealth, overall utility satisfaction would be increased by transfers from the rich to the poor. This seems a powerful utilitarian argument for equality, but its practical implications are whittled away when Bentham turns his attention to the fourth end of legislation, security of property. This he insists is its prime end, and the first duty of the legislator is to maintain the established distribution of property. In this context, any conflict between security and equality must be decided in favour of security. Again Bentham argues this on aggregative utility grounds. Whilst for any given volume of wealth equal distribution will bring the greatest utility satisfaction, any larger-scale redistributive measures which undermine existing expectations will in time diminish drastically the total volume of wealth by destroying incentives to labour.

This discussion of the ends of legislation suggests that, for Bentham, the range of government intervention should be narrow; and indeed many have seen the utilitarians as advocates of the 'night-watchman' state, the minimal state. This characterization of the general disposition of Benthamite political thought is reinforced by their views on the relationship between state and economy and by Bentham's theory of punishment.

How far should legal regulation extend? It might be thought that the Benthamite answer would be that what could be left to moral discipline, to the individual's own disposition to act for the greatest happiness, should be so left; and what could not should be subject to state regulation. However, the Benthamite answer was not so clear cut. For the Benthamites subscribed to the general arguments of classical political economy, and these arguments suggested that there was one context – the market-place – in which individuals' amoral pursuit of their self-interest could achieve the general good. This theme has been developed through a distinction between a natural and an artificial identity of interests; on this view, utilitarians believed that in one area – crudely that of economic relations – the activities of rational egoists would naturally, automatically, harmonize, but in another – crudely that of politics – rational egoists would have to be forced through sanctions to act in a socially beneficial manner. Gunn – with others – rejects this separation of economics and politics; but perhaps the rejection is too abrupt. Classical political economy, in whose development utilitarians played an active role, had as a central concern the construction and exploration of the concept of the market, and it was for them a normative truth universally acknowledged that free exchange relations would achieve socially desirable end results. Individuals, seeking the means to their own satisfactions, produce goods and services which they can exchange with others for the goods and services they desire. The market mechanism itself, the laws of supply and demand, will promote the efficient investment of resources and labour. So rational egoists, thoughtless of any general social objectives, nevertheless generate a productive and commercial system maximizing the general utility; and any direct government intervention in economic activity was unnecessary to, might indeed be destructive of, a reconciliation between individual self-interest and the general good. Of course, the separation of economics and politics was not complete. It was accepted that, at least in modern commercial society, a complex market required considerable legal underpinning. The state must, for instance, provide for the safeguarding of contracts and other forms of transfer, establish a reliable common means of exchange, and above all secure property rights. The state must, in other words, establish the preconditions in which people could freely indulge their propensity (in Smith's words) to truck and barter; but it had no more direct interventionary role in the economy.

How can government perform this limited role? Men can be regulated, Bentham argued, in only two ways, by the carrot and the stick, by incentives and sanctions. Government had little choice between the two, since it must perforce rely on threats and punishment to win consistent conformity to legal rules. Since punishment involves the infliction of pain, legal intervention is almost always an evil in itself. Here Bentham states the classic liberal doctrine that non-restriction of liberty needs no defence but intrusion on it always requires justification. These assumptions are the grounds on which Bentham based his theory of punishment. The legislator should be niggardly with intervention and legal threats, and punishment can be justified only if the disutilities of its threat or imposition are outweighed by the disutilities of those anti-social actions the law is intended to counter. In developing this deterrence theory of punishment, Bentham returns to the postulate of the rational egoist and to his faith in the possibility of summing both individual and social utility values. The legislator can calculate what behaviour is detrimental to the general utility and can, by the imposition of sanctions, inhibit or even (if the detection of crime is certain) prevent that behaviour. Given that subjects are rational and punishment is an evil in itself, the sanctions neither need nor ought to be higher than necessary. The pains threatened need only be slightly greater than the benefits promised by the commission of the crime for the potential criminal to refrain, and any excess is morally unjustified. It was this argument that made Bentham one of the greatest legal reformers of his time.

This view of law and theory of punishment raises a number of questions which are still matters of philosophic debate. Can laws be characterized as commands backed by threats? Does the deterrence theory justify the minimal punishment argument? How far does it answer alternative justifications of punishment such as the retributive theory? Is it compatible with commonly accepted claims of justice, such as that only the guilty should be punished?

A problem this theory of punishment does seem to avoid is one that, as has been seen, arises from utilitarian ethics; there seems to be no incompatibility between the theory and utilitarian psychological assumptions. Men, subject to law, remain self-interested; it is merely that the legislator weights the utility values of the options before them. But the problem does creep back when the question is raised of why the legislator should act for the general utility. In his early writings, Bentham assumed the possibility of the disinterested legislator, an enlightened king or aristocrat, who would act for the general interest once he was instructed in what it required. Only when Bentham accepted that rulers could not escape the general self-interested character of humanity did the constitutional problem emerge, how to ensure that egoistic rulers would seek the general interest.

The answer reached by Bentham and the Benthamite Radicals

during the second decade of the nineteenth century was through representative democracy. Now, it was argued that to hope that rulers will, without some inducement, refrain from using their power to further their own ends is to hope for a breach of the laws of human nature. An inducement could be mounted if rulers' possession of power was made dependent on control from below through, in Bentham's words, 'Democratical ascendancy or the Ascendancy of the people'. Only when the whole community can check government through a representative democracy will the general interest become the actual end of government.

Different views can be taken about the general character of Benthamite democratic theory and two are presented below by Gunn and Ryan. For Gunn, Bentham is a precursor of modern pluralist theorists of democracy, and what he hoped for from democracy was the participation of all the varied social interests in the political process, which could be attained only by an extension of the political public. One difficulty in this reading is the constant complaint by Benthamites about the intrusion of 'sinister interests' in the political arena; this difficulty Gunn attempts to answer. Another difficulty is that there was just such a pluralist theory available in Bentham's own time, and the Benthamites deliberately and specifically rejected it. The conventional view, accepted by Whigs and Tories alike, was based on the notion of the representation of interests. The House of Commons should comprehend representatives of all sectional interests; the debate between Whigs and Tories on parliamentary reform centred on what sort of electoral system could best achieve this full representation of interests and more particularly on how the new interests emerging from industrialization could best be incorporated. The Benthamites consistently attacked this notion of the representation of interests and, conversely, it was the basis of Whig critiques of utilitarian democratic theory.

Ryan, in his examination of James Mill's ideas, recognizes this ideological conflict and poses, as the modern parallel to utilitarian democratic theory, not pluralism, but so-called economic theories of democracy. The political system the Benthamites desired was one analogous to the perfect market. The political market should be open to all and rational self-interested voters would establish consumer sovereignty by exchanging votes for those policies they judged most conducive to their individual interests. The market analogy drawn by Ryan was in fact used by James Mill himself, and it does capture well the flavour of classical utilitarian democratic theory, but, as Ryan notes, it creates problems of consistency within the utilitarian theory itself. A democratic system is supposed to ensure that the greatest happiness is the actual end of government. But how far can a democracy of egoistic voters accurately compute the greatest happiness? If the end were the greatest happiness of the majority, a democratic procedure might enforce it on governments; but, if the general utility principle has no such majoritarian implications, such a procedure might produce a faulty computation.

An examination of how the utilitarians attempted to overcome these inconsistencies produces a third, and rather different, characterization of Benthamite democratic theory, which moves it closer to the Rousseauist position rejected by Gunn. The need to overcome them was acute. Their critics repeatedly argued that, if universal suffrage was instituted, the poor majority would be vested with political power; if the poor majority acted as the utilitarian theory supposed they must act, to further their own interests, they would attack the existing distribution of wealth; but this would involve the undermining of what the utilitarians themselves saw as the central requirement of the general interest, the security of property. In answer, the utilitarians were pushed to the assertion that concern for the general interest would be the motivating factor in the minds of voters in a democracy; and this brought them to a position close to that of Rousseau – democratic governments would be shackled to the general interest since they would be subject to a general will expressing a common good. This seems, as Macaulay pointed out, to involve the replication in the utilitarians' democratic theory of the paradoxes of their ethical theory. If the Benthamites were saying that men, either as moral actors or as voters, should pursue the general happiness regardless of their own, they were preaching what was, on their own assumptions, psychologically impossible. The response to this was the assertion of a distinction between the individual's real, long-term and his apparent, short-term interests. Whilst there may be a conflict between short-term and communal interests, in the long term there is no tension between self-interests and the claims of the community. The really rational voter will sacrifice possible immediate benefits to the long-term interests of the community, and consequently of himself. Bentham, starting from a faith in an enlightened king or aristocracy, ends, at least on this characterization of Benthamite thought, with a faith in an enlightened, and therefore socially aware, democracy.

Whatever the general character of the utilitarians' views of democracy, it is clear that we are entering a different intellectual world when we look at the ideas of John Stuart Mill on representative government. One of the main issues in the discussion of this, and other aspects of his thought is how new this world was, how far his own claims to be following in the utilitarian tradition of Bentham and his father can be taken at face-value.

Ryan argues that, at least in relation to democratic theory, the claims have little substance and that J. S. Mill's conception of the nature and purpose of democracy are far distant from that of his father. Whereas James Mill's expectations of democracy were that it would instate the utility principle as the guiding rule of legislation and public policy, would ensure good government, his son's concerns were primarily with the educative functions of democracy, with its potentiality for a progress defined in terms of a heightening of the quality of the life and character of citizens. The main virtue of democracy, in his eyes, was its encouragement of the active, public-spirited, independent citizen. It would thus provide a necessary bulwark against the tyranny of public opinion, a dread of which Mill shared with Tocqueville. For both thinkers, the most pressing threat in their own society was the possible triumph of the timid, the conformist, the outer-directed personality; and this explains their common attachment to any means by which large sections of the population could be drawn into active participation in public life – representative democracy, local self-government, the growth of voluntary, intermediary associations.

Put another way, Mill valued democracy for the possibility it offered that the masses might be moved towards the largeness of mind of the best within his society. This concern for the great and the good, and the protection of their influence, can be seen in, for instance, his advocacy of a Coleridgean clerisy – a secular, spiritual priesthood – and in his defence of plural voting. This 'élitist' character of his thought, which is certainly constantly exhibited, is for some evidence that he cannot qualify as a democrat.

Ryan rejects this, but argues that J. S. Mill's hopes for democracy are so distant from those of his father that he had effectively abandoned at any rate 'traditional' utilitarianism. On this view, Mill is left with at most a commitment to an attenuated form of utilitarianism, a form in which the achievement of the progressive improvement of the quality of individual life plays a much larger role than the simple maximization of happiness. The question posed by Ryan in relation to Mill's theory of democracy – how far his central concerns with progress, liberty, individuality are compatible with the claimed utilitarian base – is repeated in interpretation of all of his writings. Put more generally, interpretation has been largely concerned with the question of Mill's consistency, how consistent and coherent are the ideas of this eclectic thinker, who was so influenced by such a variety of thinkers, so sympathetic to such a variety of values.

The particular question posed was faced most directly by Mill in his essay on *Utilitarianism*. Here, he distanced himself from some parts of Bentham's full theory – particularly the psychological postulates and any suggestion that an individual's own utility could define his moral obligations. But he does commit himself clearly to the basics of utilitarian ethics, that pleasure and freedom from pain are the only things desirable as ends and that the standard of right conduct is its effects on the happiness of all concerned. However, ambiguities and, some would argue, inconsistencies arise when he attempts to counter the objection that this poses a degrading conception of the good life. For he then introduces a qualitative differentiation between types of pleasure. Of course, Bentham himself, despite his claim that pushpin is as good as poetry, could distinguish between the desirability of different pleasures; but the measures of this desirability were quantitative (the intensity of the pleasures, their durability, and so on). Mill specifically rejects such a quantitative assessment and so leaves open the question of how a utilitarian could favour the frustration of actual (even if debased) wants and advocate the promotion of aspirations which (however noble) might for many be unattainable.

Similar problems emerge in interpretation of Mill's liberalism. At the beginning of his essay *On Liberty*, he commits himself to utility as the ultimate arbiter in ethical questions, qualifying this by insisting that utility must be 'grounded on the permanent interests of man as a progressive being'. How far he maintains this commitment is at the centre of much of the controversy over interpretation of the essay. His argument there starts from the famous dictum that 'the only purpose for which power can be rightfully exercised over any member of a civilized community, against his will, is to prevent harm to others'. The limits of social control are to be decided on the basis of a definition of a sphere of private action in which the individual should be safeguarded against intrusion.

This 'very simple principle' asserted by Mill has been the subject of persistent debate. One problem, which Williams takes up in the first part of his article, is what can be understood by the distinction between self-regarding and other-regarding actions. If the distinction is merely between actions which affect the actor alone and those which affect others, it is of little help in deciding the limits of social control since there are no, or few, actions or classes of action which could in principle affect only the actor himself. As Williams points out, the problem is exacerbated by the variety of terms Mill himself uses to identify the distinction. The formulation Williams concentrates on, following Rees, is that other-regarding actions are those which harm the interests of others; and, by reference to the discussion of justice and rights in *Utilitarianism*, he equates these with actions which violate the rights of others. However plausible this may be as an explication of Mill's meaning, it still leaves, as Williams notices, problems of consistency. If the rights at issue are legal rights, then Mill is attempting to define the proper limits of social intervention (and so, in part, the rights which should be guaranteed to the individual) in terms of existent legal rights. If the rights at issue are certain moral rights (deriving perhaps from the requirements of justice), how is this to be reconciled with Mill's initial disavowal of any appeal to 'the idea of abstract right' independent of utility?

Problems of the same order emerge in Mill's particular applications of his simple principle. One consequence of the principle seems to be a clear rejection of state paternalism, intervention in order to prevent people harming themselves. One question at issue here among commentators is how far in the course of the essay Mill sticks to this clear rejection, given the exemptions he allows, of for instance children, 'barbarians', the ignorant, and so on. Another is how far this rejection of paternalism is compatible with a utilitarian stance. Why, from this standpoint, should the harms people may inflict on themselves be distinguished from those they may inflict on others, and, if such self-inflicted harms are preventible, why should they not be prevented?

For Mill, the most important corollary of his simple principle was probably freedom of conscience and discussion. His defence of such freedoms is in large part founded on utility, at least in the extended sense he gives to the term. Freedom of discussion and public challenges to accepted beliefs are necessary to counter erroneous ideas and to vivify generally held true opinions; and the continued progress of society is dependent on an incremental grasp of truth and on popular beliefs being held critically and self-consciously. In the same way, Mill defends what he calls liberty of tastes and pursuits in utilitarian terms. Social progress, at least in the sense of the improvement of the quality of individual life, is achievable only if individuals are capable of both framing and acting upon plans of life that they have decided for themselves.

Yet, although Mill uses the language of utility to justify these central freedoms, questions are often raised about how far such freedoms are compatible with utilitarianism in any strict sense. In the main, Mill insists that constraints upon the expression of opinions or upon private behaviour cannot be justified by the fact that such opinions or behaviour run counter to general tastes or moral beliefs, no matter how strongly held. Whatever distaste and shock might be felt by people faced with what they regard as the aberrant and abhorrent ideas and practices of others, these feelings should not be taken as grounds for legal interference or even for the exercise of the more strenuous forms of social pressures to conformity. But why, from a utilitarian standpoint, should such morality-dependent harms, as they have been called, be discounted? For some commentators, there are good utilitarian arguments for the general exclusion of such harms from any legislative felicific calculus. On Williams's reading, their exclusion would be justified because they are not harms to the interests of others; but this again raises the question of how far Mill, in this definition of interests, had moved from his claimed utilitarian base.

Problems of consistency such as these have led some to conclude that Mill's deference to utilitarianism was no more than an act of filial piety and that his liberalism was centred on social values only tenuously connected with utility. For Williams, its core was a concern for 'the free spirit', the vigorous, critical, self-aware character, intent upon self-improvement, the heightening of his sensibilities and intellectual awareness. In this context, Mill's defence of liberty as the absence of restraint stemmed, not from the desire for utility maximization, but from a concern for individuality.

This kind of characterization of Mill's thought has been challenged. Some have indeed questioned Mill's 'liberalism', portraying him as primarily an advocate for a particular set of values and beliefs who seized on liberal objectives as a means of achieving the hegemony of his own viewpoint. More particularly, on this view, his plea for freedom of discussion, for the rational and critical examination of all received opinions, was based on the expectation that his own brand of rationalist humanism would be the victor in such public debate at the expense of those beliefs, such as Christianity, which rested, not on rational persuasion, but on acts of faith or deference to custom. Certainly, such a portrait has some substantiation in the tensions in Mill's thought between his advocacy of 'the free spirit' and his firm conviction that intellectuals such as himself had a peculiar purchase on social and moral truths. Whatever the apparent relativism of his defence of liberty of conscience, he believed his own social values and understanding to be more than provisional or subjective. However fierce his attack on the tyranny of the majority, he did allow for, even urge, the social influence of enlightened opinion. Whatever his pleas for experiments in living and for independent, non-conformist persons, he did expect that, at least in a progressive society, individual plans of life would be increasingly and commonly fashioned on the pursuit of the higher pleasures as he saw them. However strong his distrust of older priesthoods, he did hanker after a secular clerisy. What is at issue here, however, is whether these tensions are evidence of the hypocrisy, conscious or unconscious, of the intellectual imperialist; or whether, as has been claimed alternatively, they are the marks of the civilized man, able to recognize the existence and legitimacy of alien values yet none the less firm in his own convictions and commitments.

## ACCESSIBLE EDITIONS

J. Bentham, *An Introduction to the Principles of Morals and Legislation* (London and New York, Methuen, ed. J. H. Burns and H. L. A. Hart)

J. S. Mill, *Utilitarianism, Liberty, Representative Government* (London, Dent, Everyman's Library)

## SUGGESTED READING

M. Cowling, *Mill and Liberalism* (Cambridge, Cambridge University Press, 1963)

E. Halévy, *The Growth of Philosophic Radicalism* (London, Faber & Faber, 1949)

R. J. Halliday, *John Stuart Mill* (London, George Allen & Unwin, 1976)

A. J. Hume, *Bentham and Bureaucracy* (Cambridge, Cambridge University Press, 1981)

J. Lively and J. Rees (eds), *Utilitarian Logic and Politics* (Oxford, Clarendon Press, 1978)

J. C. Rees, *John Stuart Mill's On Liberty* (Oxford, Clarendon Press, 1985)

F. Rosen, *Jeremy Bentham and Representative Democracy* (Oxford, Clarendon Press, 1983)

\* A. Ryan, *J. S. Mill* (London, Routledge & Kegan Paul, 1974)

\* J. Steintrager, *Bentham* (London, George Allen & Unwin, 1977)

D. F. Thompson, *John Stuart Mill and Representative Government* (Cambridge, Cambridge University Press, 1976)

## Chapter Thirteen

# JEREMY BENTHAM AND THE PUBLIC INTEREST*

## J. A. W. GUNN

Posterity pays major political thinkers the dubious compliment of cherishing their failings as well as their insights, the choice between them being dictated by the prevailing interests of the age. This truism is especially well illustrated by the treatment accorded Jeremy Bentham and, in particular, his famous aggregative definition of the public interest. The concept was central to Bentham's work on economics, law, and politics, bridging demands for specific reforms and more theoretical notions about social and political processes. Its applicability to so many contexts is a major reason for continuing ambiguity about Bentham's intentions.

The standard criticisms of the 'sum-of-particular-interests' have been that it sprang from an untenable psychological hedonism and readily lent itself to a *laissez-faire* individualism incompatible with social responsibility and a strong sense of community. An 'invisible hand' of some sort has seemed not only a natural, but a necessary, implication.[1] Sometimes the emphasis has been that particular interests were irreconcilable, sometimes on the resulting disharmony between the satisfaction of at least some particular interests and the preservation of the public good.[2] As R. B. Perry has put it, all particular interests do not 'add up'; rather, such individualism suggests trains approaching each other on a single track – and the implication of diminished, rather than augmented good, is obvious.[3] Such criticisms have usually pilloried the utilitarian idea of public good as reducing community to jarring bundles of appetites.[4]

Another interpretation has always been available in the evidence, for one might absolve Bentham of advocating near-anarchy by assuming that all interests were meant to be similar, not in the same sense that all men sought the same few tokens of success, but that they were united by a common will. Growing concern with

* Previously published in the *Canadian Journal of Political Science*, vol. I, no. 4 (December 1968).

the 'classical theory of democracy' has contributed to this new perspective, giving us Bentham, the populist, a somewhat different figure from Bentham, the extreme individualist.[5] For while this more recent interpretation is not incompatible with elements of the first, it certainly suggests that, far from being dissolved, the public interest voiced by a unanimous people might become too pervasive and demanding a standard. To some contemporaries this concern for public power may suggest a state of mind useful for reviving a complacent, pluralist democracy; more frequently, however, the radical-democratic strain is taken as a sinister force intolerant of the normal diversity of interests and eager to reduce them to unity.[6]

An adequate account of Bentham's position must then assess both interpretations. It is now well established that the traditional distinction between a natural and an artificial harmony of interests, corresponding to economic and political affairs respectively, is ill-founded.[7] The problem cannot then be dismissed by referring to these different sectors of activity; they were not so differentiated by Bentham, and rightly not. This being so, it is important to examine evidence drawn from legal and political writings in understanding Bentham, the individualist, and current interpretations of his political attitudes will benefit from consulting economic works. Indeed, it can never have been thought that the 'sum of interests' referred alone to economic processes, since the expression was always placed by Bentham in some broader, political context. Even so, this has prompted no second look at the Benthamite version of a public interest. Before dismissing the doctrine as dangerous nonsense, we should take that second look.

## NOMINALISM

Bentham's formal definition of the public interest did not alter over a period of forty years. His best-known statement was his first, when he asked: 'The interest of the community then is, what? – the sum of the interests of the several members who compose it.'[8] It is clear that the context of similar remarks and their purpose varied a good deal, and hence some versions are more comprehensible than others. However, later works contain the same assumption that the interest of the community was, in some sense, an 'aggregate' of particular interests.[9] The community was but a fictitious body and the public interest an 'abstract term' covering a mass of individual interests.[10] Public advantage had to be reducible, in some manner, to 'private and personal advantage'.[11]

In all such statements we see Bentham's nominalistic distrust of fictions and abstractions. His was a mind that delighted in displaying the rich variety of concrete particulars cloaked by the quaint fictions of the law. States were best viewed as collections of individuals. Just as the public interest was founded upon the satisfaction of particulars, so the wealth of a nation was to be calculated as a 'sum of the particular masses of wealth belonging respectively to the several individuals of whom the political community . . . is composed'.[12]

One way of alluding to wealth in whatever form was to speak of 'property' and its rights. Bentham observed that hymns in praise of property would often appear less plausible were one to substitute the concrete equivalent 'rich men'.[13] However, he remained a ready defender of property rights supposedly belonging to all. On examining a number of Bentham's statements about the community and its individual members, it becomes apparent that in this area as well his nominalism was more intelligent and less mechanical than is usually supposed.

Here, economic examples are most instructive. In the same work in which Bentham said that the national wealth was a compound of individual masses of wealth, he allowed that it in no way followed that an increase in the wealth of individuals necessarily added to the national total. For this there were two reasons. If some individuals could somehow double their supply of money, they might be said to have increased their wealth in proportion. This was not, of course, true of the nation as a whole, for an increase in the money supply unaccompanied by an increase in goods would simply lower the value of money.[14] Second, one could not infer public benefit from an increase in an individual's stock until it was ascertained whether anyone else had lost a corresponding amount in the same transaction.[15] This commonplace of the welfare economist was not a Benthamite discovery: it had been the opinion of all but the most irresponsible of economic individualists. There was yet a third qualification. Bentham distinguished carefully between wealth in private and public hands: 'States have no persons distinct from the persons of individuals; but they have property. . . .'[16] There were thus limits to the facile, nominalistic habit of dissolving every unity into an aggregate, for sometimes the members of the supposed aggregate would not add up to form the unity. It all depended upon what predicates were applied to the constituent parts; the context was important. This was certainly the case in the treatment of wealth and property. Was it also true of the political concepts?

## THE REALITY OF THE COMMUNITY

True to his basic philosophy, Bentham refused to attribute to the public any personality distinct from those of individuals. To do so was to invite 'false and pernicious consequences'.[17] Sustaining this attitude was the long-standing liberal and radical distrust of foreign adventures other than trade. A policy of foreign conquest for the aggrandizement of the state was thus dismissed as a trick of foreign despots who cheerfully sacrificed their concrete citizens for a chimera such as national honour.[18] In war the state towered over its citizens, sacrificing their lives and property to its survival. Of course, territorial integrity would sometimes have to be defended, and Bentham admitted that this might involve sacrifices by private persons as the smaller mass of security was traded for the greater.[19] He went farther, and observed that in times of 'extraordinary public danger' individuals would develop a 'social interest' stronger than the interests peculiar to themselves.[20] Still Bentham retained his suspicion, not only of warfare, but even of national defence. These were all too easily made pretexts for arbitrary government, while in fact citizens were in greater danger from their 'professed protectors' than from 'foreign and declared enemies'.[21] War was a crime, against foreigners as against one's own subjects, and rulers were warned against pursuing the 'frivolous honours of the flag'.[22] Thus Bentham shunned the absolutist understanding of the public interest with its emphasis on *arcana imperii*. Bentham did not employ the expression 'reason of state', for it had already become unfashionable both for defenders and critics of dynastic ambition.[23] However, he was quite aware of the continuity between the tactics of absolutism and those of his own day. This is made clear in a plea for publicity in the making of foreign policy:

> The good old Tudor and Stuart principles have been suffered to remain unquestioned here. Foreign politics are questions of state. Under Elizabeth and James, nothing was to be inquired into . . . everything was a matter of state. On other points the veil has been torn away; but with regard to these, there has been a sort of tacit understanding between ministers and people.[24]

For all his suspicions about state personality, Bentham was sometimes led very close to such a fiction in his own argument. In the process of trying to dissociate individuals from the pursuit of national power, he remarked that 'a nation has its property – its honour – and even its condition. It may be attacked in all of these particulars without the individuals who compose it being affected.'[25] While this involved no softening of his attitude toward national aggrandizement, the statement did give the community some being independent of its constituent parts. Of course, Bentham would never have considered national honour as the right measure of the public interest. He was saying merely that matters such as diplomatic reversals were less vital than some statesmen supposed, since they need not touch the interests of individual citizens. The argument demonstrates that when Bentham's individualism conflicted with his nominalism, he was willing to embrace the fictions condemned by the latter.

A clearer indication of Bentham's position comes in his treatment of the various sorts of offences that were, or should be, recognized by the law. His views were summarized in the statement that 'An action cannot be detrimental to a community but by being detrimental to some of or more of the individuals that compose it. These individuals may either be assignable or unassignable.'[26] By assignable, he meant distinguishable from the rest of the population. Hence the statement quoted above might better have said that a nation could also be attacked in its condition with the individuals composing it being affected, although one could not assign detriment to specific persons. This is what one would understand from his treatment of the categories of offences. Bentham recognized public offences 'against the state in general', and these included acts detrimental to external defence, internal order, and 'sovereignty', or preservation of the regime against 'rebellion'. All such offences were described as those 'by which the public interest may be affected'. Particular individuals would presumably suffer through these acts, but they could not be identified, for the mischief tended to be 'comparatively unobvious', and so no private citizen had a 'particular interest' to bring the offenders to justice.[27]

We have seen that one of the traditional criticisms of Benthamite notions about the public interest rests upon a supposed failure to distinguish purely private interests and activities from the welfare and public institutions of a community. It seems, however, that Bentham was more perfectly aware of the distinction than were most political thinkers. In one of his most detailed considerations of contemporary political argument he assailed the authors of the Declaration of the Rights of Man for their ambiguous use of the word 'autrui'. So loosely had they used it that there was 'no distinction between the community and individuals', thus depriving lawmakers of any recourse against acts 'by which no individual sufferers are to be found'.[28] Elsewhere, he accused the French writers of failing to say whether rights were to be exercised 'each in his individual capacity, or only together in their collective'.[29]

What is lacking here is any sign of that contempt for community institutions ostensibly belonging to liberal social doctrine. There is no celebration of private satisfaction at the expense of the whole; instead we find a strong affirmation of the virtues of community. This discovery is important because in his most famous comment on the public interest Bentham had said that it was 'vain to talk of the interest of the community without understanding what is the interest of the individual'.[30] But here we have seen a number of areas of policy in which, while the public interest was involved, it was unnecessary, and indeed impossible, to begin with interests of individuals. Such interests were not consciously involved in this public interest, and Bentham was primarily concerned with the interests of individuals as they conceived them, since any other assumption invited despotic government.[31] Here the condition of individual awareness did not obtain, and diffused and indirect detriment to individuals could only be inferred from damage to the community of which they were members.

In order to preserve the public interest as dealt with here, there was no question of allowing private persons to pursue their private interests: it was not even necessary for a legislator to consider each person's particular interest. In the prevention of 'public offences' few persons had an interest in the sense of a strongly felt personal concern, while if one understands interest to refer to anything which added to an individual's pleasures (or diminished his pains), all citizens had an interest of sorts, which was the same for all. The process was also apparent when evils of a semi-public nature involved certain forms of 'national debilitation'. Such evils might even take the form of offences by the government when it restricted civil liberties. In these circumstances the immediate sufferers were determinate, but most of the evil was suffered by unidentifiable fellow citizens: 'through the sides of one individual the public is wounded: that is to say, all other individuals are: as well those who do not feel the wound as those who do.'[32]

The public interests treated here consisted in the avoidance of certain conditions, a negative good that could be seen as benefiting all individuals, even though the connection with some interests might be rather attenuated. Bentham portrayed the evils of 'political gagging' as an example of a misfortune which might only afflict some members of the community in any immediate sense. He argued, however, that through such infringements on liberty the

nation, considered as an 'aggregate', would suffer, since the formation of intelligent public opinion would be obstructed.[33]

Anyone who was willing to contemplate national debilitation as
something affecting individual interests had surely conceded all that
most exponents of national strength might desire. Bentham was
quite prepared to recognize offences against the 'public' which either
had no immediate impact on individuals or in some cases had their
major effects on the anonymous mass of the people. He retained
this sole proviso that individuals, albeit unidentifiable individuals,
had to be affected. Indeed, he went so far as to allow that the public
was concerned in offences against God, were it possible to establish
some connection between His pain and pleasure and the realm of
human affairs.[34] Tories and others might well have objected to
Bentham's description of the community as an aggregate, and they
would certainly have been displeased with his insistence that it was
absurd ever to sacrifice present generations to posterity. Nevertheless, so broadly did he define individual concerns that, in the name
of these individuals, the community gained its full share of consideration. Now it is important to examine Bentham's use of the public
interest in other contexts, asking especially what sorts of interests
belonging to individuals together formed this public good.

## THE NATURE OF PRIVATE INTERESTS

An attempt to identify those interests coming together to form the
public interest must begin with exclusions. Some criticisms of this
sort of individualism rest upon the assumption that Bentham envisioned a public interest consisting in the satisfaction of all private
interests. The critics in question are quite correct in saying that
such an idea was unrealistic nonsense. Bentham would have agreed.
Certainly his benevolence led him to state that it would be an
excellent thing if, on all occasions, the felicity of each person could
be guaranteed. But, as he immediately confessed, this was impossible: 'Thus it is that to provide for the greatest felicity of the greatest
number, is the utmost that can be done towards the maximization
of universal national felicity, in so far as depends on government.'[35]
The closing qualification is very important. National felicity
consisted in that of individuals, but only some forms of felicity were
deemed the responsibility of government.

Writing in 1780 of the 'sum of the interests' of individuals,
Bentham appeared to be concerned with individual satisfaction in
all its forms. However, in his later writings he was increasingly
the radical reformer laying down a programme of action for an

enlightened government and specifying how such a government might be obtained. Clearly there were many forms of individual felicity that might be freely enjoyed without government intervention; many activities that give people pleasure are freely open to all, and, producing no conflict, require no authority to allocate shares. When we recall that Bentham wanted to replace government control by private initiative in certain sectors of the economy, it should occasion no surprise that he should also feel that people contributed to the national happiness as they went about their tasks of securing private happiness. Still, it remains true that Bentham was most often concerned with aspects of the public interest that bore an immediate connection with government. Often he claimed that the public interest was subdued by lesser interests and that the law had yet to realize a genuine public interest.[36] This carried no suggestion regarding a great range of innocuous private pleasure. Rather, he was saying that certain interests, realizable through government, had been thwarted. What were these interests?

According to Bentham, the 'common interests' to be furthered by his schemes for reform 'correspond to the immediately subordinate right and proper ends of government, maximization of subsistence, abundance, security and equality'.[37] 'Subordinate' in this context meant subordinate to the greatest happiness of the greatest number. These four ends of government served to spell out the content of the greatest happiness principle in concrete form. Security and subsistence were accorded higher priority than the others, with security being quite the most important. This was because all four goods could not simultaneously be maximized, and without security both subsistence and abundance would be endangered and equality would exist only as equality of misery.[38] The all-important principle of security applied to that of person, property, reputation, and condition in life.[39]

Significantly, the quality shared by all of these conditions, except perhaps abundance, was that they could simultaneously be realized in some measure for all citizens. Bentham especially emphasized that security in person and property was one interest that was truly universal. In his estimation, no one stood to gain by an attack on property, the foundation of abundance and of civilization itself. He challenged those who warned that democracy would lead to an assault upon property. It could not happen, he said, because to level property was to destroy it by weakening incentive and by wasting resources which often had to be concentrated for efficient use.[40] To attack property was a 'universal-personal-security-destroying act' and of this 'no human being sensible of anything ever failed of being sensible'. One could only believe that the poor sought to destroy property by believing that they placed less value upon their own possessions, however few, than the rich placed on theirs. This Bentham denied.[41]

But how could he deny it? It seems implausible to deny to the poor a motive for plundering the rich; Bentham's argument here was infirm in some ways, although it would be well to remember that history, on the whole, has proven him right in his claim that property would survive democracy. The argument serves to illustrate Bentham's enormous concern for security, a concern buttressed by his conviction that to be effective it had to be universal. Once government was used to effect a redistribution of property by seizing that of some individuals, the genie would refuse to go back into the bottle. In such matters 'the interest of the first is sacred, or the interest of no one can be so'.[42]

The point also becomes more plausible if one recalls that Bentham wanted security of person and the enjoyment of civil liberties, not just protection of middle-class possessions. Each invasion of the principle of inviolability weakened its hold and eventually governments and rapacious citizens would pose a danger to the foundation of society. While government remained the most dangerous enemy, Bentham had to admit that some few citizens might also want to attack property. What he refused to admit was that this could really be in the interests of the poor or that the great majority could ever believe that it was. The basic principles remain unscathed: 'If you shake the principle of security as to one class of citizens, you shake it as to all: the bundle of concord is its emblem.'[43]

The argument had nothing to do with a *laissez-faire* attitude to the use of property, for Bentham's concern was more for future security than for unlimited appropriation. By way of emphasis, he noted that it was everybody's interest 'to possess, to retain, and upon occasion acquire property'.[44] Here then was a set of interests deemed to belong to more or less all private persons, which, at the same time, was clearly for the good of the community. Governments, when tyrannous, ignored this universal interest, wasting the subject's money in places, pensions, and general inefficiency; sacrificing lives and property in war and robbing all those who were subjected to arbitrary and expensive judicial processes. If one treats the interests of most citizens in ending these abuses as the public interest, the alleged conflict between individual and community interest disappears. The great mass of citizens were seen as joining to repair these faults in the polity. In this context their interest did add up, or harmonize, for they were all the same.

## INTERESTS IN THE POLITICAL PROCESS

It has now been established that Bentham recognized community needs, and further, that he expressed this sort of common good in such a way that it could be seen as embodying certain interests belonging to all individuals. To complete the picture, we must see how the public interest could be realized on issues where everyone's concern for security provided no immediate answer, since particular interests were in conflict.

Bentham was aware that, in positing a public interest that consisted in an aggregate of particular interests, he risked being misunderstood. Once when lamenting how 'the general interest is sacrificed to the particular interest' he anticipated an obvious objection:

> But it may be retorted, this prevalence of particular over universal interest being, according to yourself, so general, the necessary consequence is, that no ultimate mischief ensues – everything is as it should be; for what is the universal interest but the aggregate of all particular interests?[45]

He conceded that men were indeed self-seeking, wishing to give preference to their own interests. The whole problem was that some people had the opportunity to exercise this self-interest and others had not: 'The wish is everywhere – the power not so.' The answer was to change the political system, not human nature: 'The sum of all the several distinguishable interests being thus framed and ascertained would constitute the universal interest; in a word, the principle of universal suffrage would be applied.'[46] Presumably, such interests produced no such universal interest until reform was achieved.

Now this cannot have been what Bentham meant when, in the *Introduction to the Principles of Morals and Legislation*, he called the public interest a sum of particular ones, for he was not then a democrat. At that stage in his development Bentham does not seem to have enquired very closely about how particular interests were to meet in the public interest. His slogan for describing the public interest had previously been employed by other reformers and Bentham apparently accepted it without dwelling on the implications.[47] In some of the later writings the slogan about a sum of particular interests was tied to the extension of the franchise. Thus Bentham came to accept a view of the public interest that involved giving all individuals the opportunity to articulate their interests. This could not mean, of course, that all interests, without exception, would find satisfaction: some private interests were irrelevant to governmental and legal reform and others were positively detrimental to it. The meaning of Bentham's later formula differed little from that of the Civil War radicals who had claimed that in a monarchy one man's interest was effective, while in a commonwealth those of all citizens were put forward – no one interest 'rampant', but all 'passant', as one contemporary of Harrington had put it.

Since Bentham was not a political innocent, unaware of conflicts of interest, the charge that he sought to subordinate all particular interests to that of the people deserves consideration. This interpretation has deep roots in modern political theory, finding support in our regard for social pluralism and the corresponding rejection of the abstract, unaffiliated individual of some earlier theories.[48] The new interpretation gains further plausibility from the indisputable fact that Bentham, supposedly the arch-individualist, was extremely hostile to some forms of privilege enjoyed at the expense of the community. The villains altered with the occasion. Sometimes it was the monarch and the lords who trampled on the people's rights; sometimes the sinister interest was that of agriculture.[49] Did he then only avoid a blind clash of interests to fly to a demagogic faith in a spontaneously generated general will? Was the radical individualist really a precursor of what is sometimes called 'totalitarian democracy'? Some political scientists apparently feel that this description would be no great exaggeration.

In point of fact, it is simply untrue that Bentham saw a few sinister interests opposed by the 'people', visualized as a single, homogeneous group. Sometimes, his rhetoric suggested this, since one could scarcely expect him to claim that reform would be unpopular, but usually the context supplied necessary qualification.[50] We have already seen why he felt that most citizens would be of one mind about the great end of security, and if he was extravagantly optimistic about each man's stake in the property system, certainly his opponents' pessimism has proved even less correct. While unconvincing in absolving the poor from a desire to seize property, Bentham was surely right in saying that civil liberties were most secure for all when there was no precedent for their restriction. Apart from this one common interest, Bentham placed realistic limits on the homogeneity of the public.

In addition to those already mentioned, he identified numerous interests that might, under some circumstances, prove subversive of the public interest. These include lawyers, the ecclesiastical establishment, standing armies, banking houses, manufacturers, Whigs,

Tories, and even the common gossip.[51] While this might be taken as an indication of the reach of a fanatical striving for unity, the more sensible conclusion is that any group, left unchecked, would prove a menace to the community. Usually Bentham called such interests 'sinister', the pejorative term referring not to the quality of the actor's motives, but to the consequences, or 'direction', of the interest.[52] This was consistent with his general philosophy and meant that it was the fact of incompatibility with the public good that made interests sinister. The answer was neither to proscribe the sinister interest nor to reform the character of its members, but simply to prevent its unopposed progress. This was the recommended course of action in dealing with King, lords, and placemen. In large measure the disquiet caused by Bentham's opinions has proceeded from a failure to appreciate that not all particular interests were sinister, but that any interest might be, under certain circumstances. Bentham has hindered our understanding by occasionally calling sinister interests by other names – 'partial' or even 'particular' interests. But from this we must not conclude that the 'People' was a greedy Moloch, jealous of all competitors.

Far from hypostatizing the 'People' as a single, irreducible interest, Bentham provided a most sophisticated analysis of society as a congeries of different interests. Particularly instructive is the analysis of the way in which commercial interests were formed, as those similarly situated laid aside their rivalry to form a 'coalition'. He explained how the success of such an alliance depended upon the mass of capital and number of individuals involved, as well as on the ease with which they might be organized. Thus he specifically noted how large manufacturers 'concentrated in small districts' might form a regional interest that could easily overpower a numerically larger group that was unorganized.[53] Of course, one might simply interpret this as an indication of the prevailing liberal animus against men acting in concert. It is conceivable that Bentham could be quite aware of the existence of well-organized sinister interests while seeking only to dissolve them into a homogeneous mass.[54]

It seems most unlikely that this was what Bentham was advocating. Certainly, he was most concerned about the fate of those groups and categories of citizens that came closest to embodying the whole nation. With this in mind, he espoused the cause of the unorganized consumer against organized producers; the latter were 'a chain of iron', the former, 'a rope of sand'.[55] However, he often challenged organized interests in the name of other specific interests that lacked organization, and not in the name of a unanimous public. Writing of producers, Bentham complained that only those groups with the largest resources were powerful. Who, he asked, spoke for 'Bakers, butchers, tailors, shoemakers, farmers, carpenters, bricklayers, masons . . .'? There was no objection to groups striving to defend or advance their interests; indeed, universal suffrage was portrayed as a situation where 'every one individual in every class' would be allowed to protect his interest by political means. Instead of insisting that all partial associations should be abolished, Bentham contented himself with the observation that 'even of the manufacturing interests, it is not every class that has the power to associate and combine in support of the common interest of the class'.[56]

It is not difficult to see why Bentham saw the vote as a panacea for this political imbalance. The groups which he saw as uninfluential were those which, by their very size, were unable to concentrate their power and were thus unable to avail themselves of the avenues of access enjoyed by the powerful friends of administrators and politicians.[57] It would thus be pointless for him to exhort them to organize; had they been able to, they would have done so already. However great his concern for small producers, Bentham was even more solicitous of those interests whose size made them less well defined. Paralleling his treatment of the consumer, Bentham wrote of the litigant. The opposition to arbitrary law taxes was inchoate, for, by the nature of the situation, parties at law had no obvious common interest, but were paired off against each other. The eventuality of going to court could not be anticipated, and hence opposition to administrative insolence was ineffective. While 'shopkeepers' and 'glovers' were 'compact bodies' appearing in force at the House of Commons, suitors for justice had 'no common cause and scarce a common name'.[58] Short of writing of 'potential interest groups', one wonders what more Bentham could have said.

It is not then true that Bentham tried to reduce all interests to a single one. His aim was rather that of giving all particular interests expression. Still less can we say with one critic that Bentham reviewed the community 'as a single group out of which issues a will for the greatest happiness of the greatest number, not as a dynamically obtained compromise but a continuing single will'.[59]

Bentham did not claim each individual desired the greatest happiness of the greatest number at the expense of his own good. Nor was Bentham the nominalist likely to forget that the public or community consisted only of individuals: 'Who is that public that is to be distinguished from individuals?'[60] Admittedly, he recognized a form of public welfare irreducible to that of specific individuals, but this is a very different matter from reifying the community as a political agent. The notion of a general will of some sort is no doubt hopeful for the interpretation of some thinkers who consistently reified the public, and this would include some in the British Radical tradition.[61] Applied to Bentham, it represents a curious and unwarranted misunderstanding.[62]

Bentham was no value-free scientist. He had a programme that he wished to see implemented and this entailed imputing certain interests to the electorate. Quite as important, though, were the interests from which the electorate was to be shielded. If electoral corruption by proponents of misrule could be prevented, Bentham was confident that the voter would be moved primarily by his 'share in the universal interest'. That is to say, in the absence of an opposing 'sinister interest', a citizen's conception of the universal interest would determine his electoral conduct.[63] Significantly, Bentham drew no distinction between the pursuit of interests in protecting individual rights and the concern for a universal interest. Such interests were the essence of the public interest and certainly not 'sinister'. It is incorrect, then, to assume that citizens fashioned a general will. However impotent the voter might be in pursuing only his selfish interests, opinions about the public interest would necessarily differ. Bentham did not say this, but were it not assumed, his concern for extending the electorate would be pointless.

Knowing that, at best, the voter would have a concern for the community as the best guarantee of his own welfare, Bentham realized that it was the legislature which would have to discover this public interest. Individual legislators were also in a much better position than the private citizen to promote selfish interests. Of the individual legislator, Bentham wrote: 'insofar as his aim is to serve such of his interests alone as are theirs as well as his, he finds all hands disposed to join with his.'[64]

These common interests were our old friends security, subsistence, equality, and abundance. It was accepted that all public men would normally feel a stronger pull from private or parochial interests than from that of the whole.[65] However, the very ubiquity of self-interest was the preservation of the public interest, as the aims of one individual or group would be checked and moderated by others.[66] The result might then centre on truly common concerns. This description remains unsatisfactory in failing to explain exactly how Parliament would act to secure the general interest. But we have yet to agree on how any legislature may be said to do that. Bentham actually wrote a treatise on legislative tactics, but confined himself to technicalities of procedure.

While Bentham was an early critic of balance as a principle of domestic and international order,[67] his own theory of politics rested on an equilibrium of forces in society and in the legislature, a treatment of political processes more realistic than the prevailing ideas about the balanced constitution. We are now aware of the pitfalls in the equilibrium assumption, but Bentham's problems are still shared by theorists of modern pluralism.

## THE SUM OF INTERESTS

It is never easy to write of interests: protean and all-pervasive, definable at any level of generality, multiple and conflicting even within a single individual – their coherent description strains our command of language and forces us at times into dubious metaphors. Bentham cannot be said to have avoided these difficulties, as his remarks about the public interest attest. He wrote of a sum of interests in at least three different contexts, the first of which was very ill-defined. In the *Introduction* he claimed simply that the public interest was the sum of interests of particular persons. He explained neither what these interests were nor how they were combined. At this point Bentham came closest to the fault of trying to calculate utilities where there was no common unit. One can think of aggregating interests belonging to different people if they are compatible; the vocabulary of modern political science still does so. However, to speak of a 'sum' of conflicting interests requires some explanation, and in this earliest statement of Bentham's position none was provided.

Bentham did indeed believe that private happiness was the basis of public good, but not in the way so frequently imagined. The security of property and allied rights was very different from numerous highly personal interests that were not shared with the rest of the community. All of this only becomes clear when Bentham repeated the 'sum' formula in treating the security of property. In this context he was able to say that it was an 'obscure and false notion that private interest ought to give way to the public interest'.[68]

This in no way legitimized anarchy, for the interest in question was that of preserving rights, not of gaining anything at others' expense, and so was shared by all citizens. Elsewhere, he frequently showed how private interest must of necessity give way to the needs of the majority. There was no objection to private interests being put forward, but this was not to say that all were simultaneously to be successful.

Difficulties arising from the treatment of property rights may be largely removed by reference to the public interest and universal suffrage. Here Bentham insisted that in order to advance the public interest, 'all particular interests must be comprehended and advanced'. To banish all doubt as to the meaning of the 'universal-interest-comprehension principle' he added that this meant that 'with exception to as small an extent as possible, interests all to be advanced: without any exception, all to be considered'.[69]

Some modern writers would have us believe that the unity of interest perceived in relation to property rights was meant to be universal, with all citizens swept forward by a single legitimate will. An examination of Bentham's understanding of the political process has displayed the difficulties in any such claim. When he visualized the public interest under universal suffrage as the product of a mass of particular interests, he was recommending nothing unusual from the perspective of modern politics. He wished only to establish a policy-making process in which all interests were participants, thus leaving ample scope for a variety of competing interests. This suggests an understanding of the public interest far removed both from a crude sum of individual pleasures and from a single popular will, closer to modern conceptions of a process or set of procedures.

In the notion of an aggregate of particular interests, Bentham had a brilliant slogan that served to convey many of the characteristics of the classical democratic tradition – its individualism, nominalism, suspicion of *raison d'état* – even its eventual concessions to political equality. The slogan was embedded in a theory of politics consistent both with a concern for community problems and with a realistic acknowledgement of the prevalence of legitimate social diversity.

All too often the obscure remarks at the beginning of his best-known work have provided the sole text for Bentham's comments on the public interest, and for this we should perhaps blame Bowring, who made a difficult writer unreadable. In recognizing that he was not an egoist of the Max Stirner variety, we must avoid the opposite danger of making Bentham into an English Rousseau – and an extreme one at that! But to declare Bentham innocent of certain faults can only leave us pondering applications of the concept central to his thought. Bentham grasped the notion of a public interest with his usual confidence and seemed to speak strongly on at least two sides of the question. Since the question still arises, both sides remain relevant.

## NOTES

1   At times the connection is only suggested by passing directly from comments about the definition of the public interest to Bentham's recommendations on economic policy. See J. H. Hallowell, *Main Currents in Modern Political Thought* (New York, Holt, 1950), p. 214. Others are more explicit, while recognizing that Bentham was thinking about more than just economic processes. See Hanna F. Pitkin, *The Concept of Representation* (Los Angeles and Berkeley, University of California Press, 1967), p. 199.

2   Examples are cited in Nathan D. Grundstein, 'Bentham's Introduction to the Principles of Morals and Legislation', *Journal of Public Law*, 2 (1953), pp. 344–69 at p. 352.

3   Ralph Barton Perry, *Puritanism and Democracy* (New York, Vanguard Press, 1944), pp. 500–2.

4   Writers who tax classical liberalism with this defect include the following: R. M. MacIver. *The Web of Government* (New York, Macmillan, 1947), p. 187; T. P. Neill, *The Rise and Decline of Liberalism* (Milwaukee, Bruce Publishing Co., 1953), p. 59; Sister T. A. Corbett, *People or Masses: A Comparative Study in Political Theory* (Washington DC, Catholic University of America Press, 1950), p. 88; G. Jarlot, 'Personne et humanité', *Archives de Philosophie*, XII, Cahier I (1936), p. 58; Guido de Ruggerio, *European Liberalism* (Boston, Beacon Press, 1959), pp. 101–2; and, from a more secular perspective than most of the above, Andrew Hacker, *Political Theory; Philosophy, Ideology, Science* (New York, Macmillan, 1961), p. 403. All of these deal either with Bentham or the formula of an aggregate of particular interests.

5   Bentham's place in the classical democratic tradition seems secure, even though interpretations differ widely. See Louis Hartz, 'Democracy: myth and reality' in W. N. Chambers and R. H. Salisbury, eds, *Democracy Today* (New York, 1962), pp. 27, 31; and Lane Davis, 'The cost of realism: contemporary restatements of democracy' reprinted in C. A. McCoy and J. Playford, eds, *Apolitical Politics: A Critique of Behavioralism* (New York, 1967), p. 186.

6   Some political scientists adopting this position are R. Cranford Pratt, 'The Benthamite theory of democracy', *Canadian Journal of Economics and Political Science*, XXI (1955), pp. 20–9; Alfred de Grazia, 'The nature and prospects of political interest groups', in S. S. Ulmer, ed., *Introductory Readings in Political Behavior* (Chicago, Rand McNally, 1961), p. 205; J. D. B. Miller, *The Nature of Politics* (London, Duckworth, 1962), p. 48; and D. J. Manning, *The Mind of Jeremy Bentham* (London, Longman, 1968), pp. 78–9.

7   See Shirley R. Letwin, *The Pursuit of Certainty* (Cambridge, Cambridge University Press, 1965), p. 146.

8   'Introduction to the Principles of Morals and Legislation' in *Works*, ed. J. Bowring (London, 1843) I, p. 2. Hereafter cited as *Works*.

9   'Leading Principles of a Constitutional Code for any State', *Works*, II, p. 269; 'Constitutional Code', *Works*, IX, p. 7.

10  'Principles of the Civil Code', *Works*, I, p. 321.

11  'Handbook of Political Fallacies', *Works*, II, p. 416.

12 'Manual of Political Economy', *Works*, III, p. 40. See too 'Principles of International Law', II, p. 549.

13 'Constitutional Code', p. 76.

14 'Manual of Political Economy', p. 69.

15 ibid., p. 40.

16 'Principles of International Law', *Works*, II, p. 544.

17 ibid., p. 539. This fear was shared by many people less radical than Bentham. Cf. Benjamin Constant, *Oeuvres* (Paris, Gallimard, 1957), pp. 1082–4.

18 'Principles of International Law', p. 551; 'Constitutional Code', pp. 130, 137.

19 'Principles of the Civil Code', p. 313.

20 'Constitutional Code', p. 127.

21 'Leading Principles of a Constitutional Code', p. 271.

22 'Principles of International Law', p. 545.

23 For a brief treatment of the movement of vocabulary from common good to reason of state and from that to national interest, see Luigi Sturzo, *The International Community and the Right of War* (London, Allen & Unwin, 1929), pp. 183–6.

24 'Principles of International Law', p. 559. See too the passage on 'state secrets' quoted in C. B. R. Kent, *The English Radicals: An Historical Sketch* (London, Longmans, Green & Co., 1899), p. 190.

25 'Principles of International Law', p. 539.

26 'A General View of a Complete Code of Laws', *Works*, III, p. 163. I am grateful to Professor John Plamenatz of All Souls' College, Oxford, who first made me aware of this aspect of Bentham's thought.

27 ibid., p. 174.

28 'Anarchical Fallacies', *Works*, III, p. 506.

29 ibid., p. 520. A somewhat similar objection is contained in Bentham's earliest critique of Sir William Blackstone. See *A Comment on the Commentaries*, ed. C. W. Everett (Oxford, Clarendon Press, 1928), p. 77.

30 'Introduction to the Principles of Morals and Legislation', *Works*, I, p. 2.

31 But he was aware of an objective sense of the term, writing of 'Interests, real or supposed' ('An Essay on Political Tactics', *Works*, IX, p. 45). A recent commentator has objected that in making each man's subjective interest absolute, Bentham's system required unanimity or government would be placed in the difficult position of forcing people to act against their interests. See R. E. Flathman, *The Public Interest: An Essay Concerning the Normative Discourse of Politics* (New York, Wiley, 1966), p. 22. Here it is only necessary to recall that Bentham did recognize some long-term interests of citizens that governments would care for without their being consciously affected. At the same time, Bentham often noted how 'public opinion' would be formed through the assistance of opinion-leaders, many people not knowing how best to promote their legitimate interests (see 'Plan of Parliamentary Reform', *Works*, III, pp. 445–50). Finally, the emphasis on unanimity is misplaced; for, as we shall see, Bentham promised all interests a hearing, not instant gratification.

32 'Securities against Misrule Adapted to a Mohammedan State', *Works*, VIII, p. 559.

33 ibid., pp. 559, 584–5.

34 'Letters to Count Torreno', *Works*, III, p. 524.

35 'Leading Principles of a Constitutional Code', p. 269.

36 'Anarchical Fallacies', p. 533; 'Plan of Parliamentary Reform', pp. 440, 442.

37 'Constitutional Code', p. 63.

38 'Principles of the Civil Code', p. 307.

39 'Leading Principles of a Constitutional Code', pp. 269–70.

40 'Principles of the Civil Code, Appendix', pp. 358–9.

41 'Plan of Parliamentary Reform', pp. 470, 475.

42 'Principles of the Civil Code', p. 321.

43 ibid., p. 320. The early liberals' faith in the rules of the game as a genuine common interest has been ably criticized by H. J. Blackham in his *Political Discipline in a Free Society* (London, Allen & Unwin, 1961), p. 92. One must admit though that a cogent argument may be made for universal provision of certain procedural liberties and this with no class overtones.

44 'Plan of Parliamentary Reform', p. 470.

45 'Manual of Political Economy', p. 98.

46 ibid., p. 99.

47 Mercier de la Rivière, the Physiocrat, and Sir James Steuart were amongst the widely read authors who popularized the expression.

48 See R. A. Nisbet, *Community and Power* (New York, Oxford University Press, 1962), pp. 176–80 and *passim*.

49 'Plan of Parliamentary Reform', pp. 440–2; 'Manual of Political Economy', p. 99.

50 As in the ominous sounding insistence that 'all particular interests put together will not prevail for the rejection of a measure beneficial in a superior degree to the whole' ('A Plan for Saving All Trouble and Expense in the Transfer of Stock . . .', *Works*, III, p. 137). However, even here, he avoided *a priori* unanimity by taking the interests of a large group of stock-holders as a better indication of the general good than those of a small number of powerful people. Neither group involved the whole public. We must also be aware of the tactical advantages to reformers, whatever their view of society, in claiming popular unanimity. This was certainly a large factor at the time of the Reform Bill. See Joseph Hamburger, *James Mill and the Art of Revolution* (New Haven, Yale University Press, 1963), p. 73 *et seq.*

51 For the curious last example, see 'Constitutional Code', p. 53.

52 See 'Rationale of Judicial Evidence', *Works*, VI, p. 258. Numerous other texts record the same meaning.

53 'Manual of Political Economy', pp. 97–8.

54 An example of the sort of division of opinion which he hoped to end is Bentham's comment in an unpublished manuscript about morality 'determined by class interests'. See M. P. Mack, *Jeremy Bentham; An Odyssey of Ideas* (London, Heinemann, 1962), p. 218. As the proponent of a new ethical system, Bentham naturally favoured

replacing a chaos of standards with his own; but this is a far cry from proclaiming the illegitimacy of all interests but one.

55 'Manual of Political Economy', p. 98.

56 ibid., p. 99.

57 ibid., p. 98.

58 'A Protest against Law-Taxes', *Works*, II, p. 581.

59 Pratt, 'Benthamite theory of democracy', p. 22. Professor Pratt also admits here that Bentham did occasionally appreciate the necessary plurality of social interests, but the concession is weakened by Pratt's approval of Sir James Mackintosh for being much more cogent on that point. On consulting Mackintosh, we find reference only to the interests of rich *versus* poor and country *versus* town. Thus he sacrificed Bentham's recognition of the great variety of commercial interests, without coming any closer to a coherent account of class interests. For Mackintosh's review of Bentham, see Anon, 'Universal suffrage', *Edinburgh Review*, XXXI (1818–19), pp. 165–203.

60 *Jeremy Bentham's Economic Writings*, ed. Werner Stark (Allen & Unwin, 3 vols, 1952), III, p. 215.

61 It can be argued that James Mill, and especially his followers, had this tendency. See Joseph Hamburger, 'James Mill on universal suffrage and the middle class', *Journal of Politics*, 24, no. 1 (1962), pp. 167–90 at pp. 188–9.

62 On the supposed parallel with Rousseau see D. P. Crook, *American Democracy in English Politics* (Oxford, Clarendon Press, 1965), p. 19. Bentham soundly criticized the concept of a 'general will' in its French application (see 'Anarchical Fallacies', p. 507). Elsewhere, he expressed concern lest a 'pretended general will' be produced by coercion. In unfree nations 'unanimity' might 'glitter on the surface', but would have little in common with genuine expression of public opinion (see 'Essay on Political Tactics', *Works*, II, p. 332).

63 'Constitutional Code', p. 7. This sort of statement has led some commentators to assume that Bentham was inconsistent in expecting normally self-interested people to become altruistic as citizens, sinking all personal concerns in the common good. See Pratt, 'Benthamite theory of democracy', p. 23, and Pitkin, *Concept of Representation*, p. 202. However, there is ample evidence that Bentham did not expect to cleanse electors of all private ambitions; he sought only to prevent their being bribed in the literal and characteristically pre-reform sense. See 'Plan of Parliamentary Reform', p. 485, where he explained that the great danger was 'spuriousness of suffrage', or a situation where voters were moved by greed or fear to promote the interests of others. Bentham's recognition of selfish interests, apart from one's share in the general interest, was quite compatible with his hope that 'sinister interest' could be ruled out. For, deprived of immediate pecuniary profit, voters would have no certain course of action by which to gain at the expense of the public. The difficulty of anti-social calculation on the part of voters was a consideration familiar both to Bentham ('Handbook of Political Fallacies', pp. 453–4) and, curiously enough, to one of his critics: see Pitkin, *Concept of Representation*, p. 199, n37.

64 'Constitutional Code', p. 63.

65   'Handbook of Political Fallacies', p. 475.
66   These 'counterforces' operated both inside the legislature (see
     'Constitutional Code', pp. 53, 63) and in society at large, where he
     visualized small commercial 'fraternities' banding together to combat
     the influence of larger interests (see 'Manual of Political Economy',
     p. 99). Perhaps his most elaborate description of the 'counter-
     balancing' nature of interests was in the 1816 manuscript of the
     unpublished 'Political Deontology', quoted by Werner Stark in *The
     Fundamental Forms of Social Thought* (London, Routledge & Kegan
     Paul, 1962), p. 141.
67   See 'Handbook of Political Fallacies', p. 446; 'Plan of Parliamentary
     Reform', p. 450.
68   'Principles of the Civil Code', p. 321.
69   'Plan of Parliamentary Reform', p. 452.

## Chapter Fourteen

# TWO CONCEPTS OF POLITICS AND DEMOCRACY: JAMES AND JOHN STUART MILL*

## *ALAN RYAN*

As an introductory note to the substance of this paper, I should like to start by not apologizing for begging in my own favour the major problems involved in interpreting historical texts in political theory. It will be obvious from the body of the paper that James Mill and his son appear here to illustrate a wide thesis concerning two contrasting images of the nature of politics, images that are important in their own right, and especially so in the context of recent Anglo-American political science. It might be complained that thus to use them involves riding roughshod over historical accuracy, or – to change the metaphor – that I have thrust my protagonists into a Procrustean bed of my own devising, ignoring the eccentricities, the quirks of doctrine that any biographer has to stress. A real defence against such a charge can only lie in the insights hopefully provided by the paper itself; but I should at once state that if I must plead guilty, I remain unrepentant. For my purpose is not to re-create exactly what James Mill or J. S. Mill thought he was saying, but rather to elucidate with all the assistance that hindsight can give us what kind of case each of them was making.

It is possible – it is certainly often asserted – that nothing useful can be said about *the kind of case* that is made, that the exceptions and qualifications are always so numerous and so important that respectable work can only come from considering the particular case in its particularity.[1] I do not believe this to be true, and for that reason I am not persuaded that there is any reason of principle why the kind of enterprise here attempted should prove fruitless. But it is obvious enough that taking liberties with history in this manner cannot extend to faking the evidence nor yet to overlooking evidence that might either strengthen the case here made or less

* Previously published in Martin Fleisher (ed.) *Machiavelli and the Nature of Political Thought* (London, Croom Helm, 1973).

fortunately demolish it outright. In this sense what is argued here is vulnerable to the historian's expertise. And to the extent that this paper concentrates rather narrowly on only two essays by prolific writers, both of whom wrote a good deal about closely related issues to those discussed here, and both of whom spent their professional lives in political administration, it obviously runs rather large risks in this direction. It is no part of one's duty to regret taking risks; but it is perhaps part of that duty to admit that they are taken.

The wider thesis, in the light of which I want to look at the two Mills, is this: there is visible in the political thought of the past century and a half a division of opinion over the point or the goals of political and social life in general. This division lies between the adherents of what one might call an 'economic' or 'market' account of social life on the one hand and the partisans of a 'participant' or 'self-developmental' account on the other.[2] These are not self-explanatory terms; indeed at this point they are only gestures towards explanations that will appear in due course. The distinction is very closely allied to that which Hegel noted in the *Philosophy of Right*, where it forms the basis of the distinction between civil society on the one hand and the state on the other. Civil society forms that area of social life which adequately satisfies the capacities of human nature so far as it is a subject for political economy; the state, on the other hand, satisfies the non-economic need to belong to a community of rational beings, the need to be absorbed into a life of loyalties that cannot be traded in or bargained over. There is a version of the distinction in much of what Marx says about bourgeois society and again in much of what the English Idealists had to say in criticism of their utilitarian predecessors. It is, however, a dichotomy which cannot in the nature of things succeed in ranging all political thinkers unequivocally on one or other side of the divide. Thus to represent J. S. Mill as concerned only with the quality of citizen participation in a common life, as if he had nothing whatever to say about the accommodation of interests, the eliciting of bargains, and the like would plainly be preposterous. It is of course a general truth that any picture of what is involved in political participation must make some assumptions about the nature of the political system within which the citizen is called on to participate; and it is equally true that a concern for the stability and efficiency of the political system as a quasi-economic order must make some assumptions about the participation or non-participation of those who come to market.

A potentially more damaging objection to the dichotomy as

drawn is the claim that anything said in the 'economic' vocabulary can be said equally well in the 'self-developmental' vocabulary and vice versa, so that the distinction between them is merely verbal. A proper reply to this objection would involve a careful account of the relationship between fact and theory in political science. Here we can do little more than illustrate what the objection amounts to. Let us take an issue central to this paper, the difference between 'market' and 'self-developmental' accounts of political participation. On a market theory of politics, participation appears to the citizen as a cost that he incurs in gaining for himself some part of those private goods in the enjoyment of which his happiness consists. Participant accounts, on the other hand, regard such participation as a gain to the individual in that it hopefully increases his self-awareness, strengthens his sense of belonging to a community of moral equals, and increases his sense of rational mastery over the environment. Now it is undeniable that a concern with these latter qualities is a central preoccupation with a distinctive political tradition of which Rousseau, Hegel, Marx, and the English Idealists are typical spokesmen. Such concepts lie at the heart of their account of the social world, a world that is praised by Hegel for its supposed adequacy in making such goods available to us, but is damned by both Rousseau and Marx for the obstacles it offers to their wider diffusion or more perfect possession.

It seems equally obvious that these concerns are alien to 'classical' utilitarianism, as preached by Bentham or James Mill. But, must we conclude that this is a matter of the theory? May it not be a matter of the theorist only? Can we not – as we see J. S. Mill asking himself after his exposure to Coleridge – accommodate within the economic categories of the empiricists the insights of the Idealist theorists of self-development? Thus, over participation, can we not simply add into our account such previously unthought of benefits as increased self-awareness, perhaps so many of them as to make it no longer a net expense but a net benefit, independently, that is, of its instrumental efficacy? My own view is that in the end such an attempt runs into so many difficulties as to render the revised account incoherent, but there is no simple proof of this point; the tautological results of such attempts in the literature of politics and sociology amount at best to weak inductive arguments on my side.

And doubts about the efficacy of the translation in one direction presumably apply with as much or as little force to translations in the other direction. Thus, suppose we attempt to translate the conclusions of a cost-benefit account of political participation into the language of self-development – a translation that we might ascribe to Hegel in his account of civil society. The individual in civil society alienates one aspect of his character to the business dealings of commercial life; indeed in bourgeois society he may find great fulfilment in leading the life of the good bourgeois. It looks initially, of course, as if a Rousseauist concern with constant involvement in the life of the community is a necessary consequence of any 'self-developmental' view; yet Hegel takes some pains to escape this consequence. It is not that he drops the typically Hegelian mode of analysis to argue suddenly for the merits of apathy on a cost-benefit basis; what he does instead is to claim that rationality and self-realization do not require that we spend much, perhaps any, of our time actively engaged in political or any other form of public life. He does not on the face of it renounce the goal of self-development; rather he argues that for most of us the way to self-realization is to do just those things that our station in our society calls upon us to do. We may, thus, express ourselves completely in leading just the life which a utilitarian, non-participant, market theorist of politics would have commended to us as the way to minimize costs and maximize benefits. Here, too, I think the idea that we can simply translate the conclusions of the one theorist into the words of another is eventually incoherent. At the very least, we have on our hands the historical problem of explaining how it is that Hegel's views were regarded as a very real betrayal by the Young Hegelians; the obvious answer is that the conclusions he came to *did* betray the moral concerns that the theory is centrally engaged with. At best, the translator is faced with awkward overtones which seem inevitably to attach to one way of speaking; at worst he is faced with two radically different images of human nature.

One thing, however, must be conceded. The dichotomy with which we are working does not readily categorize thinkers as more democratic and less democratic. It is a matter of brute historical fact that not all the thinkers who make so much of self-development are wholehearted democrats. Hegel, plainly, was concerned to argue *against* democracy, and it was scarcely an enthusiasm for industrial democracy that Mill picked up from Coleridge. In part, this is only to concede an old point, that there is no very direct connection between the social and political *Weltanschauung* of a thinker and the detailed social and political prescriptions he may issue. Indeed, it is only to admit that a central problem for political thought is to try to elicit the connection between the far-ranging theory and the substance of political action. And what this seems to mean at this point in the debate about the condition of contemporary democratic theory is that we need to find a way to utilize the insights of both the utilitarians and the Idealists – that we need to make Rousseau talk *to* Hume rather than at him or past him, that we need to make Mill and T. H. Green speak a common language, or for that matter Robert Dahl and the Students for a Democratic Society. Still, this is to be too concerned with wider goals and deeper anxieties; it is time to move on to the *dramatis personae* of the paper.

The first thing I want to do is to elucidate through the *Essay on Government* what I mean by saying that James Mill's essay is a classical economic model of democracy, a complement to classical economics and to utilitarian ethics. In general, commentators have made rather too little of this aspect of the essay; Elie Halévy's distinction between the natural and the artificial identification of interests tends rather to differentiate between politics and economics.[3] Most critics of the essay have relied heavily on Macaulay's devastating attack on it; and it is true that this demonstrated very clearly the ambiguity inherent in the axiom that everyone pursues his own self-interest, the dubiousness of the concept of human nature as there utilized, and the apparent absence of any sort of common sense.[4] Where they have not used Macaulay's arguments, they have pointed to Mill's hope that political power would fall into the hands of the new industrial and professional middle class, to his intention of denying the vote to women and to men under forty, as if such departures from the institutional and ideological pieties of twentieth-century Britain and America render all argument superfluous. I do not precisely set out to 'defend' James Mill's *Essay*; indeed, it seems to me an eminently dislikable document. But it has virtues that ought not to be neglected. Its most important claim to intellectual stature is that it provides a classical economic model of democratic government, and thus stands at the head of a line of thought extending down to Joseph Schumpeter or Anthony Downs, a line of thought that provides many of the explicit or implicit assumptions with the aid of which we still practise political science. In other words, Mill displays in a very clear shape the intellectual model underlying much that is presently written about the operations and the difficulties of American and British government. Of course much of what he says has been improved upon, and much has been rendered obsolete since, in particular, the growth of mass parties. For all that, many of the premises and not a few of the conclusions of recent writers are there. Although this paper concentrates on the issue of political participation, it by no means exhausts the possible issues.

Mill assumes, in the fashion of all economists (and of Thomas

Hobbes, their greater grandfather), that the natural goal of each man is to maximize his own wellbeing.[5] He says, rightly enough, that political truths ought to be culled from the widest possible examination of human nature; but he concludes after a strikingly cursory inspection of the evidence that human happiness or wellbeing consists in maximizing one's pleasures and minimizing one's pains, that we are happy in proportion as our pleasures are many and our pains are few.[6] To belabour the obvious, this account of happiness closely resembles the picture of economic motivation assumed in classical economics; we suffer work in order to gain an income, and in this process we obviously want to maximize the difference between the gratification we can purchase through the money we earn and the pain it causes us to expend our efforts in securing that money. Similarly, in *any* walk of life, we want to maximize the surplus of pleasure over the pain incurred in securing it or (to cater to the gloomy side of Mill's character) at any rate to minimize the deficit.

But Mill's theory is not economic only in this sense. It is an economic theory in a more explicit sense too. An important fact about the world we live in is that it is a world of scarce resources; and this means that we have to work for our pleasures. But work by definition is a pain and we cannot therefore wish to work more than we have to. What this must entail is that each person wants to receive as large a proportion of the product of his efforts as he can.[7] Now, to belabour the point again, it is a theorem of classical economics that in a perfect market all factors are rewarded precisely according to what they are worth to the market at large – leaving aside such complications as rent. Even without the refinements of marginalist analysis, the broad outlines of this conclusion were available to Mill. Now, if it is a free market that allows men to receive as much as possible of the product of their own labour, we have already reached the point in the argument where we can say that the overwhelmingly important task for a government is to ensure that a free market operate. In the light of this consideration, it is no wonder that one very great difference between Mill and his successors like Schumpeter is in their attitude to groups; Mill rejected the proposals for corporate representation current at his time with complete contempt.[8] In his eyes these proposals were merely ways of handing a political monopoly position to groups that already enjoyed a monopoly position in the economy. Thus, of course, Mill invoked a politics founded on the principles of perfect competition to defend a market founded on the same principles; but Schumpeter's defence is of a politics founded on the principles of oligopolistic competition, whose main task is the regulation of an economy based on the principles of oligopoly not perfect competition. This is plainly an important difference; none the less, the important identity is the extent to which they are both economic theorists of politics in this double sense.[9]

Men, then, are bent on maximizing their individual happiness, on piling up a surplus in the psychic bank. The major means to this goal is the market. But the market can only function if contracts are observed and enforced, if there is proper control over the currency, and if fraud is suppressed. If men could get what they wanted without having to accept the restraints put on their actions by the market, they would presumably do so; thus the major aim of government is to stop them. But both the establishment and the exercise of governmental authority are threatened by another fact about human nature, which again is Hobbesian in origin. Put simply, it is that men are insatiable and will want to acquire goods ad infinitum; but crucially it is not of all goods that this is true, but especially of power.[10] Power is the one thing that enables men to be sure of the future in a world filled with competitors, a world in which outcomes are otherwise unstable. It seems to be Mill's view, as it is certainly Hobbes's, that the reason lies not in any viciousness inherent in human nature but simply in the exigencies of a competitive situation. Unlike Hobbes, Mill wastes no time on the intellectual fantasy of the state of nature; indeed, unlike Hobbes, he is not so much concerned to show that all men everywhere are insatiable as to argue that there is no guarantee that our rulers will be less insatiable than their subjects. Thus is created the problem which Hobbes presumed to be out of the way; if we can locate in any pair of hands power sufficient to protect us from each other, will this power not be used to plunder us instead, for the benefit of him who holds the power? In essence, most of Mill's essay is devoted to solving this puzzle.

One way of explaining Mill's solution would simply be to summarize what he has to say about the traditional types of government and their weaknesses. It can, however, be more adequately elucidated in terms of the market model. It is plain enough that Mill's assumptions rule out any form of monarchy or aristocracy; such governments amount to handing ourselves over to what are by definition 'sinister interests'. If a firm could charge whatever prices it liked on the market, it would charge monopoly prices; similarly a monarchy amounts to a monopoly in politics and will take monopoly gains out of the political system. And the same thing applies to any aristocracy that contrives to avoid quarrelling about how to divide the spoils among its members. These governments will be such as to maximize only their own good and not that of the people as a whole.[11] Mill dismisses almost as rapidly the traditional arguments for checks and balances and for a system of separation of powers;[12] any such separation is illusory, since a coalition will instantly form to take over a monopoly of power – if power is divided among three groups, any two will combine against the third, supposing that all three do not rather combine against the public.[13] It is usually, and in general rightly, urged against Mill that if all governments were as careless of constitutional forms as he supposes, then no form of government whatever could secure us against the oppression of our rulers. Against this, it does not seem unfair to suggest that the Anglo-American enthusiasm for the separation of powers and for the doctrine of checks and balances may well have blinded us to the extent to which coalitions between interests have formed and flourished, and not always for the general good. Mill's conclusion, at any rate, is simple enough; what we require is some method of ensuring that power is placed only in the hands of persons who are unable to use it for any purposes contrary to the interests of the people at large. Were the whole nation able to take decisions on its own behalf, there could be no question of the dominance of sinister interests; but this is plainly impracticable. The problem thus amounts to securing the same result by other means; and the means according to Mill is through the device of representation.[14] We the people, who would act rightly – who could not under processes of free bargaining act otherwise – but who are disqualified by our numbers from actually gathering together, delegate persons to act on our behalf. We are too many to take decisions, but our delegates are few enough to decide and act; if they are appropriately selected and properly controlled, they cannot but act in the public interest. Of course, there are some extremely awkward questions raised by a bald assertion of this sort. On the premises of any one so empiricist as Mill, who are 'the people', and how can this entity or nonentity take decisions, control anyone, or fail to control anyone? There is surely an ambiguity here created by Mill's basic premise of the natural proclivity of each man to pursue his own individual interest; what can the 'public' interest be, and how could anyone be led to pursue it? Without answers to these questions, how can we give a plausible account of how the public interest is served by the device of representation?[15]

The answer is to account for the processes of representation in quasi-economic terms, by representing the political system as a market, and the behaviour of voters and those for whom they vote in a manner analogous to that in which we represent the behaviour of buyers and sellers of goods. The individual voter is in the market for a policy that will be in his own interest, i.e., that which maximizes his utility, just as he shops about in the economic market for goods that will yield him a maximum of utility.[16] Representatives in a democracy thus turn out to be delegates in the search for utility maximization, a view that entirely coheres with the radical view of representation in the early nineteenth century. Their platforms are, so to speak, the shopping lists according to which they seek at the level of national policy-making to maximize the welfare of their electors. There is a natural connection between such an account of representation and the view that politics exists in order to harmonize the activities of rational egoists; and it is important to see that representation as a device does not look anything like so centrally important once we conceive of politics in other terms. For Rousseau, to take an obvious example, representation can solve nothing, since the object of social and political activity is in large part to integrate the individual in communal action, a thing that simply cannot be done at second hand.[17] That we can delegate a man to go and vote as I and others decide he should is an important fact when we think of political activity as essentially self-interested in the utilitarian manner – or in the way in which most pressure-group theorists think of it now. But if social and political life is concerned with such goals as self-expression and self-realization, it is on the face of it hard to see how anyone else can express *my* self on my behalf or can through his activities realize *my* capacities. If politics cannot be reduced to a form of quasi-economic bargaining, then the fact that I can get someone else to bargain on my behalf ceases to be the central fact about the possibility of mass democracy. For James Mill there seems to have been no problem, but only because he chose not to face it. Although a good deal of his talk about the people and the visibility of a 'public interest' looks more Rousseauist than reductionist or Benthamite, the logic of his position is surely that he would have to give an account of the people's choice and the public's interest that was individualist and reductionist. The general interest must be derivable by way of some process of summing the gains and losses of individuals under alternative policies.[18] To work out what kind of policies would be in the general interest we must presumably make the kind of calculations that John Rawls has investigated concerning the kinds of bargains that could be struck by rational egoists.[19] Long-run considerations about uncertainty, vulnerability, and the like might well lead us to accept all the major institutions of the free market and the policing arrangements that attend it; in the absence of clear information about our prospects under given procedures, we should all have to accept policies in the general interest rather than our own. In the short run, we can expect to see much more clearly how we could make gains; but since everyone else can see this and move to cut the gain off from us, we should once again be forced to espouse the general rather than our sectional good. And it goes without saying that the real world will yield less of this desirable state of affairs to the extent that the real world departs from the assumptions embodied in the model, in respect of differential access to information, inequalities of power, and the like.

For this account of Mill, I do not want to claim any great novelty; it may push Mill rather fiercely into the market mould, but at the level of doctrine rather than biography it is no injustice. There are all manner of things about Newton that a biographer would tell one about, which do not concern the physicist; and what is here being claimed is that about Mill's doctrines we can crystallize many of the commonplaces – and some of the more startling recent assertions – about the way in which liberal democracy can and should work. A good example here is the issue of political partici- pation, on which a lot of recent attention has been focused. On the market theory, participation is a cost to the individual since it requires much the same activities to vote rationally as to shop sensibly – we need to expend time and energy in gaining infor- mation, i.e., we have to work. To expend energy on work is itself a pain and is costly in terms of diverting energy from other activities with a higher direct yield in pleasure.[20] From this it follows that a person would not desire the suffrage, let alone desire actually to use it, unless he thought that his vital interests would suffer if he did not – or, but very implausibly, that direct political action would yield him a high utility compared with other activities. It might be argued that a *utility maximizer* (i.e., an optimist), as distinct from a *disutility minimizer* (i.e., a pessimist), would find this less convincing; the ambitious and the optimistic will want to be active just as they will cheerfully take risks and work harder in order to pile up fortunes over and above what they can reasonably think they need to avoid hardship. There is no simple answer to this point; for the purposes of this paper it is enough to point out how little of an optimist James Mill was and how unlikely he thought it that any rational man would be an optimist; again, his conception of what politics could achieve may very well have been such to leave little room for ambition.

For more general theoretical purposes, it is of course very

important to remember that any cost-benefit analysis of behaviour is very vulnerable to speculation about temperament. For Mill anyway, the way ahead is simple; we work to avoid the evil of starvation; if we could eat without working we should do so, and similarly if we could have the benefits of the suffrage without voting, we should do so. Thus Macaulay's attack on Mill's refusal of the suffrage to women is not entirely well taken. It is not, as he so contemptuously asserts, a case of dogmatizing away the interests of half the human race.[21] For Mill's defence, if it could hardly be word for word, is at any rate thought for thought that of a writer like Downs,[22] and to some extent much like that of Bernard Berelson and indeed any of dozens of consensus theorists in the 1950s.[23] If someone will look after your interests for you, then there is no earthly reason why you need engage in political activity at all – not even to the extent of trying to find out who are the candidates for office nor what their policies are. The effort you do not expend on this sphere, you can expend to better effect elsewhere. After all, political activity is only one of those activities which may increase your utility-flow, and possibly not the most effective by a long way. This argument is not a defence of 'functional apathy', be it noted; our argument here is only concerned with the gains and losses to the individual, not with the needs of the political system as a whole. The arguments for functional apathy only consider the utility to society at large of the abstention of a class of persons whose entry on to the political scene might cause chaos. So far as those individuals are concerned, their own interests might indicate something else altogether, for if they are sufficiently ill-provided for under the present arrangements, it is likely that any degree of social disruption will affect them only marginally for the worse and possibly much for the better. The case made by Mill is different; it is much more akin to the defences of 'privatization' or 'depoliticization' – other forms of satisfaction are so readily available, and the satisfaction they yield is so great that politics can safely be ignored. On Mill's analysis, then, we can say that anyone who can safely do without the vote will not want it, or will not use it; and this is individually and socially rational, since elections are expensive and Mill envisages their being frequent, which would be very costly indeed if there were universal suffrage and universal use of the suffrage.

But, what Mill has become known for as much as anything is the defence of concentrating power in the hands of the middle classes; this may resemble, but is certainly not quite the same as the defence of the political entrepreneur by Robert Dahl and others. Mill's argument is that the interests of the middle class are identical with the interests of society as a whole. It is not clear what sort of an argument he thinks he has to back up this assertion. The usual commentator's ploy is attractively easy and is even employed by J. S. Mill in discussing his father's politics; we are to see the *Essay on Government* as primarily a piece of propaganda against such long-standing bugbears of the radicals as civil-list pensions, duties on food and raw materials, and the like, and thus we do not have to look for arguments at all. A certain amount of philosophical paint is often applied to political programmes; that is what is happening here. J. S. Mill says rather plaintively that his father was a practical man who would have dealt with the facts as he found them, as he did in the course of his experience at India House.[24] But to my mind this defence yields too much. James Mill knew perfectly well that he could not state as an empirical truth that all good governments had been those managed by the middle classes – it could not be true, if for no better reason than that the middle class that Mill defended was a historical novelty. But the way out of the apparent concession is obvious. All good governments can be accounted for as the result of checks of a non-institutionalized sort upon the power of the ruling group to rule in its own selfish interest; wherever the general good was promoted we would expect to find a process like that of bargaining taking place in however covert a way. A society may manage to work some sort of market economy in the absence of a conventional currency because people adjust their behaviour accordingly – the case imagined by Locke of a pre-monetary state of nature where barter flourished shows that the case is anyway conceivable. So, equally, a political system other than representative government may achieve many of the utility-maximizing objectives we set ourselves. The advantages of a formally constituted representative system are those that always attach to institutions with specific purposes, advantages mostly of a division of labour. Still, does even this guarantee the truth of Mill's assertion about the harmony of middle-class interests and the general interest? Surely not; but we can go further. It may not be a general truth that representative government only works well with middle-class control; but the general argument rests on the qualities which Mill ascribed to the middle class of his day. These qualities are of course those of economically rational man – and they can be summarized as industry and knowledge.[25] Mill's belief that education and the wider dispersion of knowledge would be forces for stability rather than for chaos seems to be explained on this view. We have no need of spectacular personal qualities in a world that is managed by rational well-informed people, since the calculations of such people should always yield identical results in terms of public policy. Mill believed that, as things stood when he wrote, the middle class had more or less a monopoly of these desirable virtues, so that it was from the middle class that the rational bargainers that democracy needs would mostly be drawn. As rational men, they could see that it was in their long-term interest to create a working class in their own image – diligent, provident, and intelligent; and this of course was what was in the interest of the working class also. Thus, on Mill's premises, the most rational political policy for the working class as a whole was to accept the leadership of the middle class, while for individual members of the working class, it was rational to follow the direction set by middle-class 'opinion leaders'.

Putting the argument as briefly as this makes it look hair-raisingly simplistic. This is not entirely a vice, since many good theories have this kind of simplicity about them at first sight. What is important is what can be done with them, and what can be done, as we have seen, is that we can show how Mill's argument underlies much of the recent acceptance of such phenomena as deference voting, voter ignorance, low involvement, and the like as not regrettable but desirable phenomena. Another current debate on which the utilitarian theory is illuminating is the validity of taking stability as in some sense a measure of political democracy. The demonstration of this point shows interestingly how political and economic theory can come together to reinforce what must have partly been a non-theoretical response to Cold War alarms about subversion and civil war. Like any piece of classical economics, Mill's picture of politics rests on an ambiguity in its basic premises which leads to some doubt about how to evaluate his conclusions. The proposition that all men try to maximize their own welfare hovers uncertainly between the status of logical truth and empirical falsity.[26] In consequence, there is a good deal of difficulty in applying the notion of optimality to the performance of an entire economy – we simply cannot tell whether an economy is maximizing welfare or not. As is well known, there are two ways out of this problem: one is to set up what looks like rational standards for overall performance and to assess the actual performance of an economy by these; the other is to work with the notion of Pareto-optimality and say that any situation is optimal where there are no desired trades left to be made. In other words, a situation is optimal where no one can better his position after he has compensated anyone made worse off by his move.[27] The attractions of Pareto-optimality are obvious in that it enables us to dispense with making our own judgements about what would be a desirable social mix of products and to leave the arbitration to the people involved. But to call any situation optimal, we must make two assumptions – firstly that people are free to make any trades they wish to make, and secondly that people have adequate information, since otherwise there will be possible moves not taken up. There are many complications over and above these, and many more in the field of analysing moves between one Pareto-optimum and another; but these can be ignored here. The basic point is that it is very plausible to equate stability under conditions of freedom as being the same thing as democracy; for what can stability indicate except that the trades possible in the circumstances have been made? This is not to say that democracy entails stagnation, since it is obvious that new goods will appear, tastes will change, and there will be a good deal of bustle in the market-place. None the less political stability indicates that the public interest is served.[28] It is true that James Mill was no conservative; he was willing to use the threat of mob terror to get concessions from the political incumbents of his day.[29] None the less, his theory is non-dynamic in the same sense as most of classical economics – normality is the situation where equilibrium is achieved and the market is cleared of unwanted policies and unsatisfied demands. And such an equilibrium situation is for Mill market democracy, even if large numbers of people take very little part in the processes by which this equilibrium is achieved and maintained. To make the picture fully coherent and convincing, we should have to explore at greater length the various qualifications here left implicit; for instance, we have said nothing about the requirements of free access to the market, nor about the analogues to the requirements of perfect information. It is, however, notable that many of Mill's occasional writings were precisely about those topics that such qualifications involve – popular education and the freedom of the press among them.

James Mill has generally had a bad press from the critics, and it is not hard to see why. If there were no other reason, we should probably dislike him for the education which he inflicted on his son. Most of us – Alexander Bain is a notable exception in this – take an uncritical attitude to J. S. Mill's account of his education and a correspondingly critical attitude to the father who devised it. For those who dislike utilitarian politics he is a cherished *bête noire* – and the class of those who dislike utilitarian politics is a very large one, including almost all forms of nineteenth- and twentieth-century conservatives, almost all forms of revolutionaries, and many forms of reformist socialists. He seems tailor-made for abuse – to be accused of advocating 'steam engine government', 'anachronistic syllogising', 'heartlessness', 'doctrinaire narrowness', and so forth. To redress the balance a little, it is worth saying a few words in defence of at any rate the *kind* of case he was making. The various forms of classical economic theory have been in many ways the most dazzling achievement of the social sciences; to see how true this is, one has only to think of the longevity and vigour of this one branch of the social sciences. Classical economics brought large numbers of hitherto unexplained phenomena under intellectual and to some extent social control and set up standards for other social sciences to aim at. The use of notions akin to homeostasis in economics long antedates their use by cyberneticists and then by political scientists. What is even more to the point is that classical economics was tied in very closely to a scientific theory of individual psychology and to a moral philosophy that were themselves attractive for quite independent reasons. It seemed, therefore, that a social science was in the making that would allow important questions both of explanation and policy to be answered, no matter in what society they were asked. Even where the answers that were found were not those expected, progress was made; for the theory enabled social scientists to make mistakes they could explain. And that is a neglected but very vital function of all theory. The fruitfulness of the approach would take a lot of documenting, but in the context of democratic politics, surely the evidence is simple enough – and it is sufficient to cite the work of Schumpeter or Downs. An obvious weakness of Mill's initial model is that he has nothing to say about parties, or about groups, save to mistrust them as sinister interests. If the market theory of democracy were to survive, it had to be brought to face the reality of less than perfect competition. In essence, Schumpeter's revision of the theory of democracy is applying the democratic model to the situation of oligopoly. And the new model as much as the old leaves us with the same questions. We no longer have to justify a curtailed suffrage, but we do need to explain a limited use of the vote; we no longer bother about the power of landlords nor about civil-list pensions; but we still worry about the rake-offs of well-entrenched chairmen of Congressional committees; in other words we still perceive democracy as an instrument for utility-maximization, and thus we still have to concentrate on what look like exorbitant prices being asked for political action, and we still try to remove obstacles to the making of reasonable bargains. Naturally, we employ much the same intellectual categories as the Mills for this purpose and make much the same assumptions about the goals of the citizenry and their rulers. James Mill remains no less dislikable for his place in such a tradition, but it would be folly to deny the intellectual appeal of so long-lived and flourishing a tradition.


None the less, our next task is to turn precisely to the dissatisfaction with this tradition which agitated the younger Mill. In other words, in terms of the categories we initially began with, we must turn from economic to self-developmental democracy; away from utility as a central notion and on to the idea of progress, self-realization, and growth. But before we do so, it is necessary to say a preliminary word about whether J. S. Mill was a democrat at all. A number of writers have questioned whether Mill would have thought of himself as a democrat; perhaps the longest and most careful statement of these doubts was offered by J. H. Burns some twelve years ago in two articles on the history of Mill's changing views on the subject.[30] It seems to me, however, that all such doubts are fairly futile; Mill's last word on the subject in his *Autobiography* certainly describes him as a democrat[31] – we may choose to refuse the title to him in the light of his defence of plural voting and the like inegalitarian provisions of *Representative Government*, but if the question is one of his self-ascription, there is no good reason to ignore the evidence. If, however, the question is one of whether he *ought* to have thus described himself, the matter is wide open to dispute over the essential and non-essential tenets of democracy. The trouble with an account such as Burns's is that it hides the fact that beneath a remarkable willingness on Mill's part to experiment with practical devices of one sort and another, there was an almost equally remarkable consistency in basic aim. The point that I wish to establish is that J. S. Mill was at once more ambitious for democratic politics than his father had been and at the same time more pessimistic about those areas where his father had been most cheerful – notably in his estimate of the harmony of interests between the middle class and the labouring poor, and again in his estimate of the willingness of the labouring class to submit indefinitely to the leadership of the middle class. This means that more is at issue than any simple maximization of utility, while the dangers of mass tyranny are constantly present to him – dangers that are all but ruled out of his father's account by definition. Save to the extent that it reminds us that liberalism and democracy are by no means inevitably allies, arguing that J. S. Mill was not a democrat serves little or no purpose. What obviously does matter is that we should see clearly in what way the goals he defends in *Representative Government* and elsewhere differ quite radically from those that his father valued, and how right his Idealist successors and critics were to think these goals more than a little at odds with traditional utilitarianism.

Where James Mill's *Essay on Government* is very brief and apparently very simple, *Representative Government* is a great deal longer and more complex. Moreover its length and complexity do not mean that it is a completely adequate guide to Mill's reflections on the essay's premises. Many of these have to be culled from his long wrestling with Saint-Simon and Comte, from his attempts to do justice both to Bentham and to Coleridge, from his efforts in the *Principles of Political Economy* to separate out the area of free choice from that of economic necessity. Mill's famed inconsistency derives from a less famed but more consistent belief in the importance of doing justice to a great variety of goods, rather than to one at the expense of all others. The consistency of his interests means that the high and sometimes rather absurd faith he places in technical devices – the defence of 'fancy franchises' in *Representative Government* and in his occasional writings – is part and parcel with the grave fears he expresses in *Liberty*. The importance of *Liberty* in the light of *Representative Government* is plain from the outset; for both works illustrate the extent to which progress replaces utility as the key conception. In the essay *On Liberty*, Mill insists that he appeals only to utility; but he immediately moves away from any simple utilitarian defence of individual freedom by qualifying the claim: the utility in question is that which is founded on man's permanent interests as a progressive being.[32] But this, manifestly, is to make the principle of maximizing utility logically dependent on the principle of maximizing progress. So, equally with *Representative Government*, the goal is no longer that of maintaining a stable and efficient administration in the service of maximum general utility; now it essentially involves notions of change and progress.[33] So emphatic is Mill upon this point that he makes it the text for a criticism of the doctrine common to Coleridge and to Comte that societies involve principles of change and principles of rest, and thus that there ought to be parties of order and parties of progress. For him, order is desirable only in the limited sense that if there is to be progress, then certainly we must not slip backwards; but the value of order is solely its value as a condition of progress. The criteria of progress, too, are not very obviously utilitarian, for the progress Mill defends is scarcely related at all to economic goods, nor to the aim of piling up an ever larger supply of things to be consumed by the members of a society. Primarily the progress desired is improvement in the quality of the human beings composing the society. It can be fairly objected that James Mill also was concerned to improve the quality of the human character, and that an emphasis on what is now called socialization – a concern for the educative effects of the political system – was common to both the Mills and to most utilitarians. But what this objection misses is the difference in the aspects of character that J. S. Mill cared about. So far as he was concerned, his father and Bentham had systematically neglected the most important aspects of human nature – the list of their shortcomings is given in the famous essay on Bentham and is fairly extensive.[34] We might in James Mill's world take pains to socialize men into industry and probity and into a calculating kind of intelligence; we should not care to make them bold, imaginative, individual, and sensitive. Yet it is these qualities that J. S. Mill most wants to preserve and encourage; a flock of honest and businesslike sheep would be total failures as a society of developed human beings.[35]

To say that by comparison with his son James Mill worked with a static and timeless picture of human nature and of social and political life is in no way to contradict what was earlier said about his radical politics. What is at issue is somewhat similar to what is said to be at issue when equilibrium theorists in sociology are accused of building conservatism into their explanations of social life; they reasonably retort that the sort of equilibrium involved can change radically – the stability required is at a fairly high level of abstraction.[36] Similarly, when James Mill is said to have a static view of human nature, there is no suggestion that he would have denied that men can come to develop new tastes or to change their minds about what they want. His emphasis on the insatiability of one desire – that for power – shows that there is dynamism in the picture. None the less, the differences between father and son remain untouched. For the father, power is a special case, in that the desire for power is parasitic upon the desire for goods in the usual sense; and even compared with Hobbes he is imperceptive about humanity's apparent tendency to accept 'fancy' values – as for example the desire to win for the sake of winning and not for the sake of the prize. But for the son, we simply fail to understand human nature if we ignore the fact that men use the satisfaction of one desire as a mere stepping-stone to the acquisition of new desires, quite often incomparable with the old. James Mill tends to lump men's choices together; but the younger Mill's account concentrates much more steadily on the personal and the idiosyncratic. For him, the choices a man makes are what go to make up his self; and the ability to choose one's own character is for him practically an obsession.[37] Since our choices both reflect and create our characters, the need to have the widest possible range of choices available becomes paramount. The point is illustrated most clearly by a negative consideration – what the fears were that agitated them. James Mill, in essence, desires to keep the hands of the rulers out of the national till; democracy is as much as anything a means of ensuring that our rulers do not misconduct themselves with the funds they take out of our pockets. But J. S. Mill's great fear is of mass despotism. It is not a fear of what has recently obsessed theorists of 'mass society'; in spite of the spectacle of Louis Napoleon, he does not fear the aroused mass that blindly follows the charismatic leader. It is not the frenzy of the masses but their lethargy which chiefly frightens him. We could say, however, that he shares a fear of totalitarian democracy, for he certainly fears the overwhelming pressures of a united public opinion, an opinion whose answer to all social and political problems is summed up in the imperative to be like everyone else. But as *Liberty* makes clear, it is not that such a despotism will be brutal or violent – its effectiveness may well be the greater for the gentleness with which the pressure is applied. The ills to guard against are passivity, inertia, timidity, and intellectual stagnation. *Liberty* and *Representative Government* are of a piece in their concerns, with the difference that the former essay is concerned with the total social and psychological problem, the latter with its more directly political implications. Thus, if we must sum up the basic political goals of the younger Mill in contrast with the elder, it is that social and individual existence must be kept open-ended, that the potentialities for growth, change, and development must receive the first priority. It is the view of the educator in an extended sense, that of the defender of an education that is received not as a preparation for some further goal, but for its own sake.

An illustration will serve to flesh out so summary a statement. Among the views that are defended in *Representative Government*, perhaps the most mocked is the defence of open voting and a non-secret ballot.[38] Its interest is that though the conclusion may seem merely quaint by now, the argument underlying it is disquieting still. For Mill, voting is an act with two aspects: aggressive and defensive we might call them, or other-regarding and self-regarding. The vote is an instrument with which to defend our rights and with which to make our claims felt. But it is also an instrument of control over the lives of others; when we vote we necessarily help to bring about the implementation of policies that bind others as much as ourselves. If we are willing to accept the task of controlling other people to any extent, we must in reason be willing to account to them for how we propose to exercise that control. To vote is to commit oneself to courses of action for the whole community; if the choice is not merely frivolous or merely selfish, it can be defended on principle in front of other people; if it has to be thus defended, the knowledge of this fact will very likely make voters think more carefully about what it is that they are doing. It hardly needs emphasizing how different a demand upon voter's motivation this makes from that made by James Mill. Plainly there are lots of practical objections to be raised against the idea of open voting. On the available evidence of what voters *do* know, *do* feel, and – given their education, employment, and general life-style – could plausibly be expected to know and feel, Mill is asking much too much. He overestimates the extent to which most of us are able or willing to defend our views – if we have any – in front of a potentially hostile audience, even if that audience is armed with nothing more than words. Again, it may be said that no audience would long confine itself to words once it was invited to have strong feelings about matters. Any government as predicated on dispute as this one, would move from democracy to anarchy in very short order. On the other side it can be replied that our evidence all comes from a form of democracy not much like that desired by Mill; we do not know, and we are forced to speculate on rather little evidence, how much more controlled and reasonable people would be if they were brought up to argue about public matters. But whatever the evidence will reveal, Mill makes a point of some importance in these days of 'other-directed' man. Is there not something slightly peculiar when people equate the secrecy of the ballot with the belief that political opinions are a private matter? On any possible view of the distinction between private and public life, voting is an element in one's public life – so is Mill right in seeing secrecy as at best a concession to human frailty and to the inadequacy of legal safe-guards? Certainly the argument clarifies the differences between the two Mills. For the elder Mill voting involves trying to get what you can in the political competition; for J. S. Mill it involves defending your own perception of society and its needs, and thus it involves exposing yourself to new influences, competitive views of the world, new demands on your capacities. It thus seems to be quite unlike shopping for policies in your interest; it is a – on the face of it gruelling – piece of social and political education.

Given that much of the recent literature on political participation has in fact been a literature on the voting – and non-voting – habits of the English and American public, we ought now to explore further the view of political participation which characterizes J. S.

Mill's politics. We have already seen that a utilitarian may well decide that a rational man would fare excellently were he to ignore politics altogether. The so-called 'apathetic' individual may very well be promoting his own interests, even where there is no question of his having reasoned his way through to such a conclusion. The conclusion will still be true, so long as the increased costs of participation are larger than benefits got from it. James Mill's argument about the costs and benefits to women may be thought to have received support from the facts so far known about feminine political behaviour, even though few of them have heard of James Mill.[39] The arguments offered by J. S. Mill on this score amount to a repudiation of the view that participation is a cost to the individual, and it is this argument we must clarify. On the market view, participation bears costs because it involves an allocation of time and effort away from other sources of pleasure; like all activities, it bears an opportunity cost by definition – all activities involve not doing those things that are strictly ruled out by doing them; it also bears a cost above its opportunity cost, namely the pains of work. To reject the applicability of the notion of opportunity costs here is to reject the applicability of cost-benefit analysis to human behaviour; to reject the added costs of 'work' in this instance is to part company to some extent with the axioms of political economy. Thus, in arguing for the view that participation is a good to the individual, J. S. Mill has at least to part company with the usual utilitarian views on work. And indeed it comes as no surprise to find that he does just this. The defence of participation as a good is paralleled by the emphasis placed by Mill on the moral value of public-spirited work. An important instance of this occurs in Mill's discussion of the industrial and military life – a point on which he had learned from Comte.[40] An army is a body of men devoted to an intrinsically evil end – namely destruction and killing; by contrast industrial life is devoted to the praiseworthy goals of creating more goods for people to enjoy. And yet the effects of these ways of life on those who take part in them are very different from what we should expect. The army can call upon intense loyalty, devotion, individual courage, and a sense of common purpose among all its members; the factory can call on nothing of the sort, and Mill in fact was very disenchanted with the grabbing, meanness, and selfishness of industrial and commercial life. Mill's advocacy of co-operatives was part of the hope that communal ventures other than military ones could call out the same sort of loyalties as only armies had done in the past. To introduce considerations such as these was to alter drastically the inherited political stance.

Political participation thus becomes important because political life is part of an irreplaceable public life and because the life of common action is different in kind from our private pursuits. An aspect of the essay on *Liberty* that is usually overlooked in this context is the extent to which Mill's defence of individual freedom against social constraint rests on the firm belief that an unconstrained involvement in the affairs of the community could thereby be liberated. Mill believed quite as firmly as did antithetical figures like Hegel that a man can only have an adequate concern for himself by having an adequate concern for others, and that isolation from the common life of the society was stunting even to individuality. Of course *Liberty* would not be what it is if this were its main point, and Mill's emphasis on *free* involvement, *uncoerced* interest is not in question. But to infer from Mill's libertarian views that he cared little for co-operation is quite as foolish as to infer from the fact that he was dedicated to many of the goods that Comte was concerned for that he shared an equal enthusiasm for Comte's follies. It would be equally a mistake to turn Mill into a hack liberal-conservative as to turn him into a disguised Comte or Marx.

The stress on the educative aspect of political life recurs very clearly in Mill's treatment of local government.[41] Mill had very mixed feelings about the growth of centralized government; on the one hand he valued expertise and saw quite plainly that 'big government' had come for good; moreover he accepted the need for a permanent civil service with whose work the political authorities ought not to interfere once clear instructions had been issued. With the desire for efficiency there blended the natural pride of the Examiner of the East India Company who knew that its administration was the most efficient in Britain and the Coleridgean concern for the maintenance of a clerisy of enlightened intellectual leaders. This was an alarmingly élitist combination, even if it was only one side of Mill's politics. It was, however, much modified by an enthusiasm for local loyalties, gained from sources as diverse as de Tocqueville and Adam Ferguson. The saving virtue of de Tocqueville's America was the initiative and the vigour displayed in local self-government; and it was this that Mill hoped to retain for democracy in England. He was quick to argue that at a local level men could govern themselves in the most literal sense of the words; they could not only vote other people in, they stood a good chance of holding office themselves.[42] In other words, the old Aristotelian criteria for citizenship could genuinely be fulfilled. And where they could be, they should be, since self-government was its own best preparation. The educative effects of this kind of citizenship were

241

much emphasized by Mill; and his arguments are increasingly repeated by people working in exactly this sphere. Welfare workers, poverty programme leaders, community project advisers tend to accept increasingly that only where the poor and unorganized take an active part in the management of their own rehabilitation is the programme really effective. And equally true to Mill's anxieties are the accountants and the administrators who fear they will have no books to balance and no account to give. But at the very worst Mill's argument is no worse than the belief that a child who is taught to play a musical instrument will almost certainly not be a musical prodigy but may still grow up with a greater appreciation and enjoyment of music. Equally, the average voter may be quite unlikely ever to become a national figure; but he will be better able than at present to make rational and considered judgements about what the national figures do. There is nothing peculiar to Mill about the claim that local politics and local concerns can most readily offer the chance of sustained popular participation; as a long-standing pluralist position it is to be found in Jefferson as well as Montesquieu; and as the example of Rousseau indicates, it is not a prerogative of the pluralists to hold the belief. Yet it is in the end an argument resting on beliefs about what will satisfy people that can only with some difficulty be made to look remotely utilitarian.

Along these dimensions, then, *Representative Government* emerges as a critique of the older Mill's essay. Where the political search leads James Mill to a political order which will maximize utility by harmonizing the strivings of rational egoists without any great call on their political virtue, it leads his son to the advocacy of measures that will keep society on the move both intellectually and emotionally, that will strengthen society as a community of evolving individuals. For James Mill the dispensability of political life – for example the establishment in its place of a permanent but honest bureaucracy – is both logically and morally a possible undertaking; in his view satisfaction is essentially something inner and private, a sensation of pleasure that is causally linked with the events in the outside world. There is no hint that the source of pleasure matters for any other than causal reasons, that is, for reasons connected with how much pleasure it will give, and how certain it is to give it. All that the theory allows room for is questions of efficiency – the goal is that our pleasures be many and our pains be few. There is here no room for those criteria which J. S. Mill was later to call the aesthetic criteria of appraisal, which he regarded as being ultimately the most important.[43] The politics of James Mill is the politics of the consumer, not the politics of the agent, no matter how activist he himself was. Politics is dispensable, because politics is a means to an end, in principle replaceable by a more efficient means if one should be found. For the younger Mill, things could hardly be more different. He was always desperately hampered by the atomistic psychology inherited from Bentham and before him Locke; but he was so sure of the facts to be explained that he was ready to allow confusion to overtake the theory rather than to deny the undeniable. And the crucial fact was that pleasures differed in kind as well as in quantity; the kind of pleasure is determined by the source from which it comes, so that more pleasure taken in a less worthy object cannot begin to count against less pleasure taken in a more worthy object.[44] The highest pleasures, therefore, are those that are taken by the best kind of person; and such a person takes pleasure in the worthiest objects. And for Mill, the best kind of man is one who is rational, active, open-minded, socially engaged. It is a commonplace how uneasily Mill's moral views repose upon their psychological base; more interesting than that commonplace is to elucidate what it is that he incorporates so uneasily. And in essence, the things he brings in are elements in a political life whose merits are more at home in the universe of a mid-nineteenth-century Aristotle than a middle-class philosophical radical. And even where the two Mills agree in their views, this agreement is often illusory. Thus, they seem almost equally inegalitarian in their view of the working class; but where the older Mill thinks that the working class will be indefinitely willing to take its cue from the middle class, much as he thought that India would indefinitely be content to be administered by an English company, the younger Mill does not agree. Moreover, although he was alarmed about the effects of class-dominated government and anticipated all sorts of foolishness from an uneducated democracy, John Stuart Mill did not in the end want to see middle-class tutelage continue for ever, just as he was willing to see India outgrow English government. For in the last resort, the desire to make one's own decisions, to be one's own master, is constitutive of a peculiarly human excellence, and in its absence life would be flat and worthless. There are, of course, many other areas into which such a comparison eventually leads us; among those most urgently in need of some exploration are those which cluster round J. S. Mill's slow but steady evolution towards an individual kind of liberal socialism.

Finally, there is a last word to be said about the importance of the contrast which this paper has been concerned with. It is not only a question of trying to become clearer about where the two Mills stand in the history of democratic thought – interesting though this would be at the level of intellectual history alone. It is rather that behind our more down-to-earth thoughts about politics there stand larger preoccupations, which are both historically more stable than many of our factual beliefs and less amenable to ready factual testing. It is thus that elucidating the ideas of James Mill and J. S. Mill can contribute to our present need to be self-conscious about the ideological preconceptions that we bring to the study of politics. And what, hesitantly, I want to suggest is that democratic theory in the past century and a half has operated, not within *an* ideological framework, but within two rather ill-fitting conceptual schemes. And this perhaps goes some way to explain why it is that political science hardly ever yields the conclusive answers that its practitioners hope for. If two conceptual schemes depict man as on the one hand a private being, a consumer who comes into the market for goods, whose behaviour is to be understood in contractual and bargaining terms, and on the other hand as an agent, a being whose need is to make the world conform to plans he shares as a member of a community, then it is no wonder that we are still in difficulties about simple questions, such as whether we live in a democracy. Of course, we may dismiss such considerations as many political scientists do and take refuge in institutional definitions of one sort and another, stipulating that such things as the presence of more than one political party, the bloodless transfer of power, the unforced turnout of a certain number of voters, and the like cumulatively entitle us to call a state a democratic one. But this 'definitional stop' will only work for one move; it simply serves to raise the question of why we should choose these criteria as the important ones, what sort of relation they bear to the goal of self-government or whatever it may be. And at this point the problem appears all over again, for we shall surely have to explain why the existence of these institutions enables people to have – or impedes them from having – what they want more successfully. And this entails having something for which the shortest title is 'a view of political human nature'. And what this brief account of James and John Stuart Mill's ideas indicates is that we seem to have not *a* view of human nature, but two not obviously compatible views.[45]

## NOTES

1  I take it that this is one of the tenets of Michael Oakeshott and his supporters.
2  Anthony Downs, *An Economic Theory of Democracy* (New York, Harper,

1957), yields me this label; but the account is, as he notes, provided in, e.g., Joseph Schumpeter, *Capitalism, Socialism and Democracy* (London, Allen & Unwin, 1943), chs 22 and 23.

3   E. Halévy, *The Growth of Philosophic Radicalism* (Boston, Beacon Press, 1967), pp. 486–90.

4   *Macaulay's Complete Works* (London, Longmans, Green & Co., 1906), 7, pp. 327–71. [Also in Jack Lively and John Rees (eds), *Utilitarian Logic and Politics* (Oxford, Clarendon Press, 1978), pp. 99–129].

5   *Essay on Government*, ed. C. V. Shields (Library of Liberal Arts, Indianapolis, Bobbs-Merrill, 1955), p. 48 [Lively and Rees, p. 56].

6   ibid., p. 48 [Lively and Rees, p. 57].

7   ibid., p. 49 [Lively and Rees, p. 56].

8   ibid., pp. 77–82 [Lively and Rees, pp. 82–6].

9   I hedge at once by agreeing that the analogies between economic and political life can at best be partial; for a useful argument about one point of breakdown in the analogy see D. Stokes 'Spatial models of party competition', *American Political Science Review* (1963), pp. 368–77. I ought also to hedge by emphasizing Schumpeter's hostility to pressure groups of all kinds, op.cit., pp. 288–9; Schumpeter's attachment to the Weberian theory of 'leadership democracy' is at least as important a part of his work as his attachment to the economic theory of democracy.

10  *Essay on Government*, pp. 58–9 [Lively and Rees, pp. 63–4].

11  For a recent discussion of the activities of 'interests' in something like Mill's sense, see Mancur Olson, *The Logic of Collective Action* (New York, Schocken Books, 1968), chs 5 and 6.

12  *Essay on Government*, pp. 63–6 [Lively and Rees, pp. 59–61].

13  ibid., p. 63 [Lively and Rees, pp. 68–72].

14  ibid., p. 67 [Lively and Rees, p. 72].

15  Mill's case for the belief that simple representative democracy will maximally serve the 'common' (or the 'general' or the 'public', for there seems no clear distinction here) interest is never stated. It is therefore not clear what it is, in spite of the hostile attention it has received from the time of Macaulay onwards. In *Political Argument* (London, Routledge & Kegan Paul, 1965), p. 241 n., Brian Barry suggests that Mill thought that everyone except the sinister interests shared a 'common net interest'; this he says, and quite correctly, is untenable since it is all too likely that a certain stable majority will have an interest in policies detrimental to a certain stable minority. Obviously, the examples of American Negroes and Ulster Catholics support Barry here. A possible alternative reading is that Mill thought of governments as only concerned to hold the ring between competing interests, so that in effect it would only be a very limited class of policy that was ever under discussion. Of course, it is just possible that Mill was simply muddled and that he equivocated between aggregative and distributive senses of *all*, thus believing that if the people pursued each his own interest, this would somehow mean that each pursued the interest of all. The only thing to be said unequivocally in Mill's defence here is that he is at least engaged in a serious attempt to protect the public interest against private interests, which is more than can be said for such

books as D. B. Truman, *The Governmental Process* (New York, Knopf, 1951). See, e.g., Olson, op. cit., pp. 122–5.

16  Cf. Downs, op. cit., ch. 3, especially pp. 36–45.

17  *Social Contract* (Everyman Library, 1910), Bk. 3, ch. 15, pp. 82–5.

18  But, of course, the objections to any such procedure have been devastatingly put in Kenneth Arrow, *Social Choice and Individual Values* (New York, Wiley, 1951).

19  See, e.g., 'Distributive justice' in P. Laslett and W. G. Runciman, eds, *Philosophy, Politics and Society*, series 3 (Oxford, Blackwell, 1965), pp. 58–82.

20  Downs, op. cit., chs 11–13.

21  Macaulay, *Works*, 7, p. 354 [Lively and Rees, p. 116].

22  Downs, op. cit., ch. 14: 'The causes and effects of rational abstention'.

23  Berelson *et al.*, *Voting* (Chicago, University of Chicago Press, 1958), pp. 305–13. But of course there can be perfectly good utilitarian arguments for *increased* participation as well; thus, S. Verba has recently argued that the acceptance of low levels of participation that he and his co-author shared in *The Civic Culture* (Princeton, Princeton University Press, 1963) was a mistake, in the context of the US at any rate, since there is an irreducible minimum of accurate information about the needs of the poor, the aged, the unemployed, and the racially oppressed which no authority, however benevolent, can dispense with if it is to relieve their distress. Verba, however, rejects in explicit terms the New Left argument for 'participatory democracy' as in itself conferring a good upon the participant (*Annals*, September 1967).

24  J. S. Mill, *A System of Logic* (London, 1906), Bk. VI, ch. 8, sec. 3.

25  Cf. Robert Dahl, *Who Governs?* (New Haven, Yale University Press, 1961) and J. Schumpeter, loc. cit., for what is in essence a similar defence of the entrepreneurial role in political life.

26  Mill, *A System of Logic*, Bk. VI, ch. 8, sec. 3; Macaulay, *Works*, 7, p. 365 [Lively and Rees, p. 125].

27  See J. M. Buchanan and G. Tullock, *The Calculus of Consent* (Ann Arbor, University of Michigan Press, 1965), for the incessant employment of this device.

28  This tendency of argument is particularly marked in Robert Dahl, *A Preface to Democratic Theory* (Chicago, University of Chicago Press, 1956), ch. 5, where it is argued that the persistence of stable 'polyarchy' is to be accounted for by its success in attending to all legitimate interests.

29  See J. Hamburger, *James Mill and the Art of Revolution* (New Haven, Yale University Press, 1963), for the elaboration of this point.

30  *Political Studies* (1957), pp. 158–75 ['J. S. Mill and Democracy, 1829–61', I] and pp. 281–94 [ibid., II]; see in particular the final sentences on p. 294.

31  J. S. Mill, *Autobiography* (New York, 1956), p. 199.

32  *On Liberty*, in *Essential Writings of John Stuart Mill* (New York, 1961), p. 264 [*Utilitarianism, Liberty, and Representative Government* (London, Everyman edition), p. 74].

33  *Representative Government* (New York, 1965), pp. 32–9 [Everyman, pp. 186–92].

34   *Essays on Politics and Culture*, ed. G. Himmelfarb (New York, Doubleday, 1963), pp. 97–9.

35   Thus the final words of *On Liberty, Essential Writings*, p. 360 [Everyman, p. 170].

36   Thus see for hostility to equilibrium notions, D. Easton, ed., *Varieties of Political Theory* (New York, Prentice-Hall, 1966), pp. 145–7, and for a defence, G. C. Homans, *The Human Group* (New York, Harcourt, Brace, 1950), pp. 304–5.

37   e.g., *A System of Logic*, Bk. VI, ch. 2, sec. 3, where Owen's fatalism is the target.

38   *Representative Government*, ch. 10, especially pp. 202–5 [Everyman, pp. 298–300].

39   *Essay on Government*, p. 74 [Lively and Rees, p. 79].

40   J. S. Mill, *Auguste Comte and Positivism* (Ann Arbor, University of Michigan Press, 1962), p. 149.

41   *Representative Government*, ch. 15, especially p. 286 [Everyman, pp. 347–8].

42   ibid., pp. 286–7 [Everyman, p. 348].

43   *Essays on Politics and Culture*, p. 116, cf. *System of Logic*, Bk. VI, ch. 12, sec. 6.

44   Cf. the agonized discussion in *Utilitarianism*, ch. 2 [Everyman, pp. 7–11].

45   Steven Lukes, to whom I am much indebted for comments on this paper, complains that this conclusion is disappointingly equivocal. He is quite right; it is equivocal; but it faithfully reflects the doubts I feel about the status and validity of the distinctions I have tried to draw. I must also thank Melvin Richter, Julian Franklin, Quentin Skinner, and Michael Freeman for their advice, their questions, and their encouragement.

## Chapter Fifteen

# MILL'S PRINCIPLE OF LIBERTY*

## *G. L. WILLIAMS*

In this paper I wish to do three things: to expand on the interpretation given by John Rees[1] of Mill's principle of liberty; to discuss what status this principle is meant to have in Mill's thought; and, lastly, to examine the relationship between this and Mill's views on the character of individual man. Put differently, can Mill's principle be clarified by reference to the essay on *Utilitarianism?* If so, what can we expect of such a principle in relation to action, and what connection does his principle have to his views on man as a creative, independent, and innovating character?

Following Rees's suggestion in the Postscript[2] to his article, we must turn to the essay on *Utilitarianism* for clarification of the essay *On Liberty.* First let us remind ourselves of the problem. Mill sets himself the task of maximizing the liberty of the individual. His solution, *or at least part of it*, is to regulate social control over the individual by marking off the sphere of the individual from that of society. He attempts this by means of his famous principle that the 'only purpose for which power can be rightfully exercised over any member of a civilised community is to prevent harm to others'.[3] Rees argues, correctly I think, that Mill's principle is best viewed in terms of 'harm to the interests of others' rather than simply 'harm to others', and he adds that the notion of violating a man's rights is crucial to a full understanding of this. If we turn to chapter V of *Utilitarianism* we should gain the necessary enlightenment.

In this chapter Mill sets out to show how justice is a part of general utility, and yet is distinguished from it. What does distinguish the unjust from the inexpedient? What objects fall into the category of just or unjust? Legal rights clearly do; so do moral rights which may conflict with the law. It is considered just that

* Previously published in *Political Studies*, vol. XXIV, no. 2 (1976).

each person should obtain what he deserves, unjust to break faith, to be partial, to treat others unequally. Briefly these six areas will be found to contain the common attributes of justice, but what is 'the mental link which holds them together, and on which the moral sentiment adhering to the term essentially depends'?[4]

Etymologically, justice meant conformity to law, yet in its growth 'it is true that mankind consider the idea of justice and its obligations as applicable to many things which neither are, nor is it desired that they should be, regulated by law'. Thus justice covers both constituted rights, regulated by law, and other actions not so regulated. Surely this is a division similar to that which Mill makes in *On Liberty*:

> [The] fact of living in society renders it indispensable that each should be bound to observe a certain line of conduct towards the rest. The conduct consists, first, in not injuring the interests of one another; or rather certain interests, which, either by express legal provision, or by tacit understanding, ought to be considered as rights; and secondly, in each person bearing his share (to be fixed on some equitable principle) of the labours and sacrifices incurred for defending the society or its members from injury and molestation. These conditions society is justified in enforcing, at all costs to those who withhold fulfilment. Nor is this all that society may do. The acts of an individual may be hurtful to others, or wanting in due consideration for their welfare, without going to the length of violating any of their constituted rights. The offender may then be punished by opinion, though not by law.[5]

Both types of action come under the head of justice: why, therefore, should some unjust acts fall outside the scope of punishment by law? Mill's answer is that though such punishment would afford pleasure 'we forego [such] gratification on account of incidental inconveniences' – fear 'of trusting the magistrates with so unlimited an amount of power over individuals'.[6] But the notion of compulsion in matters of justice remains, and legal punishment is replaced by personal and public disapprobation. Thus the extent of those matters in which society is entitled to interfere are those which fall within the notion of justice. But what distinguishes the obligations of justice from moral obligation in general? Justice is a part of morality while also being a distinct category, along the following lines:

duties of perfect obligation are those duties in virtue of which a correlative *right* resides in some person or persons; duties of imperfect obligation are those moral obligations which do not give birth to any right. I think it will be found that this distinction exactly coincides with that which exists between justice and the other obligations of morality.

The supposition implies two things – a wrong done, and some assignable person who is wronged.

Justice implies something which it is not only right to do, and wrong not to do, but which some individual person can claim from us as his moral right.[7]

So for Mill justice is that category which justifies the limitation of freedom and that class of actions in which rights are involved. He develops this further: the sentiment of justice, the desire to punish some definite individual for harm he has done is a natural feeling arising from the desire to retaliate, but 'it has nothing moral in it; what is moral is the exclusive subordination of it to the social sympathies, so as to wait on and obey their call'.[8] This is an important aspect of the idea of justice as Mill explains:

For the natural feeling would make us resent indiscriminately whatever any one does that is disagreeable to us; but when moralised by the social feeling, it only acts in the directions conformable to the general good; just persons resenting a hurt to society, though not otherwise a hurt to themselves, and not resenting a hurt to themselves, however painful, unless it be of the kind which society has a common interest with them in the repression of.[9]

This is far removed from the idea that Mill's principle sanctions interference whenever harm is done to an individual, taken in the subjective sense; 'a hurt to themselves, however painful' does *not* sanction interference unless society has an interest in asserting a rule for the benefit of all.

The idea of justice supposes two things: a rule of conduct, and a sentiment which sanctions the rule. The first must be supposed common to all mankind, and intended for their good.

[A] hurt to some assignable person or persons on the one hand, and a demand for punishment on the other . . . include all that we mean when we speak of violation of a right. When we call anything a person's right, we mean that he has a valid claim on society to protect him in the possession of it, *either by the force of law, or by that of education and opinion.*[10]

Here we have the division noted above from *On Liberty* – the protection by society through law or opinion of a person's rights whether constituted or not. It is this protection which distinguishes rights from everything else. The limitation of freedom is only justified in a certain range of action – where justice is involved.

> Justice is a name for certain classes of moral rules . . . which forbid mankind to hurt one another (in which we must never forget to include wrongful interference with each other's freedom) . . . which concern the essentials of human well-being more nearly, and are therefore of more absolute obligation, than any rules for the guidance of life; and the notion which we have found to be of the essence of the idea of justice, that of a right residing in an individual, implies and testifies to this more binding obligation.[11]

We can find confirmation of our view that this discussion based on *Utilitarianism* is closely allied to the principle Mill expounds in *On Liberty* by reference to chapter three of *On Liberty*.

> As much compression as is necessary to prevent the stronger specimens of human nature from encroaching on the rights of others cannot be dispensed with . . .
> To be held to rigid rules of justice for the sake of others, develops the feelings and capacities which have the good of others for their object.[12]

Thus the justification for and limitation of restraint is in terms of rights and justice, as in *Utilitarianism*. However, though this latter work does clarify the former, it is true that the matter is far from straightforward, mainly because of the multiplicity of terms Mill uses in *On Liberty* to explain his principle. Whereas in *Utilitarianism* acts which are painful, or acts which hurt or injure do not themselves call for intervention unless rights are violated, in *On Liberty* on the other hand the categories are much less clear. He talks of actions which are harmful, hurtful, do evil, injury, affect others, concern others, concern the interests of others, as though these are synonymous. It is obvious that *On Liberty* alone is insufficient, though even here there are places where the analysis in terms of *Utilitarianism* can find support: 'When, by conduct of this sort, a person is led *to violate a distinct and assignable obligation* to any other person or persons, the case is taken out of the self-regarding class.'[13]

Therefore I think Mill's principle is indeed best seen in terms of justice and rights, and it is this which explains his notion of interests. In both essays we have a range of actions or conduct with which society can interfere and a range where it should not; it is by seeing that the range of actions in both essays coincide that we can understand Mill's position. Where the rules of justice are transgressed and rights violated there society may intervene, through law or opinion; in other cases the individual is to have the freedom to act as he chooses. This is not meant to imply that the alternative to intervention is complete indifference, rather it is 'disinterested exertion'. Mill's belief in individual liberty rules out the imposition of his will on others but his respect for their rights does not lead him to withdrawal or passiveness. Where compulsion is ruled out, conviction and persuasion need not be; encouragement and stimulation are to be distinguished from the penalties of society. Toleration does not mean the suspension of judgement, nor an equal opinion of everyone alike.

It is often easily assumed that, whatever formulation we give to Mill's principle, the principle itself can be shown to be inadequate by a discussion of exceptions or borderline cases, as though the citing of one difficult case renders the principle useless. It must be admitted that Mill himself seems to give some support to this view in *On Liberty*:

> The object of this Essay is to assert one very simple principle, as entitled to govern absolutely the dealings with the individual in the way of compulsion and control, whether the means used be physical force in the form of legal penalties, or the moral coercion of public opinion.[14]

However, if we look to Mill's writings where he explicitly discusses the character and role of principles or rules of conduct we find no evidence for an 'absolutist' view but a much more sensitive interpretation of the part rules play in moral and social life. In Book VI, chapter xii of the *System of Logic* he discusses this point:

> To the judge, the rule, once positively ascertained, is final; but the legislator, or other practitioner, who goes by rules rather than by their reasons, like the old-fashioned German tacticians who were vanquished by Napoleon, or the physician who preferred that his patients should die by rule rather than recover contrary to it, is rightly judged to be a mere pedant and the slave of his formulas.
>
> By a wise practitioner, therefore, rules of conduct will only be considered as provisional. Being made for the most

numerous cases, or for those of most ordinary occurrence, they point out the manner in which it will be least perilous to act, where time or means do not exist for analyzing the actual circumstances of the case, or where we cannot trust our judgement in estimating them.

How much greater still, then, must the error be of setting up such unbending principles [universal practical maxims], not merely as universal rules for attaining a given end, but as rules of conduct generally, without regard to the possibility, not only that some modifying cause may prevent the attainment of the given end by the means which the rule prescribes, but that success itself may conflict with some other end, which may possibly chance to be more desirable.[15]

This point is, of course, one frequently made by modern writers – that principles are not straightforward indicators to actions. No rules tell us how to apply them or, to put it differently, all rules are defeasible; there are no necessary and sufficient conditions which can be laid down beforehand. Thus the level of generality on which principles such as Mill's operate leaves open the important problem of what follows in specific circumstances. The application of principles to action demands both an understanding of the principles and a knowledge of the situation. We do not decide problems in a vacuum of principles as we do not decide them in a vacuum of experience. Indeed, rules are often not even the way round a problem but are the reason for it. Mill's principle is not just a tool with which to deal with social problems but is one of the values which make the problem what it is. If we did not hold the principles we do then many matters would cease to be seen as difficulties. In our treatment of a situation insight and sensitivity are as important as rules; nevertheless, the eyes with which we see the world in the sense of seeing what is important and what is not, and the process by which we arrive at judgements on which to act, are very much dependent on principles or rules of conduct.

What then has this to do with Mill's principle, and how does it affect the way we view and evaluate it? The first point to stress is that a realization of the difficulties involved in applying a rule even when clearly formulated should not lead us to discard it. There are always difficulties; principles remain:

It is not the fault of any creed, but of the complicated nature of human affairs, that rules of conduct cannot be so framed as to require no exceptions, and that hardly any kind of action can safely be laid down as either always obligatory or always condemnable.[16]

For example, even with truth-telling 'this rule, sacred as it is, admits of possible exceptions',[17] but Mill is emphatic that in the field of morals and politics 'though the application of [a] standard may be difficult, it is better than none at all'.[18]

[With regard to Mill's views on freedom I think he is saying more than that we *should* be guided by such a principle as he describes. However unclearly, he seems to be saying that a principle of liberty is necessary if moral and political views and actions are to be justified at all. Mill's view of the good life involves certain obligations to respect a person's freedom which are akin to the logical rules of argument. I would not claim that Mill is clear in distinguishing between the moral and logical elements in such a principle as his but I do think it possible to make such a distinction. He is clearly concerned that people be allowed freedom in certain areas of their lives; he also sees that talk of goodness or justification demands the recognition of a *prima facie* case for individual freedom. Unless interference is *exceptional*, it is difficult to see what is morally justifiable in it. If one could take the reverse position, what sort of view of the individual and of moral justification would it lead to? (I think this point reinforces the belief that for Mill freedom is good in itself, or rather it expresses the same thing slightly differently.)]

If Mill's principle is best interpreted in terms of rights, what are the rights to which it refers? The preceding comment on the relationship of rules to action still leaves open this question. However sensitive we are prepared to be in applying his principle, we still need to know more about his notion of rights in terms of their content. The first point to stress is the one already made – that it is not simply legal rights which are being referred to. If it were, then Mill's idea would simply be a defence of the existing state of the law. The principle is meant, on the other hand, to be one by which to judge the law and to be one by which to change it. Given this, how do we discover the rights which Mill talks of? He does refer to them as though they can be recognized independently of his own writings, but in fact it is impossible to outline them except by looking again at his two essays and especially his notion of justice. So that we are left with a circularity: the individual should be free in those areas where rights are not affected; rights are defined by reference to justice; justice is the area where society has an overriding interest and the individual is secondary. However narrow this category, it rests, of course, on Mill's own views of society and the individual; there is no independent definition or methods of discovery. I do not want to accuse Mill here of a weakness or a mistake; a degree of circularity is an unavoidable element in the moral discourse of one who no longer derives everything from a fundamental or ultimate principle. His effective break with the rigidity of a utilitarian framework means that while retaining some of the language he has lost the simplicity of such a process of argument. So I see Mill here much more as someone exploring a moral point of view in terms of justice and freedom than as someone reducing things to a Benthamite rationalism. His discussion of freedom in terms of rights cannot be fully appreciated outside his moral framework. Given his complex and at times difficult version of happiness, including as it does truth, diversity, freedom, and so on, then his discussion of freedom cannot be divorced from his view of man. In some ways this is an obvious point; I want to use it to suggest that the proper test of Mill's principle is the role it plays in his view of a creative society, that the best criterion for judging its adequacy is how far it brings about a state of affairs which Mill would regard as good. It is to an examination of this wider perspective, this fuller context, that I will now proceed.

The first issue to raise is of a corrective nature. In treating a principle which we might wish to see incorporated in or adopted by the machinery and rules of government and society it might seem that we are giving up to the state the care of and the responsibility for freedom. The desire to limit society can lead to society being responsible for those limits. Mill does not intend to do this; the defence of freedom is essentially in individual hands, even if social recognition is one of the means used. I think Mill would be sympathetic to the idea expressed by Camus in a speech 'Bread and Freedom':

> whoever blindly entrusts them [the authorities] with the care of freedom has no right to be surprised when she is immediately dishonoured. If freedom is humiliated or in chains today, this is not because her enemies had recourse to treachery. It is simply because she has lost her natural protector.[19]

Mill directed his essay to a strengthening of the 'barrier of moral conviction' against social tyranny, intending to check excessive domination over the individual. So his principle is one that men should cherish rather than one left to society to care for; it is a right not a privilege, a claim not a concession. It is not simply meant to regulate relationships; it is aimed at maximizing liberty. The defensive element is bound up with the assertive, as I hope to show in a moment. His principle in defence of freedom is a standing challenge to tyranny and the attack must be launched by those who suffer under that tyranny.

The second and related issue is the relationship between a principle of freedom such as Mill outlines in terms of rights and what I will call a spirit of freedom or independence. I shall try to show that Mill's principle is best seen as an encouragement to the free spirit and that in this light his principle must be one of challenge, not one to institutionalize. If this is so then his talk of justice and rights is an aid to combating social oppression rather than an inflexible and absolute rule which stands or falls depending on the possibility of giving it precise meaning.

Mill does have a notion of freedom as independence as well as the more obvious notion of freedom as absence of restraint. This is not a new point but I want to explore it further and discuss the relationship between the two. If we see freedom as individual independence, perhaps the best way to describe it is in opposition to man's desire for security. While Mill would uphold the need for a certain amount of stability in social and individual life, he would see this as a basis not as an end in itself. Indeed even with ends which are worthwhile like happiness Mill does not recommend deliberate and single-minded pursuit. He would surely find the belief in security an odd one, and more important, a dangerous one, opposing as it does so much that he values. This explains his attack on custom as the proper guide to conduct, and his praise of individual expression:

> the evil is, that individual spontaneity is hardly recognised by the common modes of thinking as having any intrinsic worth, or deserving any regard on its own account.
>
> The human faculties of perception, judgement, discriminative feeling, mental activity, and even moral preference, are exercised only in making a choice. He who does anything because it is the custom makes no choice.

Mill's idea of man as an independent individual is very close to von Humboldt's, as quoted by Mill:

> the object 'towards which every human being must ceaselessly direct his efforts . . . is the individuality of power and development;' that for this there are two requisites, 'freedom, and variety of situations;' and that from the union of these

arise 'individual vigour and manifold diversity,' which combine themselves in 'originality.'[20]

While Mill recognizes the importance of experience as summarized in custom he believes a life guided simply by custom needs only the employment of one faculty, 'the ape-like one of imitation'. This has led to an increase in the 'low, abject, servile type of character',[21] so that 'society has now fairly got the better of individuality'. Mill is quite clear as to the results of such a situation: 'human capacities are withered and starved: they become incapable of any strong wishes or native pleasures, and are generally without either opinions or feelings of home growth, or properly their own.' Against such servility he puts the state of 'habitual rebellion' where the proper questions to ask are: 'what do I prefer? or, what would suit my character and disposition? or, what would allow the best and highest in me to have fair play, enable it to grow and thrive?'[22] Mill puts this differently and more concisely when he says: 'It really is of importance, not only what men do, but also what manner of men they are that do it.'[23]

It would seem then that this independent character, or his free spirit as I have called it, is a varied, original, spontaneous, vigorous, developing character. I hesitate to call this a positive concept because Mill leaves open the paths that such an individual might follow; it is the *manner* of life that he is concerned with here. I would call the notion described here as *assertive* rather than positive. What connection does it have with the notion of freedom as absence of restraint? It is clear that the latter can exist without the former; Mill's plea was for both in moral, social, and political life. To an extent the spirit of freedom can exist where freedom as absence of restraint is lacking, but Mill believed that the latter gives increased opportunity to increasing numbers to exercise the former. This does not mean, however, that freedom as absence of restraint is conditional on using it to develop the free spirit; Mill denies freedom to no one, he only encourages and advises that we use it independently. He values both the defensive (negative liberty) and the assertive (the free spirit); the former is valued for itself *and* as being the condition for, amongst other things, the development and assertion of the free spirit. The two notions are separately valued though connected.

This is an important point to make in that it warns us against seeing a principle of freedom, such as Mill outlines, as some sort of complete answer to the problem. Formal rules do not lead by themselves to spontaneous feelings of liberty; clearly for Mill choice, struggle, and protest are an essential environment for the free, independent man. Such a context is not necessarily weakened by the idea of a principle defending freedom, unless desire for such a principle and acceptance of it become in themselves the end of action. But Mill's principle is designed to protect the individual, not wrap him up in cotton wool; it leaves him a wide sphere of action – what he does from then on, whether he is independent or servile, is his own decision, revealed in countless actions and on countless occasions. To do less for him would be despotic, to do more would be paternalistic; in both cases it would be contrary to Mill's view of the free spirit.

Thus the notion of struggle as an essential background to freedom as independence does contain a truth, but it can be put in a misleading manner. If this struggle is seen solely in terms of a conflict between the state and the individual, then obviously a rule aimed at reducing this conflict, and in one sense harmonizing their relationship, will indeed decrease freedom. However, this is to view the notion of struggle in a narrow and limited way; Mill's view of struggle is as wide as his view of individual character, and it is only one kind of struggle which he regards as being illegitimately oppressive. A principle of liberty will not mean the solution of all man's problems; it will leave free man's resources for other struggles, for the difficult pursuit of his own good in his own way.

Neither of the senses of freedom mentioned above include all that Mill values; freedom as absence of restraint is a condition for freedom as independence, but not everyone will use it so, and everyone who does may choose a different path. Both these notions are important and it is my view that a full understanding of Mill's principle of liberty demands an appreciation of his idea of the free spirit. The success of his principle can best be measured by reference to this. His work is directed to the end of human liberty in the two senses outlined here; it is above all a challenge from individuals against social tyranny. If the end of freedom as independence is to be attained, then the principle of freedom in terms of rights must remain in the hands of its 'natural protectors'. We cannot expect it to operate without constant vigilance, and so it goes hand in hand with the free spirit. Without this wider perspective Mill's principle is limited and limiting.

Thus our formulation of the principle in terms of rights is not alone enough. Though his principle is clearer and less vague than is generally accepted, to view it without the context of the free, independent spirit is to see it simply as a defensive principle, ignoring the importance to Mill of individuality, spontaneity, and development of character. Individualism does not come simply by adopting Mill's principle. It is a necessary condition for most of us, but not a sufficient one, to have freedom from tyranny in order to achieve freedom from servility. The defensive position is of value in itself but also a means to the assertive one. To see it simply as protective may well be to sacrifice independence and creativity. The possession of Mill's principle in terms of individual rights is a part of the struggle against custom, tyranny, and oppression – and this struggle is itself part of freedom as independence. Mill's work is directed towards giving the oppressed a weapon, creating a strong barrier of moral conviction, and encouraging the free spirit.

## NOTES

1  J.C. Rees, 'A re-reading of Mill on Liberty', *Political Studies*, VIII (1960), pp. 113–29.
2  See *Limits of Liberty*, ed. P. Radcliffe (California, Wadsworth Publishing Co., 1966), pp. 106–7.
3  *On Liberty* (Everyman edn, London, Dent, 1931), p. 73. All references to this edition.
4  *Utilitarianism* (Everyman edn, London, Dent, 1931), p. 43. All references to this edition.
5  *On Liberty*, p. 132.
6  *Utilitarianism*, p. 44.
7  ibid., p. 46.
8  ibid., p. 48.
9  ibid.
10  *Utilitarianism*, p. 49 (my emphasis).
11  ibid., p. 55.
12  op. cit., p. 121.
13  ibid., p. 137 on (my emphasis).
14  ibid., p. 72.
15  *System of Logic*, (London, People's Edition, 1891), pp. 616–18.
16  *Utilitarianism*, p. 23.
17  ibid., p. 21.
18  ibid., p. 24.
19  Printed in *Resistance, Rebellion, and Death* (London, Hamish Hamilton, 1963), p. 66.
20  *On Liberty*, pp. 115–16.
21  ibid., p. 110.
22  ibid., p. 119.
23  ibid., p. 117.

# KARL MARX

## Chapter Sixteen

# INTRODUCTION

Marx's social theory offers the prospect of man's realization of his true nature, a nature distorted by industrial capitalism. But industrial capitalism has both negative and positive features. On the one side, it is to be vehemently condemned as distorting man's nature; on the other, it is to be welcomed because it provides preconditions of material abundance which will enable those very distortions to be removed. Marx was by no means unique in condemning capitalism (because of the poverty, inequality, or unfairness with which it was associated) but arguably he was unique in developing a theory of technologically-inspired abundance which would end class divisions, and, for the first time, at least in modern history, enable all (rather than merely some) persons to realize their true nature. Like Rousseau and Hegel before him, Marx did not see human nature as irretrievably disfigured, but saw that disfigurement as a symptom of a particular historical epoch. Rousseau's diagnosis of man's contemporary *malaise* was given point by a hypothetical history of man's loss of natural independence; Hegel's diagnosis by a conception of the movement of the Idea in history; Marx demanded, by apparent contrast, concentration on man's empirical history, and in particular on his material conditions. The readings below focus mainly on the coherence of that conception of history. They also raise questions about the possible survival in Marx's thought of Hegelian categories and methods. An understanding of Marx's social theory requires an understanding of his approach to history, but that approach was worked out in part by a reaction to Hegelian thinking. It is therefore necessary to consider briefly Hegel's conception of history and its connection to estrangement. We can then move on to the relationship between Marx's theory of history and his broader social thought. In particular, aspects of that relationship draw attention to the connections between the materialist conception of history and both scientific socialism and scientific social analysis.

Hegel's philosophy aimed to provide man with a self-understanding. This self-understanding would overcome the apparent 'otherness' of the world. It would do so by showing that, properly understood, human history could be seen as a movement which begins from immediate unity between man and his world. That immediate unity would give way to estrangement during which man was separated from the world. That estrangement, however, would itself give way to renewed unity, but a unity at a higher level. This renewed unity would be 'higher' because of the experience of *overcoming* the duality: the unity was not merely unreflective and immediate. This application of the idea of estrangement to historical experience is merely an example: the estrangement might be expressed in other forms as well, and there is an interesting question about the relation between Marx's notion of 'alienation' and Hegelian estrangement. Perhaps the most general concern for Hegel is man's lack of unity with the natural world. In the context of one of the debates introduced below, a crucial question is the relationship between the development of man's ideas about the world, on the one side, and the 'development' occurring in the world, on the other. Another application of the idea of separation, and its transcendence, may be found in Hegel's political philosophy. Here the separation is between one person and another, and the claim is that the separation has been overcome, or could be overcome (a crucial distinction), by political arrangements. The issues here are, first, the nature of Hegel's dialectics, and later of Marx's. The second problem is how the relation between the two should be characterized. At a more obviously political level, the status of Hegel's purported reconciliation of man with man, or of the individual with the community, in the state, is contentious. So, too, is Marx's reaction to all this, and his alternative path to a similar reconciliation in future society. The implications of Hegel's political philosophy are disputed partly because of his own insistence that the task of philosophy is to explain what already exists, not to prescribe what should be. Philosophy is *post festum*, enabling a rational grasp of what is, not ruminating about what might be or what should be. It therefore offers a retrospective appreciation of the rationality of the world, making man once again at home in it. If we apply this idea to Hegel's political philosophy (and it is in the Preface to *The Philosophy of Right* that Hegel gives his most eloquent expression of the idea), we must conclude that the institutional structure of the state he there explains already exists in the world. Hegel's critics have alleged that he was trying to justify the contemporary institutions of Prussia. The alternative reaction was to deny that the institutions Hegel described were already fully operative, and to interpret the work as a claim about the possibility of a reconciliation so far unrealized. This raised the further question of whether the method Hegel proposed would be sufficient to achieve the goal, or whether an alternative should be pursued.

Hegel's philosophy, including the political philosophy, employs dialectics. It is difficult to render this uncontroversially, since the vocabulary commonly employed has been criticized as misleading. That vocabulary talks of a thesis, an antithesis, and a synthesis: a starting point which somehow gives rise to its negation, and the overcoming of that negation by taking account of both previous 'moments' and yet moving beyond them. This third 'moment' then forms the starting point for another such triad. This vocabulary may mislead, however, first because perhaps it is not Hegel's own; and second, because it fails to convey sufficiently the sense in which the third moment goes beyond the first two. It is not so much a mixture of opposites, as grey is a 'mixture' of black and white, but something which, while including or acknowledging the opposition, incorporates it and transcends it. This notion may be exemplified by turning to *The Philosophy of Right*.

In the last section of Hegel's exposition, concerned with 'Ethical Life', the three 'moments' of immediate interest are 'the family', 'civil society', and 'the state'. These may be seen as developmental in a number of ways – for example, they represent successive forms of freedom, forms of experience, or relationships between institutions. To talk of development, it should be emphasized, does not imply temporal succession. The state properly so called, the third moment in the triad, includes yet goes beyond the first two. It is not merely a synthesis of two opposing principles or forms of experience because while the state 'includes' the family and civil society, it yet offers something of which both are incapable. That is a full reconciliation of the individual with the community. The family is incapable of this, not least because of its small size; civil society is incapable of it, because it is a sphere of self-interested individualism. Although the state 'draws upon' the ethical experience of family life, and the interdependence characteristic of civil society, it offers more. Hegel distinguished between civil society and the state. The distinction contrasted the kinds of experience embodied in these moments: on the one hand, needs, labour, and contractual exchange; on the other hand, public interest, citizenship, and collective decision-making. That contrast led on to his exposition of the proper relationship between civil society and the state. Marx was to present an alternative view of that relationship, both in capitalist society and in future society, but the readings below illustrate dispute about both what that formulation was, and its coherence.

The dialectical movement which *The Philosophy of Right* has been used to exemplify may be taken to operate in our conception of the world. Philosophy, for Hegel, indeed, assists us to move from a level of mere 'understanding' to a level of 'rational' comprehension by explaining this relationship. While a superficial observer might mistake civil society for the state, the proper relationship between them is given to us by dialectical reasoning. This expository or conceptual application of the idea of dialectical movement can be contrasted with the supposition that there is some dialectical movement actually present in the world, and that, if there is, the expository movement is tracing this real movement. Hegel's philosophy seemed both to be teleological and to presuppose the working out of the dialectical oppositions in the world. Man's consciousness and social arrangements were consequences of the activity of the Idea. Feuerbach's critique of Hegel proposed the inversion of this, so that Man, not the Idea, was the active agent. The central concern of the readings below is the characterization of Marx's theory of history, acknowledging this inversion. There has been considerable discussion whether dialectical progression was for Marx an expository device or in some fuller sense present in the world. We may now examine the debate between Professors Acton and Cohen about the theory of history, before indicating some of the important areas of controversy about Marx's social theory on which these readings have a direct bearing.

Cohen and Acton are concerned with the interpretation of 'historical materialism', primarily by reference to Marx's 'Preface to *The Critique of Political Economy*'. There is, however, a difference in approach between the two authors. Cohen's project is to defend a reading of the 'Preface' against criticisms made by both Acton and Professor Plamenatz; his focus is quite specifically on a key passage in that Preface. Although Acton addresses the major issue of interest to Cohen, he also has more to say about aspects of historical materialism with which Cohen is not directly concerned, and he therefore appeals to more of Marx's writings. The issue between them is the coherence of the account of the relationships between aspects of social life which appears in the 'Preface'. The passage is justly famous as a concise exposition of the materialist conception of history, but in some ways its very conciseness makes the work of interpretation more difficult and, perhaps, contentious. As Cohen remarks, the short section with which he deals contains a large number of unexplained concepts. These refer both to elements of social organization – for example, 'production relations' – and to connections between particular elements – for example, $x$ 'conditions' $y$. For the English reader, there is also the problem of the correct translation of the German, a point which arises in one of Cohen's responses to Plamenatz.

The central disagreement between Cohen and Acton, both of whom accept that historical materialism has to be understood by reference to technology, is the extent to which these 'unexplained' concepts interpenetrate. Acton takes the view (p. 291) that productive forces, production relations, the legal and political super-structure and ideologies are 'factually and conceptually so closely implicated in one another that the attempt to show that the basic ones can explain or bring into existence the superstructural ones is hopeless'. It is this that Cohen denies. He argues that these concepts are sufficiently separable by careful analysis. The first two important questions are, what is included in the economic structure of society? and, how is the relationship between law and 'production relations' to be conceived? On the first question, Cohen argues that the economic base consists only of production relations, not of production relations and productive forces. Those forces 'strongly determine' the economic structure without being part of it. On the second question, Cohen argues that production relations can be expressed without reference to law. He opposes the view that since the law defines production relations, it is impossible to divorce the economic structure, composed of production relations, from the superstructure, which includes the law. Cohen further employs his view of production relations to show how property relations can be causally explained by production relations while at the same time being an expression of them. Acton's reply rejects Cohen's claim that the apparently 'legal' notions involved in production relations can be reduced to non-legal ones.

An important part of any interpretation of the materialist concep-tion of history is its account of historical change, and in particular of the process by which one mode of production replaces another. From the standpoint of the analysis of capitalist society, the two most important transitions are from feudalism to capitalism, and from capitalism to future society. Marx's analysis of the origins of capitalism focused on the forcible separation of individuals from their own means of production, while his analysis of contemporary capitalism led him to suppose that it would experience deepening crises as the relations of production came more and more into conflict with the forces of production. This conflict would ultimately issue in a social revolution, inaugurating future society. There has been considerable disagreement about the sense, if any, in which Marx saw this outcome as *inevitable*. An assessment of the conflict between the relations of production and productive forces requires, of course, a clear idea about the meaning of the concepts involved. The debate between Acton and Cohen brings out many of the central problems. For Acton, the interpenetration of the concepts extends to legal relationships entering the productive forces themselves, a dialectical connection which precludes the explanation of one by the other, even if it is consistent with a conflict between them.

The argument about the conception of history is further complicated by the attempt to distinguish between Marx's own thought and that of his collaborator, Engels. For example, it has been suggested (by Gunn) that a dialectical view of nature is incompatible with materialism, as it involves attributing the goal-directedness of human action to natural processes. Engels did write about a dialectics of nature, but Engels and Marx are, we have been reminded, not one person but two. (The intellectual relationship between Marx and Engels has been further explored by Terrell Carver.) To describe nature as dialectical presupposes the presence of negation and contradiction within nature itself. This, it has been pointed out, imports Hegelian idealism into an allegedly materialist theory. Marx is said to follow a dialectical method, but not to subscribe to a dialectical conception of nature. Contradiction and negation arise in human thought and action, because of its goal-directedness. So we may speak of a dialectic in history *only* because we are dealing with the consciousness of human actors in it. An important aspect of such consciousness, for Marx, is class-consciousness, especially as it is connected to the overthrow of capitalism, a point to which we shall return.

Marx's development of a materialist conception of history, especially in the *German Ideology* (1846), has been used to suggest a radical disjuncture between his early writings and his later 'scientific' writings, informed by that conception. It has been suggested that the early Marx had a humanist focus on the alienation which prevailed in capitalist society, while his later writings exhibited a scientific analysis of capitalism. The *Grundrisse* (1857), to which Acton refers, has a special place in this dispute. It became available to scholars relatively recently, and represents a plan of work of which *Capital* is but a part. Those who see no radical disjuncture in Marx's writings point out that the notion of alienation is still central in *Grundrisse*, and therefore claim that it provides evidence of continuity between the concern with alienation in the early works and the mature analysis of capitalism. As we have seen, Hegel was concerned with some notion of estrangement, a concept which may be associated with that of alienation, and the debate about the continued importance of the idea of alienation to Marx is part of a larger discussion of the extent to which Hegelian influences survive in his writings.

The materialist conception of history was invoked by Engels, together with the theory of surplus value, in his discussion of the distinction between 'scientific' and 'utopian' socialism. The scientific character of the socialism developed by Marx and Engels, on Engels's account, was guaranteed by both those intellectual tools and by their ability to deal with capitalism in its developed form. Earlier socialists, or contemporary ones who did not use those tools, were necessarily projecting schemes for future society on the basis of an inadequate understanding of capitalism. Early socialist reformers were likely to conjure schemes out of their heads, without reference to the real material development of society. The status of the materialist conception of history, and of the theory of surplus value, is therefore crucial in any assessment of this claim that socialism could be 'scientific'.

The labour theory of value has, of course, a central place in the analysis put forward in *Capital*. But a further element in the argument about the distinction between 'scientific' and 'utopian' socialism is the question of whether Marx (and Engels) in fact adopted different procedures from those they attributed to the utopians. Here the envisaged transition from capitalism to future society is critical, and three related aspects of it may be very briefly mentioned. First, to what extent will future society be capable of overcoming the alienation associated with capitalism? Marx's early writings appear to offer an artisanal ideal, in which alienation is overcome primarily because individuals may choose their own self-directed activity within a fluid division of labour. Later works, however, suggest that future society will be able to harness the productive forces which capitalism has developed, and this implies that an industrial division of labour will be maintained. Hence freedom may be found only when work ends, not in work itself: the emphasis passes from the character of work to the length of the working day, and to increased leisure. Secondly, even if alienation does disappear in future society, would exploitation have been abolished as well? The key dispute here is whether Marx's characterization of exploitation in capitalist society depends upon the theory of surplus value, and, if so, whether it is coherent; or whether it rests on the idea of differential access to the means of production, in which case the terms of that access in future society require investigation. Thirdly, what is the relationship between the objective conditions which make revolution possible and the human action which brings it about? Property relations are the basis of Marx's definition of class, and class has a central role in historical explanation. Whereas for Hegel the universal class was the bureaucracy, for Marx it was the proletariat. And while Hegel had been concerned with estates, social groups defined by a legal status conferred by the state, Marx was concerned with social classes, defined by the economic relationships subsisting in society. Future society will be classless; the transition to future society from capitalism depends upon both the objective existence of the proletariat and its consciousness of itself as a class. Class consciousness is necessary but not sufficient to achieve a social revolution. It sometimes appears that the circumstances of a class will themselves promote the necessary consciousness, but sometimes too that political action is required to develop it.

To explore fully these aspects of Marx's social theory requires an investigation of the notions of ideology, false consciousness, and political action. But all these notions are subsidiary aspects of the theme of these readings: the relationship between movement in history and movement in ideas. This relationship is problematic both in Hegel's retrospective and passive rational grasp of the world, and in Marx's anticipatory and active call to unite theory with practice. The problem for Marx is to change the world, but the theory of how the world will be changed appears to announce its own redundancy. Hegelian estrangement is overcome by a rational grasp of the world as it actually is, a form of reconciliation. For Marx overcoming alienation demands that we take action to change the world. Such a transformed world will be transparent to us, and we would no longer need Marx's theory to penetrate its opacity. The theory of history, therefore, is fundamental both to Marx's own perception of his scientific socialism and to our assessment of his social theory.

## ACCESSIBLE EDITIONS

Jon Elster, *Karl Marx, A Reader* (Cambridge, Cambridge University Press, 1986)

David McLellan (ed.), *Karl Marx: Selected Writings* (Harmondsworth, Penguin, 1977)

## SUGGESTED READING

Shlomo Avineri, *The Social and Political Thought of Karl Marx* (Cambridge, Cambridge University Press, 1968)

Terrell Carver, *Marx and Engels: The Intellectual Relationship* (Brighton, Wheatsheaf, 1983)

* Terrell Carver, *Marx's Social Theory* (Oxford, Oxford University Press, 1982)

G.A. Cohen, *Karl Marx's Theory of History – a Defence* (Oxford, Clarendon Press, 1978)

Jon Elster, *Making Sense of Marx* (Cambridge, Cambridge University Press, 1985)

* Michael Evans, *Karl Marx* (London, Allen & Unwin, 1975)

Richard Gunn, 'Is Nature Dialectical?', *Marxism Today* February 1977, pp. 45–52.

Steven Lukes, 'Can the base be distinguished from the superstructure?' in David Miller and Larry Seidentop (eds), *The Nature of Political Theory* (Oxford, Clarendon Press, 1983)

Raymond Plant, *Hegel* (2nd edn, Oxford, Blackwell, 1983)

William Suchting, *An Introduction to Karl Marx* (London, Macmillan, 1986)

## Chapter Seventeen

# ON SOME CRITICISMS OF HISTORICAL MATERIALISM*

## *GERALD A. COHEN*

I was grateful when Professor Acton agreed to comment on this paper, since it concerns topics to which he has made a number of contributions. Professor Acton is among a small number of philosophers who have enriched the study of historical materialism by imposing on it standards of rigour and clarity not native to Marxism, but developed within the positivistic and analytical philosophy of the present century. I firmly support those standards, but I also support Marxist theory more firmly than those who have applied them think they are able to. I believe that very often they reject the theory because they apply the standards not too severely, but not severely enough. Sometimes they evince a reluctance to make Marxism answer to principles with which Marx had little acquaintance, but I think such kindness is misplaced. In this paper I aspire to a meticulous and where necessary pedantic use of antiseptic principles of conceptual construction and empirical verification, and I hope their employment in the limited area of historical materialism I shall have room to explore will ground a judgement that their application can be favourable to the theory.

1. I begin by exhibiting a portion of Marx's Preface to *The Critique of Political Economy*.[1] I then report and criticize Professor Acton's account of 'the economic structure', a concept introduced in the Preface. I provide my own characterization of the economic structure, and it is intended to be exegetically adequate, conceptually clear, and scientifically fertile. Though clear, my formulation also generates a clear difficulty, which is associated with a familiar criticism of historical materialism, deployed at length by Professor Plamenatz, but mentioned by Professor Acton as well. I deal with the criticism under the heading 'The Problem

* Previously published in *Proceedings of the Aristotelian Society*, supplementary vol. XLIV (1970).

of Legality', and I rebut it. I cannot say that I refute it, because the instrument of my rebuttal is only finally adequate if a certain condition, which I indicate, is fulfilled. I mark one instance where the instrument is satisfactory, but I do not prove its universal validity here. After propounding my solution to The Problem of Legality, I dilate on its relevance to the correct articulation of historical materialism.

2. In the social production of their life, men enter into definite relations that are indispensable and independent of their will, relations of production which correspond to a definite stage of development of their material productive forces. The sum total of these relations of production constitutes (*bildet*) the economic structure of society, the real foundation, on which rises a legal and political superstructure. . . . At a certain stage of their development, the material productive forces of society come in conflict with the existing relations of production, or – what is but a legal expression for the same thing (*was nur ein juridischer Ausdruck dafür ist*) – with the property relations within which they have been at work hitherto.[2]

Many unexplained concepts occur in the passage above. Some are easily explained; others are less tractable. In my opinion the 'economic structure' belongs in the former group, and this paper is intended to support that opinion. The economic structure is said to be composed of production relations and of nothing else. Hence the concept 'economic structure' will be clear when the concept 'production relation' has been explicated. For there would remain only the relation of 'constitution' which Marx posits between them, and though this relation is not simple identity, it is unproblematical, since the structure is explicitly defined as whatever the relations, *in toto*, compose or constitute. (Compare 'kinship structure' as a name for what kinship relations compose.) In this paper I shall explain what production relations are, and hence what the economic structure is.

The economic structure is also referred to, in apposition, as 'the real foundation' (*Basis*: sometimes translated 'base', or 'basis'). 'Structure' and 'foundation' denote the same thing, but to refer to it as a 'foundation' is to claim that it has causal or explanatory primacy over something else. The word 'structure' carries that claim less automatically.

I have recently consulted four documents in which Professor Acton describes and criticizes historical materialism: (1) 'The materialist conception of history'; (2) *The Illusion of the Epoch*; (3) *What Marx Really Said*;[3] (4) 'Historical materialism', in the Edwards

Encyclopaedia. In all four Acton comments on the portion of the Preface excerpted above, and in all except (3) he correctly reports that the economic structure is composed of production relations. But in all four he also adds to the content of the economic structure, in a manner which evidently violates the Preface, and which is, except in (3), indirectly inconsistent with his initial correct report. And he commits other errors of different degrees of importance.

For example. On p. 213 of (1) Acton makes these attributions to Marx: (i) *The Critique of Political Economy* divides social processes into those which are basic and those which are superstructural; (ii) Marx calls the set of production relations the 'economic structure'; (iii) the basis is identified with the material conditions of life, and the latter is made up of productive forces and productive relations. It would follow that the basis or economic structure is made up of productive forces as well as production relations.

Attribution (i) fails because the base/superstructure distinction does not divide *processes*. Basic is not a set of processes but a set of relations. This is proper, since the base is a structure, and whereas relations can compose a structure, processes cannot. This is important, because relations explain differently from the way processes do, a fact which vitiates many criticisms of Marxian explanatory theses.

Attribution (ii) is only marginally defective. It turns the relations/structure connection into identity, whereas Marx has the first constituting the second. In some contexts the difference matters, but not in ours.

Attribution (iii) is a mistake. It contradicts attribution (ii) and it contradicts Marx's text. It is repeated in (2) (137–8), in (3) (50), and in (4) (13), where the mistake is compounded, since Acton says that in the Preface Marx *wrote* that productive forces and production relations are the basis. He wrote no such thing, in the Preface or anywhere else.

Professor Acton is constrained to admit that he has misreported the words of the Preface. But he might argue that what he forced into the Preface was warranted by Marxian doctrine taken as a whole, and that I have focused unfairly on a terminological triviality. Here I can say only that I would not have bothered to advertise a merely verbal error. I believe that to locate productive forces in the economic structure is a serious misunderstanding of the shape of Marx's anatomy of society, but I cannot prove it here.

Why did Acton install productive forces in the economic structure? I offer a surmise. He propounds a technological interpretation of historical materialism, one which assigns primacy to the productive forces, and he may think that they cannot be primary unless they form part of the economic structure. Now I too support the technological interpretation, and I am grateful for Acton's lucid exposition of it [(2), 133–41]. But that interpretation does not require that productive forces be lodged in the economic structure. There is no reason to forbid the question, What causes a particular economic structure to obtain? and the answer, on the technological reading, is that the productive forces are strongly determining in the formation of the economic structure, while constituting no part of it.

In the remainder of the paper the economic structure is treated as consisting of production relations only. I now explain what they are.

3. To know what production relations are we have to know what terms can stand in production relations and how they can relate to each other. I am forced to supply that information dogmatically and I cannot deal with all the problems even the dogmatic statement raises.

For purposes of simplicity I consider dyadic relations only. By no means are all production relations dyadic. But nothing would be gained here by discussing those which are not. Henceforth I shall almost always be speaking about dyadic relations.

Persons and productive forces are the only terms that figure in production relations. All production relations are either between a person (or group of persons) and another person (or group of persons), or between a person (or group of persons) and a productive force (or group of productive forces). In other words: in any production relation, there is at least one person(s)-term and at most one productive-force(s)-term, and there is no term of any other kind.

The idea of a person is familiar. The idea of a productive force is not. The following catalogue clarifies the idea of a productive force, by listing all the types of things that can be one:

Productive Forces
- Means of Production
  - A  Tools
  - B  Raw Materials
- C  Labour-power (i.e., the producing agent's faculties: strength, skill, knowledge, inventiveness, etc.)

The items in the catalogue are unified by the fact that each is, in a wide sense, *used* by a producing agent to make a product. A denotes what he works with, B what he works on, and C what enables him to work with A on B.

The formulation above allows no entry into the category productive force of many items which have been placed in it, as a result of misreadings of Marx that cannot be documented here. Thus although Professor Acton is right when he says that 'good laws, good morals and good government can help production' he is wrong to infer that they can therefore be treated as means of production [(2), 167]. A means of $\emptyset$-ing is something used in order to $\Psi$, or in $\Psi$-ing. Laws, morals, and government are not used by men to produce products. They are used to get men to produce. They are means not of production but of mobilizing producers.

We now know the terms of production relations. I have to indicate what relations between them are production relations. I begin by providing a list of representative production relations. The list is divided into two columns:

1 $X$ is the slave of $Y$

2 $X$ is the master of $Y$

3 $X$ is the serf of $Y$

4 $X$ is the lord of $Y$

5 $X$ is hired by $Y$

6 $X$ hires $Y$

7 $X$ owns $Y$

8 $X$ does not own $Y$

9 $X$ leases his labour-power
to $Y$ (9 is a triadic relation, to be
construed as dyadic for present purposes)

10 $X$ is required to work for $Y$

11 $X$ works in association
with $Y$

12 $X$ works with $Y$

13 $X$ works on $Y$

14 $X$ supervises the work on $Y$

15 $X$ supervises the work of $Y$

What terms can the relations listed above combine? 1–10 can all combine persons and persons. 7 combines persons only in slave societies. 1–4 and 9–10 can combine only persons. 5–8 can also combine persons and things: men can hire and own both persons and productive forces.

I intend 11 as a relation binding persons only. I intend 12 as a relation which binds only persons and productive forces: e.g., Eric works with a hammer. Similarly with 13: Eric works on cotton. 'With' links a producer to a tool. 'On' links a producer to raw material, sometimes, as in 14, through the mediation of another producer. 15 is a mode of 11.

Note the tense of the verbs I use for capturing the relations which for Marx constitute the economic structure. '$X$ is now hiring $Y$' (as contrasted with 6) and '$X$ is now working with $Y$' (as contrasted with 12) are not relations forming part of the economic structure. The economic structure is composed not of transactions but of the relatively enduring relations within which transactions take place.

Earlier I excluded productive forces from the economic structure, and I would exclude persons as well. Yet production relations form the economic structure, and productive forces and persons are their terms. This generates only an apparent inconsistency. A full description of an economic structure would employ variables in place of all expressions referring to persons or productive forces. It would thus contain no names or definite descriptions designating particular persons or productive forces. Hence the contemplated inconsistency does not obtain. (It follows that one and the same economic structure can be present in different societies. An economic structure is a *form*.)

The relations in the left-hand column will be called 'o-relations'. They are relations which stipulate ownership by persons of productive forces or of persons OR relations (e.g., $X$ leases his labour-power to $Y$) which entail such ownership relations ($X$ owns his labour-power).

The relations in the right-hand column will be called 'w-relations' ('w' for 'work'). They are relations between persons and persons or between persons and productive forces which obtain when persons employ productive forces to make products.

Further analysis, not provided here, is required to make the characterization of o-relations and w-relations more precise. It is also required to show sufficient continuity between them to justify their common appellation 'production relations'. Acton and Plamenatz have criticized Marx for giving that name to relations which are too different. The presentation I have sketched reveals why that criticism is natural. I do not refute it here, because the problem of legality, which will exhaust the rest of my space, arises whether or not it is valid. In discussing the problem of legality, I engage against Professor Plamenatz, who treats relations rather like w-relations and o-relations as *candidates* for the title 'production relations'. That treatment suffices to situate the debate I shall have with him. His unwillingness to grant that both candidates can turn out to be production relations is irrelevant to the problem of legality, to which I now turn.

4. In the present section I explain how the problem of legality arises

out of Marx's formulations, on the construction I have given to them. In section 5 I consider difficulties in Plamenatz's statement of the problem. In section 6 I propose a solution to the problem.

The problem: we are committed to each of the following four positions, but we cannot consistently hold more than three of them:

1. The economic structure consists of production relations.
2. The economic structure is separate from (and explanatory of) the superstructure.
3. Law is part of the superstructure.
4. At least some production relations are defined by means of legal concepts.

Comment on 2: the parenthetical phrase is not required to generate inconsistency among the positions. I include it because I wish to show not only that production relations are separate from legal relations but also that explanation of the latter by the former is coherent.

To secure consistency, one of the positions must be abandoned. I shall abandon 4, by providing a means of eliminating the legal terms I used when introducing the idea of production relations. It was convenient to use those terms, but they were not essential. I indicate why they were convenient in the course of my solution to the problem of legality.

The legal concepts which, in section 6, will be eradicated, are conspicuous in the description of o-relations, which are either ownership-relations or not analysable without reference to ownership-relations. '$X$ is the slave of $Y$' entails '$Y$ owns $X$'; '$X$ hires $Y$' (where $Y$ is a person) entails '$X$ hires the labour-power of $Y$' which entails '$Y$ owns labour-power'; etc.

(If my scheme, not expounded here, for bringing w-relations into close connection with o-relations is well-founded, then legality would seem to affect w-relations as well.)

After presenting Plamenatz's account of the problem of legality, I shall expel legal concepts from the characterization of o-relations, and thereby render production relations legality free (or '*rechtsfrei*').

5. In *German Marxism and Russian Communism* Professor Plamenatz maintained that according to the Preface property relations are the expression of production relations.[4] Plamenatz suggested that two kinds of relation might be meant by 'production relation', the first similar to our w-relations, the second similar to our o-relations. He then argued, in effect, that (i) w-relations are distinct from property relations but incapable of legal expression in them; and

(ii) o-relations *are* property relations, and hence also incapable of legal expression in them, because where $X$ is an expression of $Y$, $X$ and $Y$ are never identical. He concluded that the idea that property relations are the expression of production relations is a confusion.

In this section I question Plamenatz's reading of the Preface, and I state a doubt about the first part of his argument. I am more interested in the second part of his argument, and the submissions of section 6 are an attempt to refute it.

Plamenatz complains that in the Preface Marx gives 'no certain clue to the identity' of production relations. This is so. He then says:

> What else does Marx tell us about them? That the system of property is their 'legal expression'. This cannot mean that the system of property is the same thing as these relations, since an expression and what it expresses are not one thing but two.[5] ['System of property' is a synonym for 'property relations' in this passage. – G. A. C.]

I shall now argue that the remarks above depend on a dubious translation of the relevant sentence of the Preface; that on a more defensible translation that sentence does not support the idea that Marx even intends property relations to be different from production relations; that the more defensible translation therefore makes it even more difficult to support Marx; but that we can nevertheless sponsor both Marx and the more defensible translation. Given the doctrine that law is superstructural, the relevant sentence is even more vulnerable than Professor Plamenatz thinks, but we shall find a way of securing it against attack.

Here is the original Preface sentence:

> Auf einer gewissen Stufe ihrer Entwicklung geraten die materiellen Produktivkräfte der Gesellschaft in Widerspruch mit den vorhandenen Produktionsverhältnissen oder, *was nur ein juristischer Ausdruck dafür ist*, mit den Eigenthumsverhältnissen, innerhalb deren sie sich bisher bewegt hatten.

I have italicized the clause in dispute. Plamenatz translates it as follows: 'what is but a legal expression *of* the same thing.' The standard, more defensible, translation is: 'what is but a legal expression *for* the same thing.' I have italicized the prepositions which differentiate the translations.

Plamenatz's translation suggests that Marx is positing a causal relation between production relations and property relations. The standard translation suggests a naming relation: 'Property relations' as another name for production relations. The preposition 'of' renders the word 'expression' a near-synonym for 'effect'; the preposition 'for' renders it a near-synonym for 'locution'.

Had Marx used the prepositional phrase '*davon*' Plamenatz's translation would have been correct and the standard translation wrong. But Marx used '*dafür*', a phrase whose most natural interpretation is the standard translation. We require a special reason for adopting Plamenatz's translation. Since I can think of none, I shall retain the standard translation.

To clarify the difference between the two translations, consider the following statement:

> *A* took from *B* an object belonging to *B*, without *B*'s knowledge, and without intending to return it, or, what is but a legal expression for the same thing, *A* committed a theft.

This intelligible statement does not entail that theft-commission is a legal expression of taking an object belonging to another, etc. The idea that theft-commission is a legal expression of that behaviour is, in addition, quite unintelligible.

But it is not true that whenever '*X*' is a legal expression *for Y, X* cannot be a legal expression *of Y*. And where *X* = property relations and *Y* = production relations, I would maintain that for Marx both connections hold, and the first is explained by the second. I think Marx intends a naming connection in the Preface sentence, but I allow that he also believes in the connection Plamenatz thinks he intends there. He does believe that property relations are expressions of production relations, that the prevailing production relations explain the prevailing property relations. At one place[6] he implies that property relations are products of production relations, and this is the view Plamenatz ascribed to him. Marx does not introduce a causal relation in the Preface sentence, but he does so elsewhere, and he employs it extensively in historical narrations.

I also believe that for Marx the causal relation grounds the naming relation: property concepts can refer to production relations because property relations are expressions of production relations. Compare: the fact that complaint is an expression *of* illness has rendered 'complaint' an expression *for* illness. But this does not prevent us from distinguishing the complaint and the illness whenever it is desirable to do so. Similarly, that Marx intends a naming relation in the Preface does not disable us from identifying and describing Marxian production relations without exercising the concept of property. This is compatible with the fact that in a society whose economic behaviour is law-abiding legal phrases refer to production relations, for in such a society a property relation to a productive force *is* a legally valid production relation. That is why Marx sometimes uses legal (superstructural) concepts to describe 'basic' facts. His practice is as compatible with the base/ superstructure distinction as is calling rheumatism a complaint with a sharp distinction between illnesses and behavioural responses to illnesses.

I now leave the naming relation and examine Professor Plamenatz's arguments against the possibility of a causal relation.

As I reported on p. 277, Plamenatz envisages two candidates for the role of production relations which have property relations as their legal expression. The first candidate is introduced on p. 24 of *German Marxism*: relations which relate men into a division of labour. Relations between foremen and their charges, and between architects and building contractors are given as examples. Plamenatz says that these relations 'do *not* find legal expression in the system of property'.

I believe that they generally do, by a route too indirect to describe here. I merely point out how unsuited one of Plamenatz's examples is to his argumentative purposes. For the phrase 'building contractor' imports a legal relation. It hints at how a position in the division of labour can enjoy a legal expression. Compare the idea of apprenticeship, which covers both a legal status and characteristic work-tasks.

Plamenatz's second candidate for production relations turns out to be, on his view, the property relations themselves. He claims this candidate fails because (i) property cannot be allowed to enter the economic structure, and (ii) an expression cannot be identical with what it expresses.

In indicating how a linguistic expression may name a phenomenon which is expressed in what the linguistic expression in the first instance names, I have supplied a basis for qualifying claim (ii). But that qualification aside, I now address the major issue, which concerns the production relations Marx usually described in legal language, our o-relations, which Plamenatz finds indistinguishable from property relations, and which he treats as an illicit presence in the economic base of facts which belong in the legal superstructure.

6. The problem of legality has two connected parts: (i) To formulate a non-legal interpretation of the legal terms in Marx's characterization of production relations, in such a way that (ii) we can coher-

ently represent property relations as expressions of, or effects of, or explained by production relations.

The programme for solving the problem has four stages. First, I display ownership as a matter of enjoying rights. Then for each such right I formulate what I shall call a 'corresponding power'. Next, I similarly describe production relations which 'correspond' to property relations. Finally I show how production relations, thus identified, may be represented as explaining property relations. I do not argue in this paper that they do explain property relations. I show only that such explanations are conceptually impeccable.

To own an object is to enjoy a number of rights with regard to the object. (I use 'right' widely, to cover the legal advantages Hohfeld distinguished as claims, privileges, powers, and immunities.)[7] The rights depend on the character of the object and of the rules governing ownership of it. A diminution in the number of rights I have over what I own is *ipso facto* a reduction in the extent to which I own what I own. Today individual capitalists have less legal discretion over their holdings than they did one hundred years ago. This can be expressed in the assertion that they have fewer rights over what they own. It is at least as correct to say that they own what they do to a lesser extent than they used to. (Note that I have not said that the capitalist class has less control over the means of production. A reduction in the individual capitalist's control can result from increased control by capitalists as a class.)

A. M. Honoré has challenged the view that to own an object is to enjoy a number of rights with regard to the object. He contends that ownership involves prohibitions or duties as well as rights.[8] His position would require that our programme be made more complicated, but its essence would be unaffected. For reasons of simplicity, I shall retain my original formulation. But it may not be irrelevant to question the adequacy or at least the inescapability of Honoré's proposals. I mention two issues: (1) A prohibition on the use of my property in a particular way may be construed as a reduction of my ownership of it. Prohibitions may be regarded as entering the definition of ownership only in this negative manner. It is difficult to see what could forbid us to treat them in this fashion, and so protect the formulation Honoré challenged. (2) Some (not all) of the prohibitions Honoré mentions apply only *per accidens* to what I own. It is true (p. 123) that I may not use my car to run my neighbour down, but this applies to any car, not just the one I own.

We can transform any phrase of the form 'the right to Ø' into a phrase that denotes a power by dropping the word 'right' and replacing it by the word 'power'. Let us call the power we derive a power which *corresponds* to the right we begin with. Possession of rights entails possession of their corresponding powers when and only when the rights are effective. (This does not mean that a man cannot have a power which corresponds to an ineffective right he has. For example: A man has the right to travel, but a gang of hoodlums do not want him to. They seek to prevent him from travelling, and they are too strong to be restrained by the legitimate authorities, who are weak. But the man has a stronger gang at his disposal, which defeats the gang that would block his movement. So he is able to travel but not because his right to travel is effective.)

I am using 'power' as follows: A man has the power to Ø if and only if he is able to Ø, where 'able' is non-normative. 'Able' is used normatively when a remark like 'He is not able to Ø' need not be withdrawn in face of the fact that he is Ø-ing. This logical feature characterizes legal and moral uses of 'able'.

The ordinary use of 'able' remains elastic and context-variable even after normative uses have been excluded, but that does not vitiate our programme. The concept of a production relation may be elastic, without being at all vague. Elasticity affects the concept of *effective* rights as well.

I now list some rights involved in ownership of productive forces, together with their corresponding powers:

| | |
|---|---|
| 1   right to use means of production or labour-power | 1   power to use means of production or labour-power |
| 2   right to withhold means of production or labour-power | 2   power to withhold means of production or labour-power |
| 3   right to alienate means of production or labour-power | 3   power to alienate means of production or labour-power |
| 4   right to let means of production decay | 4   power to let means of production decay |

A comment on correspondence 3: the specification of the power contains the legal term 'alienate'. The phrase designates a power rather than a right, but the power is described by reference to a legal notion. Since we aim to eliminate legality from production relations, we cannot be content with powers specified in a legal way. The remedy is to locate the rights contained in the concept of alienation, and to continue the translation, as follows:

To alienate is to arrange for another to have over an object the rights I now have over it. The right to alienate is therefore the right to arrange for another to have over an object the rights I now have over it. The power corresponding to this right is the power to arrange for another to have over an object the powers I now have over it. (It follows that the power corresponding to the right to alienate is not the same as the power corresponding to the right to arrange for another to have over an object the rights the alienator now has. This is unembarrassing. The correspondence-relation is 'intentional', or 'opaque'. That is, it is invalid to argue as follows – power $p$ corresponds to right $r$. Right $r$ is the same as right $s$. Therefore power $p$ corresponds to right $s$.)

A critic might question the meaningfulness of some of the phrases which denote corresponding powers. Consider correspondence 4. A critic might wonder how one could *lack* the power to let a (decayable) thing decay, and might therefore question the idea of such a power.

Reply: (i) Powers need not be difficult to secure or maintain. The power to breathe does not lack status as a power because it is universally enjoyed. (ii) In fact one *could* lack the power to let an object decay. For one might be forced to keep an object in good health or good repair. A woman might force her husband to water the plant in the hall. And the state forces people to keep certain of their chattels in good order, by legally obliging them to do so. In law-abiding societies the imposition of obligations – a reduction in rights – is a generally effective means of reducing powers.

In a manner analogous to our construction of powers corresponding to rights we could construct constraints corresponding to legal obligations. By such an expansion of our programme we could accommodate the views of A. M. Honoré.

We now have a method of excising legal terms from the description of production relations. We can construct *rechtsfrei* production relations which correspond to property relations in just the way powers correspond to rights. I shall now exemplify the use of the method. The method will be serviceable only if the *rechtsfrei* characterizations of production relations do not alter the significance of the claims Marx expressed in legal concepts of production relations.

Consider the contrasting relations of production, described in legal terms, which distinguish the ideal-type slave from the ideal-type proletarian. (We shall reflect on ideal types only.) Neither owns any means of production. Marx differentiates them by pointing out that whereas the proletarian owns his labour-power, the slave does not. Unlike the latter, the former has the right to withhold it.

Our programme enjoins us to translate as follows: the proletarian has the power to withhold his labour-power; the slave has not.

Objection: The reason for saying that the slave lacks this power is that if he withholds his labour-power he is likely to be killed, and he will certainly die. But a similar fate awaits the proletarian who withholds his labour-power, for he thereby loses the means of his subsistence. Therefore the proletarian is unable to withhold his labour-power in just the way the slave is. Therefore the production relations characterizing slave and proletarian no longer contrast when purged of legality as required by our programme.

Reply: It is not insignificant that the withholding slave is liable to be killed and the proletarian is not, but I shall not rely on this difference. I concede that the withholding proletarian dies. But note that the proletarian can withhold his labour-power from any given capitalist, including his current employer, without fear of death. The slave cannot similarly withhold his labour-power from his particular master.

The proletarian is constrained to offer his labour-power not to any particular capitalist, but on the labour market to the whole capitalist class. And this accords with the Marxian thesis that the proletarian is owned not by any given capitalist, but by the capitalist class.[9] The corresponding non-legal statement of the proletarian's position is true.

That indicates how to carry out the programme in one case. I have not demonstrated the general viability of the programme. I submit it, and I commit myself to its defence against objections.

I now turn to the second part (see pp. 280–1) of the problem of legality. Can we coherently maintain that property relations are expressions of, or effects of, or explained by production relations, on a legality-free construction of the latter? I shall give a schema for *some* explanations of the desired kind. In assessing them it is essential to recall the truism that discrepancies can obtain between rights and their corresponding powers. A man can possess ineffective rights, and he can possess powers which are acquired and/or sustained illegally.

Suppose that at a certain time (t1) property relations of type $P$ prevailed, and at a later time (t2) property relations of a different type, $Q$, prevailed. Here are two possible explanations of the required kind for this sequence.

I: Around t1 new productive forces were encouraging employers to organize production relations which violated the law, for at t1 the law forbade employment by anyone of more than twenty men, and the new productive forces could only be exploited with more than twenty men in a workshop. Because the law thus 'fettered' the productive forces, it was broken. By t2 those who had broken the law secured changes in it which restored conformity between property relations and production relations.

Summary: that production relations were changing after t1 and had changed by some time between t1 and t2 explains the change in property relations from *P* to *Q*.

II: Around t1 new productive forces were available, but the law on employable numbers was too well enforced to allow production relations appropriate to those productive forces to be formed. Those production relations were envisaged by men who strove between t1 and t2 to change the law, and who succeeded by t2. When the law had been changed, the new production relations were established.

Summary: the need after t1 to effect new production relations explains the change in property relations from *P* to *Q*.

We find patterns of kinds I and II in transitions like that from the medieval to the modern order. Usually they are both applicable: some powers are exercised illegally, others must await a change in the law. The legal change typically consecrates achieved powers and permits the formation of unachieved powers. The history of the decline of the guild system abundantly corroborates this conception, as does the following diagnosis by Paul Mantoux, which is patterned in accordance with our schema I:

> What destroyed [the law of settlement] was the irresistible pressure of the new conditions brought about by the industrial revolution. For large-scale production on modern lines a free circulation of labour was absolutely necessary. The new industries had been able to develop only because the law of settlement had been constantly broken.[10]

The productive forces demanded 'large-scale production on modern lines', which entailed new w-relations of production. These in turn required new o-relations of production ('free circulation of labour'). The law forbade that, so it was broken, ignored, and finally scrapped. Then conformity between property relations and production relations was re-established.

A functionalist rationale underlies this species of explanation. In human society might frequently requires right in order to operate or form itself. Might without right is in some contexts inefficient and/or unstable. Powers over productive forces are a case in point. Their exercise is uncertain when it is not legal. So production relations, for maximum order and efficiency, require a legal expression in property relations.

The Marxist makes the further claim that property relations have the character they do *because* actual or envisaged production relations require them to have that character. He can defend his position by recourse to historians who report how men fought hard, and successfully, to change the law so that it would legitimate powers they had or envisaged as available; or how percipient legislators altered the law to eliminate actual or potential instability the old laws fostered.

To say that production relations require legal expression for stability and efficiency is to say that the foundation requires a superstructure, and thus to cast doubt on the architectural metaphor – foundations are normally stable without superstructures. The doubt is dispelled by choosing the right architectural image. One slab resting on another would be incorrect. One correct picture is as follows.

Consider four struts driven into the ground, each protruding the same distance above it. They are unstable. They wobble at winds of force 3. Now attach a roof to the four struts, which renders them stable at all winds under force 6. Of this roof one can say: (i) it is supported by the struts, and (ii) it renders them more stable. That gives the right relation between Marxian base and Marxian superstructure. (The further Marxian claim not represented in the image, is that when and because struts are unstable a roof which stabilizes them tends to be imposed. The base does not merely support the superstructure. It explains its character.)

7. I now deal with two highly general objections to the programme I have proposed.

(i) A critic familiar with the thought of Engels might complain that I have replaced the legal conception of production relations by the 'force theory', which Engels, presumably with Marx's approval, condemned in *Anti-Dühring*. The complaint would be misdirected, because my way of defining production relations does not stipulate how the powers they enfold are obtained and sustained. The answer to that question does involve force, but also ideology and, as we have seen, law. But it is not the question that the programme answers, for it exhibits what production relations are, not how they are maintained. The following comparison should clarify my meaning.

An illegal squatter who tills the land he occupies might secure his dominion by hiring retainers who use force illegally on his behalf, and/or by propounding a myth that anyone who disturbs his tenure of his land damns himself to eternal hellfire. The squatter has something in common with a legal owner of similarly tilled land whose tenure is protected by the legitimate authorities. Both have the power to use their land. That one employs force and the other relies on the law to sustain his position in that production relation is in neither case part of the content of the relation. This comparison shows that I am not advocating a variant of the 'force theory'.

(ii) A critic might find no fault in our programme, but might be puzzled that in fact Marx gave legal characterizations of production relations. The puzzle is solved by the naming relation between legal characterizations and production relations in settled society. The naming relation makes it convenient to describe production relations, even illegal ones, in legal terms, particularly because ordinary language lacks a simple apparatus for describing them non-legally. If ordinary language had that apparatus it would not be necessary to propose our somewhat complicated programme.

It should be added that Marx frequently used legal terms in non-legal senses. This procedure is overwhelming evidence that he would have embraced our programme. At *Capital*, III, p. 660 he refers to means of production which were 'in fact, or legally, the property of the tiller himself', and, on p. 777, to those means of production becoming his 'property' first in fact, then also 'legally'. Since 'property' is a legal concept, it might be argued that there cannot be property which is the tiller's in fact but not legally. That argument would be extremely scholastic. Marx can perhaps be accused of speaking in a misleading way, but the point of his phrasing is to achieve concision, and our programme shows that the same propositions can be expressed quite unmisleadingly, at the cost of a certain prolixity.

8. In *The Illusion of the Epoch* (pp. 164–5) Professor Acton provides an argument which purports to prove that factors Marxism places outside the economic structure cannot be separated from it. I shall not review the argument. It shows only that non-basic institutions are functionally necessary to basic arrangements. So far from disturbing historical materialism, this conclusion about non-basic institutions is, I have argued, a thesis it purveys and has a right to purvey.

Extending his argument, Professor Acton writes: 'The "material or economic basis" of society is not, therefore, something that can be clearly *conceived*, still less *observed*, apart from the legal, moral and political relationships of men' (ibid., p. 167, emphasis added).

I have submitted a method of *conceiving* the economic structure which excludes from it the legal, moral, and political relationships of men. Professor Acton must argue either that I have constructed a defective concept or that I have been unfaithful to Marx's intentions.

I have not, however, tried to show that the economic structure can be '*observed* apart from' superstructural relationships. It is not immediately clear what *observation* of an economic structure amounts to. Consider, for comparison, a divorce rate. A divorce rate in a given country is identical with the number which is the ratio of divorces to marriages in that country. Can a divorce rate be observed? In a sense, yes: it can be determined by observation. In a sense, no: it is a number, and a number cannot be observed. Can we make the observations necessary to discover it without at the same time observing the factors leading to marital breakdown, or the manner in which divorces are effected? Even if we say no, our answer does not entail that the fact that a certain divorce rate prevails cannot explain or be explained by other facts about society or individuals, including facts which obtain when divorces obtain. For example: if the divorce rate is some high figure, this may explain the fact that an unusual proportion of divorces are effected by unusual means, recourse to which is necessary only because so many are seeking divorces.

Similar comments apply to the economic structure. It is determined by observation, but it is not felicitous to say that it can be observed. Yet even if we say that it can be observed, but not apart from the relationships Acton mentions, we do not rule out an explanation of those relationships which draws on features of the economic structure. The claim that economic and non-economic variables are presented together in experience cannot inhibit an attempt to explain one set in terms of the other.

The contentions I have expressed in this awkward fashion are banal. They are evidenced by the practice of theorists in any developed science. If the molecules which make up a certain biological organism never occur outside that organism and hence cannot be observed unless the organism is observed, no molecular biologist will be deterred from explaining the nature of the organism by appeal to the nature of the molecules, which are not themselves organisms. Professor Acton's strictures on the capacity of a *rechtsfrei (moralitätsfrei*, etc.) economic structure to explain law (morals, etc.) depend on a conception of explanation alien to science. Why should historical materialism be concerned about those strictures?

## NOTES

1 David McLellan, ed., *Karl Marx Selected Writings* (Oxford, Oxford University Press, 1971), pp. 388–91.
2 ibid., p. 389.
3 'The materialist conception of history', *Proceedings of the Aristotelian Society*, vol. 42 (1951–2), pp. 207–24; *The Illusion of the Epoch* –

*Marxism–Leninism as a Philosophical Creed* (London, Cohen & West, 1955); *What Marx Really Said* (London, 1967).

4   Longmans Green, 1954, repr. London, Greenwood Press, 1975.

5   ibid., p. 22.

6   *Capital* (Moscow, 1957–62), vol. I, p. 615 n2.

7   W. N. Hohfeld, *Fundamental Legal Conceptions as Applied in Judicial Reasoning* (New Haven, Yale University Press, 1919), p. 71 *et passim*.

8   'Ownership' in A. G. Guest, ed., *Oxford Essays in Jurisprudence*, first series (Oxford, Clarendon Press, 1961), pp. 107–47 at pp. 123, 134.

9   *Capital* I, pp. 573–4, 613–14.

10  *The Industrial Revolution in the Eighteenth Century: An Outline of the Beginnings of the Modern Factory System in England* (London, Cape, 1928; revised edn, 1961), p. 434.

## Chapter Eighteen

# ON SOME CRITICISMS OF HISTORICAL MATERIALISM* A REPLY

## *H. B. ACTON*

How do we interpret the exposition of Historical Materialism given by Marx in the Preface to his *Critique of Political Economy?* Mr Cohen disagrees with various accounts of it that I have given, and he thinks that Marx's view can be defended against criticisms by Professor Plamenatz in his *German Marxism and Russian Communism* and by me in *The Illusion of the Epoch* and elsewhere.[1] The criticism that Mr Cohen has chiefly in mind is that Marx says that legal relationships belong to the superstructure of society and yet has to describe the basis or foundation in terms that include legal concepts.

Nothing is more boring and few things are less profitable than defensive analyses of what one intended to say, and I do not propose to undertake anything of the kind. I confess that I found and still find the famous passage in the *Critique of Political Economy* very difficult to understand and to interpret, and I shall have more to say about it later. It should be emphasized, however, that my main concern in *The Illusion of the Epoch*, as is indicated by its subtitle, *Marxism–Leninism as a Philosophical Creed*, was to discuss what is called Marxism–Leninism, a view which takes its origins from the writings of Marx and Engels but has developed in ways that not all admirers of Marx find acceptable. I understand that Mr Cohen agrees with me that Marx's own theory, as well as that of his Marxist–Leninist successors, is to be interpreted as a technological theory of history. Nor is he criticizing my account, intended as a more precise specification than that given by Marxists, of how technological invention can *necessitate* changes in job-relationships but only *favour* changes in para-technological relationships. If I am right, Marx and Engels failed to distinguish between the way in which technological change necessitates changes in how men work, and the way in which it influences legal and political changes to

---

* Previously published in *Proceedings of the Aristotelian Society*, supplementary vol. **XLIV** (1970).

the extent that the prevailing institutions permit it to do so. I am not sure what Mr Cohen thinks about this, but one thing in my discussion of Historical Materialism that he wishes to criticize is my suggestion that the various social elements, as I called them, distinguished by Marx, i.e., productive forces, productive relationships, political and legal superstructure, the ideologies, are factually and conceptually so closely implicated with one another that the attempt to show that the basic ones can explain or bring into existence the superstructural ones is hopeless from the very beginning.[2] I shall consider his arguments on this later.

First, however, let us consider what Marx himself meant by those words in the Preface to the *Critique of Political Economy* that have been so often quoted. Mr Cohen, of course, reproduces only a part of this Preface, and from what he does reproduce he omits, as not germane to his theme, some famous sentences to the effect that the means of production determine 'the social, political and spiritual life-process generally', and that it is man's 'social being that determines his consciousness'. This close concentration on Marx's account of productive forces and productive relations, and on the legal and political superstructure, may, however, leave out of account elements of the theory that are of prime importance, and I therefore propose to try to put the passage into its context, in the hope that its meaning will thereby appear more clearly.

Marx's line of thought is as follows. Referring to his article on Hegel's *Philosophy of Right* that had appeared in the *Deutsch-Französische Jahrbücher* in 1844, he says that the first stage in his enquiries led him to the conclusion that 'legal relationships and forms of state' must be understood in terms of, and 'have their roots' in, 'the material conditions of life, the aggregate of which Hegel . . . grouped under the name of "civil society" ', and that 'the anatomy of civil society is to be found in political economy'. Marx's wording seems to suggest that he had come to this conclusion before the deeper study of political economy which he started in Paris in 1844 and continued in Brussels afterwards. If this is so, the passage quoted by Mr Cohen and what follows it would refer to a later and more developed view. In 1844, Marx seems to be saying, he had already come to believe that 'the anatomy of civil society is to be found in political economy', and after his study of political economy he came to the conclusions about productive forces, productive relations, and the rest. The first sentence of the passage quoted by Mr Cohen indicates that each individual is *forced* to enter into *pre-existing* relations of production which correspond to a stage of development of 'material productive forces'. It is important to notice this, because

Marx later suggests that individuals need not always have to conform themselves to institutions over which their will has no control. The totality of relations of production constitutes the 'economic structure of society', which is basic. On this arises 'a legal and political superstructure', and – now I come to what Mr Cohen has omitted – to it correspond 'definite forms of consciousness'. The 'mode of production of material life', Marx goes on, 'determines the social, political and spiritual (*geistigen*) life-process as a whole', and therefore men's 'social being . . . determines their consciousness', and not vice versa. There follows the sentence saying that the productive forces come into 'contradiction' with the existing relations of production, which are said to be legally expressed as 'property relations'. Continuing now beyond the passage already quoted, Marx says that the conflict between the developing productive forces and the lagging productive relationships gives rise to 'social revolution' in which 'the whole huge superstructure is slowly or rapidly revolutionized'. In general, social revolutions consist in a series of basic, 'material', 'economic' changes, which can be investigated by the methods of the natural sciences, and of the arguments about legal, political, religious, and artistic matters which many suppose are playing a large part in effecting or delaying the course of the revolution but are in fact ideological and hence subsidiary. It is the former that are the moving forces in terms of which the latter must be explained. As long as a social system can enable all the forces of production which are its basis to come to fruition, that social system continues in existence. Productive relationships of a higher level can only come into existence as a result of the development of adequate 'material conditions' (presumably 'higher' productive forces). There is always a solution for the major problems which beset a society, because the problem itself arises in a conflict between emerging productive forces and already existing productive relationships which constrain them, and the solution must consist in bringing the old productive relationships into line. In the past there have been Asiatic, Ancient, and Feudal 'modes of production' which have determined the social orders of different and developing epochs. The mode of production at the time when Marx was writing was 'the modern bourgeois type'. The corresponding bourgeois productive relationships, according to Marx, were 'the last antagonistic form of the social process of production'. The forces of production 'developing in the womb of bourgeois society' will create at the same time 'the material conditions for the resolution of this antagonism', and with the collapse of the bourgeois system the pre-history of human society will be brought to an end.

(a) If we take this passage as a whole I think we may say that Marx's view should be described as Prehistorical Materialism rather than as Historical Materialism. Pre-history will end and history will start only when the antagonistic conflicts between progressive productive forces and lagging productive relations have come to an end. This will occur when the antagonisms in bourgeois society have resulted in a higher social form. Although Marx does not say so in this passage, we know from his other writings that Marx held that this higher form of society would be a communistic society. Nor does he here say in so many words that in all earlier societies there were class divisions and antagonisms and that the communist society with which history will commence will have no class divisions.[3] His central point appears to be that in all societies up to and including bourgeois society individuals are forced to live their lives in constricting bonds of productive relationships over which they have no control. They have to spend their lives as labourers, craftsmen, machine-minders, and the like, and are hence limited and confined. The implication is that when the productive forces of bourgeois society have been fully developed, there will be a 'social revolution' out of which a society will emerge in which there are no more productive relations of a constraining type. Hegel, in his *Lectures on the Philosophy of History*, had argued that *history*, not pre-history, is the development of various forms of freedom, which he traced through Oriental society, in which one man is free, through Ancient society, in which some men are free, to Post-Reformation and Post-French Revolutionary society, in which all men are free. The freedom which Hegel claimed to see developing in human history Marx claimed to foresee in an emancipated society of the future. Freedom would be achieved when technology has developed to such an extent that individual men would no longer be forced to submit themselves to pre-existing social institutions. The pre-history of man just is the necessity of submitting to them.

(b) Marx, then, had argued that 'legal relationships and forms of state cannot be understood from themselves nor from the so-called general development of the human mind', and he extended this idea from the society of his own day to the forms of society that had preceded it. There are forces of production operating in a framework of relations of production on which arises 'a juridical and political superstructure' and associated with this are 'definite forms of social consciousness', the various ideologies. A 'legal expression' for the productive relations is the 'property relationships' of the society.

This raises two important questions. How can a juridical and political superstructure arise on something and also be an expression of it? Why should 'property relationships' be only a legal expression for the relations of production? Let us first consider the second question.

(c) In an Introduction to a version of the *Critique of Political Economy* written in 1857–8 but not published by Marx[4] there is a discussion of the relation between production and property. Marx here says that

> All production is appropriation (*Aneignung*) of nature on the part of the individual within and by means of a definite form of society. In this sense it is a tautology to say that property (*Eigentum*) [Marx here adds in brackets the verb '*Aneignen*'] is a condition of production. But it is merely laughable to make a jump from this to a definite form of property, e.g., private property. (To this is subordinated as a condition *non-property (das Nichteigentum)* as a contrary form.) History shows rather common property (*Gemeineigentum*) (e.g., among the Indians, Slavs, Celts, etc.) as the earlier form. . . . That nothing can be said about any production and also about any society where there is no form of property is a tautology. An appropriation that does not appropriate anything [does not make anything of its own – *die sich nichts zu eigen macht*] is a *contradictio in subjecto*. (*Grundrisse*, p. 9)

Later in the manuscript Marx refers to the period prior to the introduction of wage labour when, he says, the worker may have been the free owner of a small piece of land or a member of 'an oriental communal landownership system'. Such a worker is quaintly described as living in his own 'natural laboratory' and as enjoying 'the natural unity of labour with its factual presuppositions'. Living thus, 'The individual is related to himself as owner, as master of the conditions of his actuality' (*Grundrisse*, p. 375; Hobsbawm, p. 67).

We should resist the temptation of supposing that Marx is merely punning on the root that is common to 'appropriation' and to 'property'. If he were doing this his argument would consist in saying that in work the individual has to seize hold of some tool or material or animal or plant and in so doing makes it his own property. But neither assimilation nor possession is ownership, and Marx was well aware of this. We can, I think, see what Marx had in mind if we consider Adam Ferguson's *Essay on the History of Civil Society*,[5] which Marx refers to a number of times in *Das Kapital*.

Ferguson held that among savage peoples the only things owned are 'the arms, the utensils, and the fur, which the individual carries', and that the food acquired by hunting or primitive agriculture 'accrues to the community, and is applied to immediate use or becomes an accession to the stores of the public'. Furthermore, the land that savages hunt over or plant 'is claimed as a property by the nation, but is not parcelled in lots to its members', 'while the cabbin [*sic*] and its utensils are appropriated to the family'. Among such peoples there are no 'distinctions of rank or condition', and 'personal qualities give an ascendant in the midst of occasions which require their exertion, but in times of relaxation, leave no vestige of power or prerogative'. But when parents begin to 'desire a better provision' for their children, the earlier co-partnership breaks up and 'the members of any community, being distinguished among themselves by unequal shares, the ground of a permanent and palpable subordination is laid'. Savagery has then passed over to what Ferguson calls barbarism. Ferguson thought, then, that among 'savages' there was private ownership of arms and tools, family ownership of houses, and communal ownership of harvests and land. With this sort of consideration in mind Marx came to the conclusion that there are many different forms of ownership, that the forms in being at any time must be related to the modes of production of that time, and that *individual* ownership should not be taken as the central or basic form. Marx supposes that whenever an individual works he must do so within a system of rules for the acquisition of the raw materials and for disposal of the product. Such rules are rules of ownership and therefore there can be no production without ownership.

This view is intended to be subversive of the liberal theory of property. Expositors of the liberal theory, after showing that in 'mature legal systems' the basic notion of ownership is that of absolute ownership (*dominium*), go on to say that ownership has never been *quite* absolute, and that various forms of social control over property have come to limit this individualistic form. Nevertheless, on this view it is the individualistic form that is 'the basic model – a single human being owning, in the full liberal sense, a single material thing'.[6] According to Marx, however, production and hence ownership is essentially social in a number of senses. Social control over individualistic ownership is not a new development but has always existed. It is, therefore, the liberal model that should be regarded as exceptional rather than the 'communal' one. The picture of Robinson Crusoe or of the isolated hunter in Locke's wilderness should not be allowed to obscure the social nature of production and of property. 'Production by an isolated individual outside society . . . is just as nonsensical (*ist ein ebensolches Unding*) as the development of speech without individuals living and speaking together' (*Grundrisse*, p. 6). Later on Marx writes: 'Language as the product of an individual is an absurdity. But so also is property.' He also says that language *is* 'the community in so far as it speaks of itself (*das selbstredende Dasein desselben*)' (*Grundrisse*, p. 390; Hobsbawm, p. 88).

My comments on this must be bald and brief. (i) The contrast between Marx's social theory of property and the liberal view is not as sharp as Marx supposes. For on the liberal view the individual owner has the right to possession, may alienate what he owns, and so on, and this is only possible within a society. I suggest that Robinson Crusoe would be faced with *economic* problems, in so far as he would have to decide how to allocate his time and effort between providing food or providing shelter, or providing for his immediate needs or for needs he expects to have to satisfy in the future. On the other hand, unless Man Friday appears, there can be no question of ownership, for unless there are, or are likely to be other people, there can be no point in talking of Crusoe's right to possess what he has. This 'proof' that there could be economic situations without law or property would not satisfy Marx, however, since he thought that *commodities*, i.e., things produced *for sale*, and hence in a society, are essential for an economic situation. (ii) Marx's account of production as involving appropriation and property gives an extremely wide meaning to the word 'property' or to the concept of 'ownership'. Even in the savage state an individual's clothes or club, his 'arms' or his 'fur' are things that are his to a much greater extent than the land or the harvest. Marx points out in the *Grundrisse* (p. 390; Hobsbawm, p. 88) that a nomadic pastoral tribe regard their territory as their property 'although they never fix this property'. It is the herd, not the ground, that is appropriated by them. Marx's difficulty in deciding here shows that his conception of ownership, leading to ownership that is not 'fixed', was getting very diluted. M. Étienne Balibar points out that in the chapter of *Das Kapital* headed 'Absolute and Relative Surplus Value' Marx, within the space of a page or two, uses the word 'appropriation' both for an individual's control of natural objects and for capital's 'appropriation of surplus value'. The second, says Balibar, is property, and the first belongs 'to the analysis of what Marx calls "the work process", or rather he places the analysis of this work process as a part of the analysis of the mode of production'.[7] If this is so, then at this point Marx was retaining the concept of property for something 'fixed' and was no longer insisting that *all* production, as social, presupposes rules of ownership, even if loose ones. These differences are connected with the legal meaning of 'alienation' and the wider meaning that Marx gives to it, which has merged so easily with the equivocal sentimentality of our time.

(*d*) Marx's statement that 'mankind only sets itself problems which it can solve' cannot be adequately discussed as part of a brief paper. I do not think that Marx has in mind the view that a properly framed question must contain indications of the type of statement that would answer it. He understands 'problem' in a practical sense, and appears to be saying that when men find themselves in a serious practical difficulty they must, by understanding what their difficulty is, already have the information that would enable them to get out of it. But this seems just as false as to say that because someone knows what form the answer to a question must be that he therefore must be able to answer it. Men tied up on a spot towards which an avalanche is moving know the conditions for saving their lives but may not be able to do anything about it. Marx believed, of course, that machine production on a large scale was incompatible with private ownership of the means of production and that if the former was to continue the latter would have to be abandoned. This assumes, however, that Marx's diagnosis is complete in its essentials and that therefore the nature of the 'problem' is in no doubt.

(*e*) We have already seen that Marx says that the situation of being forced to work under social conditions over which the individual has no control will pass away when pre-history has been succeeded by history. What will work consist of, then, when history has started? Marx gives some indication of his views on this in the *Grundrisse* (p. 505). Here he is criticizing Adam Smith's view that work or labour is a 'sacrifice', and he says that although this is so for a mere wage-earner, it was not wholly so for the 'semi-artist worker of the Middle Ages'. Slave-labour, vassal-labour, and wage-labour are 'repulsive, utterly external forced-labour, and in opposition to this non-labour is "freedom and happiness" '. But there is a sort of labour which Fourier had called '*travail attractif*', which is the 'self-development of the individual', even though Fourier treated it as a sort of joke or play, 'naïvely and loosely' (*naiv grisettenmässig*). This sort of work,

> really free work, e.g., composing, is frightfully serious, is the most intense exertion. The work of material production can

only retain this character because (1) its social character is
settled (*gesetzt*), (2) that it is also general work of a scientific
character, not the exertion of man as a specifically drilled
natural force, but as a subject that appears in the process of
production, not in a merely natural form that has grown up
naturally, but as an activity that controls all the forces of
nature.

In this account of what production will be when history has broken
the bonds of pre-history, we notice that it is to be creative, as in
musical (and presumably, literary) composition, that it is not to be
forced in any way, and yet it is to be scientifically organized.

It seems to me that these passages, written when he was preparing
the *Critique of Political Economy* of 1859, show that Marx believed
that production, law, and property are inseparable from one another
in the sorts of society that have existed hitherto. 'Property', it is
true, is understood in a very wide sense, as comprising all rules
controlling the sorts of work that is done, the tools used, and the
disposal of the product, and it then becomes tautologous, as Marx
says, that property and production are essentially connected. This
thesis has the curious consequence that the criticisms made of the
theory expounded in the Preface, *viz.*, that Marx's basis–superstructure model separates aspects of society that are inseparable
from one another, are not in opposition to what we may call the
'*Urvorrede*', the Introduction that Marx did not publish, but on the
contrary form part of Marx's own argument there. Marx himself,
when writing for himself, says that law enters into the very processes
of production, governing the mode of production and the disposal
of the product. In simple societies this would be customary, not
statute law, but law of a sort it would have to be. Yet it is strange
that Marx has so little to say about the technological processes
themselves. For the organization of the work itself must also depend
upon what is being made and how it has to be made. Job-relationships have a relative independence of legal relationships, in that,
for example, large logs have to be sawn in pits with a top-sawyer
and a bottom-sawyer, before powered sawmills were available. The
task, the material, and the tools often determine precisely how the
workers have to be organized. But this technological component
seems not to have interested Marx when he was writing these
reflections on what he considered to be the basic social activities. To
transport and set up the stones at Stonehenge was an extraordinarily
complex task, requiring the co-operation of many men. No one
knows whether they co-operated from fear of cruel masters or in

some form of organized amity. Marx seems to have supposed that an element of forcibly organized drill (see the reference in the previous paragraph) is inseparable from pre-communist arrangements, but he does not say how far this is required by the technical problems that face men in such societies, and how far it is due to the 'economic' arrangements, which he knew to be of very many different actual and possible types.

Marx believed that, in addition to what he called the 'dialectic' of the concepts of productive forces and productive relationships – a dialectic, he says, which 'does not cancel the difference' (*Grundrisse*, p. 29) – there is also a dialectic of production and consumption (*Grundrisse*, pp. 11–16). The producer, he says, consumes himself, and consumes also the raw material he works on, and the consumer, in eating or drinking, 'produces his own body'. Hence, Marx continues, 'each is immediately its opposite'. Furthermore, it is only when products are consumed that they are *really* products: ' . . . a dress first becomes really a dress through the act of being worn.' Consequently, Marx concludes,

> there is nothing more simple than for an Hegelian to treat production and consumption as identical. And this has been said, not only by socialist men of letters, but even by prosaic economists, for example, J. B. Say; in the form that when one considers a people, its production is its consumption.

In these passages Marx seems to recognize that production, taken on its own, cannot be the moving force of social change, but must be understood in terms that link it indissolubly with the products that men want. These subtleties and free reflections do not come to the surface in the Preface, but make it appear that Marx himself had thought that the relationships I have called 'para-technological' and 'market' relationships[8] are not merely secondary to productive relationships but are even essential to the productive *forces*. Perhaps Marx changed his mind about this when he published volume I of *Das Kapital*. Near the beginning of *The German Ideology* (1845–6) Marx and Engels wrote: 'As individuals express their lives, so they are. What they are, therefore, coincides with their production, both with *what* they produce and with *how* they produce.'[9] In the chapter of *Das Kapital* headed 'The Labour Process' Marx says that what distinguishes one epoch from another is not 'what is made, but how, with what instruments of labour it is made. . . '.[10] Although the two passages *might* be reconciled, it may be that Marx was placing increased emphasis on production as abstracted from consumption.

If I am right, then, in what I say about the more fully argued view that lies behind the published Preface, Mr Cohen's attempts to show that productive relations can be stated in non-legal terms miss the point of Marx's view, for the '*Urvorrede*' or Introduction lets legal relations enter right into the productive *forces*. Marx seems to have thought at that time that distinctions could be drawn, differences distinguished, but that no real separation was possible. Mr Cohen wants to retain the distinction between productive relations and the legal superstructure by talking of non-legal or pre-legal *powers* in an allegedly non-normative sense. In order to do this he has to eschew reference to slaves or to wage-earners since these imply legal rights and duties, and to refer instead to what the men are able to do in slave-owning or in capitalist society. I doubt whether such a reduction can be made. The productive relationships would have to be described in terms of what slaves or slave-owners, wage-earners or employers, are, as individuals, able to do in a factual, non-normative sense. But if the slave who refuses to work is killed by his owner, this is not a mere matter of fact, but something that is done in consequence of an entitlement on the part of the owner. (Incidentally, it would be strange for a slave-owner, especially if he were an ideal type slave-owner, to destroy his own property.) It might seem different if the ideal type wage-earner or proletarian who refuses to work merely dies of hunger because he can obtain no food. But the payment of wages requires a contract of some sort, and therefore a wage-earner is, by his very description, an individual with an entitlement of some sort. To say that *he* has the power (non-normative) to withhold his labour power is to make a statement about an individual who is identified in legal terms. We might even argue that a slave, from the very fact that he is his master's property, can (factually) withhold his labour, just because he knows that his master wants to make use of him if he can. And it might be said, on the other side, that the ideal type proletarian (in a world with no soup kitchens, no public assistance, and no prisons to get himself into) has no power to withhold his labour, because no employer has any interest in keeping him alive.

Brecht writes in the *Dreigroschenoper*:

*Erst kommt das Fressen, dann kommt die Moral.*

There is the picture of beasts in human form tearing and gobbling with no concern for anything except satisfying their hunger. There is no room for morality, it is suggested, until hunger has been satisfied and, more generally, morality cannot be more than a justification of this tearing and gobbling until the proletariat has freed mankind from the constraints of class society. '*Fressen*', however, is less appropriate for human eating than '*Essen*', a word that can mean 'meal', as in '*Abendessen*'. But meals are not merely an individual's ingestion of sustenance, but an ordered social occasion governed by rules of a more or less formal kind. Human eating involves rules which, though not legal, can properly be called moral. In this way morality is more closely linked with the elementary forms of social life than law, and if this is so the theory of degrees of social reality attributed to Marx on the basis of the Preface to the *Critique of Political Economy* is not acceptable. On this view, I take it, morality would be part of the ideological superstructure and hence more distant from the reality of the productive forces than law is. I suggest that it does not follow from the fact that men have to work in order to survive that their other activities have to be explained in terms of their work and are determined by it. Although Marx did give classic expression to this view, it was part of what may be described as a secular eschatology. It is significant and rather pleasing that when he was writing for himself alone Marx stated a 'dialectical' view according to which the various 'aspects' of social life are implicated with one another and permit no single one-way scheme of explanation.

## NOTES

1   See pp 272 and 277 above.
2   *Illusion of the Epoch*, pp. 166–8.
3   Mr Arthur M. Prinz in 'Background and Ulterior Motive of Marx's Preface of 1859' (*Journal of the History of Ideas*, vol. XXX, no. 3, July–September 1969, pp. 437–50) argues that in order that his book should not be stopped by the Prussian book censorship Marx toned down the account of Historical Materialism in the Preface by omitting references to the class struggle which had figured in the *Communist Manifesto* and in the (unpublished) *German Ideology*. According to Prinz, Marx was trying to give the impression that he had turned over a new leaf, and was also trying to gain an influence among German socialists as against Lassalle. Undoubtedly the word 'antagonism' and the expression 'social revolution' gloss over Marx's views on classes and made it less likely that the book would be prosecuted for stirring up hatred between classes. But Marx's discretion does not amount to distortion.
4   This Introduction was published in *Die Neue Zeit* in 1903 and a translation of it in N. I. Stone's version of the *Critique of Political Economy* (New York, 1904). The whole work, which runs to nearly 1,000 pages, was published in Berlin in 1953 with the title: *Grundrisse der Politischen Ökonomie*. Pages 375–413 of this book translated by Jack Cohen with an introduction by E. J. Hobsbawm appeared in London in 1964 with the title: *Pre-Capitalist Economic Formations*. A

complete translation of *Grundrisse* is available in the Pelican Marx Library (Harmondsworth, Penguin Books, 1973).

5   D. Forbes (ed.), (Edinburgh, Edinburgh University Press, 1966) from the 1767 edition. The quotations below are from pp. 82–98.

6   A. M. Honoré, 'Ownership', in A. G. Guest (ed.), *Oxford Essays in Jurisprudence*, first series (Oxford, Clarendon Press, 1961), pp. 104–47 at p. 147.

7   'Sur les concepts fondamentaux du matérialisme historique', in Louis Althusser, Etienne Balibar, Roger Establet, *Lire le Capital* (Paris, Maspero, 1967), vol. II, p. 207. ['The basic concepts of historical materialism' in Louis Althusser, Etienne Balibar, *Reading Capital* (London, NLB, 1970), pp. 199–308 at p. 213.]

8   *Illusion of the Epoch*, pp. 166–7.

9   McLellan (ed.), *Karl Marx Selected Writings*, p. 161.

10   ibid., p. 457.

# INDEX